The Comedy Studies Reader

fig 1.

fig 2.

The Comedy Studies Reader

EDITED BY NICK MARX & MATT SIENKIEWICZ

University of Texas Press ◆ Austin

Requests for permission to reproduce material from this work should be sent to:
    Permissions
    University of Texas Press
    P.O. Box 7819
    Austin, TX 78713-7819
    utpress.utexas.edu/rp-form

♾ The paper used in this book meets the minimum requirements of ANSI/NISO
z39.48-1992 (R1997) (Permanence of Paper).

Library of Congress Cataloging-in-Publication Data

Names: Marx, Nick, editor. | Sienkiewicz, Matt, editor.
Title: The comedy studies reader / edited by Nick Marx and Matt Sienkiewicz.
Description: First edition. | Austin : University of Texas Press, 2018. |
Includes bibliographical references and index.
Identifiers: LCCN 2017046018
ISBN 978-1-4773-1599-6 (cloth : alk. paper)
ISBN 978-1-4773-1600-9 (pbk. : alk. paper)
ISBN 978-1-4773-1601-6 (library e-book)
ISBN 978-1-4773-1602-3 (non-library e-book)
Subjects: LCSH: Comedy films—United States—History and criticism. | Television
comedies—United States—History and criticism. | Popular culture—United
States—History—20th century. | Motion pictures—United States—20th century. |
Comedy—Social aspects—United States. | Comedy—History—20th century.
Classification: LCC PN1995.9.C55 C664 2018 | DDC 791.43/617—dc23
LC record available at https://lccn.loc.gov/2017046018

doi:10.7560/315996

Contents

Acknowledgments

The editors wish to thank all those who have helped in the creation of this volume, including Jordin Clark, Ava Goepfert, Lynn Petrella, Max Inhoff, Ellen Burr, Cecilia Aycinena, Michael Atkinson, Julia Biango, Leslie Douglas, our anonymous peer reviewers, and the staff at the University of Texas Press. Thanks to Mary Beltrán for shaping our thinking about comedy studies a decade ago at the University of Wisconsin-Madison, and to Jonathan Gray and Jeffrey Jones for providing key insights that greatly influenced this volume early on. Finally, we wish to thank Jill Jarvis Marx and Carrie Benedon.

The Comedy Studies Reader

Volume Introduction: Comedy as Theory, Industry, and Academic Discipline

NICK MARX AND MATT SIENKIEWICZ

What makes a TV show, film, or snippet of internet video funny? It is a simple question, but one that often requires a complex answer to which no two people ever seem to fully agree. There is an old cliché that any attempt to explain a joke is an act of comedic murder. No humor, the idea goes, can survive its own deconstruction. As editors of *The Comedy Studies Reader*, we disagree vehemently. Studying comedy no more ruins a joke than knowledge of optics discounts the beauty of a rainbow. Nonetheless, studying comedy can create a certain amount of frustration for students and scholars alike. The varieties of comedic media and potential interpretations thereof are such that no singular theory or critical approach will ever suffice to give more than a partial, contingent grasp of what makes your favorite long-running sitcom or blockbuster rom-com funny, popular, and profitable. The effort to explain a joke does not kill it. It does, however, reveal the impossibility of finding one comprehensive explanation for its success.

Accordingly, it is tempting to throw one's hands up and accept the impenetrable nature of humor. Perhaps we simply know comedy when we see it, and there is nothing more to say? We argue, however, that this is the wrong approach. Yes, there is something confusing in acknowledging how little we understand about what makes us, let alone other people, laugh. There is also something terribly exciting, engaging, and important about taking the fractured pieces of human experience and struggling to arrange them into a more orderly and useful portrait. Unfortunately, there is no grand Theory of Comedy to be found. Fortunately, there are many insightful theories of comedy that can help explain the different ways in which viewers understand humor and producers reap financial rewards from it.

Consider a brief example: A crowd gathers around your roommate's laptop. At first there are nods of appreciation. Then giggles, chuckles, guffaws. The bits of laughter morph into amplifying waves of sound, and soon enough, the group is howling hysterically. You relent, walk over to the laptop, and prepare to be amazed. What you find is a YouTube video, entitled "How Animals Eat Their Food." It features a hipster hopping around like a kangaroo and colliding into a makeshift cardboard dinner table. Your friends are in stitches, as have been, presumably, the 120 million other people who have watched, shared, and liked the video.

Faced with such overwhelming firsthand and statistical evidence, you accept the fact that lots of people find the clip very, very funny. You are, however, confronted with another, somewhat disconcerting certainty. This video, the one that is currently bringing your roommate into a state of tear-soaked comedic ecstasy, is, in your estimation, irredeemably *un*-funny. It is pointless, meandering, and nonsensical. The guy in the thick-rimmed glasses does not even do particularly good animal impressions. It is not just that you don't find it funny. It is that you cannot fathom how anyone *could* be brought to laughter by this time-sucking scrap of internet ephemera.

Certainly, all forms of media have the potential to be divisive. A drama may be judged as more or less emotionally engaging. Two viewers might entirely disagree as to how coherently a documentary makes its point. Comedy, however, is particularly prone to more fundamental disagreement. Your confusion surrounding "How Animals Eat Their Food" is not simply that you and your friends disagree. It is that you seem to have been watching entirely different videos or, at the very least, applying such vastly different understandings of humor that any attempt to find common ground would be futile.

There is, however, help. A diverse array of comedy theories provide explanations for both your friends' laughter and your stoic silence. Perhaps the video's humor can be explained by the dynamics outlined in Mikhail Bakhtin's notion of "the carnivalesque," a theory discussed in chapter 1 of this reader. In this scenario, your friends are attracted to the video's exaggerated deconstruction of proper dining etiquette. Eating is an activity circumscribed by considerable social pressure to conform to codes of behavioral decorum. Keep your elbows off the table, use the proper fork, and always chew with your mouth closed. The hipster in the video is quite aggressively and remorselessly violating said rules. Such subversion of social hierarchies, bodily discipline, and linguistic norms, according to Bakhtin, can embolden disempowered people and inspire them to tackle

"How Animals Eat Their Food" delivers carnivalesque comedy by deconstructing proper dining etiquette.

the social inequalities they face on a daily basis. Joyous laughter, from this perspective, emerges from both the disruption of traditional social order and the sense of liberation embedded within even subtle acts of protest.

In "How Animals Eat Their Food," the impressionist flails and slams himself into his meal, while the straight man at the dinner table steadfastly maintains an incongruous sense of propriety. For some, this dynamic is enough to provoke a satisfying sense of the comedic. If your laughing friends grew up in an environment concerned with proper dining manners, then they understandably might find the video hilariously liberating. You, on the other hand, having grown up with three disgusting older siblings and a proudly flatulent father, cannot feel the pleasure of relief from an etiquette by which you never found yourself constrained.

Or consider another possibility, the mechanical approach, as discussed in chapter 2 of this reader. This theory emphasizes incongruity and the ways in which the human body at times disassociates itself from the human will or intellect. Writing amid the rapid mechanization and modernization of the early twentieth century, Henri Bergson argued that comedy arises when people are stripped of their rationality and intentionality. When a human being acts as though she were an inhuman machine or an unthinking animal, we laugh. This helps explain the humor behind a range of physical acts of comedy, from pratfalls to bodily contortions. Thus,

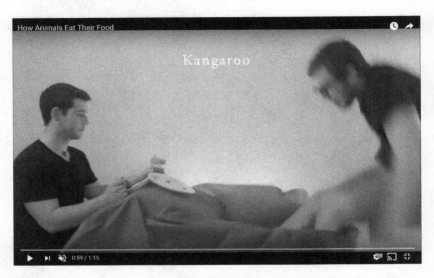

According to Henri Bergson, laughter arises when people act irrationally or inhuman.

perhaps your friends, deep down, are amused by the extent to which the animal impressionist is hopping, flopping, and falling as though he has the tiny mechanistic, five-centimeter-long brain (we looked it up[1]) of a kangaroo. Perhaps you aren't laughing because you don't see marsupials as similar to machines or because the impressionist's kangaroo movements are too lazy to effectively evoke the movements of an animal.

Of course, just as not every animal is equally skilled at eating a salad, not every theory bounces off each comedic text with equal success. A psychoanalytic reading (as discussed in chapter 3) of the video may require some stretching, but nonetheless provides us with insights into the nature of comedy distinct from those already discussed. A strange, potentially humorous detail in "How Animals Eat Their Food" resides in the choice of drinkware the creators choose to employ. From a Freudian perspective, we might read these cups as comedic "symptoms" providing a view into the inner psyche of both the creators and those who find the clip so hilarious. Although the two characters in the video are fully grown adult men, they nonetheless drink from dainty, pink and purple sippy cups. It is a distracting detail, and one that serves no obvious purpose in advancing the zoological orientation of the video's major action. And yet, the infantile table setting makes a certain amount of sense. In acting out the animal parts, the hipster is, above all, expressing a sense of childish freedom, lawlessness, and imagination that norm-abiding adults have no choice but to repress if they wish to live, work, and reproduce in contemporary society. From this viewpoint, the video is funny to your roommates because, after a long day of doing what the superego (society, more or less) tells them to do, it allows them to vicariously unleash the desires of the id (instinctive impulse) and to act like a child or an animal.

Deep thinkers such as Bakhtin, Bergson, and Freud have long pondered the diverse, surprising ways in which comedy brings pleasure to readers, listeners, and viewers. So too, of course, have scores of less intellectually inclined, but amply motivated, professional media makers. For studio executives and producers, comedy offers both a conundrum and an opportunity. As the competing interpretations above illustrate, no one knows exactly why it is that audiences find a particular show or movie funny. Comedic discourse, even when well-theorized, is a dynamic, complex system that involves countless social, political, and technological factors. Predicting if a joke will land is thus somewhat akin to forecasting weather patterns days or even weeks in advance. It's not total guesswork, but given the countless things that can go right or wrong, there is certainly a need to manage expectations. Just as the local meteorologist misses a snowstorm here and there, *Saturday Night Live*, despite recruiting the hottest joke writers in the industry, occasionally flops.

Even seemingly small details in a media text, such as the sippy cups in "How Animals Eat Their Food," reveal comedy's power to release repressed desires.

The Comedy Studies Reader offers an opportunity to consider comedy as both a theoretical concept and a commercial product, while illustrating the ways in which these things are inevitably intertwined. It grapples with the ideas of philosophers and critical theorists of comedy and tries to understand how comedic texts circulate as for-profit goods through an industry that strives to funnel their diverse meanings down singularly profitable paths. Thus it's important to note here that we've limited the book's case studies to comedic media texts including television programs, websites, and movies. Next, we consider the unique role these texts have played within American commercial media industries.

Comedy in Moments of Media Industry Transition

Humor's malleable, multi-perspectival nature opens up the potential for a tremendous return on a media producer's investment. The complex social and psychological aspects of comedy might make it unpredictable, but they also make it affordable. Comedies, be they on TV, online, or at the megaplex, generally require smaller budgets than their dramatic and action-oriented counterparts. Making a hit comedy often requires stumbling upon the right mix of relatively simple verbal and visual factors, as opposed to, for example, the creation of vast fantasy worlds or the licensing of a Marvel superhero. Furthermore, the fact that two people can find one thing funny for two very different reasons expands potential audience reach without incurring additional costs. The varied and sometimes contradictory nature of comedy theory is thus a point of simultaneous academic and industrial concern. To struggle with the complexities of the comedic is both to contemplate a core aspect of human nature and to consider a fundamental component of media economics.

Comedic media afford producers cheap sites for experimentation—particularly during times of economic and technological uncertainty—as well as distinct and edgy formats for distinguishing their products from competitors. These characteristics of comedy become especially apparent when new aesthetic, economic, and/or technological factors disrupt the previous routines of a given media industry. Comedic texts may have many textual meanings, but their circulation by producers looking for good bets in times of transition serves to narrow down interpretive possibilities. As the business of media continues to face ever-increasing rates of disruption, comedy emerges as an increasingly important area for both scholarly analysis and industrial consideration.

Funny or Die Presents satirizes the convergence of television and internet comedy styles and technologies.

Consider this example: In 2010, the premium cable network HBO premiered *Funny or Die Presents*, a half-hour sketch comedy show that mixed new pieces produced for television with viral videos already popular on the eponymous website Funnyordie.com. The opening title sequence of the show presents a curious but telling clash of imagery: amateurish graphics of a computer and a television slowly drift toward the center of the screen before merging to form the logo for the "Funny or Die Network." Upon first glance, the gag is not unlike the thousands of memes and gifs littering the internet, ones making a postmodern mash-up of today's rapid technological changes. This animation may come off as somewhat cheap and lazy, but there is a profound idea embedded within it.

The graphic points to broader changes in television during today's post-network era, a period of transition that sees the medium borrowing many aesthetic and economic practices from the internet in a desperate attempt to stay fresh and relevant for desirable young viewers. In other words, the innovation and energy of comedy on the internet is being co-opted by a television industry suddenly insecure about its place in the media pecking order. Given their comparatively low production costs and the ease with which they can be broken out across multiple media, comedy programs like *Funny or Die Presents* present the ideal forum to experiment with what works and what doesn't. *Drunk History, Tosh.o, Broad*

City, *Insecure*, digital shorts from The Lonely Island, and myriad shows and performers on Adult Swim have similarly bridged internet and television culture.

This use of comedy to negotiate industrial transition is not, however, without historical precedent. Try thinking about the relationship between comedy and media industries in a more broadly historical way: When you think of influential works from a medium's earliest period, what genres stick out? Certainly, the early film industry produced masterpieces in genres as diverse as science fiction/fantasy (Georges Méliès's 1902 *A Trip to the Moon*) and the western (Edwin S. Porter's 1903 *The Great Train Robbery*). But the early films most popularly celebrated, canonized, and revisited tend to be comedies from the likes of Buster Keaton and Charlie Chaplin. What about television? The anthology drama (such as *The Philco Television Playhouse*'s 1953 production of "Marty") is often celebrated in discussions of the medium's "golden age," but sitcoms from stars such as George Burns, Gracie Allen, and Lucille Ball bridged the transition from radio to TV and influenced broadcasting practice for decades to come. Finally, if writing a history of the early internet, it would be impossible not to emphasize humorous viral videos and other short-form comedies as central to the medium's aesthetic and economic norms. Again and again, as "new media" are brought into this world, comedy is the midwife easing their birth.

Comedy not only numbs the labor pains out of which new media are born but also guides their growth and maturation. The same properties that make comedy ideal for a medium striving to establish its early economic and aesthetic routines make it useful again when it confronts the introduction of a new technology, grapples with a new competitor, or struggles to stay relevant in the face of social upheaval. In one of its earliest roles facilitating change within a medium, comedy provided a crucial forum for working out silent film's transition to sound, one that drove producers to seek out performers who could supplement physical comedy with humorous repartee. During this period, Hollywood studios turned to vaudeville performers to meet the new demands of sound cinema. Physical comedy was thus curiously juxtaposed alongside more conventionally plot-driven scenarios and dialogue in the films of the Marx brothers, for instance. In doing so, these "anarchistic" comedies engaged in formal experimentation while still privileging classical Hollywood storytelling norms such as goal-driven protagonists and conflict resolution.[2]

If unconventional comedy provided the raucous bachelor/ette party that preceded classical Hollywood's wedding to decades of aesthetic and economic stability, then it similarly helped the television industry's later divorce from the routines of the network era. For much of television's history, the broadcast networks ABC, NBC, and CBS dominated with broadly appealing shows that won massive audience shares. Through the 1980s and 1990s, however, competitors challenged the three-network oligopoly with risqué, edgy comedies that carved up its audiences into smaller niches. The FOX network, for instance, programmed *In Living Color*, *Living Single*, and *Martin*, comedies targeted at underserved black audiences that simultaneously siphoned away young white viewers from the "mainstream."[3] FOX comedies (alongside those of Comedy Central, MTV, and many others) pioneered the template for narrowcasting to small, loyal, previously ignored audiences, a strategy that came to be de rigueur for television's multichannel transition away from the three-network oligopoly. In the television industry today, cable and streaming networks continue to counterprogram with risqué comedies such as *Transparent*, *Orange Is the New Black*, and *It's Always Sunny in Philadelphia* to attract niche audiences, as the large audience coalitions long sought by broadcasters dwindle.

In the contemporary era of media convergence, in which audiences can access film, television, and internet content alike on their own terms, comedy again helps us understand the aesthetic and economic norms of today's digitally-dominated environment. In an effort to replicate YouTube's user-generated success in the mid- to late-2000s, major media firms rushed to launch or purchase comedy-specific websites such as Dot-Comedy (NBC), SuperDeluxe (Turner), and Atom.com (Viacom) and keep them separate from their television offerings. The idea was to create internet-specific content for viewers and advertisers, maintaining a sense of medium specificity that would foster the growth of online performers at the same time that it bolstered a separate, distinct prestige for those working in "old" media like television. Comedy provided a quick and cost-effective way for television networks to dip their toes in the surging waters of original internet programming without being swept away, only to find that audiences simply wanted good (and funny) content regardless of what screen it was on.

Today, of course, media companies have broken down medium specific barriers for a variety of financial, development, and promotional purposes. Extended clips of late-night comedy shows are zealously spread online the day after they air, and advertisers for comedic content hunt desirable young consumers as they hop from smartphone to tablet to television. In this recent shift by the television industry from initial wariness to wholehearted embrace of online and social media platforms, comedy again provides the quick and cheap format for producers trying something new.

Examining comedy as a genre, as discussed in chapter 5 of this reader, helps us identify its specific industrial codes and narrative conventions, why they recur during moments of transition, and how they are related to social and cultural discourses outside of media texts. Let's return to "How Animals Eat Their Food." The video, being a product of the free-for-all, highly democratic world of YouTube home moviemaking, would seem to be a wholly organic project, divorced from any industrial standards. And yet its major textual attributes make for a nice checklist for the genre of comedic viral video. Just as genre conventions require a sitcom to be thirty minutes (with commercials) in length, viral comedy videos always seem to be two-to-five minutes in length. The cheapness and simplicity of the video may be a product of necessity, but it is also another clear marker of its genre. Adam McKay and Will Ferrell's famous viral sensation "The Landlord" looks just as cheap and loose as "How Animals Eat Their Food." The same might be said for The Lonely Island's hit "Lazy Sunday" and countless other examples in which amateurism is a clear aesthetic choice on the part of professional comedians. The transitional moment out of which "How Animals Eat Their Food" arrives sees comedy at the nexus of professional and amateur aesthetics merging and mutually informing one another.

From a bottom-up perspective, comedy remains the genre of choice for writers, actors, and producers fighting to make their voices heard across myriad social networking platforms. Created by an amateur college student who goes by the name MisterEpicMann, "How Animals Eat Their Food" quickly surged to over 100 million views and gave its creator over three million subscribers. With those kinds of viewership numbers, many YouTubers turn professional, becoming sponsored by a consumer good or lifestyle brand or by sharing advertising revenue with YouTube itself. Given this level of audience attention, it's no wonder, then, that networks are increasingly looking to the internet for cues on how to create comedy that is cost-effective, attracts a desirable young audience, and, perhaps more than anything, is actually funny and fresh. While for now the balance of power between the internet and television remains decidedly with the latter, comedy continues to be the format that best helps us understand how both media absorb bits of one another until something like the opening title graphic in *Funny or Die Presents* becomes a reality.

Critical Comedy in an Age of Crisis

Comedy plays a calming role for media industries when they reach points of financial and technological crisis. It can also have a productive, ameliorating effect on viewers facing moments of social and political turmoil. In the wake of the 9/11 attacks, numerous cultural commentators suggested that America would have to give up its joking ways, eschewing the ironic detachment of shows like *Seinfeld* for serious programs dealing with serious ideas. These commentators were, of course, utterly (perhaps even comically) wrong. The post-9/11 period has not only represented a golden age for American comedy, but it has also ushered in a vast, if somewhat narrowly focused, boom in the scholarly consideration of humor.

This apparently inverse reaction should not be terribly surprising. Moments of great trauma have, historically, often led simultaneously to serious introspection and comedic interpretation. The social and political upheavals of the 1960s and 1970s, ranging from the Vietnam War to civil rights struggles to the Watergate scandal, brought with them adventurous, boundary-pushing approaches to humor on screen. Whereas pre-Vietnam television comedy was marked largely by domestic, broadly focused humor, the 1960s and '70s ushered in a deluge of innovative, provocative programs. CBS's *Smothers Brothers Comedy Hour*, which premiered in 1967, may have looked like a traditional variety program, but its content was far more politically biting and controversial than that of its predecessors. Cutting-edge comedies such as *All in the Family* and *Saturday Night Live* similarly engaged with the crises of the era, offering Americans opportunities to debate and interpret social and political upheaval beyond the realm of traditional "serious" media. At the time, however, there was little academic attention paid to this phenomenon. Although numerous scholars have gone back and excavated the histories of these programs, few, at the time of their airing, were professionally engaged in critical approaches to the academic study of popular comedy.

The post-9/11 moment has suffered no such ill-fate. Between Vietnam and 9/11, academic media studies grew from a nonentity, to a curiosity, to a disdained but grudgingly accepted corner of the humanities, to a bona fide, booming, scholarly discipline. Whereas in the 1970s a university English department may have housed a solitary, elbow-patched film historian, the following decades brought the growth of departments and professional societies geared solely toward the critical study of nearly all media. By the early 2000s, the field had developed to the point at which scholars had become specialized into increasingly narrow subdivisions, including a group of researchers devoted to considering the meanings and import of television comedy. So, just as Stephen Colbert, Samantha Bee, Trey Parker, Matt Stone, and others aimed their satiric sights on post-9/11 cultural and political crises, a group of professionally trained analysts were ready to unearth the deeper meanings embedded within popular comedic texts.

The result was an embarrassment of scholarly riches, with numerous books and articles engaging with the subversive, politically progressive ways in which *The Simpsons*, *The Daily Show*, *South Park*, *The Colbert Report*, and other programs deconstructed the social and political complexities of the post-9/11 United States. A comprehensive list of this research would require a chapter of its own. However, books such as Jonathan Gray, Jeffrey Jones, and Ethan Thompson's *Satire TV*, Amber Day's *Satire and Dissent*, Geoffrey Baym's *From Cronkite to Colbert*, Russell Peterson's *Strange Bedfellows*, and a variety of other key works set a tone not only for the academic study of post-9/11 comedy but also for scholarly engagements with screen humor more broadly.[4] Among other contributions, these works highlighted the cultural value of long-derided comedic subgenres like animation, talk shows, and parody; demonstrated comedy's utility for fields such as political communication, philosophy, and journalism; and legitimized comedy studies itself as a "serious" scholarly pursuit within the humanities.

Comedy scholarship based on theories of satire and political power structures do, however, have their limitations. They do not, for example, fare terribly well in interpreting the ways in which hundreds of millions of people have laughed at trifles like "How Animals Eat Their Food." To illustrate the limitations of political approaches to comedy studies, let's try an exercise in irony (a theory featured in chapter 4 of this book), in which we intentionally say something in order to articulate its opposite and, in the process, attempt to create as much humor as a dusty academic volume such as this is allowed to:

> "How Animals Eat Their Food" is, clearly, a veiled political satire, pregnant with deep meanings and social importance. It is, in fact, the key to understanding all that has gone wrong in (post-) modern society and serves as a Rosetta stone for deciphering a vast constellation of contemporary geopolitical quandaries. This becomes apparent in a close analysis of the symbolism embedded in the video. The "animals," upon close consideration, represent powerful Western nations, varied in their own ways but uniformly voracious in their appetite for swallowing up the world's

resources. The "food" is the Global South, vulnerable and unable to protect itself as the whale (America, obviously) crashes into it, the kangaroo (Australia, more obviously) hops all over it, and the cow (France, maybe? They have cows there.) ineptly smashes its face into it. The second diner at the table, of course, represents the United Nations, a helpless, impotent peacekeeper who sits idly by as the postcolonial world is violently pillaged and irreparably damaged. The smashed up table is the failed universal language of Esperanto.

Or not. And if not, the study of comedic media must supplement its recent emphasis on politics, satire, and irony, no matter how well those approaches have served in making sense of post-9/11 phenomena such *The Onion* and *The Daily Show*. In the opening section of this introduction, we employed the ideas of Mikhail Bahktin, Henri Bergson, and Sigmund Freud in order to explain the appeal of "How Animals Eat Their Food" by considering its relationship to various aspects of the human condition. Certainly, these can be politicized and, just as certainly, many contemporary comedy scholars are interested in diverse approaches to studying their subject. Nonetheless, *The Comedy Studies Reader* serves as a call to expand both the scope of comedic media that scholars and students consider and the tools they use to do so.

Crucially, interrogating political power remains a key project of comedic media and scholarship, a purpose *The Comedy Studies Reader* continues to serve. Chapters 6, 7, and 8 of this volume do so by examining the power structures at work when the people involved in comedy's creation and consumption are not viewed as a single, homogeneous mass. To return to "How Animals Eat Their Food" one final, merciful time, it perhaps comes as no surprise that the two actors featured in the video are white American men. Of course, they did not have to be and there are, thankfully, increasing examples of other demographic groups producing broadly popular comedy. Yet media industry lore has long held it to be intuitively obvious that people who look and talk like the guys in this video are able to create humor that translates more broadly than that of non-white, non-male, non-Americans. Comedy by black or female performers, for instance, is nearly always marked as niche and expected to engage with the experience of people embodying those identities. Similarly, with a handful of famous British exceptions, Americans tend to create and export, and much less often import, comedy. The world of commercial comedy always has embedded within it a set of assumptions that amplify some voices while silencing others.

The final three chapters of this book interrogate the interplay of comedy and identity. They ask and, and at least partially, answer two core questions about the relationship between comedy's universal ambitions and its specific conditions of creation: How are identity categories such as race, ethnicity, sex, gender, and nationality used to construct and understand humor? At the same time, we wonder: Might contemporary scholars of comedy, by focusing so much on identity issues and political progressivism, be missing out on an opportunity to use humor to understand a broader scope of questions about the human condition?

Although there is nothing preventing researchers from considering, for example, the more personal and psychological components of screen comedy, doing so is a challenge. Scholarship is a conversation and, accordingly, new articles and ideas tend to spring from those that come before. A serendipitous, simultaneous boom in satirical American comedy and academic comedy studies has kicked off a vast and wildly productive conversation about the role of political humor in mainstream US culture. However, in doing so, a number of threads, long embedded within intellectual debates surrounding humor, have faded into the background.

In collecting, editing, and writing this book, we wish to continue the debate surrounding the political impact of comedy. Inevitably, as a book comprised of important articles from the history of comedy, media, and cultural studies, *The Comedy Studies Reader* includes material intended to introduce students and other readers to this most robust corner of the field and encourage further, deeper debate. At the same time, however, we wish to reignite conversations about the aesthetics of comedy, comedy's relationship to the lived experience of modern society, and even comedy's ability to address the joys and terrors of being a solitary human being in a vast, complex, and often deeply confusing universe. These are big, difficult, and perhaps even impossible questions to answer with any certainty. They are, nonetheless, questions we believe scholars of comedy would do well to grapple with.

The first step in doing this is to simply return to ideas that have long existed but tend not to show up in contemporary media scholarship. This book thus delves into the history of Western thought about comedy, joking, and humor, in order to encourage its reexamination in the classroom. To do so we include passages from Bakhtin, Freud, Linda Hutcheon, and other critical voices who provide systematic means of thinking about the unruly, ever-elusive nature of comedy. Although we believe this combination of classical writing on comedy serves as a strong introduction to the subject, we also hope that students and scholars of media consider returning to the original, full versions of the excerpted texts in order to expand and diversify the tools through which contemporary scholarship deals with humor on screen.

The second step is to bring fresh perspectives on comedy scholarship into dialogue with both the constraints and possibilities created by comedy in the form of commercial entertainment media. Although comedy might be our most polysemous of popular genres, its many meanings are shaped at the levels of production and distribution by a number of creative and commercial voices. To that end, we have solicited new research from media scholars who put classical comedy theory into dialogue with scholarly and industrial discourses of recent comedic television programs, films, and digital media. These original articles draw upon a range of sources, including interviews with sitcom producers, production notes from performers and executives, and promotional materials from corporate institutions. We believe such an approach—shedding new light on comedy's textual polysemy while accounting for comedy's commercial purposes—has the ability to reveal both personal and systemic insights into the relationship among humor, society, and the individual. It also, we hope, will inspire comedy studies scholars to push conversations in the field in new directions.

Volume Overview

Each of the eight chapters of *The Comedy Studies Reader* begins with an introduction that both ties together the pieces that follow and provides an illustration of the chapter's given theory through the analysis of a specific joke. It then offers a series of essays aimed at providing inspiration for both scholars and students wishing to produce original works of media comedy scholarship. Each chapter includes a return to the basics, putting forth excerpts from theoretical writing drawn from the fields of cultural studies, philosophy, psychology, and beyond. Each is meant to represent a brief literature review in which readers consider fundamental ideas about comedy, society, and the individual, as well as an acknowledgment of the inherent interdisciplinarity of the academic study of media. The chapters then gesture toward a literature review grounded in the study of media. The middle portion of each chapter exemplifies the ways in which contemporary scholars have applied comedy theory to media texts. Finally, each chapter concludes with a new, original essay that builds upon the previous excerpts, applying both deep theoretical frameworks and cultural studies forms of analysis to shed light on a specific piece of recent comedic media.

Notes

1. "Compare Brain and Body Sizes," *Serendip Studio*, accessed May 17, 2017, http://serendip.brynmawr.edu/exchange/brains/compare/size1.

2. Jenkins, *What Made Pistachio Nuts?*, 6–10.

3. Curtin, "On Edge," 181–202.

4. Gray, Jones, and Thompson, *Satire TV*; Day, *Satire and Dissent*; Baym, *From Cronkite to Colbert*; Peterson, *Strange Bedfellows*.

Works Cited

Baym, Geoffrey. *From Cronkite to Colbert: The Evolution of Broadcast News*. Boulder, CO: Paradigm, 2010.

"Compare Brain and Body Sizes," *Serendip Studio*, accessed May 17, 2017, http://serendip.brynmawr.edu/exchange/brains/compare/size1.

Curtin, Michael. "On Edge: Culture Industries in the Neo-Network Era." In *Making and Selling Culture*, edited by Richard Ohmann, 181–202. Hanover, NH: Wesleyan University Press, 1996.

Day, Amber. *Satire and Dissent: Interventions in Contemporary Political Debate*. Bloomington, IN: Indiana University Press, 2011.

Gray, Jonathan, Jeffrey P. Jones, and Ethan Thompson, eds. *Satire TV: Politics and Comedy in the Post-Network Era*. New York: NYU Press, 2009.

Jenkins, Henry. *What Made Pistachio Nuts?: Early Sound Comedy and the Vaudeville Aesthetic*. New York: Columbia University Press, 1992.

Peterson, Russell Leslie. *Strange Bedfellows: How Late-Night Comedy Turns Democracy into a Joke*. New Brunswick, NJ: Rutgers University Press, 2008.

1.

The Carnivalesque

INT. CITY HALL — DAY

LIEUTENANT FRANK DREBIN stands next to the MAYOR, addressing a group of REPORTERS.

FRANK

Thank you, your honor. Protecting the safety of the queen is a task that is gladly accepted by Police Squad. For, no matter how silly the idea of having a queen may be to us, as Americans we must be gracious and considerate hosts.

The reporters cheer. Frank, having forgotten to remove his microphone, exits the hall and enters the men's room. The mayor addresses the crowd.

MAYOR

Thank you, Lieutenant Drebin. Of course, we all have a stake in seeing that this portion of the queen's American goodwill tour is completely successful, and we can all take pride that the queen has chosen our city to visit.

The sound of Frank unzipping his fly and voluminously urinating in the restroom overpowers the mayor for a moment.

MAYOR (cont'd)

Indeed, it is for all the people who will be able to share in the, uh, celebration . . .

The sound of Frank peeing continues as the mayor struggles to keep her composure.

MAYOR (cont'd)

. . . especially exciting will be the queen's public appearances.

Frank starts singing an opera tune, his stream slows to a drip.

MAYOR (cont'd)

Um, we also —

Frank's pee returns louder than ever. He lets out a loud fart. The mayor sits down, defeated.

* * *

There is no such thing as a universal joke. Just the same, the sort of peeing and farting that punctuates the above scene from *The Naked Gun* is seen as funny across wide and diverse swaths of humanity. Nearly everyone finds bodily humor funny, even if it's only in some small and very personal way. But why? Does the embarrassing physicality of bathroom acts that we all, as humans, share privately make us laugh on its own? Or is it the naughty thrill we experience when those private acts occur publicly and disrupt the mundane propriety of being civilized beings?

Mikhail Bakhtin's notion of the "carnivalesque," which he explored most notably in his book *Rabelais and His World*, is perhaps the best-known and most useful comedy theory for explaining bathroom humor. It even dares to establish poop jokes and vomit scenes as potentially liberating on both the personal and political levels. Bakhtin was a Russian literary theorist and dissident whose political leanings greatly informed his views on art's relationship to the social order. He saw in the work of the French Renaissance writer François Rabelais an anarchic, comedic sensibility that expressed the same feelings of emancipation and subversion we might feel masquerading as someone/thing else on a debauched holiday like Halloween or Mardi Gras. Indeed, in the rigidly ordered medieval societies of Rabelais's time, Carnival provided an occasion for those outside the ruling classes to blow off steam and celebrate. Bakhtin suggests that readers/viewers of carnivalesque texts enter into a world governed not by divine power or feudal stratification, but by laughter, pageantry, spectacle, the inversion of social hierarchies, and, most importantly, the freedom for all to critique the dominant social order.

One key aspect of the carnivalesque that helps us understand *The Naked Gun* scene—and the thousands of bathroom jokes littered across centuries of popular comedy texts—is "grotesque realism." This idea posits the body as emblematic of the processes of degradation and renewal common across all forms of life. Not only do carnivalesque texts undermine the social order through mocking portrayals of royalty and authority figures, but they also flip the rules of corporeality. Polite society demands that the body remain upright and contained, with an emphasis on the head and an effacement of the nether regions. Grotesque realism and the carnivalesque expose and celebrate our basest bodily functions as consuming, excreting, stinking human animals. While we have many occasions to celebrate the seemlier aspects of bodily growth and their attendant social markers—birthdays, graduations, anniversaries, etc.—part of what makes jokes about urine and flatulence funny is that they make explicit the very *un*seemly counterparts of that growth. What makes these jokes even funnier, in Bakhtin's conception, is the way carnivalesque texts "aim" bodily excesses at those in power, as Drebin does in *The Naked Gun* scene, figuratively urinating on the pomp and circumstance of the occasion of the queen's visit.

While scholars have used Bakhtin's ideas to celebrate the subversive meanings of bathroom humor in everything from *Lolita* to *South Park*, Umberto Eco, in the second essay of this chapter, highlights the institutional and economic powers that contain the transgressive potential of carnivalesque texts. Voicing a biting critique of Bakhtin's work, Eco suggests that carnivalesque comedy provides a state-sanctioned release valve for the resentment of non-ruling classes so that they can feel sufficiently relieved before returning to their place in the social order. Citing the example of how *Animal House*'s grotesque Blutarsky (famously portrayed by John Belushi) eventually becomes a US Senator, Eco powerfully argues that "the comic is only an instrument of social control and can never be a form of social criticism."

This chapter's third essay asks us to consider darker ideas in Bakhtin's work that often go overlooked. In his analysis of the animated sitcom *Family Guy*, Philip Scepanski examines the ritualistic nature with which we have come to use comedy to talk about national traumas like 9/11. Comedic media, by employing excessive, inappropriate jokes, help us push past the disingenuous, sensationalized tone of news coverage of trauma. In doing so, Scepanski argues, carnivalesque comedy becomes an important way for us to collectively confront unimaginable acts of tragedy.

A: *Rabelais and His World*, Mikhail Bakhtin[i]

Carnival festivities and the comic spectacles and ritual connected with them had an important place in the life of medieval man. Besides carnivals proper, with their long and complex pageants and processions, there was the "feast of fools" (*festa stultorum*) and the "feast of the ass"; there was a special free "Easter laughter" (*risus paschalis*), consecrated by tradition.

i. From *Rabelais and His World*, Mikhail Bakhtin, trans. Hélène Iswolsky (Bloomington: Indiana University Press, 1984), 5–8, 37–39, 81–82. Copyright © 1984 by Indiana University Press. Reprinted with permission of Indiana University Press.

Moreover, nearly every Church feast had its comic folk aspect, which was also traditionally recognized. Such, for instance, were the parish feasts, usually marked by fairs and varied open-air amusements, with the participation of giants, dwarfs, monsters, and trained animals. A carnival atmosphere reigned on days when mysteries and *soties* were produced. This atmosphere also pervaded such agricultural feasts as the harvesting of grapes (*vendange*) which was celebrated also in the city. Civil and social ceremonies and rituals took on a comic aspect as clowns and fools, constant participants in these festivals, mimicked serious rituals such as the tribute rendered to the victors at tournaments, the transfer of feudal rights, or the initiation of a knight. Minor occasions were also marked by comic protocol, as for instance the election of a king and queen to preside at a banquet "for laughter's sake" (*roi pour rire*).

All these forms of protocol and ritual based on laughter and consecrated by tradition existed in all the countries of medieval Europe; they were sharply distinct from the serious official, ecclesiastical, feudal, and political cult form and ceremonials. They offered a completely different, nonofficial, extra-ecclesiastical and extrapolitical aspect of the world, of man, and of human relations; they built a second world and a second life outside officialdom, a world in which all medieval people participated more or less, in which they lived during a given time of the year. If we fail to take into consideration this two-world condition, neither medieval cultural consciousness nor the culture of the Renaissance can be understood. To ignore or to underestimate the laughing people of the Middle Ages also distorts the picture of European culture's historic development.

This double aspect of the world and of human life existed even at the earliest stages of cultural development. In the folklore of primitive peoples, coupled with the cults which were serious in tone and organization were other, comic cults which laughed and scoffed at the deity ("ritual laughter"); coupled with serious myths were comic and abusive ones; coupled with heroes were their parodies and doublets. These comic rituals and myths have attracted the attention of folklorists.

But at the early stages of preclass and prepolitical social order it seems that the serious and the comic aspects of the world and of the deity were equally sacred, equally "official." This similarity was preserved in rituals of a later period of history. For instance, in the early period of the Roman state the ceremonial of the triumphal procession included on almost equal terms the glorifying and the deriding of the victor. The funeral ritual was also composed of lamenting (glorifying) and deriding the deceased. But in the definitely consolidated state and class structure such an equality of the two aspects became impossible. All the comic forms were transferred, some earlier and others later, to a nonofficial level. There they acquired a new meaning, were deepened and rendered more complex, until they became the expression of folk consciousness, of folk culture. Such were the carnival festivities of the ancient world, especially the Roman Saturnalias, and such were medieval carnivals. They were, of course, far removed from the primitive community's ritual laughter.

What are the peculiar traits of the comic rituals and spectacles of the Middle Ages? Of course, these are not religious rituals like, for instance, the Christian liturgy to which they are linked by distant genetic ties. The basis of laughter which gives form to carnival rituals frees them completely from all religious and ecclesiastic dogmatism, from all mysticism and piety. They are also completely deprived of the character of magic and prayer; they do not command nor do they ask for anything. Even more, certain carnival forms parody the Church's cult. All these forms are systematically placed outside the Church and religiosity. They belong to an entirely different sphere.

Because of their obvious sensuous character and their strong element of play, carnival images closely resemble certain artistic forms, namely the spectacle. In turn, medieval spectacles often tended toward carnival folk culture, the culture of the marketplace, and to a certain extent became one of its components. But the basic carnival nucleus of this culture is by no means a purely artistic form nor a spectacle and does not, generally speaking, belong to the sphere of art. It belongs to the borderline between art and life. In reality, it is life itself, but shaped according to a certain pattern of play.

In fact, carnival does not know footlights, in the sense that it does not acknowledge any distinction between actors and spectators. Footlights would destroy a carnival, as the absence of footlights would destroy a theatrical performance. Carnival is not a spectacle seen by the people; they live in it, and everyone participates because its very idea embraces all the people. While carnival lasts, there is no other life outside it. During carnival time life is subject only to its laws, that is, the laws of its own freedom. It has a universal spirit; it is a special condition of the entire world, of the world's revival and renewal, in which all take part. Such is the essence of carnival and experienced in the Roman Saturnalias, perceived as a true and full, though temporary, return of Saturn's golden age upon earth. The tradition of the Saturnalias remained unbroken and alive in the medieval carnival, which expressed this universal renewal and was vividly felt as an escape from the usual official way of life.

Clowns and fools, which often figure in Rabelais's novel, are character-istic of the medieval culture of humor. They were the constant, accredited representatives of the carnival spirit in everyday life out of carnival season. Like Triboulet at the time of Francis I, they were not actors playing their parts on a stage, as did the comic actors of a later period, impersonating Harlequin, Hanswurst, etc., but remained fools and clowns always and wherever they made their appearance. As such they represented a certain form of life, which was real and ideal at the same time. They stood on the borderline between life and art, in a peculiar midzone as it were; they were neither eccentrics nor dolts, neither were they comic actors.

Thus carnival is the people's second life, organized on the basis of laughter. It is a festive life. Festivity is a peculiar quality of all comic ritu-als and spectacles of the Middle Ages.

* * *

Romantic grotesque was an important manifestation of world literature. To a certain degree it was a reaction against the elements of classicism which characterized the self-importance of the Enlightenment. It was a reaction against the cold rationalism, against official, formalistic, and logical authoritarianism; it was a rejection of that which is finished and completed, or the didactic and utilitarian spirit of the Enlighteners with their narrow and artificial optimism. In rejecting this spirit the Romantic grotesque relied first of all on the tradition of the Renaissance, especially on the rediscovered Shakespeare and Cervantes. It was in their light that the medieval grotesque was also interpreted. An important influence was exercised in this field by Sterne, who in a certain sense is even considered the founder of a new genre. As to the direct influence of folk spectacles and carnival forms, which were still alive though degenerate, it was appar-ently not considerable. The purely literary tradition was predominant. We should however point out the influence of the folk theater, especially the puppet show and the performances given at fairs.

Unlike the medieval and Renaissance grotesque, which was directly related to folk culture and thus belonged to all the people, the Roman-tic genre acquired a private "chamber" character. It became, as it were, an individual carnival, marked by a vivid sense of isolation. The carnival spirit was transposed into a subjective, idealistic philosophy. It ceased to be the concrete (one might say bodily) experience of the one, inexhaust-ible being, as it was in the Middle Ages and the Renaissance.

However, the most important transformation of Romantic grotesque was that of the principle of laughter. This element of course remained, since no grotesque, even the most timid, is conceivable in the atmosphere of absolute seriousness. But laughter was cut down to cold humor, irony, sarcasm. It ceased to be a joyful and triumphant hilarity. Its positive regenerating power was reduced to a minimum.

We find a characteristic discussion of laughter in one of the most remarkable works of Romantic grotesque, "The Night Watches" of Bonaventura (the pen name of an unknown author, perhaps Wetzel).[1] These are the tales and thoughts of a night watchman. The narrator describes as follows the meaning of laughter: "Is there upon earth a more potent means than laughter to resist the mockeries of the world and of fate? The most powerful enemy experiences terror at the sight of this satirical mask, and misfortune itself retreats before me, if I dare laugh at it. What else indeed except laughter does this earth deserve, may the devil take it! together with its sensitive companion, the moon."

These lines proclaim the philosophy and universal character of laughter, the characteristic train of every expression of the grotesque. They praise its liberating power, but there is no hint of its power of regeneration. Laughter loses its gay and joyful tone.

Speaking through the medium of his narrator, the night watchman, the author offers a curious explanation of laughter and of its mythical origin. Laughter was sent to earth by the devil, but it appeared to men under the mask of joy, and so they readily accepted it. Then laughter cast away its mask and looked at man and at the world with the eyes of angry satire.

The transformation of the principle of laughter which permeates the grotesque, that is the loss of its regenerating power, leads to a series of other essential differences between Romantic grotesque and medieval and Renaissance grotesque. These differences appear most distinctly in relation to terror. The world of Romantic grotesque is to a certain extent a terrifying world, alien to man. All that is ordinary, commonplace, belonging to everyday life, and recognized by all suddenly becomes meaningless, dubious and hostile. Our own world becomes an alien world. Something frightening is revealed in that which was habitual and secure. Such are the tendencies of Romantic grotesque in its extreme expression. If a reconciliation with the world occurs, it takes place in a subjective, lyric, or even mystic sphere. On the other hand, the medieval and Renaissance folk culture was familiar with the element of terror only as represented by comic monsters, who were defeated by laughter. Terror was turned into something gay and comic. Folk culture brought the world close to man, gave it a bodily form, and established a link through the body and bodily life, in contrast to the abstract and spiritual mastery sought by Romanticism. Images of bodily life, such as eating, drinking, copulation, defecation, almost entirely lost their regenerating power and were turned into "vulgarities."

The images of Romantic grotesque usually express fear of the world and seek to inspire their reader with this fear. On the contrary, the images of folk culture are absolutely fearless and communicate this fearlessness to all. This is also true of Renaissance literature. The high point of this spirit is reached in Rabelais's novel; here fear is destroyed at its very origin and everything is turned into gaiety. It is the most fearless book in world literature.

* * *

The material bodily lower stratum and the entire system of degradation, turnovers, and travesties presented this essential relation to time and to social and historical transformation. One of the indispensable elements of the folk festival was travesty, that is, the renewal of clothes and of the social image. Another essential element was a reversal of the hierarchic levels: the jester was proclaimed king, a clownish abbot, bishop, or archbishop was elected at the "feast of fools," and in the churches directly under the pope's jurisdiction a mock pontiff was even chosen. The members of this hierarchy of fools sang solemn mass. At many of these feasts kings and queens were elected for a day, as on Epiphany and on St. Valentine's day. The custom of electing such ephemeral kings and queens (*rois pour rire*) was especially widespread in France, where nearly every popular banquet was presided over by them. From the wearing of clothes turned inside out and trousers slipped over the head to the election of mock kings and popes the same topographical logic is put to work: shifting from top to bottom, casting the high and the old, the finished and completed into the material bodily lower stratum for death and rebirth. These changes were placed into an essential relation with time and with social and historical change. The element of relativity and of becoming was emphasized, in opposition to the immovable and extratemporal stability of the medieval hierarchy.

Indeed, the ritual of the feast tended to project the play of time itself, which kills and gives birth at the same time, recasting the old into the new, allowing nothing to perpetuate itself. Time plays and laughs! It is the playing boy of Heraclitus who possesses the supreme power in the universe ("domination belongs to the child"). The accent is placed on the future; utopian traits are always present in the rituals and images of the people's festival gaiety. Thus were developed the rudiments that were to flower later in the sense of history as conceived by the Renaissance.

Summing up, we can say that laughter, which had been eliminated in the Middle Ages from official cult and ideology, made its unofficial but almost legal nest under the shelter of almost every feast. Therefore, every feast in addition to its official, ecclesiastical part had yet another folk carnival part whose organizing principles were laughter and the material bodily lower stratum. This part of the feast had its own pattern, its own theme and imagery, its own ritual. The origin of the various elements of this theme is varied. Doubtless, the Roman Saturnalia continued to live during the entire Middle Ages. The tradition of the antique mime also remained alive. But the main source was local folklore. It was this folklore which inspired both the imagery and the ritual of the popular, humorous part of the feast.

Lower- and middle-class clerics, schoolmen, students, and members of corporations were the main participants in these folk merriments. People of various other unorganized elements which belonged to none of these social groups and which were numerous at that time also participated in the celebrations. But the medieval culture of folk humor actually belonged to all the people. The truth of laughter embraced and carried away everyone; nobody could resist it.

B: "The Frames of Comic 'Freedom,'" Umberto Eco[ii]

The idea of carnival has something to do with comic. So, to clarify the definition of carnival it would suffice to provide a clear-cut definition of comic. Unfortunately, we lack such a definition. From antiquity to Freud or Bergson, every attempt to define comic seems to be jeopardized by the fact that this is an umbrella term (referring, in a Wittgensteinian jargon, to a network of family resemblances) that gathers together a disturbing ensemble of diverse and not completely homogeneous phenomena, such as humor, comedy, grotesque, parody, satire, wit, and so on.

There is, however, one definition of comedy that seems to produce, as a side effect, a complementary definition of carnival: this is the one provided by the second book of Aristotle's *Poetics*. There is only a minor inconvenience: this book was either lost or was never even written—an irreparable loss, indeed. Fortunately, that which Aristotle could have said

ii. From Umberto Eco, "The Frames of Comic 'Freedom,'" in *Carnival!*, ed. Thomas A. Sebeok (Berlin: Mouton, 1984), 1–8. Copyright © 1984 by Walter De Gruyter & Co. Reprinted with permission of Walter De Gruyter & Co; permission conveyed through Copyright Clearance Center Inc.

about comedy can be extrapolated from two sources: the observations on comedy and witty manipulation of language that can be found *passim* in *Poetics* (book 1) and *Rhetoric*; and the post-Aristotelian Greek and Latin tradition, with its various more or less anonymous treatises on comedy (for instance *Tractatus Coislinianus*) which allow us to speculate about a possible Aristotelian treatment of comedy.

Following this line of thought (let me consider my attempt an exercise in the Peircean art of "fair guesses" or abductions) we can outline some basic differences between tragedy and comedy.

The tragic effect is realized when: (i) there is the violation of a rule (call it a Code, a social frame, a law, a set of social premises) which (ii) is committed by somebody we can sympathize with, since he is a character of noble condition, not so bad as to be repulsive, not so good as to escape identification, and (iii) we recognize that the rule has been broken since we feel it to be either still valid ("do not kill your father") or at least sufficiently justified by the context (in the Bible: "do not disregard the commands of God"); facing such a violation, (iv) we agree that it was bad, (v) we suffer with the hero because we understand, in some way share his remorse, and participate in his own expectation of the possible or necessary punishment (pity and fear), and (vi) we feel peaceful when we realize that the sinner has been rightly punished and has in some way accepted his punishment (we enjoy the reaffirmation of the power of the rule).

On the other hand, comic effect is realized when: (i) there is the violation of a rule (preferably, but not necessarily, a minor one, like an etiquette rule); (ii) the violation is committed by someone with whom we do not sympathize because he is an ignoble, inferior, and repulsive (animal-like) character; (iii) therefore we feel superior to his misbehavior and to his sorrow for having broken the rule; (iv) however in recognizing that the rule has been broken, we do not feel concerned; on the contrary we in some way welcome the violation; we are, so to speak, revenged by the comic character who has challenged the repressive power of the rule (which involves no risk to us, since we commit the violation only vicariously); (v) our pleasure is a mixed one because we enjoy not only the breaking of the rule but also the disgrace of an animal-like individual; (vi) at the same time we are neither concerned with the defense of the rule nor compelled toward compassion for such an inferior being. Comic is always racist: only the others, the Barbarians, are supposed to pay.

This definition of comic leads us to the idea of carnival. How do we succeed in finding situations in which we are not concerned by the rules? Naturally enough (as an entire ethnological and artistic tradition witnesses), by establishing an upside-down world (*monde renversé*) in which fish fly and birds swim, in which foxes and rabbits chase hunters, bishops behave crazily, and fools are crowned. At this point we feel *free*, first for sadistic reasons (comic is diabolic, as Baudelaire reminded us) and second, because we are liberated from the fear imposed by the existence of the rule (which produces anxiety). Comic pleasure means enjoying the murder of the father, provided that others, less human than ourselves, commit the crime.

It is for this reason that the animalization of the comic hero is so important. The tragic hero cannot be an animal (at most it can be an anthropomorphized animal: Walt Disney's Bambi). We even shed tears for Snow White poisoned by the apple; we do not cry for the seven dwarves who weep for their Princess—on the contrary, we feel relieved from our own sorrow concerning Snow White's fate precisely because of the laughable pain of the dwarves. Our tension for the tragedy is mitigated by the ridiculization of the majesty of sorrow through the ridiculization of the zoomorphic little men. They are the mask through which we can pass over in laughter the difficulty of living.

Now it is understandable in which sense carnival is connected with comedy. By assuming a mask, everyone can behave like the animal-like characters of comedy. We can commit any sin while remaining innocent: and we are indeed innocent, because we laugh (which means: we are not concerned with *that*). But now, following Bakhtin, we can go a little (?) step further. Carnival is the natural theater in which animals and animal-like beings take over the power and become the masters. In carnival even kings act like the populace. Comic behavior, formerly an object of a judgment of superiority on our part, becomes, in this case, our own rule. The upside-down world has become the norm. Carnival is revolution (or revolution is carnival): kings are decapitated (that is, lowered, made inferior) and the crowd is crowned.

Such a transgressional theory has many chances to be popular, today, even among the happy few. It sounds very aristocratic. There is but one suspicion to pollute our enthusiasm: the theory is unfortunately false.

If it were true, it would be impossible to explain why power (any social and political power throughout the centuries) has used *circenses* to keep the crowds quiet; why the most repressive dictatorships have always censured parodies and satires but not clowneries; why humor is suspect but circus is innocent; why today's mass media, undoubtedly instruments of social control (even when not depending upon an explicit plot) are based mainly upon the funny, the ludicrous, that is, upon a continuous carnivalization of life. To support the universe of business, there is no business like show business.

Therefore, there is something wrong with this theory of cosmic carnivalization as global liberation. There is some diabolic trick in the appeal to the great cosmic/comic carnival.

Bakhtin was right in seeing the manifestation of a profound drive toward liberation and subversion in Medieval carnival. The hyper-Bakhtinian ideology of carnival as *actual* liberation may, however, be wrong.

In order to better understand this point, we should now approach the opposition "tragic" versus "comic" from another point of view. It seems, according to common opinion, that tragedy and drama are more "universal" than comic. In other words, it seems that everybody ought to sympathize with the sufferings of Oedipus, while it is very difficult to laugh at disgraces of the comic heroes of Greek comedy. We feel pity and terror for the destiny of Plato's Socrates, expecting that the poison has definitely performed its lethal action, but we are uncertain why we should laugh at the Socrates of Aristophanes. We are absolutely impermeable to nonwestern comedy, while we are able to understand eastern tragedies (we understand that there is something tragic or dramatic in the story of *Rashomon*, but we do not really understand the reason behind why or when Japanese or Chinese laugh unless we are endowed with some ethnographic information). Therefore, the tragic seems to deal with "eternal" problems (life and death, love and hate), while comedy seems to be more closely linked to specific social habits.

This is, however, due to a curious case of textual *trompe-l'oeil*. In fact, why should a modern spectator be involved with the story of Orestes, who is *obliged* (according to tragic tradition) to kill his own mother? Without being compelled to think of the embarrassing situation of a member of a polyandric society reading *Madame Bovary* (and wondering why this woman had so many problems in having more than one man), it is enough to think of a sophisticated reader belonging to our own permissive western society. Should a *Playboy* reader be concerned with the sufferings of Clarissa, obsessed by remorse for having accepted the courtship of Lovelace? Why do we feel compassion (pity and fear) for characters tied to social and religious rules that are no longer our own?

In fact, every tragic or dramatic text not only tells the story of a violation of a rule, it restates the rule. *Madame Bovary* is first of all a long and passionate argument against adultery or, at least, about the impossibility of adultery in nineteenth-century bourgeois society. In Greek tragedy, one of the main tasks of the chorus is precisely to describe and to impose the majesty of rule that the hero is on the verge of breaking. Thomas Mann's *Death in Venice* is first of all a convincing lesson about the social and moral impossibility, for a middle-aged male intellectual, of falling in love with an adolescent of his own sex. It is only after the reinforcement of the rule that the tragic text informs us of the hero's violation, and to what extent he could not avoid the violation. In a way, a tragic (or dramatic) text is always a lesson in cultural anthropology; it makes even its future readers aware of a certain rule, even though this rule was previously alien to their cultural sensitivity. And only after having introjected the rule can the reader feel compassion for the hero who has violated it.

There can be a tragic description of a cannibal, belonging to a cannibalistic society, who refuses to pay homage to the customs of his own community (thus undergoing the fatal and necessary punishment) only if the tragic text has provided a convincing description of the power and majesty of that rule. Otherwise the story would sound whimsical or blatantly ludicrous (suppose: the comic vicissitudes of a dyspeptic or vegetarian cannibal unable to fill his social duties . . .).

In terms of a textual semiotics (see Eco 1979), one should say that tragic (and dramatic) texts are first of all supposed to establish both the common and the intertextual *frames* whose violation produced the so-called tragic situation. On the contrary, in comedy (understood according to our pseudo-Aristotelian definition), the broken name must be *presupposed* but *never spelled out.*

What happens in comedy also happens, according to the rules of rhetoric, in irony: irony asserts the contrary of that which is considered to be the case, and is effective only if the case is not explicitly asserted. Irony means saying "~p" when, on the contrary "p" is the case. But if one asserts "~p" and immediately afterward informs one's interlocutor that "in fact, as you know, p is the case," the ironic effect is destroyed.

Let us consider a typical example of a slapstick comedy situation: during a formal dinner somebody throws a cream pie in the face of somebody else. In order to recognize the situation as a comic one, one ought to know that (i) such behavior is *usually* forbidden by good manners and (ii) food must usually be eaten and not wasted in unreasonable *potlatches*. Additionally, to increase the comic effect, there is the animalization of the human face splattered with cream. But no one would laugh at a human face splattered with soap in a barber shop (the animalization is permitted by the frame), nor will one laugh at a human face splattered with mustard (the consumption of cream—more expensive—is more *frame-breaking*).

Years ago the magazine *Mad* published a series of comic strips called

"The movies we would like to see," in which, for instance, a gang of outlaws was tying a beautiful girl to railroad tracks. Then, in alternate shots, the customary situation takes place: the train approaches and the good guys rush on horseback to rescue the beautiful one. At the end the train wins, and smashes the girl. In order to enjoy this piece of chicanery, one must be aware of the background *genre rule* (namely, western movie) whose violation produces the comic pleasure. But the rule must be *presupposed* and taken for granted.

Many comic situations can be produced by breaking Grice's conversational maxims, provided there is no reason to presuppose an implicature of some other rhetorical usage. The maxim of quantity can be comically violated by a dialogue like:

A. Do you know what time it is?
B. Yes, I do.

The maxim of quality (do not say what you do not have adequate evidence for) can be comically violated this way:

A. I hate this philosopher! He is so confused and he writes so badly. Fortunately I have never read a single page of him! (personal communication by one of my university professors, 1953)

In the same way, one can comically violate the maxims of manner and of relation, and it is not so difficult to find adequate examples. What remains compulsory, in order to produce a comic effect, is the prohibition of spelling out the norm. It must be presupposed both by the utterer and by the audience. If the speaker spells it out, he is a fool, or a jerk; if the audience does not know it, there is no comic effect.

All this will easily explain why tragic seems to be more "universal" than comic. The *trompe-l'oeil* effect is due to the fact that in the first case the rule is explicitly outlined, and in the second it is only presupposed. But such a textual principle also explains why the so-called comic or carnivalesque "liberation" appeared so suspect. Carnival, in order to be enjoyed, requires that rules and ritual be parodied, and that these rules and rituals already be recognized and respected. One must know to what degree certain behaviors are forbidden, and must feel the majesty of the forbidding norm, to appreciate their transgression. Without a valid law to break, carnival is impossible. During the Middle Ages, counterrituals such as the Mass of the Ass of the coronation of the Fool were enjoyable just because, during the rest of the year, the Holy Mass and the true King's coronation were sacred and respectable activities. The *Coena Cypriani* quoted by Bakhtin, a burlesque representation based upon the subversion of topical situations of the Scriptures, was enjoyed as a comic transgression only by people who took the same Scriptures seriously during the rest of the year. To a modern reader, the *Coena Cypriani* is only a boring series of meaningless situations, and even though the parody is recognized, it is not felt as a provocative one. Thus the prerequisites of a "good" carnival are: (i) the law must be so pervasively and profoundly interjected as to be overwhelmingly present at the moment of its violation (and this explains why "barbaric" comedy is hardly understandable); (ii) the moment of carnivalization must be very short, and allowed only once a year (*semel in anno licet insanire*); an everlasting carnival does not work: an entire year of ritual observance is needed in order to make the transgression enjoyable.

Carnival can exist only as an *authorized* transgression (which in fact represents a blatant case of *contradictio in adjecto* or of happy *double binding*—capable of curing instead of producing neurosis). If the ancient, religious carnival was limited in time, the modern mass-carnival is limited in space: it is reserved for certain places, certain streets, or framed by the television screen.

In this sense, comedy and carnival are not instances of real transgressions: on the contrary, they represent paramount examples of law reinforcement. They remind us of the existence of the rule.

Carnivalization can act as a revolution (Rabelais, or Joyce) when it appears unexpectedly, frustrating social expectations. But on one side it produces its own mannerism (it is reabsorbed by society) and on the other side it is acceptable when performed within limits of a laboratory situation (literature, stage, screen . . .). When an unexpected and nonauthorized carnivalization suddenly occurs in "real" everyday life, it is interpreted as revolution (campus confrontations, ghetto riots, blackouts, sometimes true "historical" revolutions). But even revolutions produce a restoration of their own (revolutionary rules, another *contradictio in adjecto*) in order to install their new social model. Otherwise they are not effective revolutions, but only uprisings, revolts, transitory social disturbances.

There is neither positive nor negative connotation in this picture describing social mechanisms. Ripeness consists in acknowledging them.

In a world dominated by diabolical powers, in a world of everlasting transgression, nothing remains comic or carnivalesque, nothing can any longer become an object of parody, if not transgression itself (see *Animal House*: but finally Blutarsky becomes a US senator).

At this point one should conclude that the comic is only an instrument of social control and can never be a form of social criticism. But I have started by saying that "comic" is an umbrella term covering separate phenomena. The sort of comic we have discussed until this point is that of ancient comedy, realized in the form of peasant's festivals; it was the representation (in theater) and the self-expression (in carnival) of lower classes and "marginal" societies. The upside-down world was represented in Medieval miniatures only in the margins of manuscripts: *marginalia*. The upper classes (through their poets) depicted the peasants as animals (in comedy); then they allowed the same peasants to "freely" express themselves (in carnival) exactly as they were depicted by theater. Popular cultures are always determined by cultivated cultures.

There are other types of comic. Aristotle, for instance, speaks in the *Rhetoric* of a verbal comic, of wits, of sophisticated plays with words that seem to have a more critical power.

Since the age of romanticism, many theorists have spoken about an attitude, variously defined as irony or humor, in which the relationship between rule and violation is differently balanced.

In this essay on humor, Luigi Pirandello said that if the comic is the perception of the opposite, humor is the "sentiment" of the opposite. A case of comic is a decrepit old woman who smears her face with make-up and dresses like a young girl; facing such a picture one notices that this woman is the opposite of what a respectable old woman should be. In a case of humor, one understands why the old woman masks herself, to regain her lost youth. The character is still animal-like, but in some way one sympathizes with it. One finds oneself halfway between tragedy and comedy. This happens because humor attempts to reestablish and reassert the broken frame. It does not act in order to make us accept that system of values, but at least it obliges us to acknowledge its existence. The laughter, mixed with pity, without fear, becomes a *smile*. There is still a sense of superiority, but with a shade of tenderness. In comedy we laugh at the character. In humor we smile because of the contradiction between the character and the frame the character cannot comply with. But we are no longer sure that it is the character who is at fault. Maybe the frame is wrong. Don Quixote, unable to understand that the chivalric ideal he still follows is out of date, is a fool, but his foolishness is also due to the falsity of his ideal. He is not breaking a rule that we wish destroyed vicariously by him: we are not blindly presupposing the rule we are rediscovering and judging it as far as Quixote falls in its trap. Reading Cervantes, we are not subjugated by the majesty of an "eternal" or rediscovered law, and we are not presupposing a law that also holds for ourselves. Simply, we criticize with Cervantes a set of cultural and intertextual frames. Thus the performance of humor acts as a form of social criticism. Humor is always, if not metalinguistic, metasemiotic: through verbal language or some other sign system it casts doubt in other cultural codes. If there is a possibility of transgression, it lies in humor rather than in comic.

Semiotically speaking, if comic (in a text) takes place at the level of *fabula* or of narrative structures, humor works in the interstices between narrative and discursive structures: the attempt of the hero to comply with the frame or to violate it is developed by the *fabula*, while the intervention of the author, who renders explicit the presupposed rule, belongs to the discursive activity and represents a metasemiotic series of statements about the cultural background of the *fabula*.

Humor does not pretend, like carnival, to lead us beyond our own limits. It gives us the feeling, or better, the picture of the structure of our own limits. It is never off limits, it undermines limits from inside. It does not fish for an impossible freedom, yet it is a true movement of freedom. Humor does not promise us liberation: on the contrary, it warns us about the impossibility of global liberation, reminding us of the presence of a law that we no longer have reason to obey. In doing so it undermines the law. It makes us feel uneasiness of living under a law—any law.

Very seldom does the business of entertainment display real humor. More frequently it sells carnival. When a real piece of humor appears, entertainment becomes avant-garde: a supreme philosophical game. We smile because we feel sad for having discovered, only for a moment, the truth. But at this moment we have become too wise to believe it. We feel quiet and peaceful, a little angry, with a shade of bitterness in our minds. Humor is a *cold* carnival.

C: "Sacred Catastrophe, Profane Laughter: *Family Guy*'s Comedy in the Ritual of National Trauma," Philip Scepanski

Mikhail Bakhtin writes that, "The acute awareness of victory over fear is an essential element of medieval laughter."[2] In that era, official institutions of church and state used rituals to reinforce their dominance, but there were also parodic celebrations that mimicked and mocked the more serious ceremonies. Comedic performances represent to Bakhtin a tension between sober, serious culture, on the one hand, and more frivolous, fun culture, on the other. In medieval Europe, carnivals, feasts, and related celebrations acted as counter-rituals that imitated and counterbalanced more serious affairs. Ritual pairs—serious and frivolous—repeated throughout the calendar year, creating a rhythm in the lives of communities that vacillated between the church and state's "sacred" and the common folk's "profane" values. This created a pattern of repeated tension and release by which traditional power structures were tightened and relaxed.

Lauren Berlant, a contemporary thinker, suggests that today we are in a period of "crisis ordinariness."[3] Crises, ranging from 9/11 to school shootings, are no longer exceptional in our era but fit into a rhythm of catastrophe and recovery that increasingly normalizes a general state of crisis. Indeed, the rate at which we encounter and recover from crises appears to have sped up for many reasons, including the expansion of news outlets, a tendency towards sensationalism, and the existence of more specialized audiences.[4] Though not often discussed as a factor in today's crisis-normalization process, the growth of a parodic and satirical comedy culture plays a crucial role in engaging culturally traumatic moments, with important implications for how we remember them.[5] Academic and popular critics have raised the cultural standing of parody and satire such that certain comedy programs like *The Daily Show* blur the distinctions between serious, high culture, on the one hand, and comic, low culture, on the other. These theories can certainly help us understand comedies of higher standing, but the most telling examples arise from programs of more questionable taste.

To that end, this essay examines *Family Guy* as a notoriously base, self-consciously offensive, and largely critically reviled program that nevertheless maintains a significant popular following. *Family Guy* jokes about national traumas like the assassinations of John F. and Robert Kennedy, for example, within its larger aesthetic of provocative and offensive comedy. This essay focuses on the show's engagement with 9/11 and Columbine—the former representing the most significant collective trauma in recent American memory; the latter representing a watershed moment within an ongoing crisis of American gun violence. Although not exclusive to comedies like *Family Guy*, the show's blatant irreverence brings into sharp relief the oppositions between sacred and profane culture. By examining more closely Bakhtin's understanding of how carnival lightened the mood of medieval life and how those theories apply to contemporary comedies like *Family Guy*, we can get a better sense of how American comedy and culture respond to collective trauma in our time.

For the medieval parodist everything without exception was comic. Laughter was as universal as seriousness; it was directed at the whole world, at history, at all societies, at ideology. It was the world's second truth extended to everything and from which nothing is taken away. It was, as it were, the festive aspect of the whole world in all its elements, the second revelation of the world in play and laughter.[6]

Bakhtin uses the concept of the carnivalesque to describe art and literature that embodies the laughing spirit of carnival. Crucially, this mode of cultural engagement expresses itself outside of those particular celebrations. Authors and other artists borrowed the spirit of carnival, imitating, mocking, and laughing at all aspects of culture—most notably those things about which they *shouldn't* laugh.

Comedy and humor studies often use the concept of the carnivalesque to discuss parody and medieval carnival's focus on the body, noting its ability to disrupt cultural norms like politeness and open the way to more productive authority-questioning discourses.[7] Indeed, Bakhtin's work is at least as focused on the sociopolitical impact of these performances as on their content. Fun as it may be, a too-narrow focus on Bakhtin's applicability to poop and fart jokes ignores his insights into ritual patterns. Anthropologist Emile Durkheim says that rituals give participants a sense of what their culture holds sacred and also create a sense of community among the members of a culture.[8] For contemporary people, mass media give us a way to share a common culture across a wide population.[9] In moments of national catastrophe, these communal impulses grow even stronger as citizens consume media together at higher rates. After 9/11, for example, Americans grew notably more patriotic, displaying flags and singing "God Bless America" at sporting events, among other subtler performances of togetherness. Undoubtedly, our media culture creates a sense of sacredness around certain disastrous events. So too our media culture offers sites to discover the carnivalesque.

In his work, Bakhtin examined elements of societies very different from contemporary American media culture, meaning that his tools cannot perfectly fit the task of describing how we deal with moments of collective trauma. Most notably, he describes events that are planned and repeated at regular intervals. In the cases of collective trauma, there is an unfortunate repetition, but it is not planned in the same way as a church feast or holiday mass. Nevertheless, Bakhtin notes how serious rituals police attitudes and how comic activities can break the rules and tension created by more serious moments.

In the immediate wake of a catastrophe, news media narrates certain moments as especially important—marked not only by the attention afforded by coverage but also by the specific forms that coverage takes. Relatively recent events of this sort include 9/11, Hurricane Katrina, school shootings from Columbine to Newtown, and the 2015 assault on the Charleston Emmanuel African Methodist Episcopal Church. To varying degrees, particularly destructive and/or symbolically important events trigger a form of media coverage that sets certain acts of violence and disruption apart from more everyday bad news. Lynn Spigel notes that in the days after 9/11, television marked that period as special by broadcasting days of uninterrupted, commercial-free news.[10]

Additionally, media define traumatic events using appeals to anxiety, sadness, and other negative emotions. These feelings are not necessarily inherent to the unmediated event but instead are often constructed in media codes and coverage. Specifically, media producers cue viewers to understand material as traumatic through the use of minor-key music, close-ups of emotional faces, and slow zooms, among other formal techniques. These markers set apart the events and the periods that follow as "sacred." To Bakhtin, "sacred" meant something was the realm of the church or the king. Today, sacred events can be understood as those that are framed as symbolically important, create a sense of community, and use a respectful, serious tone.

Despite comedy's occasional role as a place to make offensive jokes about sacred events, it can also join in the call to collective mourning, reinforcing the sacred construct. Though often coming somewhat after the fact—during the time when jokes no longer seem "too soon"—comedy may also reject these frames, instead replacing anxiety and sadness with humor and mirth. In a Bakhtinian sense, the carnivalesque replaces the rituals of collective mourning. In responding to mediated catastrophe, to perform incorrectly according to a set of expectations is to invite discipline.[11] Nevertheless, humor gets some leeway. Television's fear of public and regulatory blowback and the relatively centrist ideological position of ownership and labor usually prevent immediate displays of emotional nonconformity. However, comedies like *Family Guy* suggest the value in certain environments of performing a flippant attitude towards catastrophe.

In a 2008 episode, the show's titular family, the Griffins, visit the site of the 2001 World Trade Center attacks in New York. Peter, the family patriarch, attempts and fails to understand 9/11 in discussion with the family's talking dog, Brian.

Peter: Ground Zero. So this is where the first guy got AIDS.
Brian: No, Peter, this is the site of the 9/11 terrorist attacks!

Peter: Oh, so Saddam Hussein did this?
Brian: No.
Peter: The Iraqi army?
Brian: No.
Peter: Some guys from Iraq?
Brian: No.
Peter: That one lady who visited Iraq that one time?
Brian: No, Peter, Iraq had nothing to do with this. It was a bunch of Saudi Arabians, Lebanese, and Egyptians financed by a Saudi Arabian guy living in Afghanistan and sheltered by Pakistanis.
Peter: So . . . you're saying we need to invade Iran?[12]

Peter's ignorance allows for a (rather forced) political joke at the expense of the Bush administration's perceived hawkish post-9/11 politics. Parodying post-9/11 arguments for war against ostensibly uninvolved nations, *Family Guy* mocks the attempts to blame countries based on political expediency rather than solid evidence. Imitation is an aspect of the carnivalesque, especially when it ridicules the powerful. And in some ways, this routine represents a parodic attack on inevitable attempts to find blame that are part of the post-catastrophe ritual. But more generally, Peter's ignorance, his association of 9/11 with a sexually transmitted infection (profane by its sexual nature), and the gall it takes to joke on and about the sacred ground of the attacks demonstrates the counter-ritualistic aspects of this routine.

Much like Bakhtin's understanding of the role of humor in carnival, Mary Douglas suggests that jokes act as "anti-rites," by "destroying hierarchy and order."[13] If rituals create the sense that something is sacred by framing it as symbolically important—creating a sense of community and using a respectful, serious tone—then an anti-rite must do the opposite. In practice, *Family Guy*'s contentious humor acts as anti-ritual by minimizing the symbolic importance of events, attacking the sense of community and/or subdividing the larger community, and using a nonserious and/or disrespectful tone.

Family Guy's rapid-fire style of joking offers a number of relatively self-contained gags about otherwise serious events. Slavery, the assassinations of John F. and Robert Kennedy, Vietnam, school shootings, and other traumas all become fodder for the show's humor. As discussed above, Peter seems confused about 9/11's causes, but at other times he appears to purposefully misremember. In one example, Peter recalls when, "America was attacked by mentally challenged suicide bombers."[14] Illustrating his

A Middle Eastern man fails to carry out a terrorist attack, inviting us to reimagine terrorist figures as clowns.

comment, a cut shows one side of a World Trade Center building. A caricaturized Middle Eastern man rides a bicycle into the building shouting, "Allahu Akbar." The only apparent damage is to the terrorist. Bakhtin notes how, during carnival, clowns dressed as kings. "In such a system the king is the clown. He is elected by all the people and is mocked by all the people. He is abused and beaten when the time of his reign is over. . . . The clown was first disguised as a king, but once his reign had come to an end his costume was changed, 'travestied,' to turn him once more into a clown."[15] Though the power of the medieval aristocracy is very different from that wielded by terrorism, nevertheless, there exists a similar impulse when comedies imitate these figures in order to diminish their symbolic power. In *Family Guy*'s case, the attack repaints 9/11 as a failure (that injures the terrorist no less) and the hijackers as "mentally handicapped," inviting us to laugh at these figures of terror reimagined as clowns. This gag obviously undercuts the symbolic importance of 9/11 (imagining that it was a failure) and uses a flippant tone.

Family Guy's role in subdividing community is more complex but speaks to this program's place within television's practice of "narrowcasting," the strategy of dividing audiences into small, demographically targeted markets. Although American television never treated its audience as entirely unified (treating daytime and nighttime audiences differently, for example), the longer historical pattern sees the industry targeting ever-more-specific audience segments as time goes on. Moments of collective disaster grow increasingly notable in narrowcasted television markets in that they tend to create a larger, less differentiated audience. Spigel notes that 9/11 was remarkable in this sense and that post-attack television programming fit into larger narratives of national unity. But as she also notes, these performances of collectivism were necessarily temporary, given television's and the nation's economics and culture. Rituals of collectivity like post-9/11 coverage are thus counterbalanced by rituals that help return the culture to a more "normal" state.[16] In some ways, comedy's function here as a tool for returning to normalcy runs counter to Bakhtin's notion of the carnivalesque as a suspension of normal rules, but this does not necessarily mean that carnival is the normal state in contemporary culture. More likely, it points to the fact that both the sacred and the profane are exceptional states and that these small eruptions of the carnivalesque serve as counters to our sacred moments that, compared to medieval ceremonies, are less totalizing but last for indefinite amounts of time.

Moments of collective trauma tend to draw people towards similar, if not always the same, coverage. The eventual entertainment programming that follows tends to be more narrowcasted, meaning that parodies are unlikely to address the public as a single audience, subdividing the unity of experience. Different types of programming serve different purposes using different types of appeals in the process. Even if the initial senses of anxiety, sadness, and togetherness fade, continuing news coverage as well as eventual documentary and anniversary programming tend to renew appeals to these feelings.

Parody and comedy often serve as the first sites to avoid or subtly shift the dominant moods fostered by news and drama programming. Even if Jon Stewart and David Letterman's immediate post-9/11 humor proved fairly safe, moments of even slight levity allowed for cracks in 9/11's consumingly serious media framing. In the moment, these jokes serve as relief from the emotional exhaustion that can arise from dedicated television watching of crisis coverage. Such moments play a role in television's process of moving past the overwhelming focus on the event at hand and, in doing so, they point the way towards future revisiting. Whether safe or contentious, to revisit events like these in a humorous frame instead of a mournful one is to move away from the serious tone that defines the sacred. So even when Peter Griffin references AIDS and war in addition to 9/11, the humor lightens the mood, and his misplaced blame travesties arguments made about the importance of these events. And of course, these jokes and the attacks on the Bush administration suggest that this show is not for everyone. By addressing its audience as more flippant and politically partisan, this bit acts as an anti-rite.

During celebrations like carnival, people of lower classes dressed up like kings, princes, priests, and others in positions of authority to mock established, serious rituals. Such celebrations imitated "higher" culture in order to degrade it. To Bakhtin, novels carry this spirit into literature, reformulating imitative performance into art that places all manner of accent, lingo, slang, etc. into conversation with each other.[17] Dubbed *dialogism*, Bakhtin argues that the modern novel traces back to the author's ability to "speak" in words other than his own. Crucially, dialogism also places genres in conversation with one another, highlighting the transformative power of imitation and speaking across media forms. Carrying on the spirit of dialogism, *Family Guy* draws inspiration from other media texts. In its quest to create humor by trampling on sacred moments, it sometimes mocks texts that memorialize and make sacred these types of histories. In one instance, Peter consciously tries to offend, appearing on *The Late Show with David Letterman* in order to promote a film titled *September 11, Two-Thousand-Fun*. He explains, "I play a window washer who has just finished washing the last window of the World Trade Center. And I turn around to get off the scaffold and what do I see coming? A plane! And I go, 'COME ON!' You know, it's real old-style comedy, you know? It's like two pies in the face and one in the field in Pennsylvania."[18] In this case, *Family Guy* is throwing a bit of meta-offensiveness into the mix, making a joke about a comedy that would deign joke about 9/11. At the same time, it suggests the potential for oversaturation of fictionalized narratives relating to catastrophes, offering here an imaginary ramped-up kitschiness that subtly instructs viewers in camp approaches to memorial art.

Family Guy not only travesties fictionalized accounts of catastrophe but also it satirizes news and documentary coverage. Alongside stalwarts like *The Daily Show* and *Saturday Night Live*'s "Weekend Update," sitcoms prove a fertile, if somewhat less regular, site for news parody. Perhaps most notably, *The Simpsons'* character Kent Brockman acts as an object lesson in unethical journalism.[19] Like *The Simpsons*, *Family Guy* too has a pompous, self-serving journalist in Tom Tucker. As the town's primary news anchor, Tom Tucker stands in for the ills of journalism in general. Tom's demonstrates a lack of journalistic integrity regularly, as when he struggles to pronounce a South Asian child's last name, eventually giving up, describing it as "something September eleventh-y." Besides its blatant racism, this statement betrays Tom's ignorance of the distinctions between Arab and Indian ethnicities. On top of that, it proves that he is problematically blasé about subjects which a news anchor should be respectful. This poor behavior is in keeping with Tom's general disregard for the weight of serious events. In another episode, Tom stares into the mirror practicing different inflections to one of the most significant news stories imaginable, "Good evening, I'm Tom Tucker. Our top story: the president has been shot. [clears throat] Tragedy strikes the nation: the president has been shot. [upbeat] What's the president doing in this casket? We'll tell you right after this."[20]

These examples are just a few among a larger discourse mocking news's tendency towards fearmongering. In attacking the news media's implied lack of ethics, *Family Guy* mocks the tendency of news media to self-aggrandize (a tendency often made apparent after catastrophe coverage). In a broader sense, by questioning the type of coverage that creates the posttraumatic sense of community and tone of seriousness, it operates as a counterbalance to the more serious rituals of news coverage.

Just as news media benefits from disaster and fear, so too can politicians. When Lois Griffin runs for Mayor of her town, she discovers that voters respond best to simplistic soundbites. After a voter asks "what [she] plans to do about crime," Lois responds, "a lot. . . ." The crowd applauds vigorously, prompting her to double down on this approach. ". . . Because that's what Jesus wants." The crowd grows louder in their support. "9/11 was bad," she continues to even greater support. Two more voters ask about serious problems—the environment and traffic. In both cases, she responds by saying "9/11." These jokes are less sick-for-sick's-sake than they are heavy-handed attacks on Bush's post-9/11 political rhetoric. "One could tell the story of the Bush administration," writes Sasha Torres, "as a series of more or less successful efforts to provoke and press into service the unwieldy affective intensities mobilized by 9/11."[21] Mocking strategies like those of *Family Guy* undercuts their effectiveness as rhetoric, to be sure. But laughing along with the negative rhetoric likely also helps ease the fear and anxiety that politicians seek to exploit in these moments. Jokes like these are both symbolically and emotionally useful in the process of returning to a sense of normalcy, returning, in other words, to a nonsacred state.

Bakhtin believed that, although given to celebrations of the body's more disgusting functions, carnivalesque performance also symbolized renewal through grotesque celebrations of the body. His work cites folk culture's preoccupation of the body's "lower stratum" that included defecation, urination, and procreation. Defecation connects the human body to the soil, from which peasants grew crops. More obviously, sex and subsequent birth represent renewal. For Bakhtin, humor in this vein accesses a more social pleasure of collective renewal. He quotes a 1444 circular letter at the Paris School of Theology, "Wine barrels burst if from time to time we do not open them and let in some air. . . . This is why we permit folly on some days so that we may later return with greater zeal to the service of God."[22] While one can rarely point to a particular moment where the overall rituals that mark catastrophes end, joking about these topics signals that it is no longer "too soon." They tell us that we are back to normal.

Comedy is thus not totally negative; it may attack ideas, but it often does so in the name of easing negative emotions and trying out different perspectives.[23] The gags discussed in this essay may help society get back to a place where trauma is less totalizing. Unfortunately, normalcy can be good or bad, depending on your vantage point. Sacrilegious post-9/11 humor may well have weakened Bush's ability to exploit negative feelings, but that's only a good thing if you disagree with his policies. In any case, comedy of this sort is not essentially progressive. It is often more nihilistic or even actively dismissive of any moral responsibility.

Presently, the rituals of crisis and recovery define much of our culture. If negative feelings like anxiety and mournfulness define periods of more acute crisis, then relaxing those feelings in part defines the inevitable "return to normal." Humor about trauma and tragedy is part of this process but also demonstrates the extent to which crisis in general is indeed ordinary. This repetitive pattern increasingly forms a predictable ritual, normalizing seemingly exceptional events and contributing to a culture in which publics are inured to the intensities of future traumas. And while optimists might highlight humor's ability to undercut affective arguments in favor of bad policy, it is a double-edged sword that contributes to a culture in which publics may not be moved to positive action by any crisis.

Notes

1. *Nachtwachen*, 1804 (see R. Steinert's *Nachtwachen des Bonawentura*, Leipzig, 1917).
2. Bakhtin, *Rabelais and His World*, 91.
3. Berlant, *Cruel Optimism*, 101. Berlant's thoughts on "crisis ordinariness" are broader and far more complex, ranging beyond these particularly notable catas-

trophes. Nevertheless, disasters of this nature fit into her larger schema of people feeling in a state of constant crisis.

4. Katz and Liebes, "'No More Peace!'."

5. Gray, Jones, and Thompson, "The State of Satire."

6. Bakhtin, *Rabelais and His World*, 84.

7. See, for example: Bishop, "Bakhtin, Carnival and Comedy"; King, *Film Comedy*; Thompson, "Good Demo, Bad Taste."

8. Durkheim, *The Elementary Forms of Religious Life*.

9. See Anderson, *Imagined Communities*.

10. Spigel, "Entertainment Wars," 237.

11. See Gurney, "Everything Changes Forever."

12. *Family Guy*, season 7, episode 4, "Baby Not on Board," directed by Julius Wu, written by Mark Hentemann, aired November 2, 2008, on Fox.

13. Douglas, "Jokes," 301.

14. *Family Guy*, season 8, episode 5, "Hannah Banana," directed by John Holmquist, written by Cherry Chevapravatdumrong, aired November 8, 2009, on Fox.

15. Bakhtin, *Rabelais and His World*, 197.

16. A number of differences may account for the changed role of humor as representing a state of exception versus a tool for returning to normalcy, including stronger separations between work and leisure culture, the weakened role of the church and concepts of limited government, and the postmodern dominance of popular over high culture. Suffice it to say, this chapter cannot devote the space necessary to fully explore these distinctions.

17. Bakhtin, "From the Prehistory of Novelistic Discourse."

18. *Family Guy*, season 6, episode 9, "Back to the Woods," directed by Brian Iles, written by Tom Devanney, aired February 17, 2008, on Fox.

19. Gray, *Watching with the Simpsons*. Gray devotes the fourth chapter in this book to the lessons that media consumers can learn from Brockman's troubled journalistic ethics.

20. *Family Guy*, season 3, episode 8, "The Kiss Seen Around the World," directed by Pete Michels, written by Mark Hentemann, aired August 29, 2001, on Fox.

21. Torres, "Televising Guantánamo," 45.

22. Bakhtin, *Rabelais and His World*, 75.

23. Fredrickson et al., "What Good Are Positive Emotions."

Works Cited

Anderson, Benedict. *Imagined Communities: Reflections on the Origin and Spread of Nationalism*. New York: Verso, 2006.

Bakhtin, Mikhail. *Rabelais and His World*. Translated by Hélène Iswolsky. Bloomington: Indiana University Press, 1984.

———. "From the Prehistory of Novelistic Discourse." In *The Dialogic Imagination*, edited by Michael Holquist, translated by Caryl Emerson and Michael Holquist, 41–83. Austin: University of Texas Press, 1981.

Benjamin, Walter *The Arcades Project*. Edited by Rolf Tiedemann. Translated by

Howard Eiland and Kevin McLaughlin, First Harvard University Paperback Edition. Cambridge, MA: Harvard University Press, 2002.

Berlant, Lauren. *Cruel Optimism*. Durham, NC: Duke University Press, 2011.

Bishop, Ellen. "Bakhtin, Carnival and Comedy: The New Grotesque in *Monty Python and the Holy Grail*." *Film Criticism* 15, no. 1 (1990): 49–64.

Douglas, Mary. "Jokes." In *Rethinking Popular Culture: Contemporary Perspectives in Cultural Studies*, edited by Chandra Mukerji and Michael Schudson, 291–301. Berkeley: University of California Press, 1991.

Durkheim, Emile. *The Elementary Forms of Religious Life*. Translated by Joseph Ward Swain. London: Allen & Unwin, 1915.

Eco, Umberto. *The Role of the Reader: Explorations in the Semiotics of Texts*. Bloomington: Indiana University Press, 1979.

Fredrickson, Barbara L., Michele M. Tugade, Christian E. Waugh, and Gregory R. Larkin. "What Good Are Positive Emotions in Crisis? A Prospective Study of Resilience and Emotions Following the Terrorist Attacks on the United States on September 11th, 2001." *Journal of Personality and Social Psychology* 84, no. 2 (February 2003): 365–376.

Garrett, Major. "Obama to Congress: If Newtown Moved You, Act on Guns." *CBSNews.com*, January 14, 2013, http://www.cbsnews.com/news/obama-to-congress-if-newtown-moved-you-act-on-guns/.

Gray, Jonathan. *Watching with the Simpsons: Television, Parody, and Intertextuality*. New York: Routledge, 2006.

Gray, Jonathan, Jeffrey P. Jones, and Ethan Thompson. "The State of Satire, the Satire of State." In *Satire TV: Politics and Comedy in the Post-Network Era*, edited by Jonathan Gray, Jeffrey P. Jones, and Ethan Thompson, 3–36. New York: New York University Press, 2009.

Gurney, David. "Everything Changes Forever (Temporarily): Late-Night Television Comedy After 9/11." In *A Decade of Dark Humor: How Comedy, Irony, and Satire Shaped Post-9/11 America*, edited by Ted Guornelos and Vivica Greene, 3–19. Jackson: University of Mississippi Press, 2011.

"Hannah Banana." *Family Guy*. Fox. November 8, 2009.

Katz, Elihu, and Tamar Liebes. "'No More Peace!': How Disaster, Terror and War Have Upstaged Media Events." *International Journal of Communication* 1, (2007): 157–166.

King, Geoff. *Film Comedy*. New York: Wallflower, 2002.

Spigel, Lynn, "Entertainment Wars: Television Culture After 9/11." *American Quarterly* 56, no. 2 (June 2004): 235–270.

Thompson, Ethan. "Good Demo, Bad Taste: *South Park* as Carnivalesque Satire." In *Satire TV: Politics and Comedy in the Post-Network Era*, edited by Johnathan Gray, Jeffrey P. Jones, and Ethan Thompson, 213–32. New York: New York University Press, 2009.

Torres, Sasha. "Televising Guantánamo: Transmission of Feeling during the Bush Years." In *Political Emotions: New Agendas in Communication*, edited by, Janet Staiger, Ann Cvetkovich, and Ann Reynolds, 45–65. New York: Routledge, 2010.

Zelizer, Barbie. *Covering the Body: The Kennedy Assassination, the Media, and the Shaping of Collective Memory*. Chicago: University of Chicago Press, 1992.

2.

Comedy Mechanics & Absurdity

INT. APARTMENT — DAY

JOSH sits on the couch, dejected about his failed relationship. He thinks he has set his standards too high. His sister, LIZ, is concerned.

JOSH

I don't need someone with all the bells and whistles. I just need someone safe.

LIZ

It sounds like you're talking about a car.

JOSH

Maybe I am. Maybe I am.

EXT. SIDEWALK CAFE — DAY

Liz, Josh, and Josh's best friend, MIKE, enjoy brunch.

JOSH

Mike, Liz, I'd like you to meet my girlfriend —
The camera cuts to the other side of the table, revealing a WHITE SEDAN. Josh caresses her/it lovingly — their relationship is apparently rather intimate.

JOSH (cont'd)

She's a 1998 Saturn.

LIZ

Hi . . .

MIKE

What's up, I'm Mike.

WHITE SEDAN

(Flashing high beams)
Beep! Beep!

* * *

A man cannot date a car. A car cannot make conversation. And you're lucky enough if a popular Brooklyn brunch spot has enough room for your knees, let alone a gently used midsized domestic sedan. On the surface level, the joke above from FX's *Man Seeking Woman* is full of contradiction, impossibility, and absurdity. On a basic storytelling level, it makes no sense whatsoever. These traits, however, are exactly what makes this exchange engaging and humorous.

And yet, not all nonsense is funny. Consider a lecture, or perhaps an essay in a textbook (A comedy studies reader? Never.), in which the train of reasoning derails so thoroughly that the material ceases to retain any educational value. Far from comical, this form of nonsense is likely to strike the receiver as annoying and unpleasant, evoking confusion, boredom, and other responses antithetical to laughter. The comedy theorist thus takes on the difficult job of using sense in order to catalogue and critique varieties of nonsense. Odd as it may seem, a major thread of comedy scholarship has been devoted to offering an organized, logical explanation as to why some forms of illogical balderdash descend into the oblivion of the useless while others ascend the heights of comic delight.

One of the earliest and most influential theorists of comic absurdity is Henri Bergson, whose essay "Laughter," is excerpted first in this chapter. Bergson, a thinker who came of age during the Second Industrial Revolution of the early 1900s, offers a philosophical theory of absurdity undergirded by a single, simple observation: it is funny when a living thing acts like a mechanical one. Bergson himself applies this principle broadly, using it to explain everything from slapstick humor in which people are transformed into rag dolls to animal comedy in which cats and mice act like wind-up toys, doing the darnedest things over and over again. In each case, there is an aspect of logical absurdity in which a single being is imbued with two apparently contradictory attributes: the free will of the living and the predetermination of a machine. Although it features a bit of a role reversal, the scene quoted above does just this. The car is at the same time both really a Saturn sedan and really Josh's girlfriend, capable of human emotions and expectations. To Bergson, this particular brand of incongruity has a special relationship to the human psyche that is bound up with the relief and pleasure of laughter.

Jerry Palmer, the second author excerpted in this chapter, offers a more a generalizable schema through which to understand the relationship between the comic and the absurd. Taking a formal approach to classic American cinema, Palmer argues that three conditions must be met in order for nonsense to become comedic. First, there must be some sense of surprise. The viewer understands the world to be a certain way, say, as a place in which people do not date automobiles. The surprise comes from learning that this assumption is incorrect in the fictional universe of the joke. Second, there must be a logical contradiction. In the case of *Man Seeking Woman*, the contradiction derives from the fundamental psychological and sexual incompatibility of man and machine. For reasons both social and physical, such a romantic union is an apparent impossibility. Finally, according to Palmer, the absurdity must be resolved by showing that there is some hidden logic that, in its own way, gives the nonsense some measure of plausibility, thus giving rise to the laugh. In this example, this plausibility derives from the established fact that Josh is a truly desperate guy. Perhaps he really would sleep with *anything* that moves.

Donald Crafton, in his classic essay "Pie and Chase," offers a historical analysis related to Palmer's theory, using the internal (il)logic of slapstick scenes in order to explain the narrative construction of early American screen comedies. Although American cinema is thought to be synonymous with linear storytelling, the early films of Buster Keaton, Charlie Chaplin, and others are replete with seemingly self-contained scenes that represent departures from the narrative. Understanding these gags as logically constructed sketches strung together, Crafton complicates the notion that the story is always more important than the jokes.

In this chapter's concluding, original essay, Evan Elkins takes the theories of Bergson and Palmer to their limits by applying them to *The Eric André Show*, a program whose absurdity goes well beyond that of a man dating a car. The series is marked by random bursts of violence and cruelty as it deconstructs the talk-show genre so thoroughly as to make it nearly unrecognizable. On the surface, the program is just a chaotic smash of nonsensical ideas and images. However, Elkins, in embracing the conundrum of the comedy theorist, helps explicate the method in André's comedic madness.

A: *Laughter: An Essay on the Meaning of the Comic*, Henri Bergson[i]

We laugh at Sancho Panza tumbled into a bed-quilt and tossed into the air like a football. We laugh at Baron Munchausen turned into a cannon-ball

i. From Henri Bergson, *Laughter: An Essay on the Meaning of the Comic*, trans. Cloudesley Brereton and Fred Rothwell (New York: MacMillan, 1914), 58–60, 68–73.

and travelling through space. But certain tricks of circus clowns might afford a still more precise exemplification of the same law. True, we should have to eliminate the jokes, mere interpolations by the clown into his main theme, and keep in mind only the theme itself, that is to say, the divers attitudes, capers and movements which form the strictly "clownish" element in the clown's art. On two occasions only have I been able to observe this style of the comic in its unadulterated state, and in both I received the same impression. The first time, the clowns came and went, collided, fell and jumped up again in a uniformly accelerated rhythm, visibly intent upon effecting a *crescendo*. And it was more and more to the jumping up again, the *rebound*, that the attention of the public was attracted. Gradually, one lost sight of the fact that they were men of flesh and blood like ourselves; one began to think of bundles of all sorts, falling and knocking against each other. Then the vision assumed a more definite aspect. The forms grew rounder, the bodies rolled together and seemed to pick themselves up like balls. Then at last appeared the image towards which the whole of this scene had doubtless been unconsciously evolving—large rubber balls hurled against one another in every direction. The second scene, though even coarser than the first, was no less instructive. There came on the stage two men, each with an enormous head, bald as a billiard ball. In their hands they carried large sticks which each, in turn, brought down on to the other's cranium. Here, again, a certain gradation was observable. After each blow, the bodies seemed to grow heavier and more unyielding, overpowered by an increasing degree of rigidity. Then came the return blow, in each case heavier and more resounding than the last, coming, too, after a longer interval. The skulls gave forth a formidable ring throughout the silent house. At last the two bodies, each quite rigid and as straight as an arrow, slowly bent over towards each other, the sticks came crashing down for the last time on to the two heads with a thud as of enormous mallets falling upon oaken beams, and the pair lay prone upon the ground. At that instant appeared in all its vividness the suggestion that the two artists had gradually driven into the imagination of the spectators: "We are about to become . . . we have now become solid wooden dummies."

* * *

We are too apt to speak of our feelings of pleasure and of pain as though full grown at birth, as though each one of them had not a history of its own. Above all, we are too apt to ignore the childish element, so to speak, latent in most of our joyful emotions. And yet, how many of our present pleasures, were we to examine them closely, would shrink into nothing more than memories of past ones! What would there be left of many of our emotions were we to reduce them to the exact quantum of pure feeling they contain, by subtracting from them all that is merely reminiscence? Indeed, it seems possible that, after a certain age, we become impervious to all fresh or novel forms of joy, and the sweetest pleasures of the middle-aged man are perhaps nothing more than a revival of the sensations of childhood, a balmy zephyr wafted in fainter and fainter breaths by a past that is ever receding. In any case, whatever reply we give to this broad question, one thing is certain: there can be no break in continuity between the child's delight in games and that of the grown-up person. Now, comedy is a game, a game that imitates life. And since, in the games of the child when working its dolls and puppets, many of the movements are produced by strings, ought we not to find those same strings, somewhat frayed by wear, reappearing as the threads that knot together the situations in a comedy? Let us, then, start with the games of a child, and follow the imperceptible process by which, as he grows himself, he makes his puppets grow, inspires them with life, and finally brings them to an ambiguous state in which, without ceasing to be puppets, they have yet become human beings. We thus obtain characters of a comedy type. And upon them we can test the truth of the law of which all our preceding analyses gave an inkling, a law in accordance with which we will define all broadly comic situations in general. *Any arrangement of acts and events is comic which gives us, in a single combination, the illusion of life and the distinct impression of a mechanical arrangement.*

The Jack-in-the-Box—As children we have all played with the little man who springs out of his box. You squeeze him flat, he jumps up again. Push him lower, and he shoots up still higher. Crush him down beneath the lid, and often he will send everything flying. It is hard to tell whether or not the toy itself is very ancient, but the kind of amusement it affords belongs to all time. It is a struggle between two stubborn elements, one of which, being simply mechanical, generally ends by giving in to the other, which treats it as a plaything. A cat playing with a mouse, which from time to time she releases like a spring, only to pull it up short with a stroke of her paw, indulges in the same kind of amusement.

We will now pass on to the theater, beginning with a Punch and Judy show. No sooner does the policeman put in an appearance on the stage than, naturally enough, he receives a blow which fells him. He springs to his feet, a second blow lays him flat. A repetition of the offense is followed by a repetition of the punishment. Up and down the constable flops and hops with the uniform rhythm of the bending and release of a spring, whilst the spectators laugh louder and louder.

Now, let us think of a spring that is rather of a moral type, an idea that is first expressed, then repressed, and then expressed again; a stream of words that bursts forth, is checked, and keeps on starting afresh. Once more we have the vision of one stubborn force, counteracted by another, equally pertinacious. This vision, however, will have discarded a portion of its materiality. No longer is it Punch and Judy that we are watching, but rather a real comedy.

Many a comic scene may indeed be referred to this simple type. For instance, in the scene of the *Mariage forcé* between Sganarelle and Pancrace, the entire *vis comica* lies in the conflict set up between the idea of Sganarelle, who wishes to make the philosopher listen to him, and the obstinacy of the philosopher, a regular talking-machine working automatically. As the scene progresses, the image of the Jack-in-the-box becomes more apparent, so that at last the characters themselves adopt its movements—Sganarelle pushing Pancrace, each time he shows himself, back into the wings, Pancrace returning to the stage after each repulse to continue his patter. And when Sganarelle finally drives Pancrace back and shuts him up inside the house—inside the box, one is tempted to say—a window suddenly flies open, and the head of the philosopher again appears as though it had burst open the lid of a box.

The same by-play occurs in the *Malade Imaginaire*. Through the mouth of Monsieur Purgon the outraged medical profession pours out its vials of wrath upon Argan, threatening him with every disease that flesh is heir to. And every time Argan rises from his seat, as though to silence Purgon, the latter disappears for a moment, being, as it were, thrust back into the wings; then, as though impelled by a spring, he rebounds on to the stage with a fresh curse on his lips. The self-same exclamation: "Monsieur Purgon!" recurs at regular beats, and, as it were, marks the *tempo* of this little scene.

Let us scrutinize more closely the image of the spring which is bent, released, and bent again. Let us disentangle its central element, and we shall hit upon one of the usual processes of classic comedy—*repetition*.

Why is it there is something comic in the repetition of a word on the stage? No theory of the ludicrous seems to offer a satisfactory answer to this very simple question. Nor can an answer be found so long as we look for the explanation of an amusing word or phrase in the phrase or word itself, apart from all it suggests to us. Nowhere will the usual method prove to be so inadequate as here. With the exception, however, of a few special instances to which we shall recur later, the repetition of a word is never laughable in itself. It makes us laugh only because it symbolizes a special play of moral elements, this play itself being the symbol of an altogether material diversion. It is the diversion of the cat with the mouse, the diversion of the child pushing back the Jack-in-the-box, time after time, to the bottom of his box—but in a refined and spiritualized form, transferred to the realm of feelings and ideas. Let us then state the law which, we think, defines the main comic varieties of word-repetition on the stage: *In a comic repetition of words we generally find two terms: a repressed feeling which goes off like a spring, and an idea that delights in repressing the feeling anew.*

B. *The Logic of the Absurd*, Jerry Palmer[ii]

In the second reel of *Liberty* (1929), escaped convicts Laurel and Hardy try to swap trousers on the scaffolding of a half-completed skyscraper, a process that is rendered somewhat more complicated by the fact that one of the pairs also contains a large live and aggressive crab. During these cavortings in the ionosphere they have periodically and unintentionally bombarded the cop at the foot of the half completed structure with a variety of near-lethal objects: a bag of cement, a ladder, . . . Successfully negotiating their way back to the builder's lift on the side of the skyscraper, they descend at exactly the moment that the cop decides to take shelter from the hail of descending objects—in the lift shaft. Laurel and Hardy land squarely on top of him, apparently reducing him to pulp as the lift settles on the ground; they exit rapidly. The lift goes up again to reveal a midget in policeman's uniform.

This is one of Laurel and Hardy's more audacious, surrealistic gags, and one that is entirely successful. It is also an excellent—though in no way privileged, or exceptional—starting point for a theory of gags.

The gag is analyzable into two moments, for which the terms "syllogism" and "peripeteia" are appropriate.

1. *Peripeteia*

In classical aesthetics the peripeteia is the moment when the fortunes of the principal character are reversed. The example which Aristotle gives is that of Oedipus in Sophocles's eponymous tragedy: Oedipus is eventu-

ii. From Jerry Palmer, *The Logic of the Absurd: On Film and Television Comedy* (London: BFI, 1988), 39–44. Copyright © 1988 by BFI. Reprinted with permission of BFI.

ally forced to recognize that Tiresias has seen the situation correctly, and that he himself has in fact murdered his father and married his mother in exactly the way that the prophecy foretold. In the film of *Tom Jones*, to take a modern example, the peripeteia occurs when Squire Weston cuts Tom down from the gallows at just the moment he is supposedly launched into eternity, and bears him off to marry Sophia. The peripeteias of comedy are of lesser stature, but their essence resembles that of textbook examples such as these two: it is the construction of a shock or surprise in the story the film is telling.

In the example of the lift/cop gag from *Liberty*, the surprise that the narrative constructs for us is the survival of the policeman, albeit in a changed form, when common sense tells us that the result of a squashing in a lift shaft is not reduction in size, but death. But although this surprise results from common sense (this problematic term will be discussed below), it is nonetheless constructed in the narrative of the film: in order for the surprise to occur we must know that the policeman is a normally constituted human being, not Superman or the Incredible Hulk, that the lift is a lift containing two human beings, descending at such and such a speed, etc. In other words, we have to see the immediately preceding segments of the film, in relationship to which the revelation of the cop's new status functions as does the punch line in a verbal joke. That is to say: all jokes, verbal or visual, have two stages, the preparation stage and the culmination stage; and this is true even of the most minimal gags, such as the traditional custard pie in the face, for the custard pie in the face is the culmination of a brief sequence in which the preparation consists, minimally, of the face without custard pie all over it.

Thus the first moment of the gag consists in a form of surprise, for which I have reserved the word peripeteia on the grounds that this form of surprise is constructed in the film narrative and is thus a specifically aesthetic form of surprise. However, it is clear that not all surprise, not even all aesthetic surprise, is funny: to take Aristotle's example again, the moment when Oedipus reappears on stage, his face running with blood after he has gouged out his own eyes, is certainly surprising, in some sense of the word; but it is not funny. What specific feature of comic surprise is responsible for the fact that it is funny? Or: what specific feature of comic surprise turns it into *comic* surprise?

2. Syllogism

For the second moment of the gag I have reserved the term syllogism, in order to underline its intensely logical nature.[1] In traditional logic, the syllogism is a system of reasoning in which one moves from a well-known state of affairs (called the major premise) through an empirical observation (the minor premise) to a conclusion which is as a result of the nature of the reasoning inevitably correct. A favorite textbook example was:

a) all men are mortal—major premise, a well-known state of affairs;
b) Socrates is a man—an empirical observation, the minor premise;
c) therefore—conclusion—Socrates is mortal: an inevitably correct deduction given the nature of the form of reasoning.

However, the syllogistic forms of comedy are more complex for each gag is constructed out of two, contradictory syllogisms. In the lift/cop gag one line of reasoning tells us that what we see on the screen is intensely implausible:

a) the result of squashing in a lift shaft is death—a well-known state of affairs, the major premise;
   i) the cop is squashed—empirical observation, the minor premise;
   ii) second minor premise: he survives;
b) conclusion: the event is implausible.

But a second, contradictory, line of reasoning tells us that the event does in fact have a measure of plausibility:

a) the result of squashing is a reduction in size;
b) the cop comes out smaller;
c) therefore the event has a measure of plausibility.

However, we should not imagine that these two syllogisms are of equal weight. The first of the two (implausibility) is clearly a much stronger line of argument than the second, as it has the not inconsiderable merit of being true to the world as we know it on the basis of everyday life; whereas the second is clearly only tenable on the basis of a piece of false reasoning which serves as its basis: the assumption that what is true of inorganic or non-animate forms of being can be unproblematically transposed to the realm of the animate. This manner of reasoning on the basis of a false and unstated premise was known to traditional logic as the *syllogismus in modo barocco*, the baroque syllogism; a favorite textbook example was: the grass is green, the sea is green, therefore the sea is grass.

The falsity of the second syllogism, and the fact that it is therefore of less weight than the first should not lead us to suppose that it is any the less essential, or that it is any less important in the composition, or structure, of the gag, than the first. The essence of the second moment of the gag is that it is characterized by the simultaneous presence of both modes of reasoning, which are maintained in tension, or balance with each other—provided we do not interpret balance to mean that they are of equal weight; for the tension which characterizes their relationship is based precisely on the fact that the second is a false, inferior, type of reasoning.

In summary therefore: the gag can be analyzed into two moments, thus:

1) a peripeteia, a shock or surprise that the narrative constructs for us;
2) a pair of syllogisms, leading to contradictory conclusions:
   a) that the process is implausible
   b) that the process nonetheless has a certain measure of plausibility, but that this is less than the implausibility.

The peripeteia is prepared and then sprung at a specific moment in the narrative, and this moment also unleashes the process of reflection analyzed in the two syllogisms. (It hardly needs underlining that this process is not a conscious, verbalized one on the part of the spectator: it is a spontaneous, intuitive reaction of which the two syllogisms are an elaborated, analytic form.) Finally it should be stressed that the two moments of the gag are in practice absolutely inseparable: without the moment of surprise, there is no estimation of the gag as simultaneously plausible and implausible, and without the preparation for the gag, we would have no means of knowing that the action in question is both plausible and implausible: it is only because we see the lift squash the cop that the emergence of the dwarf is to be characterized in this way. On the other hand, as we have already seen, it is the balance between plausibility and implausibility that makes the peripeteia into comic surprise, and not some other form of surprise, horrific surprise, for instance. For the totality of these processes it seems appropriate to reserve the title: the logic of the absurd.

C: "Pie and Chase: Gag, Spectacle, and Narrative in Slapstick Comedy," Donald Crafton[iii]

I contend that it was never the aim of comic filmmakers to "integrate" the gag elements of their movies. I also doubt that viewers subordinated gags to narrative. In fact, the separation between the vertical domain of slapstick (the arena of spectacle I will represent by the metaphor of the thrown pie) and the horizontal domain of the story (the arena of the chase) was a calculated rupture, designed to keep the two elements antagonistically apart. In *Narration in the Fiction Film*, David Bordwell asks, "Is there anything in narrative film that is not narrational?"[2] My answer is yes: the gag.

If we examine typical Hal Roach two-reel comedies from 1925 and 1926, we find a laboratory for what some film analysts have described as the series of symmetries and blockages that define the systematicity of classical American cinema. At the same time, it is important to differentiate these films from the contemporaneous feature. While at first the narrative structures of the shorts may resemble condensations or abridgments (features with the boring bits taken out), the high concentration of gag and spectacle defines the genre as unique. Among other features, the frequent intrusions of spectacle produce a kind of narrative lurching that often makes the plots of slapstick comedies distinctively incoherent (and delightfully so).

The Pie

Let us first look more closely at those nonnarrative gag elements that the term *slapstick* usually encompasses. This usage is appropriate when we consider the origin of that word, referring to a circus prop consisting of two thin slats joined together, so that a loud clack is made when one clown hits another on the behind. The violent aural effect, the "slap," may be thought of as having the same kind of disruptive impact on the audience as its visual equivalent in the silent cinema, the pie in the face. In fact, very few comedies of the twenties really used pies, but nevertheless their humor in a general sense frequently depended on the same kind of emphatic, violent, embarrassing gesture.

iii. From Donald Crafton, "Pie and Chase: Gag, Spectacle, and Narrative in Slapstick Comedy," in *Classical Hollywood Comedy*, ed. Kristine Brunovska Karnick and Henry Jenkins (New York: Routledge, 1995), 107–110. Copyright © 1995, republished with permission of Taylor and Francis Group; permission conveyed through Copyright Clearance Center Inc.

The lack of linear integration that offends some slapstick commentators can trace its roots to popular spectacle. For example, in his 1915 home correspondence manual, Brett Page advised would-be vaudeville writers that their scripts must account for the actors' *business.* He meant the visual, nonverbal performance component, "done to drive the spoken words home, or to 'get over' a meaning without words."[3] His pupils learned that:

> So large a part does the element of business play in the success of the two-act that the early examples of this vaudeville form were nearly all built out of bits of business. And the business was usually of the "slapstick" kind.[4]

Page defined slapstick as physical gags, and consistently emphasized its nonverbal nature:

> Every successful two-act, every entertainment-form of which acting is an element—the playlet and the full-evening play as well—prove beyond the shadow of a doubt that what audiences laugh at—what you and I laugh at—is not words, but actions and situations.[5]

Page easily generalized and shifted his focus from the nonverbal to the nonnarrative. About the vaudeville sketch he wrote,

> The purpose of the sketch is not to leave a single impression of a single story. It points no moral, draws no conclusion, and sometimes it might end quite as effectively anywhere before the place in the action at which it does terminate. It is built for entertainment purposes only and furthermore, for entertainment purposes that end the moment the sketch ends.[6]

Recalling the African projection of the fragmented Chaplin films, the movie might have been incomprehensible as a narrative, but it worked fine as a filmic sketch, an assembly of nonverbal gags. Such an aesthetic of spectacle for its own sake is clearly inimical to the classical narrative feature, but not at all hostile to slapstick cinema of the teens and twenties.

Again, we can use this concept to discriminate between the comic shorts and the comic feature. The latter purposefully (and more or less successfully) sought to produce an "integrated" spectacle. Certainly *The General* and *The Gold Rush* are exemplary in their attempt to set the hero's struggles within a determinant Griffithesque historical fiction. But when one examines the two-reelers, even late in the twenties and well into the sound era one finds a preponderance of anarchistic non- and quasinarratives that pass for movie stories.

Generally, there is a simple plot which frames the gags, with an opening premise and a closing scene which provides a resolution. The gags may or may not be thematically related. Whether this is a narrative depends on how insistently one defines it. I argue that despite a weakly structured set of causes and effects, many of these films remain, at best, quasinarratives. Although the shorts emulate feature film narrative structures, the audience is scarcely aware of it, navigating the film from laugh to laugh as though enjoying a sketch. This is gag-driven cinema.

There can be no concrete definition of a gag because it is marked by affective response, not set forms or clear logic. Further, gag and slapstick are not synonymous. Slapstick is the generic term for these nonnarrative intrusions, while gags are specific forms of intrusions. Like verbal jokes, to which they are closely related, gags have their own loose structures, systems and "fuzzy" logic that exist independently of cinema. The gag may also contain its own microscopic narrative system that may be irrelevant to the larger narrative, may mirror it, or may even work against it as parody. "Sight gags," those that depend primarily on visual exposition, still have characteristic logical structures, the same that one finds in multi-panel comic strips.[7] Think, for example, of the gag in *Jus' Passin' Through*, a Will Rogers film from 1923, produced by Hal Roach and directed by Charles Parrott (a.k.a., Charley Chase). We see a hobo checking the gates of houses for the special chalk tramp-sign that indicates whether there is a mean dog inside. One can easily see how the sequence could be presented effectively as a wordless comic strip. In the first two frames we would see images of the tramp eschewing those yards with the mark on the gate (the exposition of the nonhumorous part of the joke that vaudevillians would have called the "buildup"); in the penultimate panel we would see him fleeing a yard through an unmarked gate with a dog in hot pursuit; the final panel would show him adding his own beware-the-dog sign to the gate. Whether this corresponds to a "punch line" depends on how much visual/narrative information is perceived, and how the viewer's expectations are subverted.[8]

D: "The New Logic of the Absurd: *The Eric André Show*," Evan Elkins

Every episode of Adult Swim's *The Eric André Show* begins by literalizing the program's deconstructive aesthetic. The titular host, an actor and

A near-nude, raw-chicken-clad Eric André tests the limits of absurd humor.

comedian also known for his roles on *Don't Trust the B—— in Apartment 23*, *Man Seeking Woman*, and *2 Broke Girls*, destroys the cheap-looking, late-'60s-meets-public-access talk show's set. Consider the opening of the very first episode. After the Don Pardo–esque announcement, "Ladies and gentlemen, *The Eric André Show*!" and the familiar strains of a talk show's jazzy opening fanfare, André runs in screaming from off screen, vaults over a set chair and launches into the backdrop curtains, pulling them down. Then, he sprints over to the house band and throws the bass drum across the room into the demolished set before tackling the drummer.

Not content to merely destroy inanimate objects, André moves onto other forms of grotesque violence and self-harm. Here, his acts of destruction and mayhem become increasingly arch and difficult to watch. A shirtless André screams with two raw chickens on his hands; he pulls out his own teeth with pliers, forcibly kisses a woman—smearing his blood on her face—and shoves her onto the ground; he strips naked and destroys remaining pieces of the set. Finally, exhausted (and back in his sweat-drenched clothing), he sits down in a chair while a new set is quickly brought in and built back up around him. These sequences are different in each episode, and in subsequent episodes, they become even more creative and bizarre: dressed in a monk's robe, he covers himself in gasoline and prepares to self-immolate before a police officer enters from off screen and sprays him with pepper spray; he punches a man dressed as Benjamin Franklin in the stomach; he sexually assaults a snowman before punching its head off; he tears his own head off and throws it into a bookshelf; and so on. After these more obvious acts of destruction, the program proceeds to deconstruct the talk-show format more obliquely but no less obviously. In this first episode, after sitting down at his desk, André says, "That's all I had planned for the show. What should I do now?" Cohost and stand-up comedian, Hannibal Buress, responds, "I don't know, do a monologue or something." André then performs a half-hearted monologue before lamenting, "I'm dying." A bored Buress responds, "We all are," and suddenly falls asleep as the show switches to a public-access-quality "We'll be right back" card, complete with incongruously cheery muzak.

Several seasons in, it's clear that *The Eric André Show* is one of the strangest programs ever to air on American television. Described by its host in the press as a "talk show run by two sadists," it is a remarkably, intentionally, and gleefully off-putting piece of work.[9] It's also one of the funniest shows on television—that is, if the viewer is able to get onboard with André's warped mindset. But given all of its wanton destruction, violence, and abject distastefulness, how can we read *The Eric André Show* as a comedic work? To put it more simply, why is *The Eric André Show* funny? For many, it assuredly isn't, and André's humor rests on a high-risk/high-reward proposition: a particular brand of metacomedy that brings to mind traditional comedic conventions yet violently resists the moments of benign relief that usually accompany them. But even if the excess of André's comedy threatens to render theories of comedy and humor unsuitable for the task of decoding it, illustrating how and why audiences still might find it funny can help us understand how *The Eric André Show* plays with comedic conventions. If comedy and humor theory can help explain why certain transgressions are funny, they also indicate that it's possible to go too far. Many canonical philosophies of humor require particular sets of conditions to be in tension with each other: transgression and social mores (Bakhtin), the mechanical and the human (Bergson), plausibility and implausibility (Palmer), to offer a few.[10] However, *The Eric André Show* pulls these tensions to their breaking point, and much of its humor evokes traditional modes of comic performance and aesthetics while pushing them to their extremes. This can be explained in part by the program's industrial context. Within post-network American television's logics of escalating competition, narrowcast reach, and reliance on transgressive content, *The Eric André Show* represents an ongoing move in some televisual circles toward darker, more absurd, aggressive, and avant-garde forms of comedy. In a competitive media environment, André and company have pushed cable television comedy into a realm where traditional release valves and comforting moments are jettisoned;

almost every moment feels incongruous and random; and shock, disgust, and laughter are all on the table.

Exploding Comedic Tension

Comedy and humor have long involved destruction, bodily functions, and transgressions of both good taste and televisual conventions, but the sheer levels of excess present in *The Eric André Show* chart new territory. Although trading in the audiovisual ugliness that is part of Adult Swim's broader aesthetic and brand identity, this program represents a new extreme, taking gross-out humor to heights rarely seen on any American television program, much less a nominally comedic talk show. Virtually no episode goes by without a character vomiting, sweating, bleeding, or worse. This ugliness extends to the program's formal aesthetic; the program's sound design amplifies these elements, keeping sighs, slurps, gags, grunts, farts, and other bodily functions high in the mix. Visually, the first season of *The Eric André Show* was presented in the style of Adult Swim's long-running *Tim and Eric's Awesome Show, Great Job* —, a grimy, cheap-looking, public access–style television program, complete with degraded, analog video effects and simulated technological breakdowns. In the second season, *The Eric André Show* changed its look, abandoning the dingy analog look for HD video and a less grubby (though otherwise identical) set. However, the high-def look only amplifies the show's filth. In HD, André's flop-sweat and stained clothing are even more apparent, and the formal decrepitude of the first season is supplanted by disgusting acts presented to us in all-too-high-definition.

André's often crazed performance regularly violates the sober, wisecrack-driven mode of the late-night talk-show host. There's a Bergsonian element to André's humor in the program's opening scene, as his first appearances on screen push the limits of human performance and give the impression of a possessed machine bent on comic destruction.[11] At times, he and Buress are even replaced by actual dummies. Given that every episode begins with a manic spectacle of physical comedy that brings to mind The Three Stooges on some mixture of hard drugs, these moments can be characterized as slapstick spectacles.[12] As Donald Crafton argues, slapstick in early cinema and vaudeville relied on a "lack of linear integration," wherein slapstick functioned as comedic excess that the film could not wholly contain. Like these slapstick films, *The Eric André Show* contains a "high concentration of gag and spectacle" and features gags that function as "atemporal bursts of violence and or hedonism."

In the show's various opening sequences, André's acts of set destruction owe a debt to long-held slapstick traditions (as in moments when he tackles his drummer through the set or jumps off of a bookshelf and crashes into his desk). *The Eric André Show* also relies on the comedic power of interruption, again taking this aesthetic element to its logical extreme. Bits generally last a minute or two at the very longest, and some are only a few seconds long. Odd moments pass by with barely a moment for the audience to perceive them. Their incongruous nature follows Crafton's understanding of gags as "intrusions" on a narrative.[13] Although not a traditional narrative text, *The Eric André Show* presents every episode as a tapestry of intrusions: short, often-violent bits that disrupt any hopes of a cohesive televisual experience.

Jerry Palmer's theory of the "logic of the absurd" helps explain how André pushes the logic of comic interruptions and the slapstick gag into a more literal realm of violence. David Gurney succinctly summarizes Palmer, pointing to the kinds of tensions described above: "For humor to arise, there must be a logical balance of congruity and incongruity, plausibility and implausibility, and sense and nonsense."[14] In other words, Palmer explains how gags traditionally contain both a surprise and an unexpected result of the surprise, which is both plausible and implausible. He uses the example of a Laurel and Hardy gag where a police officer is seemingly crushed by an elevator but instead survives and is transformed into a little person in a police officer's uniform. Because it is implausible that the officer would survive, but plausible that crushing an object makes it smaller, the gag arises out of the tension between these two outcomes.[15] The audience presumably finds the humor in the simultaneous presence of expected and unexpected elements.

Often, *The Eric André Show* explodes this tension by presenting moments of extreme implausibility (bizarre, unmotivated moments that seem to come out of nowhere) or horrific plausibility (graphic displays of violence accompanied by screams of pain). Indeed, part of why we can read moments like the one Palmer describes above as humorous is because of "comic insulation," or the knowledge that the violence "isn't serious, that the character will in fact be restored to normal in a very short time, none the worse for very rough wear."[16] While *The Eric André Show*'s audience likely has some sense that they're watching a comedy program, moments when we see André scream while he bites off one of his fingers, tears his own head off, or scalps himself (all acts simulated at various points in the program's run) are considerably less insulated than your garden-variety physical gag. For participants and passersby in

André's hidden-camera stunts, the context that provides the comic insulation is often absent. These segments find André portraying outlandish characters—a "pizza ball" deliveryman dressed as a court jester, for example—who disrupt mundane events like convenience store transactions or karate classes. The disgusted and horrified responses to Andre's verbal abuse caught on camera make evident bystanders' unwitting participation in André absurd antics. André's ability to wring extreme darkness out of the trappings of physical humor makes use of physical comedy's inherent violence without providing the comic insulation that lets us know everything will be okay.

Part of what makes *The Eric André Show*'s comedy so shocking is that it walks a razor-thin line between humor and cruelty, pushing boundaries of jokes and non-jokes. Palmer summarizes a famous argument of anthropologist Mary Douglas: "A joke must be both perceived as a joke and permitted as a joke."[17] In other words, for a viewer to laugh, she must not only allow herself to find the joke funny but also she must recognize it as a joke in the first place. This awareness is key to Palmer's theory of comic insulation as well as another more recent idea, A. Peter McGraw and Caleb Warren's "benign violation" theory. As they explain, "Three conditions are jointly necessary and sufficient for eliciting humor: A situation must be appraised as a violation, a situation must be appraised as benign, and these two appraisals must occur simultaneously."[18] However, the cruel nature of some of André's hidden-camera segments, for instance, often blurs this line and further strips away comic insulation. For example, in one brief segment André asks a woman on the street, "How do you explain this?" before graphically, bloodily pretending to scalp himself (again, closing on a close-up of the woman's horrified expression). Many of these violations are not benign at all; they are hurtful and malevolent. Additionally, many of André's guerilla pranks strain legality, and he has complained publicly about needing to shoot in New York City rather than Los Angeles because of New York's looser hidden-camera consent laws.[19] André has been arrested for some of his bits, and in interviews he has also hinted at even more extreme ideas for the show that his producers and lawyers have prevented him from seeing through, including, in André's words, "a bit last year where I wanted to drive a car into a marching band and seriously injure six or seven people."[20]

By continually pushing limits of good taste and coherence, *The Eric André Show* also demonstrates how far contemporary television comedy must go in order to be truly surprising. But analyzing André's humor in the abstract, and using age-old philosophies and theories of narrative and humor based on early twentieth-century culture, will only get us so far. What happens when we consider it within the generic, textual, and industrial contexts of contemporary American television?

Metacomedic Television: The "Anti-Talk Show"

Much of *The Eric André Show*'s humor comes not from the construction of jokes in a classical sense, but from a form of metacomedy that has become part of Adult Swim's brand—one that incorporates extreme ugliness, unpleasantness, and legitimately uncomfortable moments into bits that nevertheless gesture toward comedic traditions from throughout media history. As *The A.V. Club* puts it, André's commitment to producing "a true anti-talk show" (a moniker also bestowed on the program by *The New York Times*) results in a program that is "positively apocalyptic."[21] In this way, André's humor aligns closely with a loose, avant-garde subgenre of comedy varyingly known as "anti-humor," "anti-comedy," "post-funny," or "metacomedy." Jeffrey Sconce develops the idea of "metacomedy" as "stand-up, sketch, and even narrative comedy that is explicitly about the art of comedy itself, a foregrounding of its expectations, conventions, and execution."[22] Metacomedy can be seen in Andy Kaufman's various experiments with what counts as comic performance, Michael O'Donoghue's distilled comedic evil, Chris Elliott's childlike absurdism, early David Letterman's dry, disdainful take on the late-night talk show, and Neil Hamburger's warped variation of the nightclub comic, among others. Sconce analyzes metacomedy through the work of Tim Heidecker and Eric Wareheim (a.k.a., Tim and Eric), an Adult Swim–based comedy duo who have developed a now-recognizable aesthetic based on absurdism and bodily humor presented in a low-budget, public access–style that features "odd personalities, awkward performances, technical mistakes, and obsolescent technologies."[23] *The Eric André Show*'s brand of metacomedy doesn't recall the absurdism of Tim and Eric by coincidence; it is coproduced by *Tim and Eric*'s Abso Lutely Productions (which also produces Comedy Central's high-concept prank show, *Nathan for You*, and IFC's fellow "anti-talk show," *Comedy Bang! Bang!*).

The Eric André Show doesn't fit within any standard definition of what makes a cohesive television presentation, and whenever it gestures toward the now-familiar format of the late-night talk show, it veers in unexpected directions. Everything about André and Buress's performances as talk show cohosts feels off. Lacking Johnny Carson and Ed McMahon's professional-quality banter—or even Conan O'Brien and Andy Richter's mildly absurdist take on the host/sidekick relationship—André and Buress often act as if they are barely on the same show. Their rapport is wildly inconsistent, ranging from stoned boredom to giddy playfulness to gleeful menace without any apparent motivation. While contemporary late-night talk shows tend to follow a standard format (monologue, sketch, guests, musical guest), *The Eric André Show* jerks from bit to bit without warning or explanation. Part of this comes out of the constraints of squeezing an episode into eleven minutes, but the program's frenetic pace is key to its discomfiting aesthetic. Further, in the spirit of zigging when we expect the show to zag, some bits drag on far *longer* than it seems like they should. In episode six of the first season, André abruptly interrupts an interview with Sinbad to bring out the "wheel of prizes," which includes prizes such as "Big Bucks" and "Fun Times" as well as "Move to North Korea" and "Auto-Erotic Asphyxiate." As the wheel starts to slow down, it inexplicably speeds back up while Buress and André shout with excitement. Occasionally, whatever internal logic these individual bits have breaks down on screen. In the first season's ninth episode, André introduces the next guest, nominally the musical act Grizzly Bear, and a live grizzly bear walks onto the set. Buress and André are both visibly, authentically frightened, and André nervously runs off screen as the bear proceeds to destroy his desk. In the next episode, a remote segment called "Who Can Hold the Most Babies," where Buress and André walk around a playground asking parents if they can hold their children, stops abruptly as André laughs, says he hates the bit, and ends the segment.

At the level of genre, *The Eric André Show* represents a metacomedic pastiche of several subgenres of comedy that have been promoted to the nocturnal young-adult set over the past fifteen years or so. We see *Jackass*-style pranks pulled on unsuspecting bystanders and celebrities; Tim and Eric–style absurdist, destructive humor; and a subversive and deconstructive take on the hoary late-night talk-show format (a tradition that goes back at least as far as *Fernwood 2 Night*, *Late Night with David Letterman*, and *The Larry Sanders Show* and has been taken up by Conan O'Brien, *Knowing Me, Knowing You with Alan Partridge*, and Adult Swim's earlier program *Space Ghost Coast to Coast*). The program's talk-show set is spare and dingy, and André performs versions of talk-show staples that regularly turn cruel or bizarre. In season one's "Wacky Newspaper Articles" segment, a clear parody of Jay Leno's "Headlines" bit, André showcases and riffs off dark headlines like "Killer's Maps Lead to Victim's Remains" (to which André quips, "What are we, on a scavenger hunt, folks?") and "Pastor's Daughter Struck as Gun Accidentally Goes Off." André repeats this bit in season two, but the entire segment consists of him graphically vomiting all over his desk. In another bit, which recalls Johnny Carson's Carnac the Magnificent routine, André stumbles in wearing a comically oversized turban and announces that he can predict what's in his mail. Holding the envelope up to his forehead, he mumbles gibberish, predicts nothing, and opens the envelope. The envelope is filled with spaghetti and meatballs, which André pours onto his desk and proceeds to eat with his hands.

André's demented riff on the late-night talk show is also apparent in his treatment of the celebrity interview. The program blends appearances by C-list celebrities (Tatyana Ali, *The Real Housewives of Beverly Hills*'s Brandi Glanville, Sinbad, Dolph Lundgren) and intentionally poor celebrity impersonators (such as an appearance by "Arnold Schwarzenegger" — actually Bruce Vilanch riding a scooter and smoking a cigar). The show is also notable for extending its pranks to its celebrity guests. During Glanville's appearance, André tackles and screams at a production assistant without warning, and Glanville is visibly surprised and upset. Lauren Conrad, a former star of MTV's *The Hills*, was invited to appear on an episode of the program, and André did not warn her in advance of the show's nature. As André tells it, "I puked during her interview then I ate my puke back up. She left. She was upset."[24] Indeed, this is precisely what happens on the show.

He has also boasted of using various strategies to make guests uncomfortable: putting old, smelly clams under their chairs, dripping water on them during the interviews, and even electrocuting them.[25] André regularly subjects celebrity guests to all sorts of indignities, as in a segment where Buress wakes up a sleeping Lorenzo Lamas by throwing water on him, and Buress and André force Lamas to dance for their amusement. Topping it off, they feed Lamas slop from a can (who devours it hungrily in an indication that he hasn't been fed in a while) and ask him about his involvement in Natalie Wood's death. During an interview with former MTV veejay Downtown Julie Brown, André suddenly yells, "corned beef me!" and a corned beef sandwich flies in from off screen, partially striking Brown. If an earlier metacomedic talk-show host like David Letterman "radiated dislike for the whole chatty ritual as hallowed by TV history and refined by his predecessors," André doesn't even give the ritual that much thought; he simply messes around, acts strangely, and radiates an interviewing style more akin to a mixture of sadism and apathy.[26]

André also plays with the talk-show format in more subtle ways. Whenever a guest comes out to sit in the interview chair, Buress is forced to stand awkwardly behind him or her because the chair is only big enough for one person. Questions are alternately aimless (to Brown: "I want to go on vacation. Where should I go?"), inappropriate (to Seth Rogen: "What's your cell phone number?" as André proceeds to put his number on screen), and surprisingly political (to the Spice Girls' Mel B: "Do you think Margaret Thatcher effectively utilized girl power by funneling money to illegal paramilitary death squads in Northern Ireland?"), and André regularly performs monologues that feel unplanned or veer into surrealist territory. Such incomprehensible moments can barely be considered parodies of talk-show traditions; rather, in the spirit of meta-comedy, they are Dadaist set-pieces that gesture faintly toward familiar entertainment traditions.

Conclusion: Questions of Identity and Politics

The Eric André Show ricochets between affirming and confounding traditional explanations of humor. The program is often absent of comic insulation, but it contains moments of surprising violence and implausibility that align with Palmer's explanation of absurd humor. Recalling Bergson, André's screen presence is mechanical (in his possessed energy) yet corporeal (in his excessive emphasis on bodily function). It also meets benign violation theory only about halfway, often stripping away the "benign" element. All of this is to say that the program offers a test case to see how far canonical philosophies of humor and laughter can take us. With something as extreme as *The Eric André Show*, they work only up to a point.

One reason these theories can't fully explain the dynamics of André's humor is that they don't account for the program's representational politics in the context of post-network television culture. They offer a way to assess the mechanics of *The Eric André Show*, but they evacuate politics either by focusing primarily on formal aesthetics or by presuming that André's work is purely nihilistic. But the show is hardly apolitical. For one, it has helped open up a space for black performers and performances within the comic subgenres of metacomedy and anti-humor, which have long been predominately sold to a young, white, male demographic.[27] The fact that this program is hosted by two well-known black comedians, as well as its regular appearances by rappers, such as Killer Mike, Mr. Muthafuckin' Exquire, and Chance the Rapper, indicates that *The Eric André Show* in part sees itself as addressing a black audience. At the same time, this must be considered in the context of the television industry's "use of blackness . . . as a method of cultivating brand identities with transracial appeal" in the post-network era.[28] This ambivalence is apparent in the program's presence on Adult Swim, a US cable TV channel that broadcasts in late-night time slots and mobilizes aesthetic and textual forms generally considered subcultural or "fringe" in some way. Adult Swim has long leveraged nondominant cultural forms, including black comedy and hip-hop, in order to court a long-coveted demographic of young, white men.[29] Still, the show can carry a surprising political punch, as when André asks *Battlestar Galactica*'s Richard Hatch if he thinks US foreign policy is based on imperialism. In one hidden-camera segment, André arrives at a Tea Party meeting and hands out Klan hoods and confederate flags as several meeting attendees (represented as a series of blurred-out white faces) alternately shout for the police and gleefully accept the flags. This sequence forgoes the usual violent shock-humor and inscrutable anti-comedy that have become the show's stock-in-trade in favor of a purer, more incisive satirical message.

The incorporation of black art forms and politics into a late-night, metacomedic talk show speaks to how the contemporary television industry perceives its audience as a diverse, fragmented collection of viewers and its business model as one based on narrowcasting. In this vein, André's humor comes out of a need to continually escalate TV content in order to gain viewers. As Amanda Lotz has argued, in the post-network era, "changing competitive practices among networks have borne significant adjustments in the types of shows the industry produces and expanded the range of profitable storytelling."[30] Although it would be a stretch to call *The Eric André Show* a form of televisual "storytelling" akin to what Lotz is describing, the excess of its aesthetics and content are only possible in a post-network environment where television's creators are compelled to continually up the ante. This industrial environment offers a place where the political, absurdist, nonsensical, violent, disgusting, and incongruous can all coexist with each other in an attempt to draw eyeballs.

This spirit is apparent in a quotation that opens a recent feature on André: "If [*Jackass*'s Johnny] Knoxville is a 10, I want to turn it up to 11. . . . I just want to fuckin' *push* it."[31] So, while it would assuredly be surprising to see a program come along that is more excessive in its anti-humor than *The Eric André Show*, the competitive logics of the contemporary television industry, as well as a natural artistic inclination to keep pushing the limits of comedic form, will assuredly result in something that makes André's work look tame by comparison. But in *The Eric André Show*, the twin logics of escalating competition and metacomedy have led to a piece of work that strains our ability to deploy traditional theories of humor in order to make sense of the program. At the same time, *The Eric André Show* is comedic inasmuch as it draws on traditional understandings of comedy while consciously violating them in an anarchic, metacomedic spirit.

Notes

1. The logical nature of gags was observed by French critics of the silent cinema. See Coursodon, *Keaton et Cie*, and Mars, *Le Gag*.

2. Bordwell, *Narration in the Fiction Film*, 53. Bordwell's answer is also yes, but qualified. Such elements are "excess" (citing Kristin Thompson's analysis of *Ivan the Terrible*) and "whatever its suggestiveness as a critical concept, excess lies outside my concern here."

3. Page, *Writing for Vaudeville*, 98. Fn. Thanks to Henry Jenkins for bringing this book to my attention.

4. Page, *Writing for Vaudeville*, 98.

5. Page, *Writing for Vaudeville*, 108.

6. Page, *Writing for Vaudeville*, 147.

7. Carroll, "Notes on the Sight Gag," 25–42. Noël Carroll's six categories of sight gags are a useful catalogue. His defining principle is based on the construction of conflicting interpretations in the visual organization of a scene.

8. Carroll's distinction between verbal and visual jokes ("Notes on the Sight Gag") is generally, but not always, valid. He argues: "Sight gags differ from verbal jokes. Verbal jokes generally culminate in a punchline that at first glance is incongruous by virtue of its appearing to be nonsense . . . one is initially stymied by the incongruity of the punchline, which leads to a *re*interpretation of the joke material that makes it comprehensible. Sight gags also involve a play of interpretations. But with sight gags, the play of interpretation is often visually available to the audience simultaneously throughout the gag: the audience *need not* await something akin to the punchline in a verbal joke to put the interpretive play in motion" (27). There are many examples of gags that deliver just such a "punch" due to a surprise cut or change in *mise-en-scène*, prompting a reinterpretation analogous to the one Carroll describes in verbal humor.

9. Modell, "Eric André Says a Bunch of Bullshit."

10. See Bakhtin, *Rabelais and His World*; Bergson, *Laughter*; Palmer, *The Logic of the Absurd*.

11. Writing at the beginning of the twentieth century, Henri Bergson famously theorized, "The comic is that side of a person which reveals his likeness to a thing, that aspect of human events which, through its peculiar inelasticity, conveys the impression of pure mechanism, of automatism, of movement without life" and that comedy results from "something mechanical in something living." See Bergson, *Laughter*, 87, 77.

12. Crafton, "Pie and Chase," 108, 109.

13. Crafton, "Pie and Chase," 109.

14. Gurney, "Recombinant Comedy, Transmedial Mobility, and Viral Video," 4.

15. Palmer, *The Logic of the Absurd*, 43.

16. In this way, André's humor is similar to the dark comedy of early *Saturday Night Live* writer Michael O'Donoghue. See Elkins, "Michael O'Donoghue."

17. Palmer, *The Logic of the Absurd*, 21; see also Douglas, "The Social Control of Cognition."
18. McGraw and Warren, "Benign Violations," 1142.
19. Evans, "Talking to Eric André About Season 2."
20. Modell, "Eric André Says a Bunch of Bullshit."
21. Nowalk, *"The Eric André Show"*; see also Zinoman, "The Rise of the Anti-Talk Show."
22. Sconce, *"Tim and Eric's Awesome Show,"* 75.
23. Sconce, *"Tim and Eric's Awesome Show,"* 76.
24. Branch, "Eric André Grosses Out Lauren Conrad."
25. Evans, "Talking to Eric André About Season 2."
26. Seitz, "Seitz on David Letterman's Lasting Impact."
27. In this way, André's program is of a piece with Adult Swim's *Loiter Squad*, featuring rap collective Odd Future Wolf Gang Kill Them All.
28. Fuller, "Branding Blackness on US Cable Television," 287.
29. See Elkins, "Cultural Identity and Subcultural Forums."
30. Lotz, *The Television Will Be Revolutionized*, 24.
31. Battan, "The Peaceful Madness of Eric André."

Works Cited

Bakhtin, Mikhail. *Rabelais and His World*. Translated by Hélène Iswolsky. Bloomington: Indiana University Press, 1984.
Battan, Carrie. "The Peaceful Madness of Eric André." *Grantland*, October 22, 2014. http://grantland.com/features/eric-André-adult-swim-eric-André-show-hannibal-buress.
Bergson, Henri. *Laughter: An Essay on the Meaning of the Comic*. Translated by Cloudesley Brereton and Fred Rothwell. New York: MacMillan, 1914.
Bordwell, David. *Narration in the Fiction Film*. Madison: University of Wisconsin Press, 1985.
Branch, Chris. "Eric André Grosses Out Lauren Conrad in the New Season of 'The Eric André Show.'" *Huffington Post*, October 22, 2014. http://www.huffingtonpost.com/2014/10/21/eric-André-lauren-conrad_n_6024492.html.
Carroll, Noël. "Notes on the Sight Gag." In *Comedy/Cinema/Theory*, edited by Andrew Horton, 25–42. Berkeley: University of California Press, 1991.
Coursodon, Jean-Pierre. *Keaton et Cie. (Cinema D'Aujourd'Hui, livre 25)*. France: Seghers, 1964.
Crafton, Donald. "Pie and Chase: Gag, Spectacle, and Narrative in Slapstick Comedy." In *Classical Hollywood Comedy*, edited by Kristine Brunovska Karnick and Henry Jenkins, 106–119. New York: Routledge, 1995.
Douglas, Mary. "The Social Control of Cognition: Some Factors in Joke Perception." *Man* 3, no. 3 (1968): 361–376.
Elkins, Evan. "Michael O'Donoghue, Experimental Television Comedy, and *Saturday Night Live*'s Authorship." In *Saturday Night Live and American Television*, edited by Nick Marx, Matt Sienkiewicz, and Ron Becker, 56–74. Bloomington: Indiana University Press, 2013.

————. "Cultural Identity and Subcultural Forums: The Post-Network Politics of Adult Swim." *Television and New Media* 15, no. 7 (2014): 595–610.

Evans, Bradford. "Talking to Eric André About Season 2 of 'The Eric André Show,'" Splitsider, October 3, 2013. http://splitsider.com/2013/10/talking-to-eric-André-about-season-2-of-the-eric-André-show/.

Fuller, Jennifer. "Branding Blackness on US Cable Television." *Media, Culture and Society* 32, no. 2 (2010): 287.

Gurney, David. "Recombinant Comedy, Transmedial Mobility, and Viral Video." *The Velvet Light Trap* 68 (2011): 3–13.

Lotz, Amanda. *The Television Will Be Revolutionized.* New York: NYU Press, 2007.

Mars, François. *Le Gag.* Paris: Editions du Cerf, 1964.

McGraw, Peter A., and Caleb Warren, "Benign Violations: Making Immoral Behavior Funny." *Psychological Science* 21, no. 8 (2010): 1141–1149.

Modell, Josh. "Eric André Says a Bunch of Bullshit." *The A.V. Club*, November 5, 2014. http://www.avclub.com/article/eric-André-says-bunch-bullshit-211396

Nowalk, Brandon. "*The Eric André Show.*" *The A.V. Club*, October 2, 2013. http://www.avclub.com/review/ithe-eric-andre-showi-103606

Sconce, Jeffrey. "*Tim and Eric's Awesome Show, Great Job!:* Metacomedy." In *How to Watch Television*, edited by Ethan Thompson and Jason Mittell, 74–82. New York: NYU Press, 2014.

Seitz, Matt Zoller. "Seitz on David Letterman's Lasting Impact: A Smudge on the Collective Unconscious." *Vulture*, April 4, 2014. http://www.vulture.com/2014/04/matt-zoller-seitz-on-david-lettermans-lasting-impact.html.

Page, Brett. *Writing for Vaudeville.* Springfield: The Home Correspondence School, 1915.

Palmer, Jerry. *The Logic of the Absurd: On Film and Television Comedy.* London: BFI, 1988.

Zinoman, Jason. "The Rise of the Anti-Talk Show." *New York Times*, June 7, 2012. http://www.nytimes.com/2012/06/08/arts/television/the-rise-of-the-anti-talk-show.html.

3.

Psychoanalyzing Comedy

ARCHER, the world's greatest, least self-aware secret agent sneaks into the room and prepares to assassinate his target.

ARCHER

(to himself)

I can't imagine what it would be like to know when you're going to die. Or even if.

* * *

It is difficult to agree with Sigmund Freud. His claims are pretty crazy. Sons love mothers, sure, but do they really want to sleep with them? Dads can be overbearing boors, but do their children really wish upon them violent deaths so that mom dives back into the dating pool? As hard, perhaps impossible, as such things are for most to accept, Freudian notions of the Oedipus Complex say that, deep down, people both harbor such desires and are unconsciously impacted by them. And if that wasn't belief-stretching enough, consider his methodology. Although his claims are phrased as universal, his evidence comes solely from observations of turn-of-the-century German people who had the time, money, and inclination to tell a cocaine addict what they dreamt about last night. It can thus be rather tempting to take the school of thought that Freud invented, psychoanalysis, and consign it to the realm of pseudoscience where it can mingle with healing crystals, ear wax candles, and other debunked therapies.

But then, at some point, it happens: you laugh at something that you are completely certain that you do not find funny. Or at least your conscious mind does not. Perhaps it's an Oedipal scenario or some other sexual deviance that you find appalling. Maybe it's a bit of casual sexism or racism or homophobia that you are sure that the very fiber of your being rejects. Or, like in the scene from the FX animated series *Archer* quoted above, it might be a reference to something that you find very serious, scary, and tragic: the inevitable death of you and everyone you know. Death may not be funny to you, but Archer's apparently futile denial of it is. In such moments, the idea of hidden, counterintuitive aspects of the human psyche suddenly seem much more viable. Why, when faced with that which we disdain and fear the most, do we often laugh?

For Freud and those media scholars who have followed his ideas, the answer lies in the obscure, scientifically unverified concept of psychic energy. And although the mechanism by which this works is unclear, there is something convincing, or at least intriguing, in its explanation. According to Freudian psychoanalytic theory, every person walks around every day using a tremendous amount of energy in order to repress the aspects of their psyches that get in the way of successful socialization. Deep down you want to copulate with all sorts of people in all sorts of creative, socially uncouth ways. But, in order to get through the day, you keep that fact out of sight, not only from those around you but also, at least partially, from yourself. You follow the proper rules of decorum and, in doing so, you tax yourself. Joking, according to Freud, provides a momentary opportunity to cease this exhausting act of repression. The joke brings your true, primal feelings to the surface, and the psychic sensation brought by this release of pressure manifests in the pleasure of laughter. Think of a valve releasing pent-up steam. Or perhaps a more risqué metaphor that our own repressive instincts prevent us from typing out.

As for Archer's death joke, psychoanalytic theory offers a few ways of considering why it's funny even though its subject, mortality, seems to be quite the opposite. From the perspective of Freudian joking, which is exemplified in the first essay reprinted in this chapter, Archer's comedy resides in yet another counterintuitive desire: the death drive. According to Freud, all people have a secret will to self-annihilation that, in order to function in polite society, they exert great mental energy to repress. Archer, in entertaining the possibility of his immortality, thus brings to the surface the viewer's mortality and perhaps even the fact that she has a desire for her own destruction. If this reading pushes you a bit too far, there is also the psychoanalytic theory, voiced most prominently by Otto Rank, that people spend tremendous energy simply avoiding thoughts of death for the more intuitive reason that they wish to deny its oncoming charge. In either case, Archer's joke can be seen as funny because it offers a moment in which the repressed comes to the surface, sparing us the burden of actively pushing it into the subconscious.

A second Freudian concept, distinct from that of joking, is humor, as articulated in the second essay reprinted in this chapter. Humor, according to Freud, succeeds by taking something serious and worrisome and effectively marking it as safe, thus sparing the psychic energy of despairing over it. As opposed to a momentary respite from repression, humor serves to assure us that there is nothing to worry about in the first place. Certainly, Archer's quip may also be read through this lens, by which placing the serious, scary topic of inevitable mortality in the realm of an animated spy spoof pleasurably signifies to the viewer that there is one less thing to worry about. In the concluding essay of this chapter, Andrew Owens offers a similar approach in analyzing the sexual comedy of *The Big Bang Theory*. Like *Archer*, *Big Bang*, Owens argues, both releases the viewer's psychic energy by bringing repressions to the surface and marks the viewer's deepest fears as fundamentally unserious by placing them in the mouths of fools.

The middle essay of this chapter is perhaps the most challenging in this volume. In it, Paul Flaig grapples with the oft-ignored comedy theory embedded in the work of Jacques Lacan, perhaps Freud's most prominent and difficult disciple. The essence of Lacan's comedy theory is, Flaig argues, not fundamentally opposed to Freud's theories of humor and joking discussed above. There are aspects of the reality of the human condition that lurk deep beneath the surface, and one of the pleasures of comedy derives from setting them free. In Lacan's thinking, this fundamental reality is being constantly obscured because language, the only truly human tool for expression, is inadequate for the task. Words can never express who you are at your deepest core. The character of early film comedian Harpo Marx, who is both dumb (speechless) and dumb (too unintelligent to follow the rules of language), thus brings to the surface the fact that our true selves are constantly being repressed and obscured. Once more, the psychoanalytic worldview itself might seem far-fetched, but it nonetheless serves as a useful device for untangling comedy's mysteries.

A: *Jokes and Their Relation to the Unconscious*, Sigmund Freud[i]

The case of tendentious jokes is a special one. . . . An impulse or urge is present which seeks to release pleasure from a particular source and, if it were allowed free play, would release it. Besides this, another urge is

i. From Sigmund Freud, *Jokes and their Relation to the Unconscious*, trans. and ed. James Strachey (New York: W. W. Norton, 1960), 166–167.

present which works against this generation of pleasure—inhibits it, that is, or suppresses it. The suppressing current must, as the outcome shows, be a certain amount stronger than the suppressed one, which, however, is not on that account abolished. Now let us suppose that yet another urge makes its appearance which would release pleasure through the same process, though from other sources, and which thus operates in the same sense as the suppressed urge. What can the result be in such a case?

An example will give us our bearings better than this schematic discussion. Let us assume that there is an urge to insult a certain person; but this is so strongly opposed by feelings of propriety or of aesthetic culture that the insult cannot take place. If, for instance, it were able to break through as a result of some change of emotional condition or mood, this breakthrough by the insulting purpose would be felt subsequently with unpleasure. Thus the insult does not take place. Let us now suppose, however, that the possibility is presented of deriving a good joke from the material of the words and thoughts used for the insult—the possibility, that is, of releasing pleasure from other sources which are not obstructed by the same suppression.

This second development of pleasure could, nevertheless, not occur unless the insult were permitted; but as soon as the latter is permitted the new release of pleasure is also joined to it. Experience with tendentious jokes shows that in such circumstances the suppressed purpose can, with the assistance of the pleasure from the joke, gain sufficient strength to overcome the inhibition, which would otherwise be stronger than it. The insult takes place, because the joke is thus made possible. But the enjoyment obtained is not only that produced by the joke: it is incomparably greater. It is so much greater than the pleasure from the joke that we must suppose that the hitherto suppressed purpose has succeeded in making its way through, perhaps without any diminution whatever. It is in such circumstances that the tendentious joke is received with the heartiest laughter.

B. "Humor," Sigmund Freud[ii]

In my work on *Wit and its relation to the Unconscious* (1905) I considered humor really from the economic point of view alone. My object was to dis-

ii. From Sigmund Freud, "Humour," in *The International Journal of Psychoanalysis* 9, no. 1 (1928): 1–6. Copyright © 1928, reproduced by permission of *The International Journal of Psychoanalysis*.

cover the source of the pleasure derived from humor, and I think I was able to show that that pleasure proceeds from a saving in expenditure of affect.

There are two ways in which the process at work in humor may take place. Either one person may himself adopt a humorous attitude, while a second person acts as spectator, and derives enjoyment from the attitude of the first; or there may be two people concerned, one of whom does not himself take any active share in producing the humorous effect, but is regarded by the other in a humorous light. To take a very crude example: when the criminal who is being led to the gallows on a Monday observes, "Well, this is a good beginning to the week," he himself is creating the humor; the process works itself out in relation to himself and evidently it affords him a certain satisfaction. I am merely a listener who has not assisted in this functioning of his sense of humor, but I feel its effect, as it were from a distance. I detect in myself a certain humorous satisfaction, possibly much as he does.

We have an instance of the second type of humor when a writer or a comedian depicts the behavior of real or imaginary people in a humorous fashion. There is no need for the people described to display any humor; the humorous attitude only concerns the person who makes them the object of it, and the reader or hearer shares his enjoyment of the humor, as in the former instance. To sum up, then, we may say that the humorous attitude—in whatever it consists—may have reference to the subject's self or to other people; further, we may assume that it is a source of enjoyment to the person who adopts it, and, finally, a similar pleasure is experienced by observers who take no actual part in it.

We shall best understand the origin of the pleasure derived from humor if we consider the process which takes place in the mind of anyone listening to another man's jest. He sees this other person in a situation which leads him to anticipate that the victim will show signs of some affect; he will get angry, complain, manifest pain, fear, horror, possibly even despair. The person who is watching or listening is prepared to follow his lead, and to call up the same emotions. But his anticipations are deceived; the other man does not display any affect—he makes a joke. It is from the saving of expenditure in feeling that the hearer derives the humorous satisfaction.

It is easy to get so far, but we soon say to ourselves that it is the process in the other man, the "humorist," which calls for the greater attention. There is no doubt that the essence of humor is that one spares oneself the affects to which the situation would naturally give rise and overrides with a jest the possibility of such an emotional display. Thus far, the process must be the same in the humorist and his hearer. Or, to put it more accurately, the hearer must have copied the process in the mind of the humorist. But how does the latter arrive at that mental attitude which makes the discharge of affect superfluous? What is the dynamic process underlying the "humorous attitude"? Clearly, the solution of this problem is to be found in the humorist himself; in the listener we may suppose there is only an echo, a copy of this unknown process.

It is now time to acquaint ourselves with some of the characteristics of humor. Like wit and the comic, humor has in it a *liberating* element. But it has also something fine and elevating, which is lacking in the other two ways of deriving pleasure from intellectual activity. Obviously, what is fine about it is the triumph of narcissism, the ego's victorious assertion of its own invulnerability. It refuses to be hurt by the arrows of reality or to be compelled to suffer. It insists that it is impervious to wounds dealt by the outside world, in fact, that these are merely occasions for affording it pleasure. This last trait is a fundamental characteristic of humor. Suppose the criminal being led to execution on a Monday had said: "It doesn't worry me. What does it matter, after all, if a fellow like me is hanged? The world won't come to an end." We should have to admit that this speech of his displays the same magnificent rising superior to the real situation; what he says is wise and true, but it does not betray a trace of humor. Indeed, it is based on an appraisal of reality which runs directly counter to that of humor. Humor is not resigned; it is rebellious. It signifies the triumph not only of the ego, but also of the pleasure-principle, which is strong enough to assert itself here in the face of the adverse real circumstances.

These two last characteristics, the denial of the claim of reality and the triumph of the pleasure-principle, cause humor to approximate to the regressive or reactionary processes which engage our attention so largely in psycho-pathology. By its repudiation of the possibility of suffering, it takes its place in the great series of methods devised by the mind of man for evading the compulsion to suffer—a series which begins with neurosis and delusions, and includes intoxication, self-induced states of abstraction and ecstasy. Owing to this connection, humor possesses a dignity which is wholly lacking, for instance, in wit, for the aim of wit is either simply to afford gratification, or, in so doing, to provide an outlet for aggressive tendencies. Now in what does this humorous attitude consist, by means of which one refuses to undergo suffering, asseverates the invincibility of one's ego against the real world and victoriously upholds the pleasure-principle, yet all without quitting the ground of mental sanity, as happens when other means to the same end are adopted? Surely it seems impossible to reconcile the two achievements.

If we turn to consider the situation in which one person adopts a humorous attitude towards others, one view which I have already tentatively suggested in my book on wit will seem very evident. It is this: that the one is adopting towards the other the attitude of an adult towards a child, recognizing and smiling at the triviality of the interests and sufferings which seem to the child so big. Thus the humorist acquires his superiority by assuming the role of the grown-up, identifying himself to some extent with the father, while he reduces the other people to the position of children. This supposition is probably true to fact, but it does not seem to take us very far. We ask ourselves what makes the humorist arrogate to himself this role?

Here we must recall the other, perhaps the original and more important, situation in humor, in which a man adopts a humorous attitude towards himself in order to ward off possible suffering. Is there any sense in saying that someone is treating himself like a child and is at the same time playing the part of the superior adult in relation to this child?

This idea does not seem very plausible, but I think that if we consider what we have learnt from pathological observations of the structure of our ego, we shall find a strong confirmation of it. This ego is not a simple entity; it harbors within it, as its innermost core, a special institution: the super-ego. Sometimes it is amalgamated with this, so that we cannot distinguish the one from the other, while in other circumstances the two can be sharply differentiated. Genetically the super-ego inherits the position of the parents in the mental hierarchy; it often holds the ego in strict subordination, and still actually treats it as the parents (or the father) treated the child in his early years. We obtain a dynamic explanation of the humorous attitude, therefore, if we conclude that it consists in the subject's removing the accent from his own ego and transferring it on to his super-ego. To the super-ego, thus inflated, the ego can appear tiny and all its interests trivial, and with this fresh distribution of energy it may be an easy matter for it to suppress the potential reactions of the ego.

To preserve our customary phraseology, let us not speak of transferring the accent, but rather of displacing large quantities of cathexis [mental energy]. We shall then ask whether we are justified in imagining such extensive displacements from one institution in the mental apparatus to another. It looks like a new hypothesis, conceived *ad hoc*; yet we may recollect that repeatedly, even if not often enough, we have taken such a factor into account when endeavoring to form some metapsychological conception of the mental processes. For instance, we assumed that the difference between ordinary erotic object-cathexis and the state of being in love was that in the latter case incomparably more cathexis passes over to the object, the ego as it were emptying itself into the object. The study of some cases of paranoia proved to me that ideas of persecution are formed early, and exist for a long time without any perceptible effect, until as the result of some definite occasion they receive a sufficient amount of cathexis to cause them to become dominant. The cure of paranoiac attacks of this sort, too, will lie not so much in resolving and correcting the delusional ideas as in withdrawing from them the cathexis they have attracted. The alternation between melancholia and mania, between a cruel suppressing of the ego by the super-ego and the liberation of the ego after this oppression, suggests some such shifting of cathexis; and this conception would, moreover, explain a number of phenomena in normal mental life. If, hitherto, we have but seldom had recourse to this explanation, it has been on account of our customary caution, which is surely rather praiseworthy than otherwise. The ground on which we feel ourselves secure is that of mental pathology; it is here that we make our observations and win our convictions. For the present we commit ourselves to an opinion concerning the normal only in so far as we detect it amongst the isolated and distorted features of the morbid. When once this hesitation is overcome, we shall recognize how greatly the static conditions as well as the dynamic alteration in the quantity of the energic cathexis contribute to our understanding of mental processes.

I think, therefore, that the possibility I have suggested, namely, that in a given situation the subject suddenly effects a hyper-cathexis of the super-ego, which in its turn alters the reactions of the ego, is one which deserves to be established. Moreover, we find a striking analogy to this hypothesis of mine about humor in the kindred field of wit. I was led to assume that wit originates in the momentary abandoning of a conscious thought to unconscious elaboration, wit being therefore the contribution of the unconscious to the comic. In just the same way humor would be a contribution to the comic made through the agency of the super-ego.

In other respects we know that the super-ego is a stern master. It may be said that it accords ill with its character that it should wink at affording the ego a little gratification. It is true that the pleasure derived from humor is never so intense as that produced by the comic or by wit and never finds a vent in hearty laughter. It is also true that, in bringing about the humorous attitude, the super-ego is really repudiating reality and serving an illusion. But (without quite knowing why) we attribute to this less intensive pleasure a high value: we feel it to have a peculiarly liberating and elevating effect. Besides, the jest made in humor is not the essential thing; it has only the value of a proof. The principal thing is the intention which humor fulfils, whether it concerns the subject's self or other people. Its meaning is: "Look here! This is all that this seemingly dangerous world amounts to. Child's play—the very thing to jest about!"

If it is really the super-ego which, in humor, speaks such kindly words of comfort to the intimidated ego, this teaches us that we have still very much to learn about the nature of that institution. Further, we note that it is not everyone who is capable of the humorous attitude: it is a rare and precious gift, and there are many people who have not even the capacity for deriving pleasure from humor when it is presented to them by others. Finally, if the super-ego does try to comfort the ego by humor and to protect it from suffering, this does not conflict with its derivation from the parental institution.

C: "Lacan's Harpo," Paul Flaig[iii]

Despite the importance of Jacques Lacan's thought for film theory, there is almost no scholarly engagement with the various discussions of film in his seminars. Take Seminar VII, "The Ethics of Psychoanalysis." Here, among well-known readings of Antigone, anamorphotic painting, and the poetry of courtly love, we find several film references, from Federico Fellini's *La dolce vita* (1960) to Georges Franju's *La tête contre les murs* (1959) to Jules Dassin's *Never on Sunday* (1960). Perhaps the most intriguing of such references is Lacan's analysis of the face of Harpo Marx:

> It is enough to evoke a face which is familiar to everyone of you, that of the terrible dumb brother of the four Marx brothers, Harpo. Is there anything that poses a question which is more present, more pressing, more absorbing, more disruptive, more nauseating, more calculated to thrust everything that takes place before us into the abyss or void than that face of Harpo Marx, that face with its smile which leaves us unclear as to whether it signifies the most extreme perversity or complete simplicity? This dumb man alone is sufficient to sustain the atmosphere of doubt and of radical annihilation which is the stuff of the Marx brothers' extraordinary farce and the uninterrupted play of "jokes" that makes their activity so valuable.[1]

This analysis occurs at the end of Lacan's elaboration of his concept of *das Ding*, and it is not surprising that the sole scholar to analyze this passage, Simon Critchley, has understood Harpo to embody the Thing, that forever distant object signifying human mortality.[2] Critchley relates this identity-annihilating *Fremdheit* (strangeness) to a theorization of comedy by examining Lacan's rare references to the comedic in this seminar. Critchley's argument is that, in contrast to the tragic hero's futile assumption of the finitude embodied in *das Ding*, the comic figure unwittingly "acknowledges" its finitude, an acknowledgment ratified by laughter on the part of the spectator.[3] Such recognition is produced by comic flight, a concept Lacan relates, at seminar's end, to the phallus: "[T]he element that makes us laugh . . . is not so much the triumph of life as its flight, the fact that life slips away, runs off, escapes all those barriers that oppose it, including precisely those that are the most essential, those that are constituted by the agency of the signifier. The phallus is nothing more than . . . the signifier of this flight."[4] How can we square these two passages, one on Harpo's face-as-Thing and the other on the phallic flight of a life where desire is inexhaustible? For Critchley, the connection is related to a bodily finitude, where the phallus's life-vitality represents "a sign of weakness, of the dis-possession of the phallus," which is why Harpo's comedy is dependent on the "weakness and vulnerability of the body."[5]

Despite the many merits of Critchley's reading there is a curious contradiction in it, a contradiction that may be rooted in Lacan's own scattered reflections on the comic. Lacan admits to having devoted "little time" to comedy, and perhaps as a result the curious gap between the first passage on Harpo and the second passage on the phallus's triumph is resolved by Critchley via a finitude of the body, which Alenka Zupančič, in a recent theoretical account of the comic, aptly describes as comedy's "most boring and reductive definition: comedy is about accepting the fact that we are only human, with all the flaws and weaknesses that this implies."[6] Yet the comedy embodied in Harpo's face and in the overall "radical annihilation" of the Marx Brothers' farce is not one of some humanist-imagined, mortal body, but is instead profoundly inhuman, an excessive "passion" that drives signification off its rails. Harpo, far from acknowledging the deathly mystery of the Thing, reveals that such mystery is a ridiculous object, a bit of nothing that can only end in all sorts of perverse situations. Harpo's body is not excessively weak, but indestructible, consuming everything in a paradoxically perverse simplicity. Harpo is not, as Critchley misinterprets, the fellow "who keeps tripping up and falling in the soup," but is, as Lacan states of the phallus, that which "survives" this tripping.[7] The comedy of such an image is not the fall into some bodily finitude, but the repetitive flight of falling itself, the fact that, as Zupančič argues, the comic character will get up and find new ways and new places to fall, hilariously repeating the action endlessly.[8] This survival is that part of life that seems continually to interrupt living, corrupting it with perverse enjoyment, demolishing reality's fragile order for the sake of a surreal world driven by drive.

* * *

Gookie as Comic Abyss

We might begin where Lacan does, by focusing on that essential attribute, Harpo's dumbness. The double meaning here is important, that Harpo is mute and is simultaneously an idiot, someone who cannot read, write, speak, or listen. These seeming lacks suggest that Harpo's silence is not the foundation of his idiocy, but symptomatic of it—that he is not a fool because he cannot speak, but rather cannot speak because there is something essentially foolish that cannot be meaningfully spoken, read, written, or heard, yet is also simultaneously an effect of language. Perhaps it is this muteness that first drew Lacan's attention to Harpo, given his explanation of "the dumb reality which is *das Ding*."[9]

Lacan goes on to say that "dumb things are not exactly the same as things which have no relationship to words."[10] Indeed, *das Ding*, that "first outside," "the absolute Other of the subject," only arises once a signifier attempts to signify some-Thing. The signifier is a "defense," attempting to distance itself from what refuses to speak, the Real. Something can only be considered silent once it is considered an object of signification, once a Symbolic Order exists that allows for designations to order this silence by making it speak. The hope is that signs will then move from one to the other in an orderly representational fashion, without discontinuities in the movement of the signifying chain. This process is doomed to failure from the start and that faulty starting point is the signifier, which is nothing more than "the symbol of but an absence."[11] The signifier attempts to make something speak that is already silent, and this lacuna falls away each time the signifier tries to designate, because the signifier is structurally dependent on distancing itself from this silence. It can only signify once it has absented itself from this absence, produced a distance between the Symbolic and the Real. *Das Ding* is therefore not consigned to some imaginary past, but is instead attendant with signification as such since *das Ding* is nothing other than "that which in the real suffers from the signifier."[12] The signifier carries this absence around with it wherever it goes, no matter how smooth its relation to the other signifiers in the chain may be.

On its own, then, the signifier is a rather ridiculous creature. It is, in the Real, a bit of nonsense since, cut off from its chain, it *means* nothing and therefore *is* nothing or insists structurally, but consists, in relation to discourse, of nothing. The signifier is signification's very own excess, the nonsensical materiality, the no-Thing, which signification cannot control. This excessive surplus reveals that the Symbolic Order has a stain, which is nothing other than the signifier itself, the signifier as nonsense, a primordial but perpetual nonsense bound with every bit of sense we attribute to our semiotic universe. Lacan calls this excessive surplus *objet petit a*, and any signifier has the potential to become such an object.[13] The third term here, after *das Ding* and the *objet petit a*, is jouissance, which stands in contrast to and in combat with the desire that endlessly guides the pleasure principle in the metonymy of signification. For desire, *das Ding* is always distant, sliding away as a transcendent object-cause. For jouissance, this frustration finds a kind of satisfaction, and that elusive object becomes all too present, so much so that it overruns the pleasure principle, producing a surplus waste unaccounted for in the ego's regulations. Whereas desire is geared around the purpose of the search, jouissance is "a negative instance. Jouissance is what serves no purpose."[14] The drive for jouissance does not repeat the jump from one signifier to another, trying to make meaning appear as pre-given. Instead, it formally repeats the very gesture of repetition, not the structural difference produced by the failure of repetition (that one signifier can never resemble another), but the sameness of failure, the objectified gap of the signifier as a point of fetishistic enjoyment that overwhelms the ego. This drive is always a death drive, not because of some primary masochism or a desire to become inorganic, but rather because it is what resists the living of the symbolic, that endless difference and deferral, maintaining a repetitive fidelity for the "dead letter" that initiates signification yet eludes it.[15] If jouissance "serves no purpose," then it is pre-ethical, a "primary affect, prior to any repression."[16] Hence Lacan's most succinct definition of jouissance: "It begins with a tickle and ends in a blaze of petrol. That's always what *jouissance* is."[17]

There is perhaps no better description of both Harpo Marx and the effect he has on the various chains of signification that form the narrative economy of the Marx Brothers' films. This is quite literally the case in a scene from *Duck Soup* (Leo McCarey, 1933). Following Chico, Harpo enters the ornate room of an ambassador, a tickled grin across his face.

The ambassador gives him a note to read, but he tears it up, and Chico explains, "He gets mad because he can't read." Shoving a Chico-offered cigar into his mouth, Harpo first tries to light it using a telephone only to soon pull out a blowtorch hidden in his raincoat. Sneaking behind the ambassador's back, Harpo, using scissors drawn once again from his coat, cuts the former's cigar. Asked for the records of a foreign prime minister, Harpo pulls out a phonograph record, which the ambassador throws up in the air in frustration. Harpo then takes out a handgun and shoots the flying record to pieces. Before he departs Harpo cuts off the tails of the ambassador's jacket, glues a piece of newspaper across the latter's behind to replace the missing tails, and shakes hands using a mousetrap. What begins with a tickle, a disturbing grin stretching across that dumb face, ends in "the field of absolute destruction."[18]

We are now in a good position to understand Lacan's claim for Harpo's face as "present," "pressing," "absorbing," "disruptive," "nauseating," and, most important, "calculated to thrust everything that takes place before us into the abyss or void." Lacan's language takes on a hyperbolic quality, as if Harpo's face eludes description yet simultaneously requires more and more outrageous adjectives to somehow capture his effect. Harpo's comedy does not lie in some absolute anterior/exterior relation to the Symbolic, but is rather tied to it as eruptive excess, surprising stain, and bothersome byproduct—effects perfectly captured in his expression in a Paramount publicity photo from the early 1930s. This is the classic "Gookie," the face that lay, according to an autobiographical recounting, at the origin of his comedy and career.[19] Such comedy requires meaningful signification for which he acts as an irritating excess, throwing a wrench, or any number of other dumb objects, into every narrative chain.[20] Harpo does not ignore what others say or do, but manifests the ignorance that lies at the heart of their sayings and doings. This abyss is the "abyss of the comic," which is "the revelation of what lies below. Comedy makes us rediscover what Freud showed was present in the practice of nonsense."[21] Such nonsense is disavowed by sense, and Harpo is nothing other than an apparatus for undoing this repression and making it disgustingly visible, pressingly present, in order to produce sense as nonsense and nonsense as sense. To do so he has a variety of comic techniques, on which I will elaborate.

First, there are Harpo's literalisms, which involve a miscommunication or misinterpretation between two orders of sense. In *Horse Feathers* (Norman Z. McLeod, 1932), the password to enter a speakeasy is "swordfish," and Harpo, to gain entrance, pulls out a fish and shoves a sword in it. In another scene, Harpo passes by a game of cards and hears that they need to cut the deck, which he accomplishes with an ax. Later, with Groucho in need of a seal for a legal document, Harpo brings in a live seal. In *Animal Crackers* (Victor Heerman, 1930), during a game of bridge, Harpo is told that he has the "choice of seats" and he sits on a woman's lap. Later, to see if a paycheck is good, he drops it on the ground only to see it magically bounce up. In *Room Service* (William Seiter, 1938), Harpo is sent out to get some turkey for lunch and returns with a live turkey.

Lisa Trahair and Patricia Mellencamp have each interpreted these moments as Harpo's embodying the referent ("the object signified by the signifier") or "thing presentation" which substitutes for "word presentations," but both readings misunderstand the role of the signifier in psychoanalysis, which at no point bears any relation to some actual object, but instead embodies nonreferentiality and meaninglessness.[22] As Lacan states, "[S]ignifiers are not concerned with objects but with sense." Slavoj Žižek explains the same point in relation to the nonsense of dream work: "[I]t is absolutely misleading to characterize the passage from word presentations to thing presentation . . . as a kind of 'regression' from language to prelanguage representations. In a dream, 'things' themselves are already 'structured like a language,' their disposition is regulated by the signifying chain for which they stand."[23] The comedy of literalism comes from the material gap that is the signifier, which is precisely what Harpo's visual punning and literal misinterpretations produce, the abyss between interpretations. Harpo's most brilliant literalism is his muteness, which not only interprets dumb (unable to speak) as dumb (idiot) but also understands the muteness of the signifier as the muteness of his own being as signifying subject. The literal meaning is a sense produced in excess of the ego-ordered "reality that commands and regulates" and thereby reveals that surplus in the very gesture of its polysemy.[24] Harpo's sitting on the woman or cutting the deck reveals an "extreme perversity," but each is also only the flip side of that "complete simplicity" of the turkey or the swordfish. Literalism produces a materialist comedy of the Symbolic Order, destabilizing language to the point that reality recasts itself in a surreal light.

Another technique reveals this same nonsense by cutting signifiers from ego-oriented networks of meaning. Often this cutting is literal, such as in *Duck Soup* when Harpo cuts the ambassador's jacket or in *Monkey Business* (Norman Z. McLeod, 1931) when Harpo and Chico trim a man's mustache by progressively chopping the whole thing off. On an even more literal level, Harpo in *The Cocoanuts* (Robert Florey and Joseph Santley, 1929) keeps himself busy by leisurely going through letters and tearing them up one by one. Such incisions carry signifiers away from their associations and representations. Perhaps the best example of such thievery occurs in *Animal Crackers*: Chico proves that an art dealer, Chandler, is actually a fish salesman, by exposing a birthmark on the latter's wrist. Chandler offers to pay Chico off, but instead places his cash in Harpo's pocket. Harpo soon steals Chandler's handkerchief, tie, and even his birthmark, which impossibly sits on Harpo's arm.

A signifier can only represent itself in relation to other signifiers, which is why Lacan says that the signifier "represents a subject, and nothing but a subject, for another signifier."[25] The subject is the abyss that separates one signifier from another; it is nothing but the nothing between signifiers. The signifier's metonymic relation to other signifiers, which the ego will try to tie down into conscious meaning, is dependent on this shifting, yet such shifting has to be denied for the ego to be equated, in what is the essential metonymy, with the One of the I. Harpo's thievery makes visible that all those essential attributes we associate with an ego are nothing other than fragments, arbitrarily conjured together to form an image of power. Harpo manifests not merely the muteness of the material signifier, but the very gap between signifiers necessitated by that muteness. Harpo's thievery eliminates associations and recognitions, embodying the very gap between what one says one is (whether it be via speech, clothing, office, or body) and what one is in the Real, which is to say, nothing. Perhaps the best example of such thievery occurs in *Monkey Business*. Harpo stands innocently against the wall, next to a men's room. A man walks into the bathroom and is immediately thrown out. Harpo moves along the wall to reveal that he had been covering the "WO" before "MEN." Harpo's inadvertent stealing of the "WO" in "WOMEN" suggests that the difference between men and women amounts only to two letters, which means a great deal to social norms, but nothing to Harpo. If Harpo's literalisms reveal the comedy of the Symbolic Order, then his stealing reveals the comedy of the ego, its attempt to fashion power, hierarchy, norm, or wealth, all of which Harpo can only misunderstand, miscast, and miscarry.

This thievery suggests the difference between the ego-body and Harpo's own corpus, which is revealed in his containing every signifier. In order to induce polysemy or to cut out a gap in a signifying chain, Harpo must be effectively armed with *all the signifiers* that could potentially be in play. His comedy is thus dependent on always providing untimely signifiers. This is represented by Harpo's raincoat, which has a magical ability to contain everything, including a sword, a fish, or a blowtorch. In *Horse Feathers*, a cop reveals his badge in order to make Harpo follow his commands, but Harpo opens his coat to reveal dozens of badges; in the repetitive excess of badges, the badge itself becomes meaningless, just like the symbolic authority it is intended to metonymically suggest. Later, Groucho tells Harpo that he cannot burn the candle at both ends, and Harpo pulls out a candle burning at each end, disproving Groucho's conventional wisdom. In *Animal Crackers*, Chico asks Harpo for a flash (a flashlight), and Harpo subsequently produces a fish, his flesh, a flask, and a flush (the poker hand).

Alternatively, Harpo may provide the right signifier just when such adequacy is considered impossible. In *Duck Soup*, Groucho asks Harpo who he is, and Harpo responds by showing a picture of his clownish face drawn on his arm. Groucho's response, "I don't go in for much modern art," prompts Harpo to show an obscene drawing of a woman on his other arm, which he jiggles by flexing his muscles. Harpo shows Groucho his phone number, written on a shoulder, and then his home, a doghouse drawn on his chest. In a brilliant montage, a real dog is edited onto Harpo's stomach, barking at Groucho. In the scene's final gag, Groucho says, "Well, I know one thing: I bet you haven't got a picture of my grandfather," to which Harpo responds with an excited grin, turning around and lifting up his shirt, intent to reveal this very picture on his derriere. In this scene, a virtuoso lesson in semiotics, Harpo's body acts as a writing tablet, across which any object may inscribe itself. Like the wax portion of Freud's *Wunderblock* (mystic writing pad), Harpo is a space where all inscriptions are retained, yet his comic movements reanimate them onto the wax paper screen in constantly unexpected forms. Harpo's body is a conduit; it is not merely the abyss against which signification collapses, but also the surplus where such signification falls away in its manifestation *as object*.

In Seminar XVII, Lacan describes S2, the "other signifier" which rises after S1, the master signifier in a given chain, in the following way: "[T]his other signifier is not alone. The stomach of the Other, the big Other, is full of them. This stomach is like some monstrous Trojan horse that provides the foundations for the fantasy of a totality-knowledge."[26] The difference between this big Other and the *objet petit a* is that the latter is nothing but stomach, an expulsing "organ without body," acephalous and automatic. According to Žižek, this is psychoanalysis's great discovery concerning the body: "Is not the Freudian eroticized body, sustained by libido, organized around erogenous zones, precisely the nonanimalistic, nonbiological body?"[27] The way the body speaks through its symptoms and desires has nothing to do with biological need or evolutionary adaptation. This is why it is a mistake to read Harpo as either an uncivilized child of nature or a suggestion of some natural finitude, since what separates the human from the natural is an infinite, useless, and "un-evolutionary" enjoyment. If the little other contains every signifier, it does so through a kind of consumption, a stomach full of the world's excess consumed and enjoyed. This explains Harpo's own appetite, which, like his jacket, knows no limits: ink, flowers, phones, buttons, handkerchief, coins, wax paper, and even his own finger—almost all of this eaten in his very first film scene, in *The Cocoanuts*. Here, Harpo's body is a body of the drives, one that converts language into waste. It can find enjoyment in virtually anything, by following any suggestion, the more ridiculous and contingent the better. Since Harpo cannot distance himself from the world, treating his body no differently than he would a piece of food or a telephone, we might say that he is a subject without an Imaginary, which is another way of saying that he is not a subject at all, never having secured egoic separation from the world. Treating both the world and himself as object, Harpo ultimately sees no difference between the two; therefore, what exists of himself is merely another zone for play, which is to say another zone for destruction and consumption.

One of the most famous Marx Brothers gags, derived from an old vaudeville routine, reveals this failure for self-distinguishing. In *Duck Soup*, Chico and Harpo dress up as Groucho, hoping to trick Mrs. Teasdale (Margaret Dumont) and steal secret documents. Harpo, after destroying a living room, runs into a mirror and shatters it. Groucho soon enters the room, and the two engage in a complex pantomime, with Harpo trying to prove that he is Groucho's mirrored other. After an increasingly impossible series of duplications (culminating in switching places across the threshold of the presumed mirror), Chico enters the scene, and this third Groucho destroys the illusion of correspondence and provides the climax of the joke. This sequence wonderfully illustrates the limits of the mirror stage, where a third term interrupts the binary of ego consolidation. When the third term erupts as identical to the first two, the abyss of all the terms is revealed so that the mask is nothing more than a contingent appearance, the very truth of their symbolic destitution.[28] This is most visible, as Lacan notices, in "the face of Harpo Marx," which smiles as it destroys, cries when it is forced to hear others speak, and Gookies when it reads. This face is nothing more than a mask, but a mask that, unlike other comic masks, is a kind of metasemblance, one that is *all* mask with no presumed person beneath it, only the sheer force of the signifier as empty semblance. The best instance of such masking is in *Monkey Business* when

Harpo, fleeing the police, jumps behind a Punch and Judy show and replaces a doll with his own face, which freezes into a Gookie.

No wonder, then, that Harpo, despite his constant chasing of women, is polymorphously perverse, consumed by, and consuming of, "a desire taken to be reality."[29] Since he is nothing more than a machine of the real, regurgitating sense as nonsense, necessity as contingency, authority as absurdity, Harpo cannot be considered a creature of castration. What tickles the subject is the jouissance that overwhelms the subject's defenses and perverts its desire. Harpo's polymorphous perversion takes the idiotic logic of the phallus to its extreme, the point at which he himself becomes his own object of enjoyment. This is exemplified by his most common gag, offering his leg up for another to foolishly hold. When Harpo is found unconscious in *Duck Soup*, Groucho asks, "It is male or female?" and Chico responds, "I don't think so." This excluded middle is an apt response since Harpo seems to escape any sexually situated relation to castration. Though superficially he seems like a woman-obsessed little boy, Harpo also has a proclivity for hugging men (especially Chico) and even humping objects, most hilariously in *The Cocoanuts*, where, tickled by the sound of a cash register, he humps it over and over again to produce the pleasing sound. Harpo embodies not a subject (or sexualized subject-position) driven crazy by some particular enjoyment, but rather the potentiality of enjoyment itself, its virtually infinite capacity to interrupt any order of meaning.

* * *

Conclusion

When we laugh at the Marx Brothers we are not laughing because we know better than these idiots, nor are we taking pleasure in the suffering of their victims—rather, we are laughing at the nonsense of ourselves and of our world, the nonsense that infects the sense we have of who we are and what our world might mean. Their comedy is the means by which we can enjoy the perverse destruction and surreal recombination of reality. Encountering that nothingness, the abyss of Harpo's face, and the space for play opened by that encounter, we, like the analysand, confront the stupidity of being and find a means to enjoy ourselves as its meaningless symptom.

Lacan's interest in the Marx Brothers reveals the stakes of articulating alternative forms of spectatorial enjoyment, forms that emphasize the surreal possibilities of the comic ranging from slapstick violence to screwball wordplay.[30] The constantly revolving elements in these films

undermine attempts at humanist redemption, instead emphasizing the obscene enjoyment that corrodes life beyond understanding or scopic mastery. The sheer hilarity of these films, echoed in the spectator's laughter,
hovers over that comic, annihilating abyss, which would otherwise terrify
if it did not so effectively satisfy that abyssal surplus beyond the subject's
desire. Rather than denying such surplus or converting it into sentimental
pathos, the Marx Brothers' films make it the central object of their aesthetics. The nonsense of laughter, like the nonsense of the Gookie, rati-
fies the spectator's own saintly status, the nonsensical waste of our own
preposterous being.

D: "Revenge of the Nerds: Failure, Laughter, and Liberation on *The Big Bang Theory*," Andrew J. Owens

On September 24, 2007, CBS premiered a new half-hour sitcom that has
since become a flagship property of America's second-eldest network and
one of the most culturally iconic series of its genre. Coproduced by middle-
brow auteur-extraordinaires Chuck Lorre and Bill Prady, who had previously collaborated on *Dharma & Greg* (ABC; 1997–2002), *The Big Bang
Theory* takes place in Pasadena, California, and follows both the academic
and amorous lives of genial geeks Sheldon Cooper, a theoretical physi-
cist played by Jim Parsons; Leonard Hofstadter, an experimental physi-
cist played by Johnny Galecki; Howard Wolowitz, an aerospace engineer
played by Simon Helberg; and Raj Koothrappali, an astrophysicist played
by Kunal Nayyar. Joining this ensemble of socially unskilled scientists are
female foils Bernadette Rostenkowski, a microbiologist played by Melissa
Rauch; Amy Farrah Fowler, a neuroscientist played by Mayim Bialik; and
Penny, a Cheesecake Factory waitress and aspiring actress played by Kaley
Cuoco. In a sitcom genre in which sexual innuendo has become nearly a
defining feature, *Big Bang*'s cast are employed in decidedly unglamorous,
unsexy professions.

Peppered with nerdy graces of social ineptitude at every turn, *The A.V.
Club*'s Scott Tobias dismissively wrote of the series premiere that "really
bad television shows tend to pander to the mean: in affirming the superiority of Joe and Jane Average, they mock both the egregiously stupid . . .
and the hyper-intelligent, who are struck down for the arrogant, unpar-
donable sin of . . . um . . . knowing stuff."[31] Indeed, Tobias's assessment
relies upon one of the canonical theories of comedy: that the "meanness"
of *Big Bang* is generated via comparative superiority, as viewers take plea-

sure in mocking those we deem "less than" ourselves in any variety of arenas. Yet in a more charitable appraisal, Barry Garron of *The Hollywood Reporter* argues that the series finds "endless humor in the social deficiencies of boy geniuses, albeit in a nice way. Be kind to geeks . . . because they are nice people, just socially retarded."[32] Unlike Tobias, Garron looks beyond the surface of *Big Bang*'s ostensibly vindictive veneer to offer one take on how the lampooning of geeks, nerds, freaks, and the people who love them has translated into both critical and ratings success over the series' past ten seasons and counting. In what follows, I similarly consider what might make *The Big Bang Theory* "work" comedically by proposing a theory of psychoanalytic identification that turns spectatorial discomfort into pleasurable release and comedic delight.

Taunting the outré of the Other was, of course, hardly a new cultural phenomenon on the eve of *Big Bang*'s premiere in 2007. Reaching as far back as the writings of Plato, Aristotle, and Quintilian, laughter has often been theorized as an expression of superiority over other people; an easy route to hierarchical value judgments by deftly defining "us" versus "them."[33] I argue that much of *Big Bang*'s comedy ironically revolves around the psychically discomfiting fact that the division between "us" and "them" is, at best, only ever tenuous. We, as audience members, are encouraged not only simply to laugh at these geeks but also to identify *with* them as we laugh. Putting some of the fundamental tenets of Freudian psychoanalytic theory into conversation, I offer a model of comedy's potential pleasures that is particularly illuminating when applied to this series: that of a psychically relieving release valve with liberatory potential.

Between *Jokes and their Relation to the Unconscious* (1905) and "Humour" (1927), Freud constructed what might be called a dual theory of comedy, one that articulates slight but significant nuances between laughter and humor. Laughter, in the psychoanalytic formulation, is conceived of as a somatic phenomenon, as a release of pent-up nervous energy that provides pleasure because it allegedly "economizes upon energy that would ordinarily be used to contain or repress psychic activity."[34] We often laugh, in other words, when life presents us with situations where we would otherwise have little resort other than to break down and cry. Humor, on the other hand, is a comparatively more psychic experience that allows the individual to spare her/himself "the affects to which the situation would naturally give rise" and to casually dismiss "the possibility of such expressions of emotion with a jest."[35] *The Big Bang Theory* has proven popular because its comedy is engaged at the levels of both laughter and humor. We may very well laugh at the socially unskillful shenanigans of these affable

Penny, Bernadette, and Amy admire Zack's good looks on *The Big Bang Theory*.

nerds, especially throughout their romantic and/or sexual lives, because doing so consequently allows us to circumvent coming face-to-face with a constellation of potentially ego-crushing realities: that we actually can empathize with the awkwardness of these cultural misfits; that our own comparative competency in navigating the social world is always subject to the capricious appraisal of others; and that our psychic investment in the normal equates to faith in a potentially hollow house of cards.

In his 2002 treatise *On Humour*, Simon Critchley maintains that humor is produced by a psychological disjunction, that between "the way things are and the way they are represented in the joke, between expectation and actuality."[36] The great paradox of humor is, of course, that our expectations need to be dashed in order for the joke to land successfully. The chicken cannot fulfill our desire for it to have an elaborate agenda on the other side of the road. It simply needs to cross. Undeniably, then, the sphere of humor basks in worlds in which causal chains of logic are disrupted, social practices are turned inside out, and commonsense rationality is all but torn to shreds.[37] Phenomena like the Bakhtinian carnival solicits laughter for precisely such reasons. And although countless examples exist of *Big Bang*'s ability to siphon off nervous energy through laughter and to encourage introspection through humor, the fourth season episode entitled "The Alien Parasite Hypothesis" compellingly illustrates several of the series' go-to disjunctive scenarios.

On a girls' night out, Penny, Bernadette, and Amy are casually conversing at a neighborhood bar as Penny's ex-boyfriend Zack (Brian Smith) enters to drop off new menus provided by his father's printing company. Accidentally dropping the menus out of his grasp and across the room, the three women are provided with ample opportunity to inspect the impressive musculature of Zack's rear end. After consequently emitting an involuntary whimpering that can only be aurally articulated as "hooooooooo," Amy assesses her condition with Penny:

> Amy: I'm suddenly feeling flushed. My heart rate is elevated. My palms are clammy. My mouth is dry. In addition, I keep involuntarily saying "hooooooooo."
>
> Penny: Oh, we know what's causing that, don't we?
>
> Amy: It's no mystery. I obviously have the flu coupled with sudden-onset Tourette's Syndrome.

The joke here, of course, turns on both the disjunction and deadpan sincerity of Amy's response. But whatever comedy it elicits operates on at least two levels: either a purely uncomplicated mockery of her naiveté or, at a further critical remove, an empathetic appreciation that Amy is, in a turn of phrase popularized by Alicia Silverstone in 1995, so "adorably clueless" and out of touch vis-à-vis the psychic repression of her physical urges.

Like so many other moments on *Big Bang*, the comedy of this and subsequent scenes is based upon disjunctive scenarios of sexual misrecognition, the very basis for so much of psychoanalysis's therapeutic and theoretical regime whereby psychic energy is either repressed or released with various consequences. From Oedipus and Electra complexes to neuroses, psychoses, and dreams, psychoanalysis would arguably have gained little traction if its practitioners and proponents hadn't convincingly portrayed our sexual lives as an unending series of problems in need of solutions. Pathology, Freud reminds us, has "always done us the service of making discernible by isolation and exaggeration conditions which would remain concealed in a normal state."[38] If human beings hadn't been historically forced to deny our true desires, we quite simply wouldn't need Dr. Freud to explain them to us. And indeed, the series' romantic relationship (such as it is) between Amy and Sheldon turns constantly on crossed wires; on Amy's often-desperate double-entendres and appeals to vanquishing her virginity that miss the oblivious target that is Sheldon Cooper. Yet even still, identification with either party remains comic and potentially pleasurable, encouraging both admiration of Sheldon's ability to completely shrug off the burden of sociocultural imperatives toward heterosexual coupling and sexual intercourse and inspiring empathy toward Amy's near-universal frustration at having a romantic interest whose ability to read interpersonal signals are constantly coming up short.

After engaging together in a differential diagnosis to uncover what happened to her at the bar, a procedure that produces initial explanations ranging from hyperthyroidism, premature menopause, and hosting an alien parasite, Amy and Sheldon eventually do reach a commonsense conclusion:

> Amy: My blood work shows thyroid function normal, cortisol levels normal.
> Sheldon: How about your follicle-stimulating hormone levels?
> Amy: Sheldon, I am not going through menopause!
> Sheldon: Are you sure? You said that with the testy bark of an old biddy.
> Amy: I think we need to face the cold, hard truth. I was sexually aroused by Penny's friend Zack.
> Sheldon: Hang on; I don't know that we've given the alien parasite hypothesis a fair shake.
> Amy: Let's look at this logically. I have a stomach; I get hungry. I have genitals; I have the potential for sexual arousal.
> Sheldon: A cross we all must bear.

Yet before logic can too clearly rule the day here, the comedy of this scene doubles down on psychoanalytic foundations, transitioning from disjunction to disavowal:

> Amy: Is it possible your concern for me at this moment is motivated by nothing more than simple jealousy?
> Sheldon: I hadn't considered that. Give me a moment. All right, I've considered it.
> Amy: And?
> Sheldon: I reject it.
> Amy: You reject it because you don't feel jealousy or because you are suppressing jealousy?
> Sheldon: I think I'll eat my lunch at home.

Sheldon's stubborn refusal to acknowledge his complicity in his own admission, that all human beings *do* have the capacity to experience sexual arousal, might be dismissed as simply another iteration of the arrested psychosexual development that so clearly scaffolds his man-child character and relationship with Amy. Yet at its core, Sheldon's shrugging off and making light of this awkward encounter is the ultimate instantiation of what Freud designated as the grandeur of humor: "the triumph of narcissism, the victorious assertion of the ego's invulnerability."[39] In the humorous scenario then, the ego "refuses to be distressed by the provocations of reality, to let itself be compelled to suffer. It insists that it cannot be affected by the traumas of the external world; it shows, in fact, that such traumas are no more than occasions for it to gain pleasure."[40] Packing up his sashimi, Sheldon struts out of Amy's lab with the self-assured confidence that the repression of his animal instincts has catapulted him to the moral high ground of their relationship.

Throughout a career that endeavored to scour ever deeper recesses of the mind, Freud continuously returned to several suppositions that psychoanalysis would eventually take as given: namely, that the motivating force of sexual life was known as the libido and that sexual life was dominated by the polarizing binary between masculinity and femininity. Of course, these two suppositions were also contingent upon a third: that those in possession of a penis and its symbolic counterpart, the phallus, dominated sociocultural interactions and those who lacked the penis/phallus were on a constant campaign to get one. In the psychoanalytic purview and beyond, the dichotomy between possessing (male) and envying (female) a penis is one of, if not *the* pillar upon which heteronormative society is based. Yet if rules were made to be broken, Sheldon's disavowal of amorous behavior toward Amy and the ensemble cast's general misrecognition of sexual mores may undergird much of *Big Bang*'s laughter and humor precisely because they afford us safe avenues to mock, parody, and even deride some of the most cherished ritual practices of our society.

Consider, for instance, the conversation between Sheldon and Penny in their apartment building's basement laundry room after Sheldon and Amy's embroilment:

Penny: So, how's Amy?
Sheldon: Amy's changed. I might have to let her go.
Penny: Oh no! Why?
Sheldon: I thought she was a highly evolved creature of pure intellect like me. But recent events indicate that she may be a slave to her baser urges. Like you.
Penny: I'm just going to skip over that insult.
Sheldon: What insult?
Penny: Yup, that's why I'm going to skip over it. Are you saying that Amy is . . . oh what's the scientific word . . .

Sheldon: It's not science. She's horny.

Penny: Oh. Ok. Wow.

Sheldon: It's simple biology. There's nothing I can do about it.

Penny: Are you sure?

Sheldon: What are you suggesting?

Penny: I'm suggesting there might be something you could do about Amy's urges.

Sheldon: It's illegal to spay a human being.

Penny: Yeah, that's not what I had in mind.

Sheldon: Oh . . . OH! You mean something *I* could do?

Penny: Exactly.

Sheldon: Well, I was hoping to avoid this. But I might as well get it over with. Thank you, Penny. I'll let you know what happens.

Penny: Oh Amy, you lucky girl.

It's as if, channeling *Hamlet*'s Queen Gertrude by emphatically protesting too much, Sheldon's response to this scenario reads something along the lines of, "I realize I am male. I realize I have a penis and that I am expected to use it for the purposes of sex. But I have no intention of doing so." As a solution to this conundrum, the episode ends not with Sheldon satisfying Amy's urges himself, but rather by setting her up for a no-strings sexual rendezvous with Zack, whose "ape-like expression" brings Amy back to the realm of psychic sublimation and pure intellect.

The sexual lives of *Big Bang*'s ensemble cast thus fail more often than they succeed if success in our heteronormative society equates to, as J. Jack Halberstam has written, "specific forms of reproductive maturity."[41] Sheldon is at turns both oblivious and unmotivated by Amy's amorous advances. Amy can't find a way to legitimize her sexuality in Sheldon's eyes. Raj suffers from selective mutism when talking to women. Howard goes through a veritable turnstile of romantic dead ends until marrying Bernadette at the end of season five. And it's only at the beginning of the ninth season that Leonard and Penny finally resolve their own tumultuous on-again-off-again relationship by also getting married. Yet buying into such assessments as deficiencies, even if their respective situations do eventually turn a corner, is also to simultaneously reify a host of normative metrics that this series' failures may very well be laboring to undo.

Indeed, as Halberstam elaborates in *The Queer Art of Failure*, "under certain circumstances failing, losing, forgetting, unmaking, undoing, unbecoming, not knowing may in fact offer more creative, more cooperative, more surprising ways of being in the world."[42] For example, in a later fourth season episode entitled "The Thespian Catalyst," Sheldon displays a rare moment of humility when he admits, after a disastrous guest lecture at Caltech, that teaching is the only thing he's failed at since an ill-fated attempt at a pull-up when he was a child. The comedy of this admission is bolstered by the fact that the confession is made to Amy via video chat, who can only remain silent at the other obvious thing that her boyfriend is currently failing at. Nevertheless, this conversation prompts Sheldon to take an acting lesson from Penny, a tutorial that concludes with the normally stoic scientist becoming so caught up in the repressed emotions of a scene he wrote based upon his childhood that he ends up on the phone sobbing and confessing his love to his mother.

Failure and its fallouts, then, actually have the paradoxical potential to preserve some of the phenomenal psychic anarchy of childhood and can disturb the "supposedly clean boundaries between adults and children, winners and losers. And while failure certainly comes accompanied by a host of negative effects, such as disappointment, disillusionment, and despair, it also provides the opportunity to use these negative affects to poke holes in the toxic positivity of contemporary life."[43] As Jim Parsons reflected of Sheldon's obliviousness in an interview with *Variety*'s Scott Huver,

> I don't mean to sound unromantic or unsympathetic, but I cannot stand sentimentality, and I feel very lucky to be playing a character that, nine times out of ten, when something sentimental is happening in a script, I get to be the one to burst that bubble. And that gives me such great pleasure, I cannot tell you. And I guess in a general way it relates to the thing that I loved about him from the moment I read the pilot, and for nine years now, which is just enough level of cluelessness to get away with saying some of the most outlandish and inappropriate things.[44]

By identifying with the character of Sheldon in particular, *The Big Bang Theory* allows viewers to release some level of the id's desire via laughter, while at the same time satisfying an ego that still feels it has successfully accommodated the superego vis-a-vis Sheldon's recusal from normal behavior.

Most attempts at comedy, Critchley astutely observes, are of a reactionary nature that simply serve as stalwarts to the status quo. They reinforce consensus and do not seek to criticize the established order or "change the situation in which we find ourselves. Such humor does not seek to change the situation, but simply toys with existing social hierarchies in a charming but quite benign fashion."[45] And although much of the critical literature on comedy approaches this subject from different angles, one undergirding assertion is that genuine laughter, or what Critchley calls the "true joke," has the potential to psychically relieve and even to liberate.

Humor, Freud succinctly states, is not resigned; it is actually rebellious. It signifies not only the "triumph of the ego but also of the pleasure principle, which is able here to assert itself against the unkindness of the real circumstances."[46] Whether through Sheldon's obliviousness, Amy's ineffectual feminine wiles, Raj's selective mutism, or Howard's litany of ribald quips, *The Big Bang Theory* has and continues to be a cacophony of sustained laughter at a funeral. But in this instance, the deceased is our collective and often blind faith in the logic and legitimacy of the normal.

The true comedy of Lorre and Prady's series may thus be found most obviously in how its combination of laughter and humor lays bare the "sheer contingency or arbitrariness of the social rites in which we engage. By producing a consciousness of contingency, humor can change the situation in which we find ourselves, and can even have a *critical* function with respect to society."[47] Variously aware and unaware of the rules, yet still refusing to play the game, the cast of *The Big Bang Theory* thrusts our collective unconscious out of complacence and provides us with psychologically safe avenues through which to relieve ourselves of social stress and to laugh at the supposed power of cultural imperatives. By doing so, we might just find that "what appeared to be fixed and oppressive is in fact the emperor's new clothes, and just the sort of thing that should be mocked and ridiculed."[48] After all, as Parsons's character often asserts, he isn't insane. His mother had him tested.

Notes

1. Lacan, *The Ethics of Psychoanalysis*, 55. Lacan is only one of many European intellectuals fascinated by the Marx Brothers, and by Harpo in particular. See, for example, Weber, "Vaudeville's Children and Brecht"; Artaud, *The Theater and Its Double*; Barthes, *Barthes by Barthes*, 81; Adorno, *The Culture Industry*, 49; Deleuze, *Cinema I*, 199; and Rancière, *The Future of the Image*, 51. See also Agee, *Film Writing and Selected Journalism*; and Ulmer, "'A Night at the Text.'"

2. Critchley, *Ethics-Politics-Subjectivity*, 232. Marc De Kesel's recent study of *Seminar VII* discusses Lacan's theory of comedy without ever referencing the Harpo passage, despite obvious conceptual continuities. See De Kesel, *Eros and Ethics*, 123–124.

3. Critchley, *Ethics-Politics-Subjectivity*, 224.

4. Lacan, *Ethics of Psychoanalysis*, 313.

5. Critchley, *Ethics-Politics-Subjectivity*, 230.

6. Critchley, *Ethics-Politics-Subjectivity*, 230; Zupančič, *The Odd One In*, 46. As Critchley states, "[W]hat goes on in humour is a form of liberation or elevation that expresses something essential to the humanity of the human being." Critchley, "Did You Hear the Joke," 47. See also Critchley, *On Humour*, 93–111.

7. Lacan, *Ethics of Psychoanalysis*, 313.

8. Zupančič, *The Odd One In*, 32.

9. Lacan, *Ethics of Psychoanalysis*, 55.

10. Lacan, *Ethics of Psychoanalysis*, 55.

11. Lacan, *écrits*, 17.

12. Lacan, *Ethics of Psychoanalysis*, 125.

13. Lacan would increasingly emphasize the *objet petit a* as a central concept in his later seminars, and, by contrast, *das Ding* would rarely appear after *Seminar VII*.

14. Lacan, *On Feminine Sexuality*, 3.

15. According to Zupančič, "[L]ife is the inherent gap opened up by repetition itself, the gap existing at the very heart of repetition. This is also why, for Lacan, all drive (defined by him as 'indestructible life') is ultimately a death drive—not because it aims at death, or 'wants' it, but because it is life as driven by a dead letter" (*The Odd One In*, 126).

16. Lacan, *Ethics of Psychoanalysis*, 54.

17. Lacan, *The Other Side of Psychoanalysis*, 72.

18. Lacan, *Ethics of Psychoanalysis*, 216.

19. Marx and Barber, *Harpo Speaks!*, 52–54.

20. In his memoir, Harpo tells a story about performances he gave in the Soviet Union in the 1930s. When he performed alone, the audiences did not understand what was going on and did not laugh. His handlers decided to add an additional scene involving Russian actors. Without any awareness of the language or what was being said in the preceding scene, Harpo performed exactly the same routine, this time bringing the house down. Even if totally unrelated, Harpo's nonsense often requires a point of sense-departure. See Marx and Barber, *Harpo Speaks!*, 299–338.

21. Lacan, *Ethics of Psychoanalysis*, 72, 90.

22. Trahair, *The Comedy of Philosophy*, 161; Mellencamp, "Jokes and Their Relation to the Marx Brothers," 66.

23. Lacan, *Other Side of Psychoanalysis*, 56; Žižek, *Looking Awry*, 51. Zupančič situates Harpo's literalism within this materiality, moreover suggesting that the excessive, repressed meaning acts as a stopper for the metonymic deferral of desire. Zupančič, "Ethics and Tragedy in Lacan," 190.

24. Lacan, *Ethics of Psychoanalysis*, 55.

25. Lacan, *Other Side of Psychoanalysis*, 47.

26. Lacan, *Other Side of Psychoanalysis*, 33.

27. Žižek, *Organs without Bodies*, 93.

28. Mark Winokur has provided an excellent analysis of this scene along related Lacanian lines, although he ultimately argues for the joke as "anti-Lacanian." Winokur, *American Laughter*.

29. "The Wunsch does not have the character of a universal law, but, on the contrary, of the most particular of laws—even if it is universal that this particu-

larity is to be found in every human being. We find it in a form that we have categorized as a regressive, infantile, unrealistic phase, characterized by a thought abandoned to desire, by desire taken to be reality" (Lacan, *Ethics of Psychoanalysis*, 24).

30. These films, unlike almost all other American comedies from the 1930s and 1940s, merge slapstick and screwball in a highly sophisticated way, relating the anarchic violence of the silent Harpo (a stand-in for the entire tradition of slapstick) to the at times sophisticated and at times crass zaniness of Groucho and Chico. Siegfried Kracauer emphasizes this point brilliantly. See Kracauer, *Theory of Film*, 109. For an analysis of the vaudeville source for the Marx Brothers' mixture of screwball and slapstick, see Jenkins, *What Made Pistachio Nuts*.

31. Tobias, "The Big Bang Theory."
32. Garron, "The Big Bang Theory."
33. Critchley, *On Humour*, 2.
34. Critchley, *On Humour*, 3.
35. Freud, "Humour," 162.
36. Critchley, *On Humour*, 1.
37. Critchley, *On Humour*, 1.
38. Freud, "Femininity," 121.
39. Freud, "Humour," 162.
40. Freud, "Humour," 162.
41. Halberstam, *The Queer Art of Failure*, 2.
42. Halberstam, *The Queer Art of Failure*, 2–3.
43. Halberstam, *The Queer Art of Failure*, 3.
44. Huver, "Jim Parsons on *Big Bang Theory*'s Future."
45. Critchley, *On Humour*, 11.
46. Freud, "Humour," 163.
47. Critchley, *On Humour*, 10.
48. Critchley, *On Humour*, 11.

Works Cited

Adorno, Theodore. *The Culture Industry*. Edited by Jay M. Bernstein. New York: Routledge, 2001.

Agee, James. *Film Writing and Selected Journalism*. Edited by Michael Sragow. New York: Library of America, 2005.

Artaud, Antonin. *The Theater and Its Double*. Translated by Mary Caroline Richards. New York: Grove, 1958.

Barthes, Roland. *Barthes by Barthes*. Translated by Richard Howard. Berkeley: University of California Press, 1994.

Critchley, Simon. "Did You Hear the Joke About the Philosopher Who Wrote a Book About Humour?" In *When Humour Becomes Painful*, edited by Felicity Lunn and Heike Munder, 44–51. Zürich: JRP/Ringier Press, 2005.

———. *Ethics-Politics-Subjectivity: Essays on Derrida, Levinas, and Contemporary French Thought*. New York: Verso, 1999.

———. *On Humour*. London: Routledge, 2002.

Deleuze, Gilles. *Cinema I: The Movement-Image.* Translated by Hugh Tomlinson and Barbara Habberjam. Minneapolis: University of Minnesota Press, 2007.

De Kesel, Marc. *Eros and Ethics: Reading Jacques Lacan's Seminar VII.* Translated by Sigi Jöttkandt. Albany, NY: SUNY Press, 2010.

Freud, Sigmund. "Femininity." In *The Standard Edition of the Complete Psychological Works of Sigmund Freud.* Vol. 22, *New Introductory Lectures on Psycho-Analysis and Other Works (1920–1936),* edited by James Strachley, 112–35. London: The Hogarth Press, 1964.

———. "Humour." In *The Standard Edition of the Complete Psychological Works of Sigmund Freud.* Vol. 21, *The Future of an Illusion, Civilization and its Discontents and Other Works (1927–1932),* edited by James Strachley, 159–166. London: The Hogarth Press, 1964.

Garron, Barry. "The Big Bang Theory." *The Hollywood Reporter,* September 20, 2007. http://www.hollywoodreporter.com/review/big-bang-theory-158202.

Halberstam, Judith. *The Queer Art of Failure.* Durham, NC: Duke University Press, 2011.

Huver, Scott. "Jim Parsons on 'Big Bang Theory's' Future, Why He Relishes Sheldon's Obliviousness." *Variety,* February 25, 2016. http://variety.com/2016/tv/news/big-bang-theory-jim-parsons-sheldon-oblivious-1201715273/.

Jenkins, Henry. *What Made Pistachio Nuts: Early Sound Comedy and the Vaudeville Aesthetic.* New York: Columbia University Press, 1992.

Kracauer, Siegfried. *Theory of Film.* Princeton, NJ: Princeton University Press, 1997.

Lacan, Jacques. *The Ethics of Psychoanalysis, 1959–1960.* Translated by Dennis Porter. New York: Norton, 1997.

———. *écrits.* Translated by Bruce Fink. New York: Norton, 2006.

———. *On Feminine Sexuality: The Limits of Love and Knowledge, 1972–1973.* Translated by Bruce Fink. New York: Norton, 1998.

———. *The Other Side of Psychoanalysis.* Translated by Russell Grigg. New York: Norton, 2007.

Mellencamp, Patricia. "Jokes and Their Relation to the Marx Brothers." In *Cinema and Language,* edited by Stephen Heath and Mellencamp, 63–78. London: British Film Institute, 1984.

Marx, Harpo, and Russell Barber. *Harpo Speaks!* New York: Random House, 1960.

Rancière, Jacques. *The Future of the Image.* Translated by Gregory Elliot. New York: Verso, 2007.

Tobias, Scott. "The Big Bang Theory." *The A.V. Club,* September 24, 2007. http://www.avclub.com/tvclub/the-big-bang-theory-the-big-bang-theory-12479.

Trahair, Lisa. *The Comedy of Philosophy: Sense and Nonsense in Early Cinematic Slapstick.* Albany, NY: SUNY Press, 2007.

Ulmer, Gregory L. "'A Night at the Text': Roland Barthes's Marx Brothers." *Yale French Studies* 73 (1987): 38–57.

Weber, Carl. "Vaudeville's Children and Brecht: The Impact of American Performance Traditions on Brecht's Theory and Practice." *Brecht Yearbook* 15 (1990): 55–71.

Winokur, Mark. *American Laughter: Immigrants, Ethnicity, and 1930s Hollywood Film Comedy.* New York: St. Martin's Press, 1996.

Žižek, Slavoj. *Looking Awry: An Introduction to Jacques Lacan Through Popular Culture*. Cambridge, MA: MIT Press, 1992.

———. *Organs without Bodies: On Deleuze and Consequences*. New York: Routledge, 2004.

Zupančič, Alenka. *The Odd One In: On Comedy*. Cambridge: MIT Press, 2008.

———. "Ethics and Tragedy in Lacan." In *The Cambridge Companion to Lacan*, edited by Jean-Michel Rabaté, 173–190. Cambridge, UK: Cambridge University Press, 2003.

4.

Irony

INT. WASHINGTON HILTON BALLROOM — NIGHT

STEPHEN COLBERT, dressed in formal attire, addresses a room full of Washington insiders, including the embattled US President, GEORGE W. BUSH.

STEPHEN

I believe in this President. Now, I know there are some polls out there saying this man has a 32% approval rating. But guys like us, we don't pay attention to the polls. We know that polls are just a collection of statistics that reflect what people are thinking in "reality." And reality has a well-known liberal bias.

The President laughs.

* * *

A joke is an invitation that comes with a test. If you closely follow its movements, grasp its logic, and laugh at the right moments, you become part of a club — those who get it. It is, of course, fun to feel like you are part of something. Think, for example, of a third-grade birthday party that the whole class gets to attend. That sounds fun, right? It is even more fun, however, to know that there's something special about you, as opposed to someone else. Imagine, instead, a velvet rope being lifted for your benefit, as a line full of onlookers jealously observes your ascension. Inclusion is pleasant. The exclusion of others, for better or worse, is exhilarating. A regular joke offers a chance to be entertained in the presence of others. An ironic one provides an opportunity to bask in the self-satisfying knowledge that someone else is missing out on the fun.

Irony is a term so vastly, diversely, and often incorrectly used that it is disingenuous to define it in any comprehensive sense. We can, however, state with relative simplicity what we mean by it here. For the purpose of *The Comedy Studies Reader*, irony is the act of saying something in order to communicate something else, usually the opposite of what has been said. Irony, as this definition suggests, need not always be funny. When it is, however, it has a pleasurable bite that other forms of humor rarely achieve. It also, by virtue of the stark, cruel way in which it mocks those who don't get it, can serve as a powerful political tool when aimed at the ignorance of authority figures.

In the joke above, Stephen Colbert is being mean. Ironic humor commonly employs a dynamic of degradation, but it also does much more. Colbert could have simply said that Bush is a terrible president whom no one likes. He could have mocked his dumb face and left it at that. Given Bush's presence in the room, this may have even been funny in the sort of power-inverting ways described in this book's chapter on the carnivalesque. It would not, however, have been ironic or as politically poignant.

What makes Colbert's comedy so effective is that he is able to say one thing by stating its opposite. As he does this, he not only alerts his audience to the fact that Bush is unpopular, but also emphasizes the existence of those who remain in denial of this fact. For most people it is comically absurd and untrue to suggest that reality has a political "bias." However, in communicating that it doesn't by stating that it does, Colbert allows the listener to pleasurably bask in the potential existence of partisans who blame absolutely everything on liberal conspiracy. The joke not only points to the truth but also spotlights those poor saps who remain mired in a swamp of pathetic falsehood.

As Linda Hutcheon argues in the second essay excerpted in this chapter, irony is a complex, somewhat dangerous form of comedy. There is always a possibility, perhaps even a guarantee, that a portion of the audience will simply take the ironist at her or his word. Hutcheon describes this as the "edge" of irony, noting that the ironic joke both starkly divides the world into segments and, in the process, has the potential to cause damage. Certainly, there are some, if not many, who watched Colbert and were pleased that someone was finally defending the poor president. Others might have gotten that Colbert was mocking someone, but thought the joke was meant to parody the liberal media's relentless desire to insult the brave and heroic commander-in-chief. As Hutcheon argues, the deployment of irony actively courts diverse and oppositional understandings. This potential for miscommunication, however, is exactly what allows a listener to feel pleasure and power when she believes that she's gotten it.

The last two essays in this chapter note that although irony has a potentially important political valance, it is by no means intrinsically subversive. In considering *Saturday Night Live*'s shifting comedic strategies before and after 9/11, Matt Sienkiewicz shows the ways in which irony can be used just as effectively to deny the importance of political engagement as it can be to make strong political statements. In the chapter's final essay, Amber Day turns to the clickbait-parody website Clickhole, asking whether its irony has the same subversive, progressive appeal as its parent site, *The Onion*. Considering the economic realities that underpin Clickhole, Day's essay serves as an excellent example of the ways in which comedy theory and the commercial comedy industry are more intertwined than one might think. Irony's edge not only has the potential to create loyal customers but also to expand audiences by offering single jokes with multiple meanings.

A: *Irony's Edge*, Linda Hutcheon[i]

[W]ho are the participants in this social act called "irony"? The party line says that there is an intending "ironist" and her/his intended audiences—the one that "gets" and the one that doesn't "get" the irony. What do you do, then, with the obvious fact that ironies exist that are not intended, but are most certainly interpreted as such? Similarly, there are ironies you might intend, as ironist, but which remain unperceived by others. Irony's indirection complicates considerably the various existing models of intersubjective communication between a speaker and a hearer.[1] With irony, there are, instead, dynamic and plural relations among the text or utterance (and its context), the so-called ironist, the interpreter, and the circumstances surrounding the discursive situation; it is these that mess up neat theories of irony that see the task of the interpreter simply as one of decoding or reconstructing some "real" meaning (usually named as the "ironic" one), a meaning that is hidden, but deemed accessible, behind the stated one.[2] If this were actually the case, irony's politics would be much less contentious, I suspect.

The major players in the ironic game are indeed the interpreter and the ironist. The interpreter may—or may not—be the intended addressee of the ironist's utterance, but s/he (by definition) is the one who attributes irony and then interprets it: in other words, the one who decides whether

i. From Linda Hutcheon, *Irony's Edge: The Theory and Politics of Irony* (New York: Routledge, 1994), 10–12, 14–19, 28–29, 33–36. Copyright © 1994, reproduced by permission of Taylor & Francis Group.

the utterance is ironic (or not), and then what *particular* ironic meaning it might have. This process occurs regardless of the intentions of the ironist (and makes me wonder who really should be designated as the "ironist"). This is why irony is "risky business": there is no guarantee that the interpreter will "get" the irony in the same way as it was intended.[3] In fact, "get" may be an inaccurate and even inappropriate verb: "make" would be much more precise.

* * *

The person usually called the "ironist," though, is the one who intends to set up an ironic relation between the said and unsaid, but may not always succeed in communicating that intention (or the relation). . . . Irony, then, will mean different things to the different players. From the point of view of the *interpreter*, irony is an interpretive and intentional move: it is the making or inferring of meaning in addition to and different from what is stated, together with an attitude toward both the said and the unsaid. The move is usually triggered (and then directed) by conflictual textual or contextual evidence or by markers which are socially agreed upon. However, from the point of view of what I too (with reservations) will call the *ironist*, irony is the intentional transmission of both information and evaluative attitude other than what is explicitly presented.

* * *

The interpreter as agent performs an act—attributes both meanings and motives—and does so in a particular situation and context, for a particular purpose, and with particular means. Attributing irony involves, then, both semantic *and* evaluative inferences. . . . [Irony] happens to the space *between* (and including) the said and the unsaid; it needs both to happen. What I want to call the "ironic" meaning is inclusive and relational: the said and the unsaid coexist for the interpreter, and each has meaning in relation to the other because they literally "interact" to create the real "ironic" meaning.[4] The "ironic" meaning is not, then, simply the unsaid meaning, and the unsaid is not always a simple inversion or opposite of the said: it is always different—*other than* and more than the said.[5] This is why irony cannot be trusted: it undermines stated meaning by removing the semantic security of "one signifier: one signified" and by revealing the complex inclusive, relational and differential nature of ironic meaning-making.[6]

* * *

Irony removes the security that words mean only what they say. So too does lying, of course, and that is why the ethical as well as the political are never far beneath the surface in discussions of the use of and responses to irony. It has even been called a kind of "intellectual tear-gas that breaks the nerves and paralyzes the muscles of everyone in its vicinity, an acid that will corrode healthy as well as decayed tissues."[7] Irony obviously makes people uneasy. It is said to disavow and to devalorize, usually because it distances.[8]

In fact, perhaps the most oft-repeated remark about irony—made both by those who approve and by those who disapprove of it—is about its emotional ethics, so to speak. They say that it is a mode of intellectual detachment, that "irony engages the intellect rather than the emotions."[9] But the degrees of unease irony provokes might suggest quite the opposite. Irony is said to irritate "because it denies us our certainties by unmasking the world as an ambiguity."[10] But it can also mock, attack, and ridicule; it can exclude, embarrass and humiliate. . . . Irony always has an edge; it sometimes has a "sting."[11] In other words, . . . there is an affective "charge" to irony that cannot be ignored and that cannot be separated from its politics of use if it is to account for the range of emotional response (from anger to delight) and the various degrees of motivation and proximity (from distanced detachment to passionate engagement). Sometimes irony can indeed be interpreted as a withdrawal of affect; sometimes, however, there is a deliberate engaging of emotion. . . . [A]ny use of irony or, for that matter, any discussion of the politics of irony that ignores either irony's edge or this wide and complex range of affective possibilities does so at its peril.

* * *

Needless to say, irony can be provocative when its politics are conservative or authoritarian as easily as when its politics are oppositional and subversive: it depends on who is using/attributing it and at whose expense it is seen to be. Such is the transideological nature of irony. Since this is the focus of the entire study, a few examples and an overview of the different ways in which irony can be considered transideological in its politics are in order. My operating premise here is that nothing is ever guaranteed at the politicized scene of irony. Even if an ironist intends an irony to be interpreted in an oppositional framework, there is no guarantee that this subversive intent will be realized. In a totalitarian regime (or simply in a repressive discursive context), to use or attribute irony in order to undermine-from-within is relative straightforward, if dangerous: the rules or norms are known and adhered to in the letter, though not in the spirit, of the ironizing utterance.[12] The dangers only materialize if the authorities also attribute irony and the protective cover of indirection is blown. In a more democratic situation, where different positions or "truths" theoretically coexist and are valued, irony is actually even riskier—though less materially dangerous. Those whom you oppose might attribute no irony and simply take you at your word; or they might make irony happen and thus accuse you of being self-negating, if not self-contradicting. Those with whom you agree (and who know your position) might also attribute no irony and mistake you for advocating what you are in fact criticizing. They may simply see you as a hypocrite or as compromised by your complicity with a discourse and values they thought you opposed. They might also, of course, attribute irony and interpret it precisely as you intended it to be.

* * *

However you might choose to talk about the difference between irony that is seen to exclude and finalize and irony that is seen to relate and relativize, the politics of irony are never simple and never single. Unlike most other discursive strategies, irony *explicitly* sets up (and exists within) a relationship between ironist and audiences (the one being intentionally addressed, the one that actually makes the irony happen, and the one being excluded) that is political in nature, in the sense that "[e]ven while provoking laughter, irony invokes notions of hierarchy and subordinations, judgment and perhaps even moral superiority."[13] More is at stake here, in other words, than may be the case with other discursive strategies, and that "more" has a lot to do with power. This is why the language used to talk about irony— here, as elsewhere—is so often the language of risk: irony is "dangerous" and "tricky"—for ironist, interpreter, and target alike.[14]

* * *

Whether you see the power of irony working to exclude and to put down or instead, to create "amiable communities" between ironists and their intended audiences, the social nature of the participation in the transaction called "irony" should not be ignored.[15] From the point of view of the intending ironist, it is said that irony creates hierarchies: those who use it, then those who "get" it and, at the bottom, those who do not. But from the perspective of the interpreter, the power relations might look quite different. It is not so much that irony *creates* communities or in-groups; instead, I want to argue that irony happens because what could be called "discursive communities" already exist and provide the context for both the deployment and attribution or irony. We all belong simultaneously to many such communities of discourse, and each of these has its own restrictive but also *enabling* communication conventions.[16] To pick a few relatively innocuous examples: the jokes shared by those who are parents are often lost on people like myself who do not have children, and a lot of British political satire is baffling to me as a Canadian. This is not a matter of in-group elitism; it is merely a matter of different experiential and discursive contexts. In a way, if you understand that irony can exist (that saying one thing and meaning something else is not necessarily a lie) and if you understand how it works, you already belong to one community: the one based on the knowledge of the possibility and nature of irony. It is less that irony creates communities, then, than discursive communities make irony possible in the first place.

* * *

As is often the case, I can better explain this with an example: take the various possible ways of interpreting that much cited moment in Francis Ford Coppola's film, *Apocalypse Now* (1979) when a military helicopter flight in Vietnam is accompanied by the music from Wagner's music drama, *Die Walküre* (1870) known as the "Ride of the Valkyries." Whether or not you know the precise source of the music or its particular context within the opera, you may well have heard it before, either "straight" or in one of the many parodic, mass-media versions of it that have made it into a kind of aural cliché today. Hearing its rhythmic power and strong dynamics while viewing a military maneuver might suggest to you a certain appropriateness, either because of vague suggestions of war or because the characters' response on screen reveals it as functioning "as an aphrodisiac designed to release aggressive and destructive tendencies."[17] Yet, in the context of the film, this "high-art" music is highly incongruous and clashes with the rock music that has dominated the sound-track to this point. What if, in addition to this, among your many discursive communities there was one framed by some knowledge of Wagner's work, and therefore you knew that this was called the "Ride of the Valkyries" and perhaps even that, in Wagner's mythic universe, the Valkyries were supernatural women? Then, suddenly out-of-place suggestions of the feminine and the otherworldly might well intrude on your viewing of what has so far in the film been a very male and material, not to say earthy, world. If you know even more about this, the second opera of the cycle known as *Der Ring des Nibelungen*, you might add to these now multiple incongruities, the fact that this music is used in the opera to accompany the warrior maidens as they search the battlefield for the dead bodies of those fallen heroes worthy of being taken to Valhalla, the home of the gods. However, the male-piloted helicopter, you may then notice, is just going into battle in the film: this is a killing mission, a conscious attempt to create—and not reap and redeem—dead bodies.

I have been writing "you" here but, of course, I mean "me," for this is how I attribute and interpret irony here. For me, it is the superimposition or rubbing together of these meanings (the said and the plural unsaid) with a critical edge created by a difference of context that makes irony happen. But that productive and spark-causing rubbing together is made possible in part by the context provided by my awareness of Wagner's work. Irony does not create any community here; the discursive community makes the irony possible in the first place. An American male soldier may well interpret that scene very differently; so may a Vietnamese, whether either knows Wagner's work or not. And irony may not figure in their interpretations at all.

* * *

[I]rony is seen by some to have become a cliché of contemporary culture, a "convention for establishing complicity," a "screen for bad faith."[18] What was once an "avenue of dissent" is now seen as "a commodity in its own right."[19] This position is usually articulated in terms of contrast: the "authentic" or "sincere" past versus the ironic present of the "total ironist" whose use of what is interpreted as a mode of "monadic relativism" prevents taking any stand on any issue.[20] The Hegelian and Kierkegaardian position on irony as negation is at the base of this position, as, in a very different way, it also underlies what has been called a contemporary post-apocalyptic "ironic-nostalgic" retreat from a world of "progress" in ruins.[21]

Nevertheless, even those who hold the view that recourse to irony's multivocal instability is usually at the expense of "necessarily univocal social commitments" have felt obliged to admit that there can exist ironies that point to the "necessarily unfinished, processual, contradictory nature of historical affairs."[22] Some go even further to assert that irony not only works to point to the complexities of historical and social reality but also has the power to change that reality—at least for a time: "During the revolutionary struggle irony is made welcome for it thrusts at the . . . enemy. Once the revolution is in the saddle, irony gets a prompt and dishonourable discharge."[23] Such a shift is only possible because of irony's transideological nature: while irony can be used to reinforce authority, it can also be used to oppositional and subversive ends—and it can become suspect for that very reason.

* * *

We don't have to look to the past, of course, to complicate the picture of the rewards as well as risks of irony. Entire careers are being made to this day on the ambiguities provoked by the attribution of irony: is Madonna the Empowered Woman-in-Control or the Material Girl, Complicit-with-Patriarchy-and-Capitalism? The exact same evidence is always used to argue both sides: Madonna on the cover of *Vanity Fair*, *Elle*, and *Vogue* in the fall of 1992, publishing *Sex* along with the recording of *Erotica* with a $60 million contract with Time Warner. Those who interpret her as ironically subversive see her in control of her own plural representations/masquerades—be they of vamp or virgin—through irony and artifice, though few seem willing to grant her quite the total self-ironizing camp of a Mae West.[24] Those who refuse to attribute irony see only complicity with patriarchal representations and a desire to milk them for all the (considerable) money they are worth. Madonna has attacked feminists for missing her ironies: "Irony is my favorite thing. . . . Everything I do is meant to have several meanings, to be ambiguous."[25] But ambiguity and irony are not the same: irony has an edge.

* * *

Is Madonna so successful because of her irony or her complicity? Or is that the very point? It would seem that the inability to make a clear distinction might well be what has allowed her to attract multiple audiences: those who see her as totally dominated by the masculine gaze (and either approve or disapprove); those who see her as utterly "in charge" (a positive no matter what her actual choice of self-representation); those who see only her canny commercial instincts (and, again, either approve or do not); those who see her as subversively, flamboyantly, provocatively deconstructing the "traditional notion of the unified subject with finite ego boundaries" through irony.[26]

* * *

I want to suggest, in concluding, a kind of symbolic "sign" under which a theory of irony might be written: let's call it, quite simply, the IRON. Suggestions of the familiar household pressing and smoothing device do not so much point to the incommensurability of the domains of ironing and irony, but rather to the appropriation of irony's transgressive, provocative, and subversive potentialities into women's domains.[27] But the transideological politics of irony are also encoded in such a "sign," for (as my friend, David Clarkson once suggested) the IRON can also be a branding device, one that hurts, that marks, that is a means of inflicting power. To resolve the opposite connotations of these two IRONs into a third, however, you need only think of irony in the symbolic light of the non-domestic and somewhat less violent golf club known as the IRON: it has an oblique head (the greater its number the greater its obliqueness); it is subtle (compared to the alternatives); it works to distance objects. But, it can also miss.

B. "Speaking Too Soon: *SNL*, 9/11, and the Remaking of American Irony," Matt Sienkiewicz[ii]

In this chapter I consider the question of irony and 9/11 via a close look at *SNL*'s comedic tendencies both before and after that tragic day. Although I cannot go as far as to reaffirm the overwrought mortuary declarations of Carter and Rosenblatt, I do wish to take seriously the possibility that a real change in ironic modes of comedy took place around this period of time. To do so, I offer two separate, though not entirely unrelated, conceptions of irony. In discussing pre-9/11 *SNL*, I draw upon the literary and philosophical work of Søren Kierkegaard, particularly his notion of "the ironist." According to Ronald Schleifer, this character is one who embraces "infinite negativity," and thus "is absolutely negatively free in total possibility."[28] By Kierkegaardian irony I mean a view that approaches the world with the sense that all meaning is ultimately artificial and thus nothing ought to be taken seriously. It is to deny that anything is, in a fundamental sense, important and thus to embrace a perspective through which surface level aesthetics are allowed to replace traditional ethical and religious understandings of the meaning of life. Engaging with popular critic Jedediah Purdy, I suggest that pre-9/11 *SNL* can be productively viewed as embracing a mode of comedy akin to the irony Kierkegaard describes (but, it must be said, does not like).

I then consider the moment directly following 9/11, suggesting that, for a brief period of time, *SNL*, like much of American television, really did attempt to portray a sense of sincerity and shied away from irony of

ii. From Matt Sienkiewicz, "Speaking Too Soon: *SNL*, 9/11 and the Remaking of American Irony," in *"Saturday Night Live" & American TV*, ed. by Nick Marx, Matt Sienkiewicz, and Ron Becker (Bloomington: Indiana University Press, 2013), 95–100, 102–109. Reprinted with permission from the author.

any kind. However, this irony-free moment quickly passed. Considering post-9/11 *SNL*, I suggest that, for a variety of reasons, the program turned away from the Kierkegaardian sense of irony and towards a more classical, Socratic approach. Described in the *Oxford Dictionary of Philosophy* as "Socrates's irritating tendency to praise his hearers while undermining them," Socratic irony indicates a mode of address in which a specific meaning may be twisted, but only in the service of asserting a sincerely held alternative meaning.[29] As opposed to Kierkegaard's ironist who speaks in a manner that negates the possibility for any true meaning, Socratic irony says one thing in order to passionately argue for its opposite. It is something akin to sarcasm in the common sense, but it is a sarcasm that is meant to prove a specific point. Through a careful analysis of a variety of *SNL* sketches as well as a consideration of the program's industrial and cultural contexts, I argue that although irony did not disappear on 9/11, the moment did mark a turning point at which the dominance of a nihilistic, Kierkegaardian form of irony began to slip away and a Socratic, more politically and socially committed mode of ironic address took its place.

SNL's Purdian/Kierkegaardian pre-9/11 Irony

. . . For Purdy, 1990s-era American irony is nihilistic and inherently hostile to any notion that humor could serve a productive social function. In this regard, it draws upon an important Kierkegaardian conception and denunciation of irony. Purdy's reading of Jerry Seinfeld, Wayne and Garth, in fact, suggests that during this time period Americans had become attracted to what Søren Kierkegaard (also unsympathetically) understands as the ironic or "aesthetic" mode of existence. The ironist, or aesthete, as described in Kierkegaard's *The Concept of Irony*, is a figure who, seeing the absurd seriousness with which society can treat ultimately trivial matters, resorts to a playful existence that, while light and free on the surface, nonetheless belies an "infinite negativity" at its core.[30] The ironist, for both Kierkegaard in the 1840s and Purdy in the 1990s, is someone who denies that real ethical and political values can exist and thus chooses to make up her own, knowing full well that these self-created values will not stand up to any kind of serious scrutiny.

Though Purdy does not engage with Kierkegaard's ironist in his own critique, his very brief treatment of *SNL*'s "Wayne's World" suggests that it is this particular vision of the ironic that he sees dominating American culture in the time before 9/11—a situation he feels is detrimental to US society's political and ethical health. The catchphrase-laden

"Wayne's World" sketches and films, Purdy argues, mimic a society in which "we find ourselves using phrases that are caught up in a web we did not weave."[31] According to Purdy, in the 1990s Americans felt there was little to be gained or lost on the level of fundamental moral and political issues. As a result mainstream culture became content to play the game of constant self-reference. The collage of song lyrics, catchphrases and obsession with the superficial culture of heavy metal music in "Wayne's World" never gets around to saying anything meaningful about the kinds of issues essential to a morally functioning society—what Purdy might call "authenticity."

A close look at the *SNL* episodes immediately preceding and following 9/11 provide a useful vantage point to apply Purdy's Kierkegaardian understanding of irony in a concrete fashion. In a strange coincidence, both episodes began with a segment centering on New York mayor Rudy Giuliani. The final episode of the 2000–2001 *SNL* season opens with a shot of Giuliani's Gracie mansion. The scene then cuts to Darrell Hammond doing his impression of the mayor, sitting in a leather chair addressing the camera. He introduces the audience to his "friend" Judith Nathan, a woman well-known at the time as Giuliani's mistress. Nathan, played by Rachel Dratch, hides playfully behind a plant as Giuliani describes the unfairness of his wife's refusal to allow Nathan to visit the mansion. For the remainder of the sketch, Giuliani's wife chases Nathan around with a baseball bat while the mayor makes repeated reference to rumors of his sexual dysfunction. Rather than providing a cogent critique of Giuliani's politics, the sketch's text is an exercise in the sort of free play and superficial referentiality that Purdy attributes to the ironist's worldview, albeit with a disturbing twist. In the midst of a series of jokes about his wife's attacks on him and his own obsession with Nathan, Giuliani offhandedly commends Robert Blake for "taking things into his own hands" the previous week—a reference to Blake's recent arrest for the murder of his wife, Bonnie Lee Bakley. The joke, which elicited groans from the studio audience, represents the very sort of cultural moment that Purdy bemoans and that Carter and Rosenblatt wished dead after 9/11. Absent from the sketch is any explicit connection to how Giuliani's personal foibles relate to the politics of New York City or his ability to successfully govern. Having spent some years exhausting a seemingly endless supply of Clinton-Lewinsky jokes, *SNL* seemed to be invoking Giuliani as a way of reinstating a discourse in which political scandal is primarily associated with soap-opera storylines as opposed to legitimate public concern.

Certainly, some readers may have read this scene as being politically engaged. Giuliani's conspicuously conservative approach to sex and crime in New York City may serve as a bridge from the sketch's content to more serious matters of public policy and morality. However, there is little evidence that this is the preferred meaning of the scene. No joke is made of Giuliani's ability to govern New York City or the political ramifications of his infidelities. The punchlines are fully personal and apolitical, including the culminating line in which Giuliani rejoices he's "fifty-seven with a comb over and a broken penis and the ladies still fight over" him. Dropped directly into the middle of this ironic (in the Kierkegaardian sense) play is the ostensibly very serious allusion to the murder of Bakley. Played for nothing more than a cheap laugh, this reference is an example par excellence of Purdy's understanding of pre-9/11 irony. The Blake-Bakley murder story is treated exclusively as a signifier, quickly dropped into the scene in connection to Giuliani's frustration over his wife's refusal to accept his mistress. Whether or not it is funny is somewhat beside the point. There were certainly ample opportunities for the sketch to skewer Giuliani's policies as well as his personality. As a law and order Republican who made a great show of banning "sex-oriented businesses" in New York City, Giuliani's personal foibles perhaps say a great deal about the relationship between public and private sexuality.[32] Jokes about violence may well have been connected to issues of domestic abuse or police brutality. And perhaps some viewers made these connections. The sketch, however, fails to provide them in a way that suggests the producers were concerned with the political ramifications of the sex-comedy of errors they were skewering. The bit follows Jones's observation that *SNL* political impressions place "an emphasis on physical or phonetic resemblance that focuses on the politician's presentation of self" as opposed to taking seriously the relationship between satire and matters of true political importance.[33] As Purdy might put it, the Giuliani sketch does not appear to be committed to the notion that it has an important role to play in public discourse.

* * *

As television, and *SNL* changed during the first decade of the twenty-first century, this attitude would melt away, leading to a comedy world that was more likely to embrace a sense of social engagement and to eschew any notion that humor was somehow diametrically opposed to a worldview in which questions of right and wrong were no longer relevant.

Stage Two: Giulianian Authenticity or, The Quest for Approval

SNL's return to the air on September 29th, 2001 also featured Giuliani. This time New York's mayor, now recognized as a national hero, played himself. Breaking the program's decades-old format, the episode opened with a somber, ten-minute prologue that featured an emotional musical performance by Paul Simon, a tribute to New York's firefighters and a now famous exchange between Lorne Michaels and Giuliani. Whereas in the opening of the show's twenty-sixth season a year before Giuliani had been portrayed as little more than a collection of silly signifiers often attributed to a prototypical politician—selfishness, lustfulness, obliviousness—during season twenty-seven's opener his presence anchored the show's authentic commitment to honoring the victims of September 11. As the very serious opening segment came to a close, Lorne Michaels turned to Giuliani, embracing him as the very embodiment of the pain and resilience of New York City. Michaels, following the very serious opening to the program, asked the mayor if it was ok for the show to be funny from that point forward. Giuliani's response of "why start now?" has been noted by scholars such as Lynn Spigel and Amber Day as having represented an official government sanctioning of post-9/11 laughter.[34] And it also marked the beginning of a period of transition in *SNL*'s comedy.

SNL's efforts at sincerity and its concern with asking permission went well beyond the opening segment with Giuliani. In her opening monologue for that first post-9/11 episode, host Reese Witherspoon offered a combination of promises and apologies, making clear to the audience that something about comedy had changed, at least for the time being. She began by expressing her appreciation for the audience's presence or, as one might interpret her remarks, their very existence. She then assured the crowd that, despite the circumstances, the cast and crew would "give it everything [they've] got." Finally, she asked permission to tell a joke, in much the way that Michaels had asked Giuliani. This time, however, the gatekeeper was the audience, who encouraged her to tell the joke, despite her admonition that it would contain a "bad word." The joke was not a particularly funny one, but it was delivered in a friendly, undeniably sincere fashion. The punch line involved a boy, apparently having been raised as a polar bear, remarking that he is "freezing [his] balls off."

The content of the humor, in many ways, changed remarkably little from the episode preceding it. As noted above, both the pre- and post-9/11 episodes prominently included jokes that referenced animal testicles. But the mode of address used throughout the episode was very much changed, with moments of stressed, perhaps even forced, sincerity appearing at various intervals. 9/11 had forced *SNL* to consider what role it might play in a world in which nothing, including comedy, would get a free pass with regards to moral significance. Before launching into her polar bear joke, Witherspoon acknowledged as much, saying that the cast and crew were still "figuring things out." This episode, as well as some of those that would follow, regularly broke out of comedic modes of address entirely, speaking sincerely to the audience, seemingly reminding viewers that *SNL* realized it now had to serve a purpose beyond making people laugh. During the Witherspoon episode, "Weekend Update" featured an appeal for donations to the Twin Towers Fund, alongside a declaration by Tina Fey that "New York City is awesome." A few weeks later, Drew Barrymore would mix into her opening monologue an authentic-sounding account of her fears about traveling to New York during the anthrax scare that immediately followed the 9/11 attacks. While it was acceptable at this juncture to make jokes, a few of which even touched upon 9/11-related topics such as Osama Bin Laden, humor could no longer revel in its frivolousness. The specter of something that truly did matter, something that irrefutably existed beyond the realm of the aesthetic free play embraced by the ironist, demanded a new mode of comedic address, even if *SNL* did not have time to fully adapt to this new style. Though the show would later come to integrate this sense of meaning into its comedy, it began by occasionally interrupting its previous approach to humor with moments of reference to the serious situation surrounding the program's production in New York City.

* * *

Stage Three: *SNL*, Stewart, and Socrates

A week later *SNL* took a step down the trail that the *The Onion* blazed and that would become a trademark of post-9/11 comedy. Apparently more comfortable now in taking a critical look at America's new cultural milieu, the second episode after 9/11 clearly displayed evidence of a new era of *SNL* that would feature a deeper sense of political engagement. The episode featured a variety of sketches that addressed questions of post-9/11 American life, and though they were far gentler than the humor found in *The Onion*, the episode's sketches nonetheless featured a considerably more critical brand of comedy. In one of the season's best-known sketches, Will Ferrell arrives to work wearing a red, white and blue thong in lieu of pants, claiming that in doing so he is the only person at the office displaying real patriotism. Whereas others have donned pins or kerchiefs with American themes, he has chosen to wear nothing but the old stars and stripes. The sketch is carnivalesque in the extreme, flipping societal standards by replacing casual work-attire with an outfit that prominently features Ferrell's bare buttocks and fuzzy paunch of a stomach. The target of the comedy, it seems, is the issue of authentic patriotism and the relationship that certain surface expressions, such as verbal declarations and fashion statements, might bear to it. By parodying surface expressions, however, the sketch posits, or at least asks the viewer to consider, the possibility of a true, meaningful patriotism that might consist of other more productive forms of expression. Such a reading of the sketch positions it in direct opposition to Purdy's idea of American irony before 9/11, which was premised on the notion that authenticity of any kind was not a goal worth pursuing.

* * *

These sketches, I argue, mark *SNL*'s turn towards a different sort of irony—one that stands in strong contrast to the vision described by Purdy and that I have compared to Kierkegaard's ironist. Instead, this mode of comedy draws upon a more traditional, Socratic notion of irony. Whereas the aesthetic irony of Kierkegaard and Wayne and Garth aims to negate the possibility of real meaning by relegating all communication to the level of surface appearances, the Socratic, post-9/11 version attempts a far more targeted inversion. As opposed to putting in doubt the ultimate importance of addressing an issue, as I argue the pre-9/11 Giuliani sketch did, these bits say one thing in order to prove its opposite. This form of discourse bears close resemblance to what has been called "Socratic irony." In Platonic dialogues, this approach to irony is most evident when Socrates praises his opponent's intelligence or denigrates his own. In such cases he says one thing in order to eventually, more forcefully, compel his interlocutor to switch positions. Such is the case when Ferrell declares that wearing a patriotic thong is the essence of supporting your nation or Tracy Morgan says that wearing a trash bag is a sign of celebrity humbleness. These utterances do not mean what they say, but they do have a very precise rhetorical intention. Most crucially, they do not deny the possibility of meaningful action; they simply aim to outline the parameters of such engagement by defining what is not appropriate or effective. In the world of contemporary comedy, this brand of irony is best instantiated by the persona of Stephen Colbert, whose endless irony is not meant to deny the possibility of meaning but instead to reinforce the absurdity of the positions he takes in order to argue for their opposites.

This is not to say that *SNL* never engaged in this form of comedy before 9/11 or always did after it. Clearly this is not the case. However, there was a marked turn in *SNL*'s approach to political and social engagement beginning with 9/11, even if it has subsided somewhat as memories of the tragedy have become more distant. Sketches in the post-9/11 period had a tendency to focus on policies more and political personalities less than in previous eras, although, as Jones has argued, *SNL* presidential impressions will always rely on personal foibles and simple mimesis to some extent.[35] Increasingly, however, *SNL* began to take on the minutiae of governmental practice and to devote prime slots, particularly cold opens, to sketches that required an in-depth understanding of current events in order to be fully appreciated. By the second half of the decade following 9/11, viewers could expect *SNL* to provide very specific takes on public life that implied a need for seriousness through the use of ironic comedy. The merging of *SNL* and the importance of real public engagement reached its heights with Tina Fey's scathing, uncanny, impression of Republican vice-presidential candidate Sarah Palin. Scholars Jody Baumgardner, Jonathan Morris, and Natasha Walth have gone so far as to describe a "Tina Fey effect," in which viewers were primed by Fey's *SNL* sketches and ultimately came to reject the viability of Palin's candidacy.[36] Though Fey and *SNL* never explicitly stated it, most came to read the sketch as making a direct statement on the appropriateness of Palin being a national political figure. Such a sense of sincere commitment stands directly opposed to the Purdian explanation of 1990s irony. And, perhaps just as interestingly, *SNL* has continued with this mode of engagement beyond election season.

* * *

Conclusion

It is important to note that this shift in modes of comedic irony is not solely the result of 9/11. As Spigel argues, the trauma of 9/11 hardly served as the ultimate determinant for the shape that American television would take during the first decade of the twenty-first century. Despite a brief moment in which networks focused on national unity as a reaction to the tragic events, very quickly "the competitive environment of narrowcasting . . . gave way to the 'bottom line.'"[37] In the realm of comedy, this meant a field of play inundated with specifically targeted programming geared precisely at the younger audiences *SNL* had traditionally succeeded in courting. Producing a variety of comedy programs on a daily basis, Comedy Central and Cartoon Network played a key role in shaping the comedic expectations of many viewers. At the same time, internet out-lets such as *The Onion* and *Funny or Die* provided nonstop material, much of which was pitched in terms of political and social critique. Just as *SNL* would ultimately embrace web-friendly video segments in order to keep up with the comedy marketplace, the turn towards socially engaged, often politically motivated comedy can also be read as a move necessitated by the marketplace expectations. Furthermore, there is a danger in overstat-ing the extent to which *SNL* has devoted itself to the sorts of complex, politically engaged comedy described above. With an hour and a half to fill each week and a mass audience with varied political beliefs to attract, *SNL* by necessity often relies on the silly and the simple. As Jones notes in this volume, there remains a need for the show to mock the more super-ficial elements of American life and politics.

Nonetheless, the experience of watching *SNL* episodes from before and after 9/11 does give the impression that something has changed with regards to the program's self-conception, at least in certain memorable moments. Even now, more than a decade after 9/11, the program shows a consistent willingness not simply to point out absurdities in the world, but also to make cogent, or at least provocative points regarding right and wrong. And this approach has moved beyond the realm of politics. In the February 18, 2012 episode, the cold open took on the brief but impres-sive popularity of Asian-American basketball player Jeremy Lin. During the sketch, three basketball analysts describe Lin in increasingly stereo-typical terms without a sense of impropriety. The fourth makes paral-lel statements about African-American players and is immediately repri-manded for being ignorant and racist. The bit, I would argue, is employing a Socratic mode of irony in order to point out the racist manner in which the American media was willing to essentialize and make a novelty out of an Asian athlete. This is not a mere comedic point. It is an incisive cri-tique and one that not only assumes a certain sense of right and wrong, but also suggests that a sketch comedy show ought to play a role in pursu-ing, or at least pointing to, the right. It is fruitless to claim such a sketch could never have been written before 9/11. Yet it is worth considering the ways in which it would have stood out during the 1990s and feels more natural in the show's current era. Irony did not die after 9/11, of course. It has always existed and always will exist in many different forms. The bal-ance of those forms can change, however, and it is worth noting the ways in which the decade or so following one of America's greatest tragedies has led to a golden era for comedy willing to be ironic but also not afraid to make a point.

C: "Welcome to the Clickhole: The Economics of Internet Parody and Critique," Amber Day

"When You Read These 19 Shocking Food Facts, You'll Never Want to Eat Again." The internet is full of such headlines offering unlikely promises of fascinating content in order to drive up revenues from advertisers who pay by the click. The satiric website Clickhole launched in 2014 to take on just such "clickbait" and other questionably scrupulous online tactics. Taking aim at various genres of viral internet communication, the site highlights many of the absurdities of online culture and the often-unthinking behavior of the internet users who circulate the material. Nevertheless, Clickhole's economic model, built on many of the same structures as the clickbait sites it lampoons, confusingly undercuts much of its critique, shading parody into pastiche, a form of imitation that lacks any critical bite. Its irony at once criticizes and reproduces. Sliding into this more cynical, less pointed form of irony, the site has a hard time living up to the high bar of cultural commentary set by many other contemporary forms of satire and parody, including that of its own parent company, *The Onion*. Instead, Clickhole leads us into a shiny hall of mirrors that reflects back our own actions in amusing replications, but lacks anything with which to anchor us. This essay demonstrates how the critical potential of irony suffers when well-executed parody shares the purely commercial motivations of its target.

Irony, satire, and parody are three separate but interrelated modes of communication which have together become particularly popular in contemporary life. Irony is the most general of the three. It involves pointing to incongruities and inconsistencies, making them visible through the distance between a literal statement and its implied meaning. As Linda Hutcheon defines it, irony "is the making or inferring of meaning in addition to and different from what is stated, together with an attitude toward both the said and the unsaid."[38] Parody, which can make use of irony, focuses on other works of art, creating copies that critically comment on an original. Finally, satire, which frequently employs irony, parody, or both, combines play with social or political critique, using wit to attack particular ideas or conventions. There is often good reason to speak very precisely about each one of these modes. Nevertheless, the three are frequently found in varying combinations, and it is together that they have become a dominant comedic mode of communication within contemporary culture.

In numerous countries around the world, you can now tune in to at least one irony-drenched news parody program—like *The Daily Show*. Similarly, a hefty portion of the videos, articles, and memes that are coursing through your social media feeds likely use irony as an attention-getting hook. While satiric irony has been in use for millennia, rising and falling in popularity in cultures and eras around the world, its ubiquity in contemporary media and political discourse demands more attention. In fact, it is within the realm of such comedy that we are now having some of our more interesting and incisive political conversations.

This satiric renaissance, of course, has not developed in a vacuum. As a number of theorists have argued, vigorous forms of ironic critique have risen up to fill in the lack of substantive discussion within more traditional media.[39] We live in an era in which image reigns. Armies of handlers surround public figures, while mass communication is painstakingly stage-managed. Politicians and corporate spokespeople communicate almost exclusively in carefully pre-scripted prose, and mainstream debate is controlled only by a small coterie of industry insiders. Meanwhile, journalism has, for the most part, not managed to keep pace. Rather than deconstruct a political party's talking points, television news hires representatives from either side to shout at one another over and over again. And rather than pull back the curtain to point out how a particular event has been staged and for what purpose, analysts breathlessly argue about whether it was staged more or less beautifully than the last time. In other words, there is a whole lot of media amplification without much interrogation.

It is hardly a coincidence that pointed, politically astute satire has mushroomed in such a climate. It is the ironic commentators who are highlighting the hypocrisies and deceptions in public speech, satirists who are laying bare cultural inconsistencies that have otherwise gone unremarked, and news parodists who are pointing to the ways in which mainstream journalism is failing us. Judging by the overwhelming popularity of these modes, there is a genuine hunger for this sort of critique. Faced with a real lack in public discourse, satirists have risen up to fill the void. As Geoffrey Baym explains, "the boundaries between news and comedy and between politics and entertainment have become fundamentally obscured in a discursively integrated, post-network age."[40] As the news has slid further toward entertainment, entertainment has become more political. Indeed, this is what makes contemporary satire so interesting: its success at driving much of the relevant social and political commentary of the moment.

In addition to this genuine need for incisive critique, satire's ascendency has also been dependent on the particularities of available technology. Up until at least the 1990s, television, for instance, was one of the last places where one would routinely find challenging satire. In the United States, when three networks were vying amongst themselves for audience share, programming had to appeal to large swaths of the population and guard against offending any substantial number of viewers. As cable fragmented audiences, however, the industry developed a practice of narrowcasting, aiming shows at much smaller, niche audiences who were interested in specialized material. This allowed for the development of much edgier and politically invested satirical programming.

At the same time, digital technologies have made particular forms of ironic juxtaposition and parody relatively easy to create for both amateur and professional satirists. The instant archiving and searchability provided by tools like DVRs allow for the retrieval and juxtaposition of footage of public figures contradicting themselves, while user-friendly editing and design programs make it relatively easy to create and share mashups, parody advertisements, and ironic memes. Meanwhile, as we are surrounded by an ever-expanding array of media forms, all simultaneously vying for our attention, creators must constantly be on the lookout for new ways of attracting interest and engagement. When it comes to shareable content in particular, the ultimate goal is to "go viral," becoming a momentary preoccupation of internet users writ large. Within this background, irony and parody have become extremely popular methods of attracting attention. It is little wonder then that the combined genre of satire/irony/parody has become a kind of cultural dominant, while each new entry serves to further prime audience expectations.

Against this background, Clickhole, though a relative newcomer, fits right in. At its debut, it also appeared to be filling something of a hole in taking aim at the burgeoning world of online content. However, this target has proven to be a tricky one to pin down; as the site succeeds in hilariously sending up the excesses of online culture, it undercuts itself by further reproducing many of these same excesses. As in the examples outlined by Sienkiewicz and Hutcheon earlier in this chapter, we can learn much about the operation of satire, parody, and irony in the instances in which they don't entirely live up to their aspirations. In this case, the failures also point to the limitations of satire that takes aim at largely commercial targets which have only tenuous connections to the public interest or wider social and political discussions.

Clickhole is the spinoff website developed by the very successful satirical news company *The Onion*. *The Onion* began as a parodic newspaper in

Madison, Wisconsin in 1988. From there it grew into a weekly paper distributed in a number of major cities and later on its own website, eventually transitioning to an all-online platform. The parent organization has also branched out with forays into faux television news and internet videos. Over the years, *The Onion* has received both popular and critical acclaim, winning accolades for its spot-on parody of journalistic norms, as well as its often-biting critique of social and political issues. Clickhole carries over many of the same strategies as *The Onion*, but positions itself as a parody of shareable online content produced by sites like Buzz-Feed, Upworthy, and the Huffington Post. Clickhole's site is made up of tongue-in-cheek short-form articles, slideshows, quizzes, "listicles," and blog posts: all of the forms we regularly see coursing through social media feeds and lurking at the corners of webpages.

The site finds its greatest success in crafting pitch-perfect parodies of these internet genres. Clickhole's writers are perfectly attuned to the favored themes of viral culture as well as the techniques and style of writing most commonly employed online. For instance, they regularly poke fun at the breathless headlines that over-promise shocking or touching content in an attempt to attract clicks (hence the term "clickbait"). Clickhole headlines include teasers such as "9 Mind-Blowing Things Hidden On The $1 Bill" and "Shocking: This Bakery in Saudi Arabia Refuses to Make Cakes For Gay Weddings."[41] At first glance, both sound very similar to myriad other headlines one might see on the web. The gay weddings story is a plausible enough call to outrage over a social justice issue, one that, in fact, echoes news stories about business owners and their rights to refuse service. However, in this case, it is supposedly written by someone comically unaware of the facts of social life in Saudi Arabia, where the very existence of gay weddings would be inconceivable. Meanwhile, the dollar bill headline mimics a commonly used "hidden secrets" hook that lures the reader with potential revelations, usually followed by a fairly uninteresting slideshow once actually clicked. In this case, however, the hidden details are absurdly exaggerated (and would, in fact, be quite shocking were they actually true), including marijuana leaves in George Washington's eyes and coupons for the Chili's restaurant chain in the corners.

Other targets include the self-congratulatory memes about sexism or racism circulated by sites like Upworthy that allow the reader to feel superior in his/her sense of tolerance or injustice, but that do not really challenge anyone's thinking. For instance, one Clickhole slideshow is farcically titled "This Interracial Couple Is So Beautiful You Won't Even Care One Of Them Has Coleslaw On His Shoulder," and, indeed, the series of pictures are exactly as described.[42] The favored comedic strategy on Clickhole is to create stories, quizzes, and columns that are, at first pass, almost identical to anything else one might find online, but to inject a hefty serving of absurdity. So, for example, one slideshow titled "8 Things No Guy Over 25 Should Have In His Apartment" begins exactly as you might imagine with "dirty clothes all over your room," but progresses to items like "your father's bones" and "mirror that shows how you die."[43] Another article gestures to the type of meme that purports to show how unrealistic and damaging the proportions are on toys like Barbies, but this one reads ""What Would It Be Like If A Real Woman Had Furby's Proportions?"[44] The accompanying picture is a grotesque mash-up of a real woman and one of the troll-like toys.

At its best, the site uses parody's deconstructive ability to point out the excesses and emptiness of much internet content and to point at the unthinking behavior of internet users—the majority of us who circulate the stuff. In some of the features, the pleasure is perhaps in recognizing and poking fun at one's own tendencies. One slideshow, for instance, is a collection of pictures that are precisely the sort of thing that regularly make the rounds: cute pictures of animals and babies, and uplifting images of heroism or kindness. Only, in this case, the headline reads "Go Ahead, Treat Yourself To Some Saccharine Dogshit. You've Earned It."[45] The captions under each picture remind us that the content is treacly and cliché, but also assure us that we deserve it, while hinting that, in fact, maybe we don't, and that we might do better ingesting content that would actually challenge us somewhat. The final text reads "Let every meaningful thought leave your mind as you learn this dog was saved from a shelter. There we go. Kick out the real thoughts, and let in this syrupy shit. Your life is hard. You deserve a break. Let it wash over you. There. That's good. Don't resist it. You deserve it. You are good. There, there. You are safe. Become this. This is who you are." The piece playfully but bitingly cuts to the heart of why we so predictably gravitate toward particular stories and images.

Clickhole's material sometimes lands in that irony sweet spot of recognition, wit, and insight. More often than not, however, it is not all that satiric. This is likely because it is casting with a very wide net. As opposed to *The Onion*, which frequently tackles social and political issues because of its focus on news parody, Clickhole takes on web content as a whole, including its most frivolous and inane components. There are certainly occasional examples of biting social criticism on the site (most notably, in the wake of several police killings of unarmed, black citizens, when they ran a piece titled "8 More Unarmed Teens Still At Large," consisting of pictures of individual teenagers with captions such as "May be holding up cellphone or other non-gun object, exercise caution"), but these are fairly few and far between.[46] The site is more often pitched at poking fun at trends or the sort of online quizzes that happen to be making the social media rounds on a given day.

In the case of *The Onion*, much of its appeal lies in its topicality. While a typical issue includes plenty of inspired silliness, readers have also come to expect a comedic deconstruction of current issues and debates. Click-hole's mission, on the other hand, is far more diffuse, as its targets are as broad as all internet users and the content they share. While it does track evolving web preoccupations, this tends to be a different form of topi-cality, one that exists in the ahistorical, continual present of viral culture rather than in the midst of social and political debate. Hence, satire is only an occasional part of its repertoire. Ultimately, Clickhole is far more fo-cused on the aesthetic and rhetorical quirks of online culture than it is on policy or power. Of course, Clickhole does not necessarily advertise itself as social or political satire, so it is perhaps not a great insult to say that it is only occasionally satiric. However, the lack of consistent social critique, combined with the site's particular economic model, means that it often begins to slide from the realm of parody into pastiche. Ultimately, despite its absurdity and its smart-aleckyness, Clickhole is sometimes difficult to distinguish from the material it mocks.

Clickhole's stories, quizzes, and listicles are designed to poke fun at internet clickbait, but they also are themselves examples of clickbait. As a Slate writer observes, "Clickhole's business model appears to be awfully similar to that of BuzzFeed."[47] When reading a Clickhole article, you are enticed by links to other features at the edges of your screen. Near the top of the page, these links are to other Clickhole features. If you scroll down just a tad, however, the sections titled "Lesser News From the Web" and "Poor Websites in Need of Clicks" are populated by links to articles on other sites. Whether or not this layout is designed to sow confusion, the headlines from other sites look almost indistinguishable from Clickhole's own, enticing the reader to follow these other leads. Much like, say the Huffington Post, Clickhole supports its own stories by this kind of adver-tising. And much like Upworthy, the site also includes what is referred to as "native advertising" in its economic model. Clickhole partners with clients for a fee, producing Clickhole stories or slideshows that feature their clients' products or are simply "presented by" those companies.[48] For instance, one article posted in January of 2015 is headlined "7 Slices

1. The One Who's Just There To Have Fun

VIA FACEBOOK.COM/DIGIORNO

With all the tense competition of a football game, it's always nice to have someone around to keep the mood light and not take things too seriously!

SIGN-UP FOR OUR NEWSLETTER

Clickhole, in partnership with DiGiorno Pizza, marries satire with commercialism.

Of Pizza You Should Invite To Your Super Bowl Party."[49] What follows is a series of close-up pictures of pizza slices with captions and descriptions that treat the slices like personality types, including "The One Who's Just There To Have Fun." Though there is no mention of the company in the captions themselves, a discrete tag at the top of the story reads "PRE-SENTED BY DiGiorno pizza." Partner advertisers like DiGiorno are ultimately hoping that readers will engage with the story like any other on Clickhole's site, and, ideally, that they will be amused enough to circulate it on social media.

The design of the site allows its creators to figuratively have their cake and eat it too, as it manages to provide some satisfying critique of industry norms, while simultaneously wielding these techniques in pursuit of the same monetary rewards. That is not to imply that there is anything duplicitous about it; no one is trying to hide the realities of this model. During their initial rollout of the site, Clickhole was exclusively sponsored by Jack Link's Jerky, the advertising for which was plastered all over the site. And in press releases and interviews, Clickhole highlighted this relationship, stating "We couldn't be more excited about working with Jack Link's on the creation of Clickhole. . . . They understand that to make a splash in today's advertising landscape, brands need to provide consumers with quality, engaging content. *The Onion* is the go-to place for funny and sharable stories, and we are happy to partner with Jack Link's on such a unique project."[50] Indeed, as one reporter notes, "*The Onion*'s native ad strategy is, in a word, shameless. Because millennials abhor inauthenticity, the thinking goes, the best strategy is to advertise to them in the most straightforward, transparent way possible."[51] On the one hand, this approach ensures a type of trustworthiness. We know that the site is not pretending to be something it is not. On the other hand, it does undercut the critical edge of the parody. For example, the site creates a lot of slideshows that require the reader to click through the content. Is this a means of poking fun at this ubiquitous online technique of inflating the number of "hits" a particular story receives? Absolutely. Is it simultaneously a way for Clickhole to inflate their own numbers? It would seem so.

This is where the site's content begins to confusingly vacillate between parody and pastiche, depending from which angle it is viewed. As Gray, Jones, and Thompson explain, "pastiche merely imitates or repeats for mildly ironic amusement, whereas parody is actively critical."[52] If parody has bite, pastiche is toothless. According to Linda Hutcheon, the element that makes the difference is what she refers to as "ironic transcontextualization."[53] Parody takes pieces of the source text but places them in a new context in order to provide critical distance from the original. It is this critical distance that creates its own commentary, but which is lacking in pastiche. Clickhole does, of course, place the tropes of the BuzzFeed-style quizzes and Upworthy videos within a comedic frame, which is certainly a form of transcontextualization, but that critical distance begins to narrow when Clickhole articles operate as their own form of clickbait. When we take into account that many of the articles on these other sites are highly self-aware and sometimes tongue-in-cheek, the differences between them can get particularly blurry.

That is not to say that it is because Clickhole aims to make money that its critical edge is easily blunted. Many highly insightful forms of parody and satire are also economically successful. Television programs like *The Daily Show* or *Last Week Tonight with John Oliver*, for instance, are great money makers for Comedy Central and HBO respectively. The fact that *The Daily Show* is supported by advertising dollars does not necessarily impact its parody of television news conventions or its commentary on the state of public political discussion. The issue, rather, is that crucial space of critical distance. The parodic news programs would not be mistaken for the straight news programs they critique. They do not speak to their viewers in the same way, do not rely on the same narratives or advance the same worldview. Rather, these shows have made a name for themselves by deconstructing the flaws in the way the issues are framed within mainstream news coverage and debate.

To be fair, Clickhole does at least point to the idiosyncrasies and excesses of online culture, but there are many ways in which it becomes interchangeable with that culture. As a case in point, one of the site's writers left the company a few months after its inception because he had been hired away by BuzzFeed, one of Clickhole's biggest targets. One journalist who was reviewing the site, held this up as proof of Clickhole's brilliance, arguing that "when our interactions have a basic structure that's inherently absurd . . . bits of everything flung at us through a firehose, our satire can't just point at absurdity: it has to become it."[54] I would argue, rather, that this simply makes visible the refractive hall of mirrors of contemporary culture. French philosopher Jean Baudrillard developed a concept that seems particularly applicable here. He describes postmodern culture as made up entirely of simulacra—copies of copies with no originals. In Baudrillard's description, there has ceased to be a distinction between representation and reality; rather, all that exists is representation. As he puts it, "simulation envelops the whole edifice of representation as itself a simulacrum."[55] There are many who would beg to differ, arguing that Baudrillard's outlook is nihilistic and politically paralyzing, but, in this instance, Clickhole falls right in line with this worldview. While the site theoretically offers critiques of internet culture, it also playfully indicates that there is nothing outside of it. Irony is used to simultaneously criticize and reproduce.

The problem with this approach (as far as parody and satire are concerned) is that it leads us toward the more cynical Kierkegaardian type of irony described by Matt Sienkiewicz in the previous essay. When everyone is equally implicated because there is no solid ground on which to stand, there is no real depth of meaning. It is a type of irony which "denies that anything is, in a fundamental sense, important and thus embraces a perspective through which surface-level aesthetics are allowed to replace traditional ethical and religious understandings of the meaning of life."[56] As opposed to the forms of irony and satire that tear down in order to argue passionately for alternatives, Kierkegaardian irony would have us laugh only at the destruction. As previously discussed, there are instances of earnestly communicated critique in Clickhole's material, such as the article on unarmed teens. However, there are many others that take a far more cynical tone. For instance, one video on the site is titled "Are You Ready To Make A Difference? Take The Pledge."[57] The video is a seemingly inspiring montage of people all around the world saying that they want to make a difference, all underscored by uplifting music. The joke, however, is that the video never reveals what the pledge is or how one might make a difference. In other words, it has all the components of an uplifting viral video except the actual content. The implication is perhaps that all such videos are ultimately just PR or that there is little substance to the things that we do find inspiring. Indeed, because the site's comedy does not take a strong ethical stance on much, it implies that there is little that one *should* advocate for.

I would argue that what has made blockbuster satiric programs like *The Daily Show* and *The Colbert Report* such phenomena is their staking out of a moral high ground. While these shows gleefully tear down political and journalistic foibles, they also passionately argue for something more. That form of irony and satire has been the dominant model for roughly the first fifteen years of the millennium, which is why we have experienced a flowering of comedy that is not afraid to take a stand (of which *The Onion* has been a part). Clickhole, though, takes us back to a more smart-alecky, low-stakes irony that is not only less insightful but also not in the least threatening to power, the drivers of online content, and those profiting from its structure. Because it shares discursive similarities to forms of satire like *The Daily Show* and *The Onion*, Clickhole is frequently spoken of as part of the same category. The defining difference, however, is that Clickhole aims its commentary at solely commercial targets, as opposed to the combined commercial and public-service domain of newspapers and television journalism.

While we have, as I have argued, experienced something of a renaissance of satiric critique in recent years, Clickhole reminds us that not all mockery of this sort is inherently satiric in a politically important fashion. Instead of deconstructing social issues, practices, or debates, it focuses most consistently on monetizing particular target markets. Truly great parody and satire is unafraid to consistently take a stand, push boundaries, and risk offending, ideally rousing us from our apathy and disinterest. While, Clickhole can certainly be amusing, it is happy to continue feeding the apathy that keeps us clicking. The remaining question is how things bode for satire as well as for the state of public discourse as a greater portion our lives and our communication shift to the web. There is, of course, nothing about the internet that is intrinsically reactionary (or emancipatory), but if the model of communication and exchange that dominates is a purely commercial one, there becomes less and less space for insightful commentary. As the targets become fluffier, so too does our critique.

Notes

1. See Hernandi, "Doing, Making, Meaning," 749; Adams, *Pragmatics and Fiction*, 1.

2. Booth, *A Rhetoric of Irony*; Karstetter, "Toward a Theory of Rhetorical Irony."

3. Fish, "Short People Got No Reason to Live," 176.

4. Burke, *A Grammar of Motives*, 512.

5. Amante, "The Theory of Ironic Speech Acts," 81; Eco, *The Limits of Interpretations*, 210.

6. Kenner, "Irony of Ironies," 1152.

7. Northrop Frye qtd. in Ayre, *Northrop Frye: A Biography*, 183.

8. Kaufer, "Ironic Evaluations," 25; Ramazani, *The Free Indirect Mode*, 12.

9. Schoentjes, *Recherche de l'ironie*, 153–186; Walker, *Feminist Alternatives*, 24.

10. Kundera, *The Art of the Novel*, 134.

11. Gutwirth, *Laughing Matter*, 144.

12. Benton, "The Origins of the Political Joke"; Dines-Levy and Smith, "Representation of Men and Women," 245.

13. Chamberlain, "Bombs and Other Exciting Devices," 98.

14. Lejeune, *On Autobiography*, 64.

15. Booth, *A Rhetoric of Irony*, 28.

16. Hagen, "The Rhetorical Effectiveness of Verbal Irony," 155.

17. Müller, "Wagner in Literature and Film," 389.

18. Lawson, "Last Exit: Painting," 164.

19. Austin-Smith, "Into the Heart of Irony," 51.

20. See Gitlin, "Postmodernism and Politics"; Jameson, *Postmodernism, or, The Cultural Logics of Late Capitalism*, 412.

21. Warning, "Irony and the 'Order of Discourse' in Flaubert," 263; Vattimo, *The Transparent Society*, 84.

22. Eagleton, *Against the Grain*, 152, 162.

23. Enright, *The Alluring Problem*, 108–109.

24. Birringer, *Theatre, Theory, Postmodernism*, 216.

25. Ansen, "Madonna: Magnificent Maverick," 310.

26. McClary, *Feminine Endings*, 150.

27. As suggested by Chamberlain, "Bombs and Other Exciting Devices."

28. Schliefler, "Irony, Identity, and Repetition," 48.

29. Blackburn, *Oxford Dictionary of Philosophy*, 343.

30. Schliefler, "Irony, Identity, and Repetition," 46.

31. Purdy, *For Common Things*, 11.

32. Myers, "Giuliani Proposes Toughening Laws on X-Rated Shops."

33. Jones, "With All Due Respect," 43.

34. Spigel, "Entertainment Wars," 236.

35. Jones, "With All Due Respect."

36. Kliff, "Wonkblog."

37. Spigel, "Entertainment Wars," 257.

38. Hutcheon, *Irony's Edge*, 11.

39. Baym, *From Cronkite to Colbert*; Day, *Satire and Dissent*; Jones, *Entertaining Politics*.

40. Baym, *From Cronkite to Colbert*, 20.

41. Clickhole, Onion Inc., posted February 26, 2015, http://www.clickhole.com/; Clickhole, Onion Inc., posted April 8, 2015.

42. Clickhole, Onion Inc., posted March 4, 2015, http://www.clickhole.com/.

43. Clickhole, Onion Inc., posted February 12, 2015, http://www.clickhole.com/.

44. Clickhole, Onion Inc., posted March 26, 2015, http://www.clickhole.com/.
45. Clickhole, Onion Inc., posted March 17, 2015, http://www.clickhole.com/.
46. Clickhole, Onion Inc., posted August 11, 2015, http://www.clickhole.com/.
47. Oremus, "Area Humor Site Discovers Clickbait."
48. Coffee, "New Venture for *The Onion* has Your Clickbait."
49. Clickhole, Onion Inc., posted January 12, 2015, http://www.clickhole.com/.
50. "Onion Partners with Jack Link's Jerky for Clickhole.com."
51. Bilton, *"The Onion*'s Clickhole Takes Aim at Viral Site Clickbait."
52. Gray, Jones, and Thompson, *Satire TV,* 17.
53. Hutcheon, *A Theory of Parody,* 12.
54. Berry, "How Clickhole Is Taking Over the Internet," B8.
55. Baudrillard, *Simulations,* 11.
56. Sienkiewicz, "Speaking Too Soon?," 95.
57. Clickhole, Onion Inc., posted February 12, 2015, http://www.clickhole.com/.

Works Cited

Adams, Jon-K. *Pragmatics and Fictions.* Philadelphia: John Benjamins, 1985.
Amante, David J. "The Theory of Ironic Speech Acts." *Poetics Today* 2, no. 2 (1992): 77–96.
Ansen, David. "Madonna: Magnificent Maverick," *Cosmopolitan Magazine,* May 1990, 309–311.
Austin-Smith, Brenda. "Into the Heart of Irony," *Canadian Dimension* 27, no.7 (1990): 51–52.
Ayre, John. *Northrop Frye: A Biography.* Toronto: Random House, 1989.
Baudrillard, Jean. *Simulations.* Translated by Paul Foss, Paul Patton, and Philip Beitchman. New York: Semiotext(e), 1983.
Baym, Geoffrey. *From Cronkite to Colbert: The Evolution of Broadcast News.* Boulder, CO: Paradigm Publishers, 2010.
Benton, Gregor. "The Origins of the Political Joke." In *Humour in Society: Resistance and Control,* edited by George E. C. Paton and Chris Powell. London: Macmillan, 1988.
Berry, David. "How Clickhole Is Taking Over the Internet." *The National Post,* December 4, 2014.
Bilton, Ricardo. *"The Onion*'s Clickhole Takes Aim at Viral Site Clickbait." Digiday .com, June 12, 2014, http://digiday.com/publishers/the-onions-clickhole-takes -aim-at-clickbait-and-viral-sites/.
Birringer, Johannes. *Theatre, Theory, Postmodernism.* Bloomington: Indiana University Press, 1991.
Blackburn, Simon. *Oxford Dictionary of Philosophy.* New York: Oxford University Press, 2008.
Booth, Wayne C. *A Rhetoric of Irony.* University of Chicago Press, 1974.
Burke, Kenneth. *A Grammar of Motives.* Berkeley: University of California Press, 1969.
Chamberlain, Lori. "Bombs and Other Exciting Devices, or the Problem of Teaching Irony." In *Reclaiming Pedagogy: The Rhetoric of the Classroom,* edited

by Patricia Donahue and Ellen M. Quandahl, 97–112. Carbondale: Southern Illinois University Press, 1989.

Coffee, Patrick. "New Venture for *The Onion* has Your Clickbait, Native Advertising Covered." *Adweek*, June 12, 2014. http://www.adweek.com/digital/new-venture-from-the-onion-has-your-clickbait-native-ad-needs-covered/.

Day, Amber. *Satire and Dissent: Interventions in Contemporary Political Debate.* Bloomington: Indiana University Press, 2011.

Dines-Levy, Gail, and Gregory W. H. Smith. "Representations of Women and Men in *Playboy* Sex Cartoons." In *Humour in Society: Resistance and Control*, edited by George E. C. Paton and Chris Powell, 234–259. London: Macmillan, 1988.

Eco, Umberto. *The Limits of Interpretation.* Bloomington: Indiana University Press, 1990.

Fish, Stanley. "Short People Got No Reason To Live: Reading Irony." *Daedalus* 112, no. 1 (1983): 175–191.

Eagleton, Terry. *Against the Grain.* London: Verso, 1986.

Enright, D. J. *The Alluring Problem: An Essay on Irony.* Oxford: Oxford University Press, 1986.

Gray, Jonathan, Jeffrey Jones, and Ethan Thompson. *Satire TV: Politics and Comedy in the Post-Network Era.* New York: New York University Press, 2009.

Gitlin, Todd. "Postmodernism in Politics." In *Cultural Politics in Contemporary America*, edited by Ian H. Angus and Sut Jhally, 347–360. New York: Routledge, 1989.

Gutwirth, Marcel. *Laughing Matters: An Essay on the Comic.* Ithaca: Cornell University Press, 1993.

Hagen, Peter L. "The Rhetorical Effectiveness of Verbal Irony." PhD diss., Pennsylvania State University, 1992.

Hernandi, Paul. "Doing, Making, Meaning: Toward a Theory of Verbal Practice." *PMLA* 103, no. 5 (1988): 749–758.

Hutcheon, Linda. *Irony's Edge: The Theory and Politics of Irony.* New York: Routledge, 1994.

———. *A Theory of Parody: The Teachings of the Twentieth Century Art Forms.* New York: Methuen, 1985.

Jameson, Frederic. *Postmodernism, or, The Cultural Logics of Late Capitalism.* Durham: Duke University Press, 1991.

Jones, Jeffrey P. *Entertaining Politics: Satiric Television and Political Engagement.* 2nd ed. Lanham, MD: Rowman & Littlefield, 2010.

———. "With All Due Respect: Satirizing Presidents from *Saturday Night Live* to *Lil' Bush*." In *Satire TV*, edited by J. Gray, J. Jones and E. Thompson, 3–36. New York: New York University Press, 2009.

Karstetter, Allan B. " Toward a Theory of Rhetorical Irony." *Speech Monographs* 31 (June 1964): 162–178.

Kaufer, David S. "Ironic Evaluations." *Communication Monographs* 48, no. 1 (1981): 25–38.

Kenner, Hugh. "Irony of Ironies." *Times Literary Supplement* (October): 1151–1152.

Kliff, Sara. "Wonkblog." *Washington Post*, March 9, 2012. https://www.washingtonpost.com/blogs/ezra-klein/post/the-tina-fey-effect/2012/03/09/gIQAwmjO1R_blog.html?utm_term=.ecd151ccb9ac.

Kundera, Milan. *The Art of the Novel*. Translated by Linda Asher. New York: Grove, 1986.

Lawson, Thomas. "Last Exit: Painting." In *Art After Modernism: Rethinking Representation*, edited by Brian Wallis, 153–168. New York: New Museum of Contemporary Art; Boston: Godene, 1984.

Lejeune, Philippe. *On Autobiogrpahy*. Translated by Katherine Leary. Minneapolis: University of Minnesota Press, 1989.

McClary, Susan. *Feminine Endings: Music, Gender, and Sexuality*. Minneapolis: University of Minnesota Press, 1991.

Müller, Ulrich. "Wagner in Literature and Film." In *Wagner Handbook*, edited by Ulrich Müller and Peter Wapnewski, 373–393. Cambridge, MA: Harvard University Press, 1992.

Myers, Steven Lee. "Giuliani Proposes Toughening Laws on X-Rated Shops." *New York Times*, September 11, 1994. http://www.mytimes.com/1994/09/11/nyregion/guiliani.proposes-toughening-laws-on-x-rated-shops.html?pagewanted=all.

"Onion Partners with Jack Link's Jerky for Clickhole.com" *Wireless News*, June 21, 2014.

Oremus, Will. "Area Humor Site Discovers Clickbait." Slate, June 12, 2014. http://www.slate.com/articles/technology/technology/2014/06/clickhole_the_onion_s_new_site_is_more_than_a_buzzfeed_parody.html.

Purdy, Jedediah. *For Common Things: Irony, Trust, and Commitment in America Today*. New York: Knopf, 1999.

Ramazani, Vaheed K. *The Free Indirect Mode: Flaubert and the Poetics of Irony*. Charlottesville: University Press of Virginia, 1988.

Schliefler, Ronald. "Irony, Identity, and Repetition: On Kierkegaard's *The Concept of Irony*." *Substance* 8, no. 25 (1979): 44–54.

Schoentjes, Pierre. *Recherche de l'ironie et ironie de la "Recherche."* Ghent, Belgium: Rijksuniversiteit te Gent, 1993.

Sienkiewicz, Matt, "Speaking Too Soon: *SNL*, 9/11 and the Remaking of American Irony." In *Saturday Night Live & American TV*, edited by Nick Marx, Matt Sienkiewicz, and Ron Becker, 93–111. Bloomington: Indiana University Press, 2013.

Spigel, Lynn. "Entertainment Wars: Television Culture after 9/11." *American Quarterly* 56, no. 2 (2004): 235–271.

Vattimo, Gianni. *The Transparent Society*. Translated by David Webb. Baltimore: Johns Hopkins University Press, 1992.

Walker, Nancy A. *Feminist Alternatives: Irony and Fantasy in the Contemporary Novel by Women*. Jackson: University Press of Mississippi, 1990.

Warning, Rainer. "Irony and the 'Order of Discourse' in Flaubert." In *New Literary History* 13, no. 2 (1982): 253–286.

5.

Genre

EXT. FOOTBALL SIDELINE — DAY

JENKO and ZOOK, two football players, stand side by side watching practice. Jenko holds a Q-tip. Zook holds a pastrami sandwich. A PLAYER bumps Jenko, who bumps Zook. The Q-tip and sandwich fall to the grass, the former resting on the latter.

JENKO

Dude, I am so sorry.

ZOOK

It's all right man. Don't worry about it.
The two simultaneously reach down to pick up the dropped items, comically bumping their heads as they do so. They smile and look down at the Q-tip sitting on the sandwich.

JENKO

I'm sorry I got my Q-tip in your meat.

ZOOK

I got my meat in your Q-tip. It's a whole new type of sandwich. Like a meat Q-tip.

JENKO

Like a meat-cute!
They both laugh. A bromance is born.

* * *

Think of your favorite romantic comedy, and picture its first fifteen minutes or so. The camera glides through panoramic views of the Manhattan skyline while whimsical woodwinds ease you down into the office of the film's protagonist. She glares at her computer, exhausted and exasperated,

134

her hair having unraveled from the morning's perfectly coiffed bun. She gathers a large armful of documents and stomps down the hallway, stopping to exchange pleasantries with a female coworker (funnier, but not prettier, than she) and to get a good haranguing from her boss about the Thompson account. She quickly turns a blind corner, only to slam into another body, sending the documents fluttering and the protagonist to the floor. She looks up to see a handsome (but nonthreatening) male face attached to that body, one that extends a warm, strong hand to help her up as he suavely coos a pithy remark that simultaneously assuages her embarrassment and hints at the likelihood that in another thirty minutes of screen time, their bodies will touch again.

You might call this opening scene "generic," and for good reason. We typically use this term derisively to scoff at formulaic and unoriginal storytelling, but "genre" also refers to a system of meaning-making that, when considering comedy, helps media makers to cue audiences' expectations about humor to come. In other words, comedy theory must account for the fact that jokes and other funny elements of media often need help in order to achieve maximum effect. Without the presence of established, comedic industrial codes and narrative conventions, viewers may miss humor for lack of preparation. The generic scene above, for example, is a convention known as a "meet cute," a narrative device common in romantic comedies that introduces a film's lead characters in a playful, if mawkish, fashion. This convention also provides crucial plot information and comedic setups that viewers use to understand the story and enjoy jokes as a film progresses. Most importantly, it lets viewers know that through all of the film's ups and downs, they should always be prepared to laugh. So common are conventions like the "meet cute" that their use has been parodied many times over, as in the football scene from *22 Jump Street* above.

The "meet cute" is just one staple among a vast array of production codes and narrative conventions that tell us we are watching a comedy. Codes are generic practices used by the industry, generally outside of a comedic text's storyworld. Television comedy codes, for instance, include shooting style (single versus multi-camera setups), running time (generally half an hour or less), and laugh tracks. Television comedy conventions include elements native to the text's story, such as its setting (places conducive to a light, joking atmosphere, such as a home, office, or bar), character types (such as the sitcom's wacky neighbor), and episodic narrative resolution. The presence of these attributes serves as an amplifier for humor, assuring the audience that they are getting things right when they find something funny.

The first essay of this chapter comes from Steve Neale and Frank Krutnik's book *Popular Film and Television Comedy*, one of the first scholarly attempts to define screen comedy's particular production practices and aesthetic sensibilities. The excerpt below focuses largely on identifying and defining key codes and conventions of the television situation comedy. Although many of the historical examples the authors mention use episodic storytelling, sitcoms have recently taken a turn to incorporating more ongoing, serial narratives. Accordingly, the remaining two essays of this chapter continue to look closely at the generic evolution of the sitcom. Ethan Thompson examines recent changes in the sitcom's codes and conventions through a consideration of the format's borrowing of documentary aesthetics. Kathryn Fuller-Seeley's essay goes back in time to examine the genre's roots on radio via a case study of Jack Benny's various early programs. The comedian provided one of the first templates for the sitcom, she suggests, by deftly negotiating the competing demands of his staff, network executives, and advertisers to create a familiar storyworld filled with recurring, colorful characters. On the whole, this chapter connects the sitcom both to historical antecedents and to contemporaneous discourses that provide us with a richer understanding of how and why genre matters.

A: *Popular Film and Television Comedy*, Steve Neale and Frank Krutnik[i]

The sitcom on television

The term "sitcom" describes a short narrative-series comedy, generally between twenty-four and thirty minutes long, with regular characters and setting. The episodic series—of which the sitcom is a subset—is, with the continuing serial, a mode of repeatable narrative which is particularly suited to the institutional imperative of the broadcast media to draw and maintain a regular audience. In order to examine the ideological "machinery" of the sitcom, we shall compare briefly the differential operations of the series and the serial, paying attention to their respective modalities of narrative transformation.

* * *

i. From Steve Neale and Frank Krutnik, *Popular Film and Television Comedy* (London: Routledge, 1990), 233–244. Copyright © 1990, reproduced by permission of Taylor & Francis Group.

[T]he sitcom relies upon a different form of repetition from the soap opera serial—the situation is not allowed to change but is rather subjected to a recurring process of destabilization-restabilization in each episode. The sitcom's process of narrative transformation relies much more emphatically, then, upon circularity. Whereas soap operas painstakingly maintain a sense of ongoing temporal development, the sitcom encourages the viewer to "forget" many of the events of preceding episodes. Not that the individual episodes are totally discrete, however: for example, Philip Drummond has considered the importance to the series mode in general of what he terms "synchronizing motifs," that is, regularly occurring bits of business, repeated situations, and catchphrases. . . .[1]

In other words, the sitcom relies upon a trammeled play between continuity and "forgetting," the key to which, as Mick Eaton has suggested, is maintaining the basic parameters of the situation:

> The demands of constant repetition in/of the series, needs to be one whose parameters are easily recognizable and which are returned to week after week. Nothing that has happened in the narrative of the previous week must destroy or complicate the way in which the situation is grounded.[2]

However, it is not uncommon for sitcoms to permit some modification of the basic situation—indeed, this may be necessary in the case of long-running programs, to forestall stasis or broaden the generative nucleus of the situation. The domestic sitcoms *I Love Lucy* and *Bewitched* (1964) both start out as husband-wife shows but over several series the situation is expanded: they have children, the children grow up and go to school, and so on. Additional characters may thus be incorporated to stave off overfamiliarity.

A 1988 BBC1 *Network* examination of the sitcom included a comment by Jeremy Isaacs, former chief executive of Channel 4, that "it is a form in which it is impossible to bring in new work. It is the most conventional form in British television." However, some degree of differentiation is necessary for the long-term success of any sitcom: indeed the sitcom cannot totally escape the "obligation" which marks television in general to address and incorporate changing cultural standards and a sense of its own "development" as a medium. The charges of conservatism, excessive stereotyping of racial, class, sexual, and regional differences, and so on, which are often levelled at the sitcom seem to pinpoint not so much the total imperviousness of the form but rather the particular way in which it operates as a *site of negotiation* of cultural change and difference. As such, the sitcom cannot simply repeat itself but rather its structuring mechanisms serve as a means of reaffirming norms by *placing* that which is "outside" or potentially threatening.

The term "sitcom" tends not merely to describe the formal properties of the half-hour narrative TV comedy, but it also carries pejorative connotations. It tends to be associated with its most pervasive and obviously conventionalized type, the domestic or family sitcom. Thus, in their book, *Bring Me Laughter*, Bruce Crowther and Mike Pinfold write of *M*A*S*H*, a "quality" sitcom with the serious setting of a Korean war hospital, that "to describe [it] as a situation comedy is more than a mite inaccurate."[3] Similarly, writer-producer James L. Brooks has remarked of *The Mary Tyler Moore Show* (1970): "When somebody called *Mary* a sitcom, we'd be furious. We weren't doing sitcom. We were doing character comedy."[4]

With the domestic sitcom entrenched so early in television history, and particularly suited, as we have suggested, to the priorities of the institution, one of the ways to produce a "quality," differentiated show is to appeal to a sense of "character realism" at the expense of the "triviality" and formulaic nature of the domestic sitcom. Thus, for example, some episodes of *M*A*S*H* are intentionally non-comic, and *The Mary Tyler Moore Show* and many of the quality sitcoms which followed it in the 1970s are not only set outside the conventional family household but are also marked by a mixture of comedy and "liberal" sentiment (a combination referred to in the trade as "warmedy").[5]

In the domestic sitcom itself the situation comprises what Mick Eaton refers to as an "inside"[6] which is a highly recognizable conception of the middle-class nuclear-family unit. The disruptions which provide the motor for the individual plots come either from conflicts within the family—which tend to be trivialized and disavowed of serious repercussions—or from intrusions from the "outside" which can easily be rejected. A few random examples will suggest the nature of such disruptions and how they are handled. In a 1988 episode of the BBC series *No Place Like Home*, the stability of the upper-middle-class family is threatened when the wife, Beryl Crabtree (Patricia Garwood), expresses the desire to go out to work. Furthermore, she applies for a job in the company for which her husband Arthur (William Gaunt) works. This represents a threat to the family order as it complicates the separation between home and work which such programs generally maintain, and also (in a series which rigidly centers the husband as central protagonist) represents a threat to the domestic sexual hierarchy and division of labor. However, the episode resolutely sidesteps these areas of complication—which would nudge the show into the realm of domestic drama—by throwing up a plot twist: Beryl does not get the job because the manager employs his mistress instead. Both Arthur and Beryl are angry that she has been overlooked—that is, the problems which initially threatened to divide them have now been replaced by a conflict between them and the "outside." After several plot developments, the unfair appointment is exposed (by the neighbor Trevor, so Arthur is not forced into any problematic conflict with the company), and the episode ends with an irritable Arthur impatiently hurrying Beryl so they can both get to work on time. This would seem to usher in a significantly altered situation, but in subsequent episodes there is no mention of Beryl working at all, and she is once more located firmly within the home. In other words, certain developments are allowed to be carried across episodes, while others are not.

* * *

Programs like *No Place Like Home* . . . demonstrate clearly the investment of both the sitcom and television in general in the bourgeois nuclear family as a model of stability, of "normality."[7] Sitcoms are an integral component of prime-time programming, and even when the situation departs from the "average family" setting, normative conceptions of the family operate as a framework within which to read the "aberrant" situation—as in the variously disrupted families found in *Home to Roost*, *Miss Jones and Son*, *Me and My Girl*, *Kate and Allie*, and *Steptoe and Son*, all marked by the lack of one parent. The sitcoms produced by the MTM company in the 1970s are interesting in this respect for they tend to be situated outside the nuclear family, but principles of unity, allegiance, and obligation are structured in a "surrogate" family network. *The Mary Tyler Moore Show* and programs which followed in its wake, such as *M*A*S*H*, *Taxi*, *Cheers*, and the more recent *Throb*, are structured around a "family of coworkers." In terms of their often-large casts and their concentration upon a wider range of emotional interrelationships, these sitcoms move closer to the territory of the soap opera. Jane Feuer sees such shows as a more "realistic" mirror for their time (in that they acknowledge, if only implicitly, that "the nuclear family was no longer the dominant form outside the texts") but also as utopian, "in that love and work merged in an essentially harmonious universe that represented a throwback to a less corporate age."[8] The recurring situation in such shows is that a "family" member would come to realize that "family unity represents a higher goal than personal ambition."[9] In other words there is the same emphasis upon group unity as is found in the domestic sitcoms, but a different conceptualization of the group; the machinery of the sitcom form functions in each case to preserve the stability of the recurring situation and to protect the relationships it comprises from disruption. To illustrate further the ways in which these American sitcoms work, we shall draw briefly upon a few episodes from *Taxi*, a series made for ABC in 1978 by four ex-MTM producers, James L. Brooks, Ed. Weinberger, Stan Daniels, and David Davis.

The show is set in the lower-class milieu of the Sunshine Taxi Company and features a large regular cast of taxi drivers. The generative nucleus of this show is thus quite broad, especially as many of the drivers hold down other jobs as well and represent mixed educational and social backgrounds—although there is only one regular woman, Elaine (Marilu Henner). The show continues the MTM-style "warmedy," with a recurrent attention to friendship, emotional interdependency, and loyalty, and a similar utopian conception of work. For example, despite the playfully sadistic glee of the shift supervisor Louie De Palma (Danny DeVito) the taxi drivers form an egalitarian group, willing to accept and incorporate such misfits as the drug-scarred 1960s casualty "Reverend" Jim Ignatowski (Christopher Lloyd) and the incompetent East European mechanic Latka Gravas (Andy Kaufman), each of whom is unsuited to life in the world outside.

A typical episode will posit a disruption to the unity of this group: for example, shaken after a mugging, Alex (Judd Hirsch), the principal character, decides to leave the garage for a safer and more lucrative job as a waiter; he eventually returns when he realizes that the good friends he has there provide the greater satisfaction and are worth taking the risk for. In another episode a row develops between Tony and Bobby when the latter neglects the goldfish whose care Tony has entrusted to him; the threat to the stability of group relations is overcome when Bobby realizes the responsibilities that come with friendship and Tony accepts Bobby for what he is. A further episode posits another type of threat common to the sitcom, when the diminutive and aggressive Louie attempts to reform his character, only to have his coworkers tricking him back to his old self (a similar plot is found in a 1956 episode of *The Phil Silvers Show*, "Bilko Gets Some Sleep," when Bilko's character change threatens to destabilize the situation). The sentimental character of the resolutions to this show tend, as in the "Love Me, Love My Tree" episode of *Bless This House* and many examples of *The Mary Tyler Moore Show*,[10] to be followed by a short comic "epilogue" which playfully reaffirms the "normality" of the character interrelationships: they do not dwell upon the emotional concatenations of the individual plot but "get on with their lives." The "epilogue," then, tends to underline the self-contained nature of the individual episodes.

Thus in both the domestic sitcom and such "surrogate family" shows, the regular setting and the regular characters are bonded together into a repeatable unity, with the structure of the sitcom representing an activity of "communalization," reaffirming the stability of the group and the situation. As Francis Wheen has commented:

> The abiding rule, whether in *M*A*S*H* or a "family" sitcom such as *The Dick Van Dyke Show*, is that a character must not face the world alone: she or he must experience the joys and tribulations of life as part of some larger social unit.[11]

In terms of its communalizing role, the sitcom can be regarded as a microcosm of broadcast TV in general, in that the medium attempts to inscribe the viewer as part of its own "family." Television is "allowed into" the home, and it precisely makes itself "at home," addressing itself in intimate terms to "You, the viewer." Both the sitcom and television in general are concerned with reaffirming cultural identity, with demarcating an "inside," a community of interests and values, and localizing contrary or oppositional values as an "outside" (which can, of course, be rendered comprehensible). The sitcom and TV in general seek to align the viewer with what Gillian Swanson has referred to as cultural "systems of propriety, or norms of acceptability," and to "provide a set of conventions which draw directly on an acknowledgement of a shared area of experience and cultural identity . . . [which] presupposes certain inhibitions the transgression of which implies marginality, an identity outside the norm."[12]

As we have noted, the activity of comedy tends to be integrally related to notions of conformity to and deviance from norms. The sitcom is important to television precisely because of its consolidatory function, not just in terms of the narratives as "represented" but also for the ways in which these are made meaningful for the audience. The viewer is imbricated as "part of" the scene rather than functioning as a separate "audience" to be performed to/for, because "naturalistic" comedy involves a more casual activity of "eavesdropping." In its communalizing activity the sitcom can be seen to extend the "bonding activity" of joke-telling. For example, in his consideration of the generative processes of the "smutty joke," Freud notes how the initial object of the joke—the sexual exposure of a woman—becomes transformed in the establishment of a "joking relationship" between the teller and the audience.[13] As he puts it, the one who listens

> soon acquires the greatest importance in the development of the smut
> . . . gradually, in the place of the woman, the onlooker, now the listener,

becomes the person to whom the smut is addressed, and owing to this transformation it is already near to assuming the character of a joke.[14]

The telling of a joke—and this holds for any tendentious joke, not just "smut"—serves to establish a demarcation between an "inside" ("we who share the joke") and an "outside" (in Freud's example, in the location of sexual difference). Such jokes create a communal bonding between the participants which establishes a relationship of power, of inclusion and exclusion. Of course, the object of such joking may not necessarily be a woman, for the constitution of the "outside" can include and marginalize other forms of non-normative sexuality, or racial, class, regional differences, and so on. Joke-telling in general takes the form of a "social contract": in announcing that one is to tell a joke ("Have you heard the one about . . .") one is promising the listeners a pleasure which is, as we have suggested, integrally related to a sense of inclusion, to the affirmation of communal bonds between joke-teller and audience. The sitcom, then, represents an institutionalizing of the pleasures and processes involved in such joke-telling.

Of course, as Barry Curtis has observed, "ignorance, lack of sympathy with or enthusiasm for the transgressions involved can fail to generate a comic response, and, in that case, deny the 'meaning' of the comedy."[15] Hence it is important for the TV industry to rework the generative nucleus of the sitcom in the face of social and cultural transformations—*Bless This House*, for example, incorporates and renders "comprehensible" the late-1960s/early-1970s theme of the "generation gap." It is also important for sitcoms to be generated which can engage sections of the audience falling outside the middle ground which the domestic sitcom seeks to address and reaffirm. Obvious examples of the latter tendency include such black sitcoms as *No Problems*, *Sanford and Son* and *The Cosby Show*. In the latter show, racial difference is made acceptable within the parameters of traditional family unity—the Huxtables are an idealized family who "just happen" to be black, *The Cosby Show* can flaunt its "modernity" in its positive representation of blacks but can at the same time hold this in place through a "commonplace" sense of family unity. A more obvious example of the containment and domesticization of difference is represented by those shows which incorporate "supernatural" or "otherworldly" elements into the situation: *Bewitched*, *I Dream of Jeannie*, *My Favorite Martian*, *Mork and Mindy*, *The Munsters*, *The Addams Family*, and the more recent *Alf* for example. In each case the "alien" elements which become incorporated within "normal life" are, of course, detached from the customary sinister connotations of vampires, witches, man-made monsters, and invaders from space.

B: "Comedy Verité? The Observational Documentary Meets the Televisual Sitcom," Ethan Thompson[ii]

About halfway through the first season of the FOX television show *Arrested Development* the program's narrative abruptly confronted its televisual style. As the Bluth family enters a courtroom, the presiding judge announces that no cameras are allowed, and the doors are closed, blackening the television screen and cutting off the unfettered access to the Bluths viewers have enjoyed all season. This courtroom incident is the first—and only—time *Arrested Development* overtly suggests there is an actual camera crew within the show's diegesis that is responsible for the documentary "look" of the show. No character addresses the camera or complains about the presence of the crew in his or her car and bedroom. The Bluth family may be gloriously aloof, but they are not so clueless as to fail to recognize they are the subjects of a documentary or reality television show. However, that is exactly what the program *looks like*. The televisual style of *Arrested Development*, with its handheld cameras, awkward pacing, and violations of continuity rules, looks a lot more like a documentary than it does a traditional sitcom. Still, this reflexive moment of the slamming courtroom doors is little more than a convenient transition into the commercial break. When the show returns, the cameras will go on unacknowledged, just as before. The observational style will continue to provide intimate access to the unfolding comic travails of the Bluths, with all the visual and aural cues viewers of documentary and reality television programs have become accustomed to.

Arrested Development is one of a growing number of television comedies that look different and are made differently from comedies in the past. This essay seeks to situate this emerging televisual mode of production, looking to the producers of the shows to see how they conceptualize their work and explain the mode of production, as well as mapping out how that work might be read by audiences within the traditions of both television

ii. First published as "Comedy Verité? The Observational Documentary Meets the Televisual Sitcom" by Ethan Thompson from *The Velvet Light Trap* 60, no. 1 (2007): 63–64, 67–72. Copyright © 2007 by the University of Texas Press. All rights reserved.

and documentary forms. In his analysis of a number of recent British sit-coms, *The Office* in particular, Brett Mills has appropriately termed this televisual style "comedy verité." The theoretical contexts of these two forms and the industrial context of contemporary American television, with its need for both product differentiation and standardization of the production process, are both vital to understanding comedy verité as a mode that can be selectively employed within more traditional styles or can even be embraced as a distinct alternative to the standard multicamera and single-camera modes of production. Comedy verité seems capable of reinvigorating the sitcom format because it fits the constraints of the ma-terial economy of television, and as a mode of representation its observa-tional style is peculiarly suited to the tastes of contemporary audiences. Indeed, as Jason Mittell recently argued in this journal, we have witnessed since the 1990s an unprecedented trend toward narrative complexity in television storytelling that blurs distinctions between episodic and serial narratives, that exhibits a heightened degree of self-consciousness, and that demands a higher intensity of viewer engagement "focused both on diegetic pleasures and formal awareness."[16] It is within this context that I believe comedy verité can best be understood not as a subgenre of television comedy but as an emerging mode of production that is being adopted for its efficiency, visual complexity, and semiotic clout.

Perhaps the most important and obvious industrial trend in television over the last couple of decades has been the dwindling of the network audience, as viewers are increasingly split between choices of channels and other media entertainment options. One way this has affected program-ming content is that original narrative programming is now booming on cable, which was once primarily the province of reruns. Cable programs have been willing to take greater risks, particularly with comedy, since they can appeal to a smaller audience and not abide by the same decency guidelines as broadcast television. In response to this, the networks are shifting toward a year-round calendar of original programming. Scripted programs, which are more expensive than non-scripted, have necessarily decreased in number as reality-based television programs pick up the pro-gramming slack.

On the cultural (and not economic) side of this equation, situation comedies have struggled to connect with audiences as they once did. Per-haps as a nostalgic response, combined with an antipathy for the reality programs taking their place, there has been some public lamenting that the sitcom is dying a slow and painful death. An article in the *New York Times* explained: "The trend across all of network television is sharply away from comedy as a staple of entertainment programming, pushed aside by an audience bored by a tired sitcom format, changing industry economics and the rise of reality shows."[17] At the same time, the aesthetic grammar of nonfiction TV is increasingly influencing scripted television. Nowhere is this more evident than in the emergence of sitcoms that have adopted the visual codes—even the mode of production—of the observational documentary. In the early 1960s the television networks turned to producing documentaries as a strategy to counter the bad publicity brought by the quiz show scandals and the "vast wasteland" critique of TV content. As Michael Curtin has shown, documentary programs were partially attempts to redeem the networks for lapses in good taste—both ethical and aesthetic. If the content of documentaries saved the reputations of the networks in the past, today their style breathes new life into the sitcom.

This new mode makes both stylistic and semiotic references to what Bill Nichols has described as the "observational mode" of documentary, including both cinema verité and direct cinema. Echoing the substantial difference between those documentaries, there are significant differences between the approaches of these shows, particularly in preproduction, but they all take advantage of the opportunities for improvisation enabled by embracing the observational documentary look and, with differing degrees, its mode of production. Comedy verité has become common enough, with enough self-described "handheld, improvised comedies" that it is necessary to examine the mode of production to find what is indeed "handheld" and "improvised" and what is, through its televisual style, referencing the observational documentary that audiences have learned to decode as a privileged way of representing the "real."[18]

The two primary programs that will be discussed here are the aforementioned *Arrested Development* and HBO's *Curb Your Enthusiasm*, which predates the FOX show and has outlasted it as well. Both shows developed cult followings and garnered critical raves, though neither is a hit sitcom by traditional standards. Though *Arrested Development* won an Emmy for best comedy series its first season, it couldn't connect with a large enough audience to sustain itself beyond three seasons, each with fewer episodes produced than the season before. *Curb Your Enthusiasm* has chugged along on the demographic profile of its viewers and their willingness to subscribe to HBO.

* * *

As a mode of production adopted temporarily or in totality, comedy verité combines the "don'ts" of observational documentary (manipulation, interactivity, effects) with its claim to capturing reality as it unfolds in order to create a televisual masquerade with, at least in some cases, successful comic effects. The key to these comic effects would seem to be both an undermining of the "real" access of the observational documentary with a shift in viewer engagement of the content. In their wide-ranging theoretical examination of film and television comedy, Steve Neale and Frank Krutnik usefully note Freud's distinction between the set-up joke or gag and the comic event: "For Freud a joke is made (constructed, produced); it exists only in utterance; and its immediate material is language and signs. The comic, by contrast, is witnessed (discovered, observed). It can exist, beyond the realms of formal utterances, in situations encountered in everyday life."[19] This distinction made by Freud long before cinema verité or multicamera sitcoms offers an enticing connection between observational documentary and observational humor. What comedy verité may be doing through its distinctive televisual style is shifting the source of humor in the television comedy from the constructed joke to the observation of a comic event. From the perspective of the television industry, this televisual shift made sense both in terms of product differentiation (make sitcoms that look different) and material economy (the improvised style fits the limited budget and time constraints of the production). From a theoretical standpoint, the shift echoes that made in documentary from the expositional mode of representation, with its all-knowing narrator who makes sense of events, telling the viewer what they mean, to the observational, with its suggestion that the truth will reveal itself if we watch long enough. The observational component of these sitcoms, which includes not just what they look like but also the timing of shots and the sense that at times we observe events in real time, creates a different type of engagement with the narrative. The sitcom is thus reinvigorated by a shift from the tired realm of the staged sitcom, with its three cameras, studio audience, or one-camera, coverage shooting, to an experience of observation or witness.

* * *

Handheld Improvised Comedy vs. Handheld = Improvised Comedy

Having explored the historical and theoretical contexts of comedy verité, I want to now shift to a more industrial perspective by looking at what the key creative individuals involved in producing *Curb Your Enthusiasm* and *Arrested Development* believed is made possible by their unconventional modes of production. This can be useful, I think, in understanding how the deployment of televisual style can from the industrial perspective both be a sound financial decision and have extensive textual ramifications in terms of opening up different spaces for creative expression by changing the typical mode of production. After all, the sitcom standard of the three-camera set-up, filmed live before a studio audience, was formulated by Lucille Ball and Desi Arnaz not just for financial reasons but for reasons of comedic timing and performance too.[20] These two examples are chosen in order to understand how what initially may appear to be a visual strategy of fakery or "mocking" the documentary can more importantly play a role in affecting the sort of narrative complexity Mittell describes.

Larry David's guidelines for making *Curb Your Enthusiasm*, according to coproducer and director Robert Weide, were "all location, all in-sequence and no script."[21] This was the directive the production has followed, but, like *Arrested Development*, *Curb Your Enthusiasm* has made its documentary style literal only once. The pilot was an HBO special titled *Larry David: Curb Your Enthusiasm*, a mock documentary following Larry as he starts doing stand-up after leaving his job writing and producing *Seinfeld*, which he also helped create. The pilot ends with Larry chickening out on the big concert, but *Curb Your Enthusiasm* returned as a comedy series produced with the same visual style but without the conceit of a documentary team recording it and without the "talking head" interviews of the pilot.

Prior to *Curb Your Enthusiasm*, Weide was best known as the director of a number of documentaries about comedians, including Lenny Bruce and Mort Sahl. This training in documentary no doubt influenced the approach to the visual style of the *Curb* plot, besides being appropriate for its subject matter: "Larry wanted me to do it because of my documentary background, figuring I'd know how to apply the rules of documentary filmmaking to this odd hybrid. I was very excited by the idea of purposely blurring the line between the real and the fabricated, so that viewers would actually be trying to figure out what was real and what wasn't."[22] Though Weide's documentaries were more the talking head than direct cinema variety, the improvised program that David wanted demanded a different approach to the production. "I basically shot the special as if it were an actual cinema verité documentary," says the director.[23] The series dropped the documentary conceit but stuck with the style, strictly at first, then gradually loosening up a bit to get the necessary coverage and for the simple fact that a "real" documentary crew would never go to some of the places *Curb Your Enthusiasm* needed to go. Rather than having scripts for an episode, the cast works from an outline of what has to happen in each particular scene and improvises dialogue. While the scene is improvised, two high-definition video cameras shoot the action simultaneously, with one always on David because so much of the comedy depends on his reactions. There is no rehearsal of scenes, just one quick blocking, then the first take is a general master shot. The scenes will be re-improvised several times as the director and actors sharpen the scene and get plenty of coverage to ensure it can be cut together: "We shoot scenes as many times as we have to, then continue to hone it in the editing room." Generally, each episode, he says, takes five to seven days to shoot, then three weeks to edit.[24] *Curb Your Enthusiasm* thus spends far more time in the postproduction phase than traditional sitcom modes of production, especially the multi-camera mode with its reliance on "switching" between cameras while the scenes are performed chronologically before a live audience. The program also requires more postproduction work than the traditional single-camera mode, with its standardized approach to coverage and scripted lines. The improvised scenes mean both dialogue and blocking can vary greatly between takes.

The mode of production integrates documentary and fiction methods, echoing shifts between the real and unreal in the show's content, as some actors (such as David, Richard Lewis, and real-life husband and wife Ted Danson and Mary Steenburgen) "play themselves" and other actors play characters (Cheryl Hines plays Larry's wife, Cheryl David—though his real-life wife is named Laurie; Larry's friend and agent, Jeff Greene, is played by Larry's friend—but not agent—Jeff Garlin). The program is shot on-location in "real" offices and homes that aren't "really" Larry's or Jeff's.

David Barker has usefully described the manipulations of television space as a key way in which meaning is encoded during television production. He distinguishes between two types of TV space: (1) camera space, which is the horizontal field of view (wide shot, medium, medium two-shot, close-up) and camera proximity (where the camera is placed in relation to the performers); and (2) performer space, which refers to performer blocking along axes defined in relation to the camera. Barker's categories of camera space and performer space help to analyze television production techniques by connecting them to the semiotic strategies that hold the narrative together or prompt audience reaction to the characters and story. In his comparison of the single-camera mode of production with the multicamera mode, Barker shows how these different types of space can be manipulated to structure meaning. Despite its much-vaunted relevant content, *All in the Family*, for example, is a standard multicamera sitcom, with Archie as the axial character around whom the other characters' lives revolve and upon whose reactions much of the comedy depends. Accordingly, Archie's chair sits center stage, and most of the performer blocking is across the stage, on the x-axis. The space of the stage living room is carefully demarcated, with each performer having a space that others may or may not move in to, Archie's chair being the most "off limits." As Barker points out, the cameras could move into the spaces only to make the audience uncomfortable. Barker mentions that it is absolutely necessary that the viewer is never allowed to share Archie's point of view; rather, the audience must always be looking at him. He is the object of derision, and being allowed to share his point of view—by the camera entering the performer's space and engaging in a shot-reverse-shot pattern—would undermine this.[25]

While the action may have revolved around Archie's throne in that multicamera sitcom, Larry is constantly on the prowl on LA's West Side. Archie was something of a fish out of water, a relic from another time who couldn't accept the social changes on the outside that had found their way into his home to confront him. If Archie is a social dinosaur because he is out of touch, Larry has the social clumsiness of the dinosaur. He is a cultural misfit, well-meaning, perhaps, but given to social missteps of an unending variety. Like Archie, much of the humor in *Curb* derives from Larry's reaction to his own predicament. In *All in the Family*'s multicamera mode of production, this is encoded through the well-timed close-ups on Archie's face, the cameras hitting their well-rehearsed marks like the punch line of a joke, carefully timed and switched on-the-fly during the performance. In *Curb*, that reaction is sure to have been caught on tape but will have to be mined in some assembly of rough continuity.

According to Weide, the scenes in *Curb* are restaged until all the necessary coverage is obtained and the dialogue and comedy refined and repeated during the process as well. From reading this description and by looking at the resulting scenes, it is clear that the "handheld, improvised" (observational) approach to the show is another type of coverage filmmaking. The cameras may be handheld and the content improvised, but the editing of the shots follows classical Hollywood patterns. For example, a scene that takes place at a dinner party at Jeff Greene's house begins with an establishing exterior shot of the house. Inside, a medium close-up shows Larry listening to a Russian couple; it then cuts to an over-the-shoulder two-shot of the Russians as the husband speaks and the wife translates. The next shot is an over-the-shoulder of Jeff talking to Marty Funkhauser, which is a violation of camera continuity, but, because

Larry is at the same moment talking about Marty, continuity is maintained through the dialogue, and the visual jump-cut is consistent with the verité style. Most of the scene continues the shot-reverse-shot pattern common in single-camera production. These sequences are first between Larry and the Russians, then between Larry and Jeff. Though the humor of the situation is recognizable visually, it is dependent upon sound for continuity, with connections made between events through audio cues or sound bridges. These include Larry's mentioning of Marty's name, Jeff's wife calling him away from Larry, and the scream of Jeff's daughter when she discovers a photograph of Larry's decayed tooth. A greater emphasis on dialogue continuity is more necessary than in the single-camera format, where the set-ups are carefully planned, or in the multicamera set-up, when the on-screen relations are always clear and the entire stage may easily be put in view.

While comedy verité shows share key characteristics, there can still be substantial differences (again, as in Winston's "verité" docs) in their stages of production. *Arrested Development* is fundamentally a different version of comedy verité because it is carefully scripted. The "improvisational" component is affected, thus making it an example for the verité mode of production as deliberate stylistic choice, rather than one necessitated by the lack of standard preproduction scripting. However, it is still particularly suited to the program's content. While *Curb*'s verité style is necessary to catch improvised material, *Arrested Development*'s approach allows a very dense program that doesn't have to pause to hold for studio audience laughs to pass and can "get in more" comic and narrative content, according to writer/producer Mitchell Hurwitz.[26]

Appropriately, the idea for *Arrested Development* grew first out of a question of form: Ron Howard had the idea of a sitcom that looked like a reality program. "The intent by Ron, who spent half his life in multiple-camera comedy and half his life as a single-camera director, was to marry the best of both worlds," David Nevins, president of Imagine Television, said when the deal to make the show was first announced.[27] Nevins queried Hurwitz about the possibility of a new approach to making the family sitcom: "His question was, 'What if we shot a show in digital video, so we could go very fast and didn't have to spend an hour and a half lighting for each shot, we could just go out there and start shooting, like *Cops* or *Blind Date*? Could we spend that time sharpening the jokes and making a more ambitious production? What would happen if we applied the sensibility of multi-camera to single-camera?'"[28]

The preproduction process in the multicamera sitcom, where camera positions and lighting schemes are standardized, focuses on the tightening of the dialogue and comic delivery, with repeated chances to test these out. The use of handheld, high-definition video cameras would free up more time for such tightening. Additionally, Hurwitz describes how, in striking comparison to *Curb Your Enthusiasm*'s brief outlines, the scripts for *Arrested Development* might start at sixty pages and be whittled down to thirty-two. Careful attention to the writing process on this program was expected to help tighten comic timing as well as free up some time for limited improvisation:

> Something about not waiting for the laugh of a laugh track allows you to take lines that otherwise might be seen as just direct jokes, and make them seem realistic. . . . We throw a lot of the jokes away. So it feels improvised, but we really do write these out. We write in the overlaps often. We write in the stutters sometimes, if that's important to a scene. Then, that said, a lot of the people on our cast—Will Arnett, David Cross, and Jason Bateman are really good at adding to the dialogue, and spinning things, and coming up with pieces here and there. But it's a very tightly scripted show, because we're trying to accomplish so much in such a short amount of time.[29]

Hurwitz's comments here about "direct jokes" made "realistic" echoes Freud's distinction between the set-up joke and the comic. Though carefully scripted, the comedy verité mode of *Arrested Development* makes the humor seem observational or comic. The "so much" material Hurwitz referred to may have doomed *Arrested Development* for broadcast life, though the show's density is ideal for rewatching. While the program was still in production Hurwitz fatalistically explained: "We're really making a show for the new technology here. We're making a show for TiVo, and we're making a show for DVD, and it really becomes part of our objective in making this thing."[30] Whereas television has always been considered more dispensable than films, and sitcoms especially, again, new technologies may be bringing about changes in TV form—this time because of use by the audience. These changes might not have caught up to the broadcast programmers, who are still looking primarily at Nielsen numbers at first broadcast rather than the repeated viewings of devoted fans willing to buy DVDs.

The density to which Hurwitz refers includes jokes that might be missed the first time around. However, the program was also one of the most televisually dense during its tenure on the air, and though it primarily featured the look of the observational documentary, this was accentuated by still photos and flashbacks (and even 3D!) that signified the program was putting the viewer in a position to witness not just everything that happened to the family but what might have happened to them many years prior or in front of some other camera altogether. In the first episode of the second season, for example, George Bluth's brother, Oscar, is repeatedly mistaken for George and attacked by police. When Howard's narrator tells the audience that George has escaped prison, he is quickly shown in a distorted still photo that is matted in the shape of a circle, with text that tells us we are seeing footage from an ATM machine. Just after this, another green still photo again shows George and is credited as a Newport Beach traffic light photo. Later, video footage from a "security camera" shows Oscar attacked by police in an elevator. These visual documents are lent legitimacy because they look different—they're distorted and discolored—and because they are taken not by "fly-on-the-wall" cameramen pretending not to be there but by unmanned surveillance cameras.

If from the perspective of its producers *Curb Your Enthusiasm* is an improvisational comedy necessarily captured through handheld cameras, from the perspective of the audience the mode is a strategy of "claiming the real," marked by its documentary style as well as its radical deviation from standard sitcom form. Though *Arrested Development*'s televisual style violates the "hands-off" standards of the observational documentary, these excessive, even reflexive, gestures are consistent with the masquerading televisual style. Though *Curb Your Enthusiasm*, *Arrested Development*, and *Jamie Kennedy's Blowin' Up* do not include the "making a documentary" conceit, like Christopher Guest's movies or the BBC and NBC versions of *The Office*, they all identifiably borrow the style of observational documentary. This borrowing of documentary style is about finding not just a mode of production but a method of reading as well. Whether audiences associate the look with Maysle's documentaries or *Survivor*, the connotation is understood to be the same: this is "real"—at least relative to other television.

In his essay "Toward a Poetics of Documentary," Michael Renov notes that common among all the tendencies of documentary filmmaking is the indexical relationship between the documentary and its "real" content: "The documentary 'truth claim' (which says, at the very least: 'Believe me, I'm of the world') is the baseline of persuasion for all of nonfiction, from propaganda to rock doc."[31] Will the truth claim become the new baseline for persuading viewers to laugh now that the laugh track and the studio audience signify the worn-out style of the past? More likely, comedy verité will exist as an alternative, a distinctive visual style or production strategy dependent upon the traditions of the "high" cinema verité documentary as well as the economics of "low" reality TV. That claim is rewritten in the sitcom to suggest that you are not watching comedy but are observing the comic as it unfolds before the handheld cameras. Whether the comic is improvised or carefully scripted, it *looks* like it just happened. As a mode of production, comedy verité can effectively create opportunities for producing laughter that hadn't been there before. These might range from *Curb*'s improvisation to the densely packed, carefully scripted dialogue of *Arrested Development*. The viewer is situated as a witness of the real/comic through this alternative mode of making or seeing television comedy. As a method of producing televisual masquerade, comedy verité connects the dots between the audience member's "ways of seeing" to his or her humor.

C. "Inventing the Situation Comedy: Jack Benny, the 'Fall Guy,' and the Making of a Genre," Kathryn Fuller-Seeley

The situation comedy is one of broadcasting's most stable genres. Originating in the 1930s, it arose from the radio industry's need to fill a weekly half hour with cheerful banter to wrap around the sponsor's advertising commercials (which were the program's real content). Throughout its history, critics have regularly heaped scorn upon sitcoms, in which cardboard characters, limp jokes, and stale plots have predominated. However, when producers, writers and performers have dared to experiment with the flexibility underlying the sitcom's structure, the results have been fascinating and hilarious. One of the first to develop the half-hour workplace situation comedy format, radio comic Jack Benny and his production group experimented with ways of developing characters and narratives, incorporating commercial messages, and dealing with the interference of sponsors. Benny's innovations propelled his program to the top of the radio and then TV ratings for three decades. Now, eighty years later, innovative program creators have been taking lessons from the past to resuscitate the sitcom, incorporating into it narrative twists, unusual characters, and production methods drawn from documentary, reality TV, and animation. They are also responding to the changing industrial environment of fragmented audiences, declining ad revenue, new distribution forms, and changing relationships with sponsors using some of the tactics Benny pioneered.[32]

This historical case study, examining Jack Benny's origination of a prototype of the sitcom on radio, demonstrates that the sitcom's roots (and its pleasures) lay both in innovation as well as in response to industrial pressures. Facing the daunting challenge of filling radio's unprecedented, ferocious demand for fresh content, Benny initially struggled. Working with scriptwriter Harry Conn, Benny ultimately turned his problems into strengths and thrived in the new medium, moving from relying on short vaudeville monologues and the recycling of old jokes (what other radio comics did) to crafting an ensemble-based radio comedy program. Studying Benny's development of characters and situations, especially his own hapless "fall guy" character and his efforts to manage industrial challenges, can help us better understand how contemporary iterations of workplace sitcoms (*Larry Sanders, The Office, Parks and Rec, Big Bang Theory*) and domestic family sitcoms (*The Simpsons, Modern Family*) inject new life into old forms and create innovative comedy today.[33]

The Canada Dry Radio Program: A New Mixture of Music and Comedy in 1932

NBC Radio's primetime broadcasting schedule in spring 1932 was dominated by musical programs featuring dance bands and singers. The show sponsors (who footed the entire bill for productions and produced them with the assistance of their advertising agencies) were frustrated by the limitations of this popular genre. Orchestras were expensive to hire, temperamental singers threw tantrums, and it was difficult for any single show to stand out in the crowded field. NBC executives suggested that potential sponsor Canada Dry Ginger Ale try a twist. The network proposed a half-hour program of popular tunes performed by well-known New York bandleader George Olsen's orchestra and his Ziegfeld Follies–alumna wife, vocalist Ethel Shutta. For the novelty, a comedian would serve as the show's "master of ceremonies," cracking a few jokes between song introductions.[34]

The comic that Canada Dry settled on, after a round of auditions, was thirty-eight-year-old, moderately successful vaudeville veteran Jack Benny. Over fifteen years onstage, Benny had crafted a smooth-talking, but wryly self-deprecating, kind of "stand-up" comedy routine. He was a nattily-dressed Midwestern "Broadway Romeo," who held a violin that he rarely played. Vaudevillians had honed their best seventeen minutes of material into an act that they could reuse for years, performing in different theaters every week. While some comics wrote their own jokes, Benny purchased his routines from gag writers and polished them to fit his own style. The pull of a growing entertainment medium, coupled with the push of the steep decline of vaudeville during the Great Depression, propelled the apprehensive Benny to try his hand in radio.[35]

On the first episode of the new *Canada Dry Program*, broadcast live on Monday, May 2, 1932, Jack Benny performed seven brief segments, joking about personal experiences, his Hollywood misadventures, and the meagerness of his girlfriend (material plucked from his old stage routines). He put an unusual spin on the boring commercials by performing the middle ads himself, turning them into nonsensical send-ups of Canada Dry's product.

> Ladies and gentlemen, this is Jack Benny talking, and making my first appearance on the air professionally. By that I mean, I am finally getting paid, which will be a great relief to my creditors. I really don't know why I am here. I'm supposed to be a sort of master of ceremonies and tell you all about the things that will happen, which would happen anyway. I must *introduce* the different artists, who could easily introduce themselves, and also talk about Canada Dry made to order by the glass, which is a waste of time, as you know all about it. You drink it, like it, and don't want to hear about it. So ladies and gentlemen, a master of ceremonies is really a fellow who is unemployed and gets paid for it.

After the past five decades in which the characters of TV network sitcoms functioned in hermetically sealed fictional worlds that gave no acknowledgement to the commercials that surrounded and interrupted their narratives, more recently, sitcom creators have revisited aspects of Benny's earlier relationship with sponsors' products. The cast of *Glee* made commercials for Chevrolet while appearing in character (certainly a big break for a high school singing group). In its later seasons, *Community* incorporated sponsors like Subway into the narrative. *30 Rock* constantly interweaved the reality of NBC network promotions with the fiction of the production of Liz Lemon's show. Sponsors' attempts to connect to devoted fans among shrinking mass audiences, and to overcome the tools technology gives those audiences to block out the ads, has led them to retrace their steps and embrace the innovative connections Benny made between humor, characters, and commercial culture.

Back in 1932, Benny leapt into the total intermingling of advertising pitch with the fictional narrative world of his master of ceremonies duties. But otherwise, he was quickly at a loss for what else to do on the air. In the first program, Benny exchanged a little nervous banter with orchestra leader Olsen and singer Shutta, who offered awkward, brief responses to Benny's "cheap" vaudeville jokes. By the end of the episode, Benny realized he was heading toward disaster.[36] "I didn't have any idea how important it was to have good material, and how hard it was to get," he later recalled. "The first show was a cinch—I used about half of all the gags I knew. The second show consumed all the rest, and I faced the third absolutely dry."[37] Not only Benny, but also the sponsor, the ad agency, and even NBC seemed almost shockingly naïve about how much labor Benny's performances were going to entail to constantly devise fresh material. In the second and third episodes, Benny provided brief descriptions of his fellow radio performers that again drew on standard vaudeville insult-humor—Olsen was penurious, Shutta lied about her age, the boys in the band were drunkards, and announcer Ed Thorgerson resembled a Hollywood playboy with slicked back hair and a thin mustache. (It "looked like he'd swallowed all of Mickey Mouse but the tail," Benny quipped.)[38] The others spoke little. Benny appealed to his unseen listeners directly, asking if there was anybody out there, and repeatedly reintroduced himself: "Hello somebody. This is Jack Benny talking. There will be a slight pause while you say 'what of it?'"[39] Desperate for help, Benny secured the services of gag writer Harry Conn, a former vaudeville tap dancer.[40] Conn would do the heavy lifting of writing, Benny would edit, polish and perform the material, and Benny would pay Conn's salary out of his own pocket.[41]

With Conn to write fresh jokes, *The Canada Dry Program* scripts started to become more adventurous. George Olsen now was given more straight lines as he and Benny engaged in humorous conversation. Everyone in the studio, from orchestra members, to Conn, to Benny's personal assistant Harry Baldwin, was pulled to the mike to voice fictional guests in brief one-time appearances. Benny and Conn then began experimenting to create a richer fictional world for the program, presenting sketch routines that briefly moved away from the microphone. On May 23, 1932, they finessed the problem of segueing from being live around the mike by endowing announcer Ed Thorgerson with a magical ability to tune an on-air radio to overhear cast members at a soda fountain located in the building's lobby. The show staff created sound effects of glasses clinking and ginger ale fizzing. Jack and Ethel Shutta bantered with a soda jerk (portrayed by orchestra member Fran Frey). The scene may have only lasted two minutes, but when Benny "returned" to the studio after the next song, he assumed that he had to explain to the audience what they had done: "Well folks, this is Jack Benny back at the studio. Well, to tell you the truth, we never even left here. Olsen's bass drum was the counter. And the fizz you heard was one of the boys sneezing." This significant shift for Benny and Conn away from verisimilitude toward fictional fantasy enabled them to expand the narrative spaces in which characters could interact.

Benny's early efforts at experimentation find parallels in recent sit-coms, such as when the producers of *The Office* and *Modern Family* burst out of the confines of the multi-camera mode of production and used single camera shooting in handheld-camera documentary style, with interviews of characters to complicate the story. *The Simpsons, Family Guy* and *South Park* added absurdity and the imaginative spaces of animated worlds. Innovative creators can use filming and narrative techniques to take the action and our interactions with characters outside the "present-ness" of productions centered around a microphone or a single, confining living room and into new worlds.

Experimenting with Characters, Situations, and Plot

As the Canada Dry episodes continued in summer 1932, Benny and Conn tried out a revolving mixture of comic monologues, pun-tossing repar-tee, fictional adventures, and comic sketches. (Some experiments, such as satirizing political candidates, ended after a few attempts, perhaps at the behest of the sponsor.) As dialogue exchanges expanded, the previ-ously dominant musical performances decreased. The show evolved into a comedy program interspersed with music. Benny and Conn started build-ing character relationships and conflicts. Framing the group as workers putting on a radio show, Benny and Conn began to sketch out a "person-ality" for each member of the cast that blended reality and fiction. The cast became a stable of recognizable, quirky-yet-likeable characters that could bounce off each other in informal exchanges in the studio or inter-act in "situations" from visiting the zoo to having dinner at cast members' homes. Like contemporary sitcoms that have incorporated elements of reality TV into the narrative (such as *The Larry Sanders Show, Arrested Development*, or *Louie*), in 1932 Benny's Canada Dry show began breaking the fourth wall between performers and viewers, with self-reflexive meta-comedy. Blending real events with fiction, the characters (who used their real names) might comment on the script as they performed it, and they continually blurred their real-life activities with the imaginary narratives.

At this point, Benny and Conn also determined that adding a new con-tinuing character and even a love interest might be useful directions for the program narrative. On the show, Benny looked for an assistant to handle his fan mail. This search continued over the next month's episodes, as Benny acquired first an inefficient male secretary, then an incompetent female secretary named Garbo.⁴² A teenaged fan of the program from the small town of Plainfield, New Jersey, named Mary Livingstone, wandered on to the program on July 27. She was played by Sadye Marks Benny, Jack's real-life spouse, a talented non-professional whom he'd incorporated occasionally into stage routines and film shorts in similar supporting roles as a flirtatious and flip, but none-too-bright young female companion. Radio listener reaction was favorable, and several episodes later, Mary assumed the permanent role of Jack's lackadaisical part-time secretary. Sadye even changed her real name to Mary Livingstone Benny.

Along with adding a new character to the program came questions of narrative development. How much continuing plot did Benny and Conn want to have on their show, among the sketches and monologues crammed into the interstitial spots sandwiched between the musical numbers? They toyed with the idea of developing a romantic comedy subplot. Episodes in September and October 1932 played out Jack and Mary's flirtations and comic misunderstandings and climaxed with a scene of them espousing their love for one another. Benny and Conn had written themselves into a corner. Would the show now be dominated by a love story? Where would the comic conflicts arise? They quickly did an about-face with the scripts and decided to move in an ironically unsentimental direction, backing away from romantic tensions. Mary returned to flirting with the orchestra members and announcer, performing ineptly as a secretary, ribbing Jack's foibles, and making silly comments that pegged her as a "dumb Dora" character (a convention carried through to more recent sitcom ditzes like *Friends'* Phoebe Buffay).

Other sitcoms in the years since have successfully merged drama and humor, such as *M*A*S*H*, and others have played with romantic tensions between major characters (like *Cheers* or *Friends*) but other shows faltered when those relationships were consummated (like *Moonlighting*). The writers of *Big Bang Theory* responded to critics' complaints about the one-dimensional nature of the sitcom's female characters by developing Penny from a dull bimbo into a smarter, wittier member of the cohort, and by slowly creating the romantic relationship between Sheldon and Amy.⁴³ While Benny and Conn backed away from the coupling of Jack and Mary, their decision to have her remain on the program as Jack's sometimes-secretary who became the sharpest critic of his every failing added layers of ironic humor to the narrative. It also rewarded his listeners for a paratextual understanding of both the fiction of the show and the reality behind it. Listeners knew that Jack and Mary were a celebrity married couple off stage but enjoyed the shock of hearing Mary's sharp put-downs of Jack on the air, which mocked traditional gender relationships.[44]

Commercial Constraints Drive Innovation in the Sitcom

Just when Benny and Conn thought they had achieved a successful mixture of comedy and music, as critics praised the growing complexity of characters and humorous situations, in November, 1932, Canada Dry unanticipatedly declared its displeasure with many aspects of the program. The sponsor changed networks to CBS to gain a larger and more advantageous network of participating stations. But this meant losing Olsen, Shutta, and the announcer, who were contractually obligated to work only for NBC. The sponsor also declared that the Benny program's comic elements were lackluster, and it hired an additional writer/performer, Sid Silvers. Benny and Conn suddenly had to start over from scratch—teaching a new bandleader, singer, and announcer how to become comedians and fighting off the intrusions of Silvers, who sought to turn the show into the completely fictional, continuing story of a befuddled Broadway producer and his smart-aleck assistant (Silvers). Silvers reduced Mary's part to practically nothing. These moves caused Benny, Conn, and Livingstone to threaten to quit if Silvers was not removed and they did not regain full control of the program's production. While Canada Dry relented and let Silvers go, the sponsor summarily cancelled the popular show in January 1933.

Fortunately for Benny, automobile manufacturer Chevrolet picked up sponsorship of the show, and they now billed the program as a comedy show that contained music. However, the change meant that Benny and Conn had to quickly train yet another cast to become adept readers of comic dialogue. Mary assumed a much more prominent role on the program, now as Jack's companion, the only female character on the show, and the program's main "stooge" or comic assistant. Conn expanded Mary's role by having her read letters from her Mama back on the farm in Plainfield and recite dreadful self-composed poems. A talented if untrained vocalist, Mary also occasionally performed songs with the orchestra. She flirted with band members and the announcer and heckled Benny more than ever before. Critics continued to praise Benny's humor, one writing that "Jack has the knack of making everyone on his program real and human, instead of just a lot of radio voices."[45]

Benny's radio challenges were far from over, however, as in the next year Chevrolet dropped him because the firm's new CEO preferred orchestral music. The show bounced among other Great Depression-battered sponsors that could barely afford it. The program careened to a variety of slots in the weekly broadcasting schedule, and it took dedicated fans to find the program to tune in. To further complicate matters, when Benny periodically relocated from New York City to Hollywood to shoot a film role, his cast members with ties to the East Coast could not join him. The rapidly revolving door of bandleaders, singers, and announcers wreaked havoc on the show creators' attempts to maintain a roster of interesting supporting characters. Up to this point, the sponsors and their ad agencies had selected all the performers. Benny became determined to take on the responsibilities of program producer (or what we today would call a "showrunner") to control the personnel upheavals by making more of his own cast selections, hiring the performers himself, and presenting his program as a complete package for the sponsor to fund. Benny's first hiring of a permanent cast member was new announcer Don Wilson, the tenth announcer Benny had to break in during the program's two years on the air, who joined the program in April, 1934. Conn made Wilson an intelligent (and originally pugnacious) opponent of Jack's posturing. Wilson's character became jollier as jokes about his girth abounded, and he had a warm, friendly Midwestern voice that soon made him one of the top salesmen in radio. The tensions Benny negotiated in these years between what the sponsors demanded and how he wanted to develop his program shows us that studying examples of the sitcom genre form can highlight the struggles between aesthetics and commercialism.

The recent program *Community* similarly struggled to survive in a rapidly changing broadcast television landscape. It initially labored to stand apart narratively from standard network fare in an era of declining audiences and budget cuts. It evolved into an innovative space for producer Dan Harmon to experiment—like Benny—with genre parodies, edgy characters, and self-referential humor. *Community* drew a small but devoted audience and struggled each year to avoid network interference and cancellation. It faced Harmon's firing and narrative missteps, Harmon's return, fervent appeals from fans and star Joel McHale to save the program, and finally cancellation and a new home in the experimental program-funding environment of online streaming through Yahoo.[46]

Benny's Character Becomes "The Fall Guy"

By Spring 1934 Benny and Conn rejiggered their program's humor again. In order to further differentiate it from that of other radio comics who smugly insulted their dim-witted straight men and grabbed all the big laughs for themselves, Benny and Conn experimented with the show's core character. Evolving from his role as the self-deprecating but polished master of ceremonies, Jack became increasingly fallible—vain, cheap, boastful, cowardly. Benny's character became "the Fall Guy," the unlucky fellow to whom humiliating things always seemed to happen, the butt of the joke, and the loser who always got blamed when things went wrong.[47] On the May 11, 1934 episode, to make a peace offering after they'd had an argument at the show's opening, Don Wilson invited Jack to visit his mother's home in the Bronx for the weekend. Jack suffered numerous misadventures on their journey, getting robbed three times and gladly handed over his money in each instance. The thief even awarded Benny a card identifying him as a frequent customer. When the pair finally arrived at the Wilson home, there was no food and no spare bed for the hapless "fall guy" Benny.

Benny's character began to develop more personality quirks and flaws (cheapness, boastfulness, his poor violin-playing skills, vanity, his paucity of hair and lack of masculinity). The list steadily grew longer as the Jack character lost most of that assured "Broadway Romeo" suavity he'd demonstrated during his vaudeville career, and was now depicted as inept at interacting with the opposite sex. His patriarchal authority as star of the show was more frequently challenged by his mocking radio employees. While standard joke-book-style insults about cheapness and stupidity were still bandied about by the entire cast, the jabs were refurbished so that charges were now often made by others, egged on by Mary, and aimed at Benny.[48]

Jack Benny finally achieved massive success and stability for his comedy program in early 1935. Sales of his latest sponsor's product (Jell-O) skyrocketed, propelled by the inviting, warm commercials Wilson broadcast for the dessert product, and the delightful punning references to the product that Benny and Conn sprinkled throughout the program. Newspaper columnist O. O. McIntyre lauded the show: "Benny's humor has the dry crackle of sun-burned twigs. Never explosive, he bungles along, firing the arrows of contempt at himself. He brought to the business of being a comic a combined restraint, a suavity that was something entirely different, and it clicked."[49]

LAUGH WITH JACK BENNY
EVERY SUNDAY NIGHT!

Turn your radio to Station WBZ
Sunday at 7 P. M.

DID you know that Jack Benny was voted the best comedian on the air in the 1934 poll of radio critics all over the country?

He puts on a radio show so breezy and spontaneous that it brings ripple after ripple of delighted laughter!

Tune in this Sunday. Hear Jack Benny, Mary Livingstone, Frank Parker, Don Wilson, Don Bestor and his orchestra . . . in a sparkling half hour of music and comedy.

Sponsored by JELL-O

An advertisement for Jack Benny's 1935 radio program on NBC highlights both his new sponsor, Jell-O, and his cast of supporting players.

The Benny-Conn partnership fractured in Spring 1936, however, when a resentful Conn claimed that the show's success was entirely due to his writing, and he suddenly quit one week to create his own programs (pale imitations of Benny's program which lacked the sparkling wit of the superbly acted original). Benny quickly rallied assistance from his show-business friends, and after a few shaky weeks, emerged with a new duo of young scripters (Bill Morrow and Ed Beloin). Building on the strong foundation that Conn had laid, Morrow, Beloin, and other writers worked with Benny over the subsequent years to continually add fresh ideas and inventive embellishments to the program. Every year they made Jack's foolish behavior a bit more absurd, and they continued to experiment with additional characters, benefitting from long-term narrative developments such as the feud with rival radio comic Fred Allen, the many embarrassing predicaments Jack placed his next-door neighbors Ronald and Benita Colman in, or the comic characters and sounds voiced by Mel Blanc. Even as Benny continued broadcasting his half-hour program for nearly thirty more years on radio and television, he never allowed his show to become exclusively framed as a situation comedy. Benny always claimed that he preferred to continually mix program formats, incorporating workplace situational comedy one week, parodies of popular films another, with guest stars who appeared as real celebrities to humiliate Jack, performances by singers or musicians, domestic humor at Benny's home, or intimate banter around the microphone. Benny maintained that he wanted to keep his audience guessing what form the next episode might take.

Contemporary sitcoms that have similarly endured many years, like *The Simpsons* or *South Park*, have also survived by deliberately changing over time, as the shows evolved from focusing on interactions of the family and friends to tackling political and cultural issues with comic absurdity. Homer Simpson's cluelessness reaches new levels each season, while Trey Parker and Matt Stone take advantage of their show's simple animation process to have the smart-mouthed South Park boys deal each episode with issues plucked from the week's headlines.

Conclusion

Jack Benny's bumpy entry into the evolving modes of variety and situation comedy program production in the early 1930s illuminated the ways in which the entertainer's performing identity and the shape of comedy could be impacted by structural factors of an entertainment system. Commercially sponsored network radio added new wrinkles to the construction of its entertainment, from the sponsor's desire to intersperse advertising messages into the show, to the economic efficiency of continually working with the same small group of performers, to interference of the many executives who sought to meddle in Benny's attempt to write, perform, cast, and manage his own program. The radio system also demanded seriality and live performance as opposed to stand-alone products like a feature-length motion picture. Radio configured its audience into one mass group of listeners who expected to hear new material in every iteration of a program. This system demanded constant variety of content, along with the identifiable similarity of material being produced by recognizable "stars" whose talent could be associated with positive qualities of the consumer product being advertised.

The relentless need for new material for his radio performances affected the ways in which Benny shaped his comedy. He became very dependent on one writer (Harry Conn) to provide the new material each week, which forced Benny to labor that much harder to craft his own comic point of view. Benny and Conn found that incorporating dialogue bits into their show's sketches added more variety to the single performer model. Better yet, molding individual characters for the other performers around the microphone enabled Conn to devise more humor from the quirkiness of those disparate personalities, conflicts and misunderstandings between them, and the humor that arose from putting those characters into comic situations. The development of characters and situations went hand in hand for Benny and Conn as they created the show from week to week in those early months of the radio program.

Benny and Conn's perfecting of the "Fall Guy" character (and the cast's incessant insults of him) was a very important aspect of the show's continued success, but even that character would also have to continue to change to maintain audience interest. Benny and his writers had to keep increasing the cheapness of Jack's stingy ways over the years, making his penury more hyperbolic to shock audiences. Thus Jack could get held up by a robber three times in 1934 and shrug it off, but by the late 1940s a robbery would become scaled up into the mortally serious, and hilariously famous "Your Money or Your Life" skit. As well, Jack's character would also become increasingly vain, from coyly declining to reveal his age, to the eventual determination to remain thirty-nine. With repetition and small incremental increases, Mary, Rochester, Phil, Professor LeBlanc, and other stooges could turn their insults of Jack into comic shorthand, dressing the same complaints in updated costumes over the years.

As historian Michele Hilmes has noted, in the 1930s, radio entertainers like Jack Benny were fortunate to have multiple chances to develop their personas and formats.[50] Later program producers would not have the relative luxury of time that Benny experienced in the three-to-four years during which he was able to evolve his particular comic style. Broadcasting became ever more expensive with the move from radio to television production in the late 1940s. It increasingly became a big business dependent on stricter genre and format structures, pressuring creators to reduce risk by curtailing experimentation. Benny and Conn were able to experiment and make mistakes, and to build a loyal audience of fans. Only now, in the post-network era of media convergence, when technology has allowed production costs to plummet, and the internet is creating new platforms, new spaces, and new niche audiences for programming, there exist again expanded opportunities for generic experimentation.

The generic codes that Jack Benny and Harry Conn experimented with in the early 1930s as they developed their workplace situation comedy/variety program are still being negotiated, just under a different set of commercial pressures. These include the evolution away from multi-camera to single-camera production, the growing prevalence of cutaways in animated sitcoms, and the shifting shapes of sitcom forms enabled by digital distribution. Today, after more than eighty years of sitcom history, contemporary shows have been able to once again break out of stricter molds of what a sitcom "should be," combining traditional comedy forms and characters with alternative forms of visual presentation and storytelling that rely on improvisation and looseness, mixing in stand-up, animation, sketch comedy, and documentary techniques. Comedy producers, writers, and performers are similarly using the opportunities and challenges afforded by new digital media, new distribution platforms, niche audiences, and a new comic culture to enliven the moribund sitcom genre. These new twists, innovative plot devices, and experimental framing and filming strategies combine content from a variety of genres and media forms. In doing so, they channel the creativity and problem-solving skills of Benny and his crew in order to breathe new life into an old form.

Notes

1. Drummond, "Structural and Narrative Constraints," 69.
2. Eaton, "Television Situation Comedy," 69.
3. Crowther and Pinfold, *Bring Me Laughter*, 120.
4. Kerr, "The Making of MTM," 88.
5. Feuer, "The MTM Style," 37.

6. Eaton, "Television Situation Comedy," 73.

7. As Mick Eaton has put it, "The ideology held by the institution of television as a machine for the production of meaning is that the family is a sufficiently stable situation, settled enough to be able to bear repetition, and to deal with the on-slaughts of the outside in a recognizable, characteristic way," 73.

8. Feuer, "Narrative Form," 109–110.

9. Feuer, "Narrative Form," 109–110.

10. Feuer "The MTM Style," 44–45.

11. Wheen, *Television*, 208.

12. Swanson, "Law and Disorder," 34.

13. Freud, *Jokes and their Relation*, 141–143.

14. Freud, *Jokes and their Relation*, 143.

15. Curtis, "Aspects of Sitcom," 11.

16. Mittell, "Narrative Complexity in Contemporary American Television," 38.

17. Carter, "Reality Shows, Costs and Innovative Comedy Threaten a TV Staple."

18. See Corner, "Performing the Real: Documentary Diversions" for a com-pelling discussion of what he calls "post-documentary television."

19. Neale and Krutnik, *Popular Film and Television Comedy*, 72.

20. Butler, *Television: Critical Methods and Applications*, 197.

21. Sweetzer, "No Writers, No Script, No Rehearsal."

22. Sweetzer, "No Writers, No Script, No Rehearsal."

23. Weide, "Stranger than Fiction."

24. Weide, "'Curb Your Enthusiasm' Producer."

25. Barker, "Television Production Techniques as Communication."

26. Hurwitz, "Mitch Hurwitz, Creator of 'Arrested Development.'"

27. Schneider, "New 'Development.'"

28. Hurwitz, "Interview: Focus on Television: Mitchell Hurwitz."

29. Hurwitz, "Interview: Focus on Television: Mitchell Hurwitz."

30. Hurwitz, "Mitch Hurwitz, Creator of 'Arrested Development.'"

31. Renov, *Theorizing Documentary*, 30.

32. Thompson, "Comedy Verité?"

33. Benny and Conn did not invent the "situation comedy," as of course they drew on well-known and long-standing models of situational, domestic, serialized humor in literary storytelling, comic strips, and other areas of media and popu-lar culture. My primary interest here is to chart how one particular entertainer's approach to comedy changed over time and adapted to alternative comic forms.

34. The new Canada Dry show joined a rapidly increasing number of music-and-comedy programs on primetime network radio and other vaudevillians, such as George Burns and Gracie Allen, George Jessel, Fred Allen, and Jack Pearl. The new performers and shows joined such already-popular variety programs as Rudy Vallee on *The Fleischmann Hour*, Ed Wynn for Texaco, and Eddie Cantor for Chase and Sanborn.

35. See Fuller-Seeley, "Dish Night at the Movies."

36. "Radio's Script Act Cycle," 55; Bodec, "Radio's Top Names," 59; Bodec, "Radio in '32," 58. On radio in the early 1930s, see Hilmes, *Radio Voices*; Douglas, *Listening In*.

37. Beatty, "Unhappy Fiddler," 28–29, 142–144.

38. "Were You Listening Last Night," *Pittsburgh Press*, May 10, 1932, 11.

39. *Canada Dry Program*, May 11, 1932, script in Jack Benny Collection, UCLA.

40. "Gag Writing: It's Big Business Now," *Literary Digest*, December 12, 1936, 24, 26.

41. "Air Gag Writers," *San Bernardino Sun*, May 28, 1933, 20–21. To Conn's chagrin, the radio network would not allow writers to get on-air credit, so Benny alone became the focus of public and critical acclaim, even as Benny paid Conn one of the highest salaries earned by radio writers.

42. *Canada Dry Program*, May 23, 1932.

43. Holmes, "How a thorough De-Gazing Saved 'Big Bang Theory'"; Holmes, "Baby Steps: Love and 'The Big Bang Theory.'"

44. Gray, *Show Sold Separately*.

45. "Jack Benny is Back," *Ottawa Citizen*, March 11, 1933, 7.

46. Weinman, "Back by Popular Revolt."

47. Beatty, "Unhappy Fiddler," 143.

48. *Chevrolet Program*, March 18, 1934.

49. McIntyre, "New York Day by Day."

50. Hilmes, "Where Everybody Knows Your Name," 217.

Works Cited

Barker, David. "Television Production Techniques as Communication." In *Television: The Critical View*, 6th ed., edited by Horace Newcomb, 169–182. New York: Oxford University Press, 2000.

Beatty, Jerome. "Unhappy Fiddler." *American Magazine*, December 1944.

Bodec, Ben. "Radio's Top Names—1932." *Variety*, January 3, 1933.

Bodec, Ben. "Radio in '32." *Variety*, January 3, 1933.

Butler, Jeremy. *Television: Critical Methods and Applications*. 2nd ed. Mahwah, NJ: Lawrence Erlbaum Associates, 2002.

Carter, Bill. "Reality Shows, Costs and Innovative Comedy Threaten a TV Staple." *New York Times*, 24 May 2004. http://www.nytimes.com/2004/05/24/arts/laughter-fading-sitcomland-reality-shows-costs-innovative-comedy-threaten-tv.html?mcubz=3.

Corner, John. "Performing the Real: Documentary Diversions." *Television and New Media* 3 (August 2002): 255–269.

Crowther, Bruce, and Mike Pinfold. *Bring Me Laughter: Four Decades of TV Comedy*. Columbus, OH: Columbus Books, 1987.

Curtis, Barry. "Aspects of Sitcom." In *BFI Dossier 17: Television Sitcom*, edited by Jim Cook, 4–12. London: Film Institute, 1984.

Douglas, Susan J. *Listening In: Radio and the American Imagination*. Minneapolis: University of Minnesota Press, 2004.

Drummond, Philip. "Structural and Narrative Constraints and Strategies in The Sweeney." *Screen Education*, no. 2 (August 1976): 15–33.

Eaton, Mick. "Television Situation Comedy." *Screen* 19, no. 4 (Winter 1978/79): 61–90.

Feuer, Jane. "Narrative Form in American Network Television." In *High Theory/ Low Culture: Analysing Popular Television and Film*, edited by Colin MacCabe, 101–114. Manchester, UK: Manchester University Press, 1986.

———. "The MTM Style." In *MTM, Quality Television*, edited by Jane Feuer, Paul Kerr, and Tise Vahimagi, 32–60. London: British Film Institute, 1984.

Freud, Sigmund. *Jokes and their Relation to the Unconscious*. Harmondsworth: Penguin Modern Classics, 1976.

Fuller-Seeley, Kathryn H. "Dish Night at the Movies: Exhibitors and Female Audiences during the Great Depression." In *The American Film History Reader*, edited by Jon Lewis and Eric Smoodin, 170–188. London: Routledge, 2014.

Gray, Johnathan. *Show Sold Separately: Promos, Spoilers, and Other Media Paratexts*. New York: New York University Press, 2010.

Hilmes, Michele. *Radio Voices: American Broadcasting 1922–1952*. Minneapolis: University of Minnesota Press, 1997.

———. "Where Everybody Knows Your Name: Cheers And The Mediation Of Cultures." In *Critiquing the Sitcom: A Reader*, edited by Joanne Morreale, 213–223. Syracuse: Syracuse University Press, 2003.

Holmes, Linda "How a thorough De-Gazing Saved 'Big Bang Theory.'" *Monkey See*. NPR. January 6, 2010. http://www.npr.org/sections/monkeysee/2010/01 /how_degazing_saved_the_big_ban.html.

———. "Baby Steps: Love and 'The Big Bang Theory.'" *Monkey See*. NPR. Dec 17, 2015. http://www.npr.org/sections/monkeysee/2015/12/17/460143091/baby -steps-love-and-the-big-bang-theory?utm_source=npr_newsletter&utm _medium=email&utm_content=20151218&utm_campaign=npr_email_a_friend &utm_term=storyshare.

Hurwitz, Mitch. "Mitch Hurwitz, Creator of 'Arrested Development.'" By David Bianculli. *Fresh Air*. NPR. November 3, 2005. http://www.npr.org/templates /story/story.php?storyId=4987832.

Hurwitz, Mitchell. "Interview: Focus on Television: Mitchell Hurwitz." By Tasha Robinson. *Onion AV Club*. February, 9 2005. http://www.avclub.com/content /node/24899/1/1.

Kerr. Paul. "The Making of MTM Show." In *MTM, Quality Television*, edited by Jane Feuer, Paul Kerr, and Tise Vahimagi. London: British Film Institute, 1984.

Literary Digest. "Gag Writing: It's Big Business Now." December 12, 1936.

McIntyre, O. O. "New York Day by Day." *Rochester Evening Journal*, September 1934.

Mills, Brett. *Television Sitcom*. London: British Film Institute, 2005.

Mittell, Jason. "Narrative Complexity in Contemporary American Television." *Velvet Light Trap* 58 (Fall 2006): 29–40.

Neale, Steve, and Frank Krutnik. *Popular Film and Television Comedy*. London: Routledge, 1995.

Ottawa Citizen. "Jack Benny is Back." March 11, 1933.

Pittsburgh Press. "Were You Listening Last Night." May 10, 1932.

Renov, Michael. *Theorizing Documentary*. New York: Routledge, 1993.

San Bernardino Sun. "Air Gag Writers." May 28, 1933, 20–21.

Schneider, Michael. "New 'Development.'" *Daily Variety* 26 (September 2002).

Swanson, Gillian. "Law and Disorder." In *BFI Dossier 17: Television Sitcom*, edited by Jim Cook, 32–42. London: Film Institute, 1984.

Sweetzer, Norton. "No Writers, No Script, No Rehearsal: Is This Any Way to Direct a Sitcom?" Whyaduck Productions. http://www.duckprods.com/projects/cye/cye-sweetzerinterview.html.

Thompson, Ethan. "Comedy Verité? The Observational Documentary Meets the Televisual Sitcom." *The Velvet Light Trap* 60, no. 1 (2007): 63–72.

Variety. "Radio's Script Act Cycle." May 10, 1932.

Weide, Bob. "Stranger than Fiction." *DGA Quarterly* (Fall 2005). https://www.dga.org/Craft/DGAQ/All-Articles/0503-Fall-2005/Funny-Business-Bob-Weide.aspx.

Weide, Robert. "'Curb Your Enthusiasm' Producer Robert Weide." By David Bianculli. *Fresh Air.* NPR. March 9, 2005. http://www.npr.org/templates/story/story.php?storyId=1753476.

Weinman, Jaime. "Back By Popular Revolt: Community, Ousted Creator Returns to Save His Show—Or Lose Face Rather Publicly." *Maclean's*, January 2014.

Wheen, Francis. *Television.* London: Century, 1985.

6.

Race & Ethnicity

INT. HIGH SCHOOL SCIENCE CLASSROOM — DAY

MR. GARVEY, a middle-aged black man, agitatedly paces at the front of the classroom.
                              MR. GARVEY
All right listen up, y'all! I'm y'all's substitute teacher, Mr. Garvey. I taught school for twenty years in the inner city. So don't even think about messing with me, y'all feel me? OK, let's take roll here.
Mr. Garvey picks up a clipboard, reads and mispronounces two names from the roster with increasing frustration.
                              MR. GARVEY
Dee-Nice. Is there a Dee-Nice? If one of y'all says some silly ass name, this whole class is gonna feel my wrath. Now, Dee-Nice!
DENISE, a white female student, tentatively raises her hand.
                              DENISE
Do you mean "Denise?"
Mr. Garvey furiously breaks the clipboard over his knee.
                              MR. GARVEY
Son of a bitch! You say the name right, right now.
                              DENISE
Denise?
                              MR. GARVEY
Say it right.
                              DENISE
Denise.
                              MR. GARVEY
Correctly.
                              DENISE
Denise.

MR. GARVEY

Right.

DENISE

Denise.

MR. GARVEY

Right.

DENISE

Dee-Nice.

Mr. Garvey gives a sarcastic, exaggerated bow.

MR. GARVEY

That's better. Thank you.

* * *

In the introductory chapter of this volume, we asked you to consider comedy's dual, seemingly contradictory nature. On the one hand, comedy speaks to all of us by making light of shared human experiences. The carnivalesque finds humor in common bodily functions, the absurd infiltrates into everyone's daily life, and, surely, repression and relief help explain comedy in a wide variety of cultural settings. On the other hand, the introductory chapter also reminded you that not all lives are experienced the same way, and that comedy speaks just as powerfully to individual experiences as it does to a sense of universal humanity. In other words, for as much as we'd like to champion comedy's universalizing power, so too must we remember the multitude of specific cultural, economic, and political contexts within which that power operates.

Race is among the most powerful lenses through which we discuss and analyze a variety of life experiences, from education to work to something as mundane as the pronunciation of a name. From one perspective, the *Key & Peele* sketch excerpted above appears to be striving for a universal approach to humor similar to the ones considered in this volume so far. Viewers of all races ought to be able to decode the common, cross-racial misunderstanding displayed in the teacher's struggle to pronounce his students' names. After all, the black Mr. Garvey is made to look the fool much more so than the white students are. Upon further consideration, however, the humor of the piece is clearly steeped in a racial complexity that belies the idea that all viewers will find the same humor in it. This racial power structure is impacted not only by the punchlines featured in the sketch but also by the biracial identity of the actor portraying Mr. Garvey (Keegan-Michael Key), as well as the sketch's place on a network (Comedy Central) that has historically privileged white viewers.

The sketch offers at least two plausible comedic readings if the viewer uses race as her primary analytic tool. One highlights an "otherness" of black culture, as the exaggeratedly silly mispronunciations from Mr. Garvey differentiate him from the normative expectations of his white students (and viewers), making him the butt of the joke. An alternative reading interrogates the inequality of power between the black and white creators and consumers of comedy. In this reading, the sketch mines name mispronunciation for laughs as a way to understand the constructed, artificial nature of racial hierarchy. The black Mr. Garvey is supposed to know and utilize the "correct" pronunciation of names assumed by his white students. After all, these are "normal" names in American culture, to be contrasted with more ethnically or racially marked names whose mispronunciation by a white teacher would be excusable. By not abiding by these assumed rules, the sketch confronts viewers with the arbitrary way something as innocuous as a name can create and reinforce race-based power differentials. It shows us that the naming and pronunciation norms of the dominant, largely white American culture are not natural or eternal. The sketch's humor in this reading, then, comes from making this assumed, implicitly white norm explicit and, in doing so, asking a largely white audience to grapple with this possibility.

Of course, audiences might understand both of these readings of the sketch at the same time, or they might even process it with a range of readings other than the ones discussed here. Comedians like Key and Peele have long addressed race in this manner, pairing a trenchant critique of race-based power hierarchies alongside humor "safe" for mainstream sensibilities. In the first essay of this chapter, Herman Gray describes this approach—using humorous representations of race in order to expose dominant power—as fundamentally ambivalent. Race-based comedy, for Gray, constantly negotiates two competing tensions, perpetuating and critiquing race-based social hierarchies. He describes the 1990s sketch comedy from FOX, *In Living Color,* as having the same sort of ambivalent politics of representation described in the *Key and Peele* sketch above. For some, Gray says, the ambivalence of race-based humor "contests hegemonic assumptions and representations of race in general and blacks in particular in the American social order; for others, it simply perpetuates troubling images of blacks." Racial approaches to understanding humor strive to tease out the nuances of this ambivalence, accounting for how and why different people find things funny, as well as who has the power to tell jokes to what audiences.

Felicia Henderson examines similar issues through insights gleaned from her time in the writers' room for Chris Rock's sitcom *Everybody Hates Chris*. While we've primarily considered comedic texts themselves—movies, television shows, and internet videos—throughout this volume, Henderson's work provides evidence of race-based disparity enacted at the level of media production. In considering how these disparities impact the meanings encoded in comedic media, Henderson's study highlights racial tensions that often remain invisible to viewers. The third section of this chapter, by contrast, interrogates the opposite end of a comedic text's life cycle by looking at viewer responses to the relationship between humor and racial stereotypes in the 2001 blockbuster *Rush Hour 2*. Through focus group interviews with a racially diverse audience, the authors discover that viewers tend not to be critical of comedically framed racial stereotypes. Instead, they argue, comedy helps viewers naturalize and tolerate stereotypes, increasing the risk that viewers will bring their racial prejudices into their daily lives.

Finally, although most critical race analyses of comedy have focused on texts by, for, and/or about African-Americans, the final essay of this chapter uses a similar approach to consider Indian American representation. In their examination of the Netflix sitcom *Master of None*, Bhoomi Thakore and Bilal Hussain consider how star Aziz Ansari's move from broadcast television to the streaming world has afforded him more freedom to critique television's dominant politics of representation, while at the same time reminding us that there remains much work to be done. In much the same way that *Key & Peele* negotiated their blackness on Comedy Central, so too did Aziz Ansari downplay his Indian Muslim heritage on *Parks & Recreation*, only to more fully embrace identity politics for *Master of None*.

A. *Watching Race*, Herman Gray[i]

I want to offer the case of *In Living Color* to foreground a cultural politics of representation that uses irreverence, satire, and spectacle to engage issues of multiculturalism and diversity within blackness. I also offer the show to highlight often-disturbing questions about the effects of such strategies for black cultural politics. I want to link the range of meanings activated by the show (and the response it generates) to broad social, cul-

---

i. From Herman Gray, *Watching Race: Television and the Struggle for Blackness* (Minneapolis: University of Minnesota Press, 2004), 130–131, 137–140, 145–146. Copyright © 1995 by the Regents of the University of Minnesota. Reprinted with permission.

tural, and political discourses about race, sexuality, class, and gender.[1] I suggest ultimately that *In Living Color* discursively enacts a cultural politics of representation that settles around a position of ambivalence. For some, this ambivalence contests hegemonic assumptions and representations of race in general and blacks in particular in the American social order; for others, it simply perpetuates troubling images of blacks.[2]

For many critics and admirers alike, the popular appeal and commercial success of *In Living Color* stem from its ability to appeal to audiences across a very broad gulf of racial, class, gender, and sexual difference. Indeed, the show's creator, its producer, a former black male writer, scholars, and critics seem to agree that it is the show's transgressive use of the trope of race that allows it to reconfigure audiences that are differently positioned socially. If this crossover appeal is the source of celebration, it is also the source of considerable angst and criticism. In the end, it is this constant negotiation and rearticulation that account for the show's often biting satire and its ambivalence. Both are essential for the show's commercial appeal, its cultural resonance, and its effects.

What is the show ambivalent about? It is ambivalent about representations of blackness that often come at the expense of the black working class and the poor; it is sometimes ambivalent about its representation of black difference even as it critiques white racism; it is ambivalent about gayness in the black community even when it satirizes effeminate black gay men; and it is ambivalent about black women as it reverses the terms of power in and of gender relations. Attributing this ambivalence to the disciplining power of television's commercial imperatives, Schulman puts the matter quite clearly with the suggestion that the show's "ambiguity gives it bimodal appeal—a quality deemed all-important in a commercial medium for whom the aggregate minority viewing audience is insufficient in itself to garner the kinds of ratings that yield substantial revenue."[3] Dates and Barlow also indicate that sophisticated black urban viewers have cultivated a tolerance of this ambivalence, given that they too very much enjoy the show.[4]

Ambiguity is most clearly expressed in the show's mobilization and representation, perhaps even critique, of historic stereotypes of African Americans and its parody of images of the "black underclass" with characters such as Frenchy, Anton, Benita Betrell, and the Homeboys. Even though these and other continuing characters are represented through parody and satire, the very presence of these characters (as well as the multiracial cast) set in African American contexts constantly forces viewers to jockey for a "reading position": Are these representations merely instances of inside jokes, to which African Americans have some exclusive claims? Are the show's representations harmless fun? Are the representations (and the organizations and people responsible for them) simply complicit in perpetuating stereotypical and ultimately derogatory images of African Americans? Are these representations so spectacular and exaggerated that in the end they inevitably expose and criticize the absurdity of all forms of bigotry?

* * *

To be sure, there are political lines that *In Living Color* draws, and there are stances that it takes, but the meanings the show organizes and registers are *relational*. They do not inhere in the text, and they are socially constructed, not politically determined. The politics that are enacted are therefore deeply conflicted and often contradictory. *In Living Color*'s politics range from *critical* (e.g., a sketch that parodied credit card commercials and featured a black man who could get a credit card, but who then found the card did not shield him from the suspicions and racism encountered daily by middle-class blacks) to *ambivalent* (e.g., the collection of sketches called "Men on . . .") to *transgressive* (e.g., the various sketches featuring Homey the Clown, Anton the homeless man, and Handiman, a physically challenged superhero) to *irreverent* (e.g., sketches featuring underclass black women gossips, Rick James, Louis Farrakhan, Arsenio Hall, Oprah Winfrey, Marion Barry, Jesse Jackson). In fact, for all its biting humor, the show still maintains a *utopian* vision. It leaves viewers "with an affirmation, a sense that there are signs that someday . . . there will be a time when prejudice [will be] obsolete, a time when at night it might be safe to walk down the street."[5]

Seen from the vantage point of the various discourses that enable *In Living Color* and in which it is positioned, a wide range of themes are figured. Among the most significant are *sexuality* (e.g., the "Men on . . ." sketches, sketches featuring Prince), *masculinity and gender relations* (e.g., sketches about a female animal trainer who trains men and advises women on how best to control [black] men in relationships), *racism* (e.g., sketches that make white guilt the focus of humor), *racial identity* (e.g., sketches featuring the Brothers Brothers, Tom and Tom), *social class* (e.g., sketches featuring Homey the Clown, Frenchy, Anton, the black cafe, Cephus and Reesy, Benita Betrell, two black talent agents from Funky Finger Productions in Compton), *nationalism and politics* (e.g., sketches about Jesse Jackson, Louis Farrakhan), and *black popular culture* (e.g., sketches on Arsenio Hall, Prince, Oprah, Vanilla Ice; the presence of rap music and the Fly Girls).

Aesthetically, *In Living Color* reorganizes specific images, themes, and events from America's racial past as well as contemporary African American cultural and social practices to distinguish itself from other television shows. In fact, in her inventory of the show's strategies of representation Schulman claims that the show depends on historical and contemporary stereotypes, white spectatorship, idealized visions of a multiracial order, and role reversals for its humor, modes of address, and cultural meanings.[6]

And of course *In Living Color*'s strategy of representation relies heavily on rap music and hip-hop sensibilities. Rap and hip-hop are used deliberately but quite strategically in the program to generate identifications across racial lines. From the angle of the television industry, this strategic use of rap is also a useful marketing strategy for appealing to and reconfiguring different audiences in terms of race, gender, and age. Other television shows, notably *The Arsenio Hall Show*, *Where I Live*, and *Fresh Prince of Bel Air*, have used similar strategies, as has a great deal of television and radio advertising.

But I do not want to downplay the extent to which *In Living Color* is supremely televisual and therefore at the very center of contemporary commercial media and popular culture. In other words, attention to issues of sexuality, class, race, gender, masculinity, and so on are figured in terms of television itself. That is to say, these issues serve as vehicles for commenting on the medium of television itself — advertising (e.g., the credit card commercial parody), variety shows (e.g., the Brothers Brothers), home shopping networks (e.g., the Homeboy Shopping Network), science fiction/action adventure programs (e.g., *Star Trek*), talk shows (e.g., Oprah Winfrey's and Arsenio Hall's shows), PBS (e.g., "Men on . . ."), and television news (e.g., the Rodney King beating). In an ironic twist, many of the show's sketches offer commentary on commercial television's own exclusions, exaggerations, and complicity in the construction and representation of blackness. This critical performance and intervention has been illustrated nicely in sketches parodying recent credit card commercials and the PBS staple *This Old House*.

The sketch that parodied the signature style of certain credit card television commercials playing widely at the time the sketch was aired used the popular advertising convention of the individual testimonial to construct the experience of what, on the face of it, seemed to be a typical credit card customer. In this instance, however, the customer, played by David Alan Grier, was a black middle-class professional male whose very blackness and maleness generated suspicion and harassment each time he attempted to use his "prized" "Equity Express" card. These "routine troubles" were presumably provoked because this customer was a black male and, as such, a signifier for suspicion and danger.

In a parody of PBS's *This Old House*, Anton (Damon Wayans), a home-less black man, instructed the audience on the complexities of construct-ing shelter out of cardboard. Representations in the sketch satirized the well-known series in which a host and remodeling expert instructs (white) middle-class homeowners in the challenges and joys of restoring houses. In both the commercial and *This Old House* sketches, commonsense as-sumptions about citizenship, property, and social class were parodied, and hence the ironic juxtaposition of class and race with familiar tropes of middle-class homeownership and unemployed homelessness was made ex-plicit. Politically, these images are especially effective because they disturb the presumed separation of these discourses. In effect, they are reconfig-ured and politicized by their relocation to the same discursive space.

Sketches such as those described above call attention to assumptions about race and class as the basis for idealized representations. In other words, because African Americans seldom, if ever, appear in such tele-visual spaces as credit card commercials or home remodeling programs, *In Living Color*'s staging (through parody and irony) foregrounds these cul-tural forums, calling attention to their exclusion of blacks and the normal-ization of class (middle class) and race (white). As Schulman notes, these sketches indicate that, at its critical best,

> *In Living Color* does not offer a plausible picture of American society
> as open and pluralistic. Nor does it, taken as a whole, suggest that the
> American Dream is accessible to people of color. Ironically, its subtext
> seems to be that whether individual African Americans are "deficient" or
> "gifted" has mattered little to white society, which has historically viewed
> them as "all alike."[7]

In addition to *In Living Color*'s engagement of race, class, and tele-vision in these sketches, the show also represents different subject posi-tions within blackness. This diversity within blackness is most often rep-resented through the trope of social class, although one would also have to include gender, sexuality, and race.

* * *

Conclusions

In Living Color's thematic focus and its strategies of representation in no way ensure radical, even progressive, claims on blackness and represen-tations of African Americans. The production of any kind of critical cultural politics in commercial network television cannot rest with a single series, episode, sketch, or character. The show's ability to move beyond its important but momentary effect of disrupting hegemonic representations of blackness remains at best ambivalent and contingent. But I regard even this momentary and often troubling disruption as important. *In Living Color*, like *Frank's Place*, *Roc*, and *A Different World*, cumulatively disturbs and interrupts television's own discourse, a discourse that is still too insular, self-referential, and complacent on questions of race and ethnicity. And, of course, even in a program such as *In Living Color*, television's power to normalize, trivialize, and routinize is ever present. In fact, *In Living Color* has so quickly moved to the stage of routinization that its transgressive edge has long since disappeared. Moreover, during the 1992–93 season Wayans actually left the show as executive producer because of creative and scheduling differences with Fox. Hence, I deliberately characterize the show's contributions to diverse representations of blackness with conditional terms such as *contingent* and *ambivalent*.

I continue to believe that the cultural force of *In Living Color* can be realized where there are other active practices and discourses that critique, empower, frame, and authorize its constructions and representations of African Americans. In the absence of other cultural practices and social movements aimed at transforming social relations of power both in and over representation, then, one might well be tempted (correctly, I think) to read *In Living Color* as mere distraction, as appropriated images and representations that have been softened and displaced though comedic conventions and tolerated as harmless television entertainment that re-secures the dominant terms of power. Or, in a slight variation, the show might be seen as simply providing an "authentic" black view of the world from within the sacred and privileged territory of blackness.

There are, to be sure, problems that complicate the meanings of the show and the critical cultural potential it might hold as popular culture—its use of humor, its staging of and privileging of race (as well as middle-class heterosexual dominance) as the leading edge of its critique. The attempt to represent race relations and the diversity within blackness is one of the qualities that distinguishes *In Living Color* from other representations of blacks on commercial television. The show's strategies of representation, ambivalent positions, and location within commercial network television require not just dismissal, but complex and nuanced readings. Part of *In Living Color*'s rich potential has always been its transgressive and irreverent stance, but a cultural politics based on irreverence and transgression is tricky. What the show signifies in its representations of race, gender, class, and sexuality is necessarily contingent and indeterminate. For some, the show's strategies of representation produce critical insights; for others, especially those African Americans who complained to writer Franklyn Ajaye, they produce representations that are dangerous and embarrassing. In the end, the show's meanings depend on how it organizes its audiences and negotiates the discourses, debates, and circumstances that enable and constantly reposition it within the larger society.

B: "The Culture Behind Closed Doors: Issues of Gender and Race in the Writers' Room," Felicia D. Henderson[ii]

According to television comedy writer Daley Haggar, "if you're not comfortable with sexual humor or with crudeness or with all sorts of people being really honest about certain emotions, then yeah, this job is not for you."[8] As a scholar who is also a television writer, I concur with Haggar's assessment. I have been employed on the writing staffs of six prime-time sitcoms and three one-hour dramas. By the time I embarked on my doctoral study at UCLA, I had been writing and producing television shows for thirteen years. In fact, I was a consulting producer on the CW's Chris Rock co-created sitcom, *Everybody Hates Chris* (UPN/The CW, 2005–2009), when I began the first year of the PhD program.

No experience I have had on a writing staff has been exactly like any other experience I have had. Every show's culture is unique. On one of the most wholesome family sitcoms, I encountered daily ribbing by the all-male writing staff for not laughing at every joke about male genitalia. On my first one-hour drama I found myself in a political power struggle with an executive producer who did not believe I should have input equal to his regarding the show's creative direction. (The fact that I was responsible for the creative development of the show and had written its pilot script was not reason enough to value my input.)

Because I have been writing, directing, and producing television for so many years, my critical perspective on production culture, specifically the writing of prime-time television comedy, is deeply reflexive and auto-ethnographic.

* * *

ii. First published as the article "The Culture Behind Closed Doors: Issues of Gender and Race in the Writers' Room," by Felicia D. Henderson, in *Cinema Journal* 50, no. 2, 145–147, 150–152. Copyright © 2011 by the University of Texas Press. All rights reserved.

The Writers' Workspace

The writers' room is half-hour comedy's creative ground zero. It is here that a process of collective decision making that I call "situational authorship" exists. Inside this ground zero, quasi-familial and organizational rules structure conventionalized socioprofessional activities that overdetermine the manner by which television's on-screen texts are authored. In this space, ideas are negotiated, consensus is formed, and issues of gender, race, and class identities play out and complicate the on-screen narratives that eventually air on network and cable television.

This essay aims to unpack the sociocultural rituals that are integral to situational authorship. In particular, I will examine the ritual of othering writers based on gender and race. Categorization based on difference, according to Stuart Hall, "is part of the maintenance of social and symbolic order. It sets up a symbolic frontier between the 'normal' and the 'deviant,' the 'normal' and the 'pathological,' the 'acceptable' and the 'unacceptable,' what 'belongs,' and what does not or is 'Other.'"[9] Othering becomes particularly significant when one considers how personal backgrounds and beliefs of writers influence on-screen narrative. When othering becomes a method of silencing points of view, the ideas of those who are othered effectively die on the vine. If the other wishes to survive, she or he quickly learns to present ideas that are acceptable to the more powerful writers in the room. It is this process that leads to the homogenization of ideas.

This is nearly always the process for half-hour comedies. On a daily basis, the writing staff gathers in the room and brainstorms about what the next episode will be.[10] Once a story area is "broken," or agreed upon and approved by the head writer (who is usually also the executive producer), one of the writers on the writing staff is assigned the task of outlining and writing the script. However, before that writer is released to write the script, she or he has heard many individual writers' perspectives on the story.

For example, perhaps the assigned writer had a notion to name the guest-starring character Tammy, but then he learns that the executive producer's ex-wife (to whom he grudgingly pays alimony) is named Tammy. The writer would be well advised to change his character's name. Or perhaps the writer wants to give his main character a Toyota Prius, but the senior writer who sits next to him in the room has a Prius that was just recalled and is not keen on the idea of giving Toyota free publicity unless it is bad publicity. The executive producer assures both writers that the studio's legal department would never allow the latter. Quickly, the car is changed to a Honda Civic Hybrid.

Or, as I witnessed while observing the writers' room at the CW sit-com *The Game* (2006–2009), a Jewish writer suggested a joke dependent on poking fun at a Jewish character based on his religious identity.[11] The black writer assigned to the script commented that the joke might make it into the Jewish writer's script—but it absolutely would not be in any script with the black writer's name on the title page because it would make her look anti-Semitic. "I can't get away with what you can get away with," she added. The ethnically insensitive joke did not find its way into the script, as is often the case when the bias in the joke offends the sensibility of a senior writer in the room, or when the writer of the episode can make a strong case for a particular story or joke causing harm to his or her repu-tation as a writer.

* * *

The Sanctity of Trash Talking

In 2006, the "creative necessity" of off-color jokes in the sanctity of the writers' room was upheld by the California Superior Court in its decision to dismiss the lawsuit brought by a black woman employed as a writer's as-sistant on the NBC comedy *Friends*. Although the show's studio, Warner Bros. Television, acknowledged that some of the sexually explicit talk took place, the studio argued that such talk was vital to the chemistry of the show.[12]

Amaani Lyle accused the highly rated comedy of fostering an environ-ment of sexual harassment and racial discrimination. California's Supreme Court justices, ruling 7-0, agreed with Warner Bros. Television Produc-tions that "trash talk" was part of the creative process, and that the studio and its writers could therefore not be sued for raunchy writers' meetings.[13] Warner Bros. and the *Friends* writers successfully argued to protect the room and the creative necessity of sexually coarse and vulgar language by claiming that their workspace was one "focused on generating scripts for an adult-oriented comic show featuring sexual themes."[14]

Of course, "sexually coarse and vulgar language" was not invented by the writing staff of *Friends*. Nor was other behavior that in most work en-vironments would be considered actionable. The two examples of writers' room gender politics given here—one from the early 1950s and the other from the late 1990s—illustrate how situational authorship functions and how durable its dynamics are. Through the othering that takes place in both examples, methods of homogenizing the cultural dynamics of the writers' room emerge. Humor is generated within this space through a process of inclusion and exclusion, familiarity and othering, and humor is derived from social categories such as race, gender, ethnicity, and sexuality, which become the means by which the performative space is homogenized.

Others with Opportunities

The cultural and structural stability of the writers' room over the last half century is also illuminated by how the othered are forced to function if they desire continued employment. Often, familiarity breeds opportunity in this workspace. However, for marginalized writers it is not always "who you know," as the old adage suggests. It is instead what you pretend *not* to know that determines success in highly competitive writing positions.

For example, when a series with a predominantly white cast decides to introduce a black character, and there is a black writer on the writing staff, he or she is usually assigned to write that particular script in a political dance in which the head writer/executive producer avoids discussion of why such an assignment was made. For the black writer, the dance is more complicated. If the writer refuses the assignment, she/he risks being labeled someone who is not a team player or a writer who is too sensitive about race. However, if she/he accepts the assignment, the black writer must be concerned with being pigeonholed as a writer who can only write black characters. The dilemma is a complex one. The writer becomes othered regardless of how she/he responds to the request. Agreeing to the writing assignment others the writer as being only capable of writing "black material." Refusing the assignment others this same writer as someone who racializes all encounters.

Gender is also used to other women in writers' rooms. Whereas the black writer's silence in addressing the race-related story assignment is a common strategy for combating marginalization, women writers must often let their laughter be heard as a strategy to combat being othered. A female writer who does not laugh along with off-color jokes about penis size may be labeled incapable of being "one of the guys" and therefore "not a good fit" with a predominantly male staff. This writer, if she is unable to feign a level of comfort with such jokes, will not last more than a year or two in the male-dominated world of television comedy writers.

"Uni-Culturalism": The By-Product of Situational Authorship

In her foundational 1950 text, *Hollywood, the Dream Factory: An Anthropologist Looks at the Movie-Makers*, Hortense Powdermaker hypothesized that the social dynamics of the filmmaking community exercised an important influence on the production of movies and that, ultimately, the production processes and actions "behind the scenes" influenced the content and form of films.[15] This argument can be applied to television comedy writing. The behind-the-scenes actions or rituals in the writers' room, and the roles writers play within this space, not only influence but also author the content and form of television comedy's humor and narrative. When othered writers assimilate in order to be included, what is then left out of creative discussions also affects authorship.

In a post-network era dominated by "color-blind" and "multicultural" hiring, attempts at inclusion are based more on visual difference than on cultural difference. Without consideration of cultural differences in the creative process, color-blind and multicultural casting of both the writers' room and on-screen characters becomes a means of instituting "uni-culturalism." In other words, the more race, gender, and class are used to other writers, the less comfortable these writers are with expressing creative and cultural difference. In a uni-cultural world that limits its definition of multiculturalism to visual difference, all writers and all characters may not look alike, but they all mimic the dominant group because there is little acceptance of actual difference. Moreover, in an attempt to mainstream a variety of cultural and racial differences, difference itself is treated as the antithesis of multicultural inclusion. Yet I would argue that multiculturalism should be a celebration of cultural difference on-screen, in the writers' room, and, ultimately, in storytelling. By analyzing how content is authored, we can better understand how images are created and how the process of creating such images can lead to the exclusion of gender, race, class, and cultural difference in favor of a hegemonic, uni-cultural perspective.

C: "Naturalizing Racial Differences Through Comedy: Asian, Black, and White Views on Racial Stereotypes in *Rush Hour 2*," Ji Hoon Park, Nadine G. Gabbadon, and Ariel R. Chernin[iii]

Rush Hour 2 (2001), the sequel to *Rush Hour* (1998), achieved enormous commercial success, grossing over $226 million in the United States and

iii. From Ji Hoon Park, Nadine G. Gabbadon, and Ariel R. Chernin, "Naturalizing Racial Differences Through Comedy: Asian, Black, and White Views on Racial Stereotypes in *Rush Hour 2*," *Journal of Communication* 56, no. 1 (2006): 157–161, 163–168, 171–173. Copyright © 2006 by John Wiley & Sons Inc. Reproduced with permission of Blackwell Publishing.

$329 million worldwide.[16] As of March 2005, the film ranked 45th in the all-time US box office.[17] The movie follows two police officers, one from Los Angeles (Chris Tucker as "Carter") and one from Hong Kong (Jackie Chan as "Lee"), as they pursue Asian gang members attempting to execute an elaborate counterfeiting plot. Although *Rush Hour* and *Rush Hour 2* can be classified as action-comedy "buddy movies," the films depart from convention by pairing an African American and an Asian in the lead roles. Although such a casting decision could have alienated White viewers, the film's incredible mainstream success suggests that it appealed to both minority and White audiences. Perhaps inspired by the success of the *Rush Hour* franchise, the current film landscape reveals a growing number of comedies that feature Asian and/or Black leading men, among them *I Spy* (2002), *Shanghai Knights* (2003), and *Harold and Kumar Go to White Castle* (2004).

It is possible to argue that the growing number of comedies starring racial minorities has facilitated racial tolerance, as well as the acceptance of Asian men, in particular, who have been consistently marginalized from mainstream cultural representation in the United States. However, it is premature to claim that these films represent a substantial shift in the cultural representation of race. A critical investigation reveals that not only is the racial hierarchy a crucial part of these films' narratives but also the characters consistently conform to negative minority stereotypes that can be deemed racist. The relationship between explicitly stereotypical portrayals of race and commercial success seems highly problematic and contradictory. If blatant stereotypes are embodied in films, why do people enjoy them? *Rush Hour 2*'s enormous commercial success makes it an ideal example through which to explore the apparent paradox between potentially racist representations in comedy and its widespread popularity transcending racial boundaries.

* * *

Racial stereotypes in comedy

Stereotyping serves multiple purposes, both cognitive and motivational, and it "emerges in various contexts to serve particular functions necessitated by those contexts."[18] A wide range of situations, such as cognitive overload, group conflict, power differences, or a desire to justify the status quo, can give rise to the formation and activation of stereotypes.[19] From a media industry perspective, stereotyping results from the need to quickly convey information about characters and to instill in audiences expectations about characters' actions.[20] Stereotypes are important in comedy because not only do they help to establish instantly recognizable character types but such character traits and stereotype-based jokes also constitute a source of humor.[21]

Critical attention has been paid to the ideological implications of the stereotypical treatment of racial minorities in comedy, whether stereotypes are "read as a symptom of existing social relations or as a more active component of the politics of representation."[22] With regard to the disruptive potential of comedy, King notes that comic representations of race (i.e., exaggerated portrayals of racial traits) can be identified as a parody of the stereotype and a strategy of subversion, thereby opening up the possibility of critiquing the racial norm and rejecting prejudice. Denzin suggests that the conventional narrative in the interracial buddy films, where two men of different races develop trust and friendship, can be read as an imaginary utopia in which racial differences do not matter. In fact, comedy often inverts stereotypes to generate humor.[23] For instance, in the *Lethal Weapon* (1987) film series, the Black character is middle class, conservative, and family oriented, and the White character is unpredictable and dangerous.[24] Jewish and Black comedians tell jokes about their own race to criticize social injustice and racial inequalities.[25]

Scholars, however, concede that it is often difficult to distinguish social commentary and satire from the ideological reproduction of racial stereotypes in comedy. The most frequently debated question is whether viewers laugh *at* stereotyped minority figures or *with* them.[26] For critical scholars, the distinction is less important than the negative social consequences of seemingly harmless racial jokes. Critical views on race in comedy posit that racial stereotyping serves an ideological function, normalizing racially defined characteristics and legitimating the racial hierarchy.[27] Critical scholars claim that in a social environment in which racism is deeply rooted, racial jokes and stereotypes inevitably reinforce hierarchically structured racial differences.[28] Omi argues that racial jokes told across the color lines "will, despite its 'purely' humorous intent, serve to reinforce stereotypes and rationalize the existing relations of racial inequality."[29] Schulman questions the satirical use of racial humor as a tool for criticizing racism.[30] She argues that an attempt to critique racism through comedy results in unintended consequences, namely, the reinforcement of the very stereotypes that the humor attempts to ridicule. Race-based comedy often juxtaposes racially characterized non-whites against socially dominant Whites: "[racial humor] appears at the same time to have internalized something of the very despicable images that oppressors of the black community have harbored for centuries, however blatantly it parodies their absurdity and illogic."[31] Bogle claims that although comedy is perceived as having the potential to comment on the problematic nature of stereotyping, it rarely capitalizes on the opportunity. In the world of the film, minority characters rarely resist or reject the stereotypes that are forced upon them. In his discussion of *48 Hrs.* (1982), Bogle argues that the character Reggie Hammond (played by Eddie Murphy, a Black actor/ comedian) never gets mad at Jack Cates (played by Nick Nolte, a White actor) for making racially insulting comments, thus "greatly neutralizes the inherent racism."[32]

Scholars also highlight the harmful effects of minority actors embodying stereotypes associated with their own race. King points to the enactment of racist stereotypes, particularly that of the "coon," by Black comedians, such as Eddie Murphy, Martin Lawrence, and Chris Tucker, and notes that their performances are uncomfortably reminiscent of racist ideologies that have been used to justify racial discrimination in the past.[33] Means Coleman also claims that Black actors appearing in what she terms "neominstrelsy" sitcoms, such as *Martin* (1992–1997), *The Fresh Prince of Bel Air* (1990–1996), and *The Wayans Bros.* (1995–1999), are "taking part in their own racial ridicule by adopting Jim Crow, coon, and Sambo characterizations."[34] She argues that Black sitcoms emphasize self-deprecating humor, physical comedy, provocative and flashy clothing, and "ghetto-centric" characterizations, all of which contribute to a narrowly defined portrait of African American men and women.

* * *

We contend that seemingly innocuous racial jokes and stereotypes in comedy need critical attention in the current social climate. Most people claim to be color blind and antiracist; however, race continues to serve as an important cognitive category with which people make sense of their social world.[35] Much of the existing scholarship expands the understanding of racism and racial differences in conjunction with racial stereotypes as representational devices or cognitive categories. Racial stereotypes play a significant role in maintaining the racial ideology in post–civil rights America where blatant declarations of racist views, bigotry, and violence have become uncommon and unacceptable.[36] Racial stereotypes ultimately reduce and naturalize racial differences and, thus, preclude alternative ways to think about the category of race.[37] Once the beliefs of racial differences are naturalized as objectively existent and immutable, these differences provide insight into how people see their world. Given that racial stereotypes are most frequently used to represent people of color, the reified racial beliefs help maintain the racial hierarchy and White privileges. These beliefs also lead to social consequences, including the negative judgments of racial minorities and social injustice.[38] We argue that racial stereotypes in comedy should be taken seriously because of their potential to naturalize racial differences through humor. However, the potential of comedy to subvert racial stereotypes cannot be underestimated. The purpose of the present study is to examine the ideological implications of racial stereotypes in comedy and to determine whether they humorously naturalize or possibly disrupt the beliefs of racial differences that constitute the ideological basis of the racial hierarchy.

Textual analysis

. . . *Rush Hour 2* promotes numerous Black and Asian stereotypes through characters that personify and verbalize these racial myths. Lee is a respectful but culturally ignorant and asexual Asian man who excels at Kung Fu. Henchwoman Hu Li serves as the Asian "dragon lady" who is desirable but dangerous.[39] The Chinese women at the massage parlor embody the stereotype of obedient Oriental dolls readily fulfilling Americans' sexual desire and fantasies. These two images of Asian women may seem contradictory, but they reflect two major stereotypes of Asian women frequently found in the mass media. Omi suggests that although it is possible for racial minorities to be stereotyped in multiple ways within the same text, such contradictions do not challenge the one dimensionality of minority images.[40] Carter is a loud, impulsive, hypersexual yet childish Black man who is often portrayed as ignorant and causing trouble. He constantly reinforces stereotypes associated with his own race. He tells a Chinese woman that he likes his chicken "dead and deep fried," as if it is natural that a Black man likes fried chicken. He also furthers the African American stereotype in his manner of speaking, such as "she's the bomb," "mack out," and "look fly."

A critical reading of *Rush Hour 2* indicates that racial ideology is coded both in the characters and in the narrative. First, Jackie Chan and Chris Tucker both portray likeable characters that do not problematize or transgress mainstream racial images and boundaries. Their characters are buffoons or "symbolically castrated men" that do not challenge White masculinity.[41] In contrast to Chan's Hong Kong–made action movies, where his characters are not only affable but also masculine and tough, Chan's Hollywood films, such as *Shanghai Noon* (2000) and *Shanghai Knights*

(2003), cast him in the role of the funny, desexualized, and unthreatening Oriental male.[42] Lo argues that Chan's masculinity has been toned down in Hollywood in order to ensure that his characters conform to racial conventions. Tucker as Carter is an infantile Black man who, despite his masculine physical presence, is incapable of protecting himself without Chan's help. King indicates that the Black comedian's high-pitched voice and childish tone are unthreatening to the racial status quo because they help "reduce any threat created by the spectacle of a seemingly dominating Black character."[43] Most of the racial jokes in *Rush Hour 2* are directed toward minorities, which strengthens Whites' positive self-image and their dominant position in the racial order.

* * *

Rush Hour 2 diffuse[s] viewers' potential claims of racism and promote[s] the acceptability of racial stereotypes. First, the minority status of two main characters signals that their racial jokes are acceptable and not racist. Because people of color are usually portrayed as victims rather than perpetrators of racism, they are not perceived as having power over the others (as opposed to a White character having power over a minority character).

Second, racial jokes in the film cross color lines, creating an impression that all races are subject to stereotypes. Although there are only a couple of instances in the film that could potentially be interpreted as promoting White stereotypes, the inclusion of these few quips creates the impression that all racial groups are targeted by the film's racial humor. Marchetti argues that "Hollywood films often play various positions one against the other, so that a text can appear to espouse rather liberal attitudes toward race."[44]

Third, the film's stereotypes are coded as realistic and natural and based on the characters' personality differences and the execution of the plot. For instance, Carter's impulsive behavior is used to propel the plot and causes Lee to engage in fights with the Triad gang members. Carter is also always the funny distraction when Lee is responsibly investigating the crime. The relevance of stereotypes to the plot and characterization makes the racially stereotyped content acceptable and realistic.

Fourth, the two leading men are portrayed as good friends. Because neither Carter nor Lee is hurt by the racial remarks, the film encourages viewers to interpret the humor as acceptable. They are seen singing together in the car, and they often help each other out of difficult situations. At the end of the movie, Lee gives Carter his father's badge as a symbol of friendship. This also implies that despite all of Carter's racial jokes and comments, Lee was still a true friend and there were indeed no hard feelings between them.

* * *

A discussion of the ideological limitations and possibilities of racial stereotypes in comedy cannot be complete without exploring audiences' interpretation of the text. We now turn our attention to the viewers. We examine how viewers of different races make sense of the racial stereotypes in relation to the genre of comedy and the textual devices that we discussed above. How do audiences interpret *Rush Hour 2*'s racial stereotypes? Are White, Black, or Asian audiences offended by any content in the film? Do White, Black, and Asian American audiences differ in their sensitivity to the portrayal of race in this film?

* * *

Offensiveness

Irrespective of race, the majority of the focus group participants laughed throughout their viewing of *Rush Hour 2*. They stated explicitly that they enjoyed *Rush Hour 2*, and that the film's racial humor did not offend them. Although participants gave numerous reasons for why they were not offended, several common themes emerged. First, Black, White, and Asian participants mentioned that *Rush Hour 2*'s status as a comedy dictated that the film should not be taken seriously. Many participants stated that they would have taken offense at racial jokes and stereotypes if they had been conveyed in different generic forms, such as drama.

> Jeff (White male, 19): It's not as offensive when you know it's supposed to be funny, as opposed to just coming out of nowhere, and you're like, "what?"
> Justin (Asian male, 18): I think since it's in a comedy movie, people can let it go.
> Aaron (Black male, 20): The context of putting the whole interaction with the comedy so people aren't necessarily offended when Lee says, I'm gonna bitch-slap you back to Africa or something. Like, that was funny because of the context but if he said it anywhere else, it wouldn't.

Most participants in all three racial groups acknowledged, however, that even within the context of a comedy, racial humor could potentially be racist. Several participants said that the race of the person telling a joke can dictate whether or not the joke is racist. In comedy, it is often considered acceptable for racial minorities to tell racial jokes, whereas the same jokes told by Whites would be considered racist. Most participants agreed that if a White character told the same jokes as Carter and Lee, audiences would probably be offended.

> Vanessa (Black female, 20): Well, I guess culturally people would be less inclined to take offense, in my opinion, [because of] the fact that Chris Tucker is black and Jackie Chan is Chinese. . . . They're both minorities. . . . Whereas I feel that if one of the characters had been White, there's a historical stigma of White oppressor that could maybe just not let people think his intentions don't have any racial prejudice or racial hatred or patronizing feelings in any way.
>
> Ryan (Asian male, 19): I think it's more acceptable I think. There's one line when Jackie Chan was in a truck, he's like "I'll slap you back to Africa." There's no way that a White character would ever say that in the movie because . . . you can't say that.
>
> Ethan (White male, 20): The movie works because it's two minorities. They can rag on each other. It wouldn't be acceptable if one of them was White because . . . it just wouldn't work out. People would be offended and stuff.

The White participants' discussion of racial stereotypes revealed that they were keenly aware of Whites' stigmatized position as perpetrators of racism. One White participant explained that the main characters' minority status allowed White people to enjoy the jokes without feeling guilty.

> Amy (White female, 20): Maybe the jokes are more politically correct because you're making fun of your race against someone who can also make fun of their race and White people don't have to stand back and be, like, "Oh, shit, sorry." Like, I'm sorry I'm an oppressor, or something.

Second, several of the Black, Asian, and White participants stated that the movie was not offensive because the jokes were targeted at Blacks, Asians, and Whites—and not at one group in particular.

> Stacey (White female, 20): I think a lot of it has to do with that they ragged on every race in this movie. I think if it was just focused in on

one race, and they only made fun of that one race, it would start to get a little racist. . . . If it was just only Black jokes or only Asian jokes, or only White jokes.

Even when Lee told Carter that he would "bitch-slap him back to Africa," some Black participants stated that there was no need to be offended by the comment because earlier in the film Carter had said he would slap Lee back to the Ming Dynasty. One Black participant suggested that making jokes about every race was a deliberate move by the filmmakers. Our textual analysis, however, shows that Whites were portrayed differently than Blacks and Asians in *Rush Hour 2*. The film successfully creates the impression among the viewers that all races are objects of mockery, distortion, and exaggeration.

Third, in assessing the offensiveness of the film's racial humor, Asian, Black, and White participants considered the movie's internal context of two close friends making fun of each other's race. Participants felt this type of racial humor was acceptable because neither Carter nor Lee seemed offended by any of the comments. Their banter was interpreted as harmless "inside jokes."

Nathan (Black male, 18): I think a lot of the joking about the stereotypes in the movie was kind of softened by the fact that Jackie and Tucker are friends and they're cool.

An interesting aspect of the discussions within the Black and Asian focus groups is the fact that although most participants denied being offended by *Rush Hour 2*, many were still able to label the film as offensive on an intellectual level. We propose that this happened in part because of the nature of the focus group experience; participants were forced to think about the film and its implications. However, even after they acknowledged the movie's potential offensiveness, most were still accepting of the film and insisted that they were not offended.

* * *

Regardless of race, the majority of focus group participants did not take *Rush Hour 2*'s portrayal of race seriously, stating it was only a comedy and thus not intended to offend viewers. Throughout the discussions, participants frequently commented that it would be unusual to discuss a fictional comedy like *Rush Hour 2* at length and that the moderators were reading too much into it. Although participants made light of the racial stereotypes in *Rush Hour 2*, they perceived and accepted many of its racial portrayals as real. Participants in all three racial groups felt that the racial stereotypes in the film were humorous and acceptable because they were based on a "kernel of truth" that had been exaggerated.

> Moderator: What are some of the stereotypes in the movie?
>
> Stacey (White female, 20): Tucker kicks Jackie Chan in the face and says all Asians look alike.
>
> [People laugh]
>
> Josh (White male, 21): Or that all Asians are short.
>
> Emily (White female, 20): [Quoting movie]: "I'm two feet taller than everyone else in the room."
>
> [People laugh]
>
> Moderator: And why is that funny? I can see everyone sort of giggling when they remember it.
>
> Anthony (White male, 18): It's just so true.
>
> [People laugh]
>
> Moderator: So you think there's truth in it. Is there truth in the stereotypes?
>
> Stacey (White female, 20): Yeah.
>
> Moderator: Do you remember "Carter's theory of criminal investigation"?
>
> Richard (Asian male, 23): Follow a [rich] White guy. [There's always a rich White guy behind every crime.]
>
> Sandra (Asian female, 22): When I heard that, [I thought] "Oh my God. It's kind of funny" because I guess.
>
> Steve (Asian male, 22): Because it's true.
>
> Ken (Asian male, 19): Stereotypes are based on some types of truth.
>
> Mark (Black male, 21): I think most stereotypes Tucker brings out are true. They are things that you don't usually think about or just say. But they are kind of true. . . . In general, of course you can't stereotype every single Black person, but I think Carter is supposed to be that average Black person from the ghetto.

Despite participants' emphasis on the fictional nature of *Rush Hour 2*, they perceived a sense of realism in its racial representations; few participants stated that racial stereotypes in the film were unreal or incorrect. Although many participants claimed that they could distinguish between fiction and reality, we observed strong continuity between the film's representations of race and participants' general opinions about racial traits.

As participants' comments suggest, many revealed (likely without realizing it) that they thought many of the stereotypes expressed in the film were based on truth.

Throughout the focus group discussions, many participants displayed a blurring of the distinction between the fictional characters and the actors who play them, using Lee and Chan, or Carter and Tucker interchangeably. One White participant implied that Black stereotypes in *Rush Hour 2* are likely to be true because Chris Tucker (as an actor) plays off of stereotypes and he makes jokes about his own race. As Jhally and Lewis note, fictional media are simultaneously real and unreal and therefore have a significant impact on how we perceive the social world.[45] Fiske argues that realism in the media encourages viewers to incorporate on-screen attitudes and beliefs into the real world. Although it is beyond the scope of our study to determine whether participants of our study transformed *Rush Hour 2*'s racial characterizations into their everyday common sense, we found evidence that the movie influenced how participants made sense of racial differences.[46] We observed several incidents in which participants used *Rush Hour 2* as a reference to validate their own actual racial beliefs.

> Amy (White female, 20): It was funny, because in the outtakes, Jackie Chan got his lines wrong, and Chris Tucker's phone goes off, and he's like, "No, brother, get off the phone. Get off the phone." The outtakes almost played into the stereotypes and it's the actual people, not their characters. I don't know if that was a very politically correct thing for me to say.

The sense of realism participants perceived in *Rush Hour 2* has ideological effects because it authenticates the racial stereotypes in the film and grants them an objective status. We claim that a comedy like *Rush Hour 2* can contribute to viewer's sense of the real and foster the believability of different racial characteristics. Although not all participants stated explicitly that the film's stereotypes are based on truth, most of them hesitated to claim that they were false, confessing that their first-hand experience of different races is limited. We argue that the humorous portrayal of racial traits and the sense of realism in *Rush Hour 2* encouraged participants to see or seek "true" components in racial stereotypes rather than to challenge or argue against the exaggerated and totalizing nature of stereotypes. Most participants in all three racial focus groups agreed that there are certain characteristics about different racial groups that are more common than others and that the film simply exaggerated these traits to make them funny and entertaining. In addition, the participants of all three racial groups rarely talked about White stereotypes while preoccupied with minority stereotypes. Although participants identified several jokes about White people in the film, they did not see a strong association between Whiteness and stereotypes. In the general discussion of racial stereotypes, participants of all races infrequently mentioned stereotypes associated with Whites. Our study suggests that *Rush Hour 2* successfully promotes a sense of normality of Whiteness among viewers while encouraging them to see non-whites as racially marked and different.

Conclusion

The fact that almost none of our focus group participants were offended by *Rush Hour 2*'s explicit racial jokes is revealing but potentially misleading. Viewers' claims that racial stereotyping in comedy is funny, inoffensive, and therefore acceptable do not automatically establish that it is harmless. Racial stereotypes in comedy are problematic precisely because they help validate racial differences through humor, thus rendering them natural and unchallengeable. Inoffensiveness in comedy is a necessary condition for the naturalization of racial differences because if overly antagonistic racist remarks or assumptions were presented in ways that were offensive, they would likely trigger an oppositional reading, resulting in a straightforward rejection and critical evaluation of the cultural construction of racial differences. Because racial stereotypes in comedy rarely offend the audiences and are presented in an enjoyable way, audiences are able to naturalize specific knowledge about racial minorities without resistance. The generic conventions and textual devices of comedy ensure that viewers actively consume and derive pleasure from racial jokes and stereotypes without critical and interrogative engagement with them. Comedy ultimately controls and limits audiences' critical reflection of potentially racist characterizations, thereby making viewers susceptible to the beliefs of racial difference. Our study suggests that not only do different racial audiences enjoy racial jokes and humor in comedy but they are also much more inclined to see truth in racial stereotypes than to cast doubt on them.

D. "'Indians on TV (and Netflix)': The Comedic Trajectory of Aziz Ansari," Bhoomi K. Thakore and Bilal Hussain

Introduction

In the fourth episode of the first season of Aziz Ansari's Netflix series, *Master of None*, the comedian directly addresses a range of issues faced by non-white performers in US popular media today. The episode starts with a montage of reductive and arguably offensive representations of South Asian and Indian Americans from the last several decades—the overt caricature of actor Fisher Stevens playing an Indian engineer in the 1988 film *Short Circuit*, the character Zack Morris from the television show *Saved by the Bell* speaking in a heavily-accented Indian "brown voice," and spokesperson Ashton Kutcher using both stereotypes to imitate a fictional Bollywood producer in "brownface" for a Popchips television commercial.[47] In the episode, Ansari's character, Dev Shah, traverses the world of casting, finding that producers only want him to fill token roles or play to stereotypes. By the episode's end, he is forced to choose between his integrity and playing a brown-voiced reboot of the immigrant character Balki from the 1980s sitcom *Perfect Strangers*.

Upon its release, *Master of None* was immediately met with acclaim, as critics noted that, "it picks apart the social conventions of [Ansari's] generation, [and] ponders the insidiousness of racism and sexism in entertainment."[48] However, the series' critical voice represents a significant departure from that of Ansari's previous work. Historically, Ansari relied less on his South Asian identity and experiences, and instead emphasized black cultural stereotypes in his performances. In this essay, we examine this previous stage of Ansari's career, specifically considering how he marked himself as ethnically "other" than white, drawing upon what Kristen Warner describes as the Hollywood tendency to employ superficially diverse casting strategies as "signifiers of historical progress in the struggle of televisual racial representation" that nonetheless avoid deep, critical engagement with "social and cultural specificity."[49] Forgoing a robust engagement with South Asian culture, Ansari in his early career instead drew upon his non-white identity to appropriate and re-articulate black culture to mass audiences. In doing so, Ansari played off the long-standing Hollywood tradition of ethnically marginalized comedians appropriating black culture in order to normalize themselves and appeal to commercially desirable middle-class white viewers. As Michael Rogin argues in his study of blackface comedy in the 1920s, marginalized Jewish and Irish performers often found commercial success by physically embodying blackness in order to safely deliver white audiences the perceived

Dev (Aziz Ansari) reacts in disgust at being offered the role of a stereotyped Indian in an American sitcom.

pleasures of African American culture.[50] Prior to *Master of None*, Ansari's liminal position as neither black nor white allowed him to engage in a similar dynamic.

Ansari, of course, does not don blackface in his performances. His early career, nonetheless, was marked by playful references to black culture and relatively little reflection on his own identity position. The expansion of distribution channels for comedy, alongside the "mainstreaming" of popular discourse about race in America, however, have encouraged a new turn in his humor. Ansari has recently engaged his own identity politics more explicitly and critically. We argue that Ansari's performance in *Master of None* represents a shift both in the comedian's approach to race and in industrial strategies of representing identity on American television as a means of addressing a more engaged and multicultural audience.

Race and Popular Television Comedy

Historical representations of non-whites in popular media and culture have traditionally relied on stereotypes and caricatures.[51] These stereotypes are not static but have changed over time based on social, political, and economic forces that determine the ways in which ethnic groups fall above or below each other in the racial hierarchy.[52] This hierarchy itself is also ever-changing. For example, the Irish and Italians were once considered "non-white" in US society but, through social integration and intermarriage, are now a major part of "white" America.[53] In the same way that racial formations inform social stereotypes, so too do they inform the creation and perpetuation of stereotypes in comedy.

Historically, South Asian stereotypes (in society and on screen) have generally taken one of two extreme forms—1) the foreign immigrant, often represented as a convenience store owner or taxi driver (such as *The Simpsons'* Apu), and 2) the assimilated professional, often represented as a doctor or scientist (such as *The Big Bang Theory*'s Raj). These two representations reflect the immigration trends of South Asians in the United States. The first group of immigrants, comprised of highly educated individuals with technical expertise, emigrated during the 1960s and '70s.[54] These South Asian immigrants are often perceived as "model minorities" for their high education levels and occupational status.[55] The second group, whose demographics have increased in the US since the 1980s, are much more diverse in their educational and professional backgrounds.[56] Today many South Asians in the US are the children or family members of naturalized US citizens, as are Ansari's characters in *Parks and Recreation* and *Master of None*.

When considering this trajectory of South Asian stereotypes in popular media, it is important to acknowledge the role of commercial mass media that allow these characters to make it on screen in the first place.[57] The economics and aesthetics of screen media encourage the adoption of simplified, easily identifiable character types. Given the need for efficiency of production and the requirement of wide intelligibility, mainstream commercial media productions often cut corners by putting forth such stereotypes. As Charles Ramírez Berg argues, stereotypes "require little or no introduction or explanation, and because they are so quickly and completely comprehended as signs, stereotypes are an extremely cheap and cost-effective means of telling" a Hollywood narrative.[58]

Although the economic logic of Hollywood still fosters stereotypes in popular comedy, contemporary post-racial discourses have increasingly incentivized the kinds of representational strategies embraced by Ansari for much of his early career. As Kristen Warner notes, watchdog groups have emerged to challenge both stereotypes and minority underrepresentation in popular media, often threatening to call for revenue-killing boycotts. In response, many producers have moved toward a post-racial "blindcasting" model in which roles are written without specific racial expectations for the actor. In such cases, media tends to become diverse but fails to engage critically with culturally specific minority issues. As we discuss below, blindcasting has placed Ansari in myriad supporting roles (such as his character in the film *30 Minutes or Less*) that preclude any significant dialogue with the politics of South Asian representation. When Ansari did engage with performance elements related to identity politics, he tended to draw from black, not Indian, cultural signifiers, as in the cases of *Funny People*'s Randy Springs or *Parks and Recreation*'s Tom Haverford.

There are, of course, occasional texts, including *Master of None*, that transcend the limitations of both the stereotype and post-racial blindcast models. At times this is achieved through the sheer force of a non-white performer's will and talent, as in the case of Eddie Murphy's controversial, star-making turn on *Saturday Night Live* in the 1980s. Lampooning stereotypes and provoking debates on race in America, Murphy, according to Racquel Gates, combined "social critique and crossover success."[59] Even Murphy, however, required some help from his industrial context. *Saturday Night Live*, although an NBC show, was aimed explicitly at a younger, hipper, and smaller audience than the vast majority of network programming at the time, reducing incentives to invoke stereotypes in pursuit of mass viewership. *Master of None*, emerging in the post-network online space of Netflix, represents Ansari's move into such a relatively open artistic and economic space. Freed from the broader audience expectations of *Parks and Recreation*, *Master of None* targets a smaller, younger, more diverse, and presumably more progressive, audience with a representational strategy that includes a diverse cast and brings specific attention to the South Asian American experience.

Ansari in Television and Film

Prior to *Master of None*, Ansari's comedy had long downplayed his South Asian and Muslim identity, often relying instead on the comedic incongruence between his ethnicity and the centrality of black culture in his humor. This is particularly true of his stand-up comedy. For example, Ansari's 2010 hour-long stand-up special *Intimate Moments for a Sensual Evening* features bits about his fondness for hip-hop culture, riffing on artists like Kanye West and R. Kelly. This comedic misalignment of ethnic identity and subject matter was most acutely present in Ansari's performance as Tom Haverford on the NBC show, *Parks and Recreation* (2009–2014). The show began in 2009 as a "mockumentary" sitcom focusing on the everyday activities of the Parks Department of the fictional rural town of Pawnee, Indiana. The staff of Pawnee's Parks Department includes South Carolina–native Tom Haverford, who aspires to rise in the ranks of government without really trying. As the seasons progress, Tom turns into a business mogul, starting ventures including "Entertainment 720," a hip-hop inflected media and marketing conglomerate, "Tommy's Closet," a clothing store where boys could "rent-a-swag," and a proposed animated series *Tommy and the Foxx* with Jamie Foxx. Although Tom displays a deep, diverse knowledge of black culture, his character rarely appears influenced by Indian American, Muslim, or immigrant experiences.

In the fourth season, on the episode "Pawnee Rangers," Tom and office coworker Donna (played by black comedienne Retta) kick off their 2011 "Treat Yo Self" day of celebration. On this day, Tom walks in the office with DJ Bluntz, a black man playing music from a large boom box. He shouts, "DJ Bluntz is in the building! Here to announce that Tom Haverford is in the building!" Tom shouts, "Oh! One two, One two! Donatella!" Tom walks up to Donna, hands her three cupcakes in a pink box and says, "Three words: Treat—Yo—Self." Each cupcake is covered in frosting that spells out one of the words. The interaction between Tom and Donna draws its humor from the South Asian (or racially ambiguous) Tom excitedly appropriating hip-hop slang, a dynamic that continues across much of the series.

In "Pawnee Rangers," Tom plays a bridging role between Donna and Ben Wyatt (played by white actor Adam Scott). While Donna represents a stereotypically bold and brash black femininity, Ben embodies a hegemonic whiteness often understood as "mainstream" in US commercial culture. This stark dichotomy is highlighted when Donna suggests taking Ben along on "Treat Yo Self" day. Tom is against the suggestion, holding her hand and referring to Donna as his "Nubian princess." As a non-white "other" character, Tom's presence softens the scene's potentially stark racial binary. He plays an in-between character that ultimately allows both Ben and the viewer to enter into Donna's world. In doing so, Tom gives the scene a multicultural inflection while implicitly orienting its perspective to appeal to a broadcast audience inclusive of a large, prized white subgroup.

Ansari's tendency to play characters that fail to engage deeply with his own identity can be seen in a variety of mainstream films, including *Funny People* (2009), *Get Him to the Greek* (2010), and *This is the End* (2013). In *30 Minutes or Less* (2011), for example, Ansari plays Chet, a substitute teacher on a mission to help the main character Nick (played by Jesse Eisenberg). Typical of his film work, Ansari plays the "cool nerd" that is a friend or coworker but is not given agency to express his identity in any substantive way. He adds a sense of nonspecific multicultural content to the story but does so from a background position. Even on the movie poster for *30 Minutes or Less*, Ansari stands behind Eisenberg, who occupies the center of the image. Chet is one of many thinly developed Ansari characters who, tellingly, are given names that do not allude to either Indian or Muslim heritage (e.g., Eugene, Matty, Tom, Marcus). In order to find a place in mainstream Hollywood fare that avoided clichéd Indian roles, Ansari gravitated toward blindcast roles, in which superficial diversity overcomes the ugliest stereotypes but fails to allow for deep engagement with minority experience.

Very few Indian American and Muslim American comedians have found the same level of mainstream success as Ansari, who has thrived for much of his career in blindcast roles and in playing supporting characters to white protagonists. However, a number of Indian American and Muslim American comedians, including Hasan Minhaj, Hari Kondabolu, and Dean Obeidallah, are finding success on the margins of popular American comedy today. In contrast to Ansari's pre–*Master of None* work discussed above, these comedians explicitly engage the politics of mediated representation with progressive, comedic takes on ethnicity, identity, and citizenship.

For example, Indian American comic Hari Kondabolu, a writer and performer with appearances on *The Late Show with David Letterman*, *Conan*, and *Jimmy Kimmel Live*, regularly addressed these and other issues from a minority perspective on FX's now-cancelled late-night show *Totally Biased with W. Kamau Bell*. In a 2012 bit, Kondabolu sarcastically lauds the proliferation of Indians on television, noting that all he had to go on growing up was the Indian convenience store clerk Apu on *The Simpsons*. Kondabolu highlights the offensive incongruence between Hank Azaria's whiteness and his brown-voice performance of Apu, saying that if he saw Azaria do Apu's voice at a party, Kondabolu would "kick the shit out of him." Even Indian American comedians that have occupied the same mainstream spaces as Ansari on broadcast, such as Mindy Kaling on *The Mindy Project*, see limited success. Kaling's show ran for three years to critical acclaim but low ratings before eventually moving from FOX to the streaming network Hulu. Again, it is in these newer streaming spaces occupied by "networks" like Hulu, Amazon, and Netflix where Ansari and other actors of color have been able to engage more deeply with their identity politics.

Conclusion

In discussing the Netflix program *BoJack Horseman*, Matt Sienkiewicz and Nick Marx argue that the show's genre-bending aesthetic indicates that the online streaming giant has shaken off "the restraints of longstanding industry lore and even the limitations of blunt instruments such as genre conventions and traditional demographics."[60] Ansari's turn to identity politics in *Master of None* perhaps points to a similar development for Netflix in the realm of racial representation. Free to pursue smaller, more targeted taste cultures and social groups than does broadcast television by virtue of its online distribution, *Master of None* breaks new ground in Ansari's comedic portrayal of South Asian American life. While Ansari's show does not break into the critical realm that more progressive South Asian performers like Kondabolu have gone into, his character establishes Ansari as a South Asian American actor who is aware of the inequality faced by all people of color in a biased, Eurocentric America.

The difference between the broadcast and Netflix versions of Ansari's approach to South Asian identity can be seen in the very different romantic lives of *Parks and Recreation*'s Tom and *Master of None*'s Dev. Both Tom and Dev have long-term relationships with white women. However, in the second season episode of *Parks and Recreation*, "Tom's Divorce," the interracial dynamic is subverted through the device of a "green card marriage" in its comedic storyline. Tom is presented as the empowered half of the couple, with his faux-wife, the white Canadian Wendy, taking up the position of the immigrant. There is, certainly, something very funny about the way in which the episode defies audience expectations and works to dislodge discourses of immigration from those of brownness or blackness. However, in doing so, it takes what could be a critical engagement with the identity politics surrounding South Asian assimilation and replaces it with a series of jokes in which Tom's Indianness is, at best, an amusing background element.

In *Master of None*, by contrast, Ansari's Dev uses his relationship with a white woman, Rachel, to explicitly explore his own ethnicity and the politics of interracial romance. In a scene where the two discuss Rachel's dating life, she names off the ethnicities of previous lovers: "White. White. White. White. Half-Asian. And you," referring to Dev. He responds, "So that half-Asian guy, he was kind of a gateway drug to me?" "I guess so. Who knows what'll be next?" Rachel ponders. Dev snaps back, "I do! White guy!" Although meant humorously, Dev's retort highlights the persistence of whiteness as a structuring ideology in modern romance. The scene comments insightfully on the power dynamics often embedded in interracial relationships, particularly those between whites and nonwhites. Dev's romantic relationship with Rachel succeeds in acknowledging an oft-ignored aspect of Indian American experience, though it perhaps does little to topple the longstanding hegemonic whiteness of American mainstream comedy.

Ansari has come a long way from Tom Haverford on *Parks and Recre-*

ation. Not only has he evolved into his character on *Master of None*, but he has also shifted in his conversations on the press circuit. In spots on such programs as *The Late Show with Stephen Colbert, Conan,* and *The Tonight Show with Jimmy Fallon,* Ansari openly discusses issues of diversity and South Asian stereotypes in the media. While watching this side of Ansari is refreshing and equally entertaining, it illustrates the hindrances we have examined throughout this paper, ones centered on why it took so long for Ansari to publically dive into longstanding critical issues. While South Asian and Muslim stand-up comedians such as Kondabolu and Obeidallah have been addressing these for years, Ansari is late to the party.

Netflix and *Master of None* represent a step forward in popular, mainstream depictions of Indian American life. Mocking the tropes of network-era television and defying the culturally neutral diversity model of post-network blindcasting, Ansari's Dev exists somewhere between the limiting stereotypes embodied by Apu and the critical comedy of comedians like Kondabolu and Obeidallah. Netflix, as an aspiring global distributor that combines commercial network ambitions with more adventurous aesthetic sensibilities, is a place for such a character to exist, outside of the mainstream media's (white) gaze. Although beginning by working with the same representational tactics as myriad ethnic American comedians before him, Ansari's increasingly critical sensibilities today offer unique insight into the evolving relationship between comedy, American identity politics, and the future of commercial media entertainment.

Notes

1. In the context of this discussion I use the term *enabled* in a very particular way: to specify the potential articulations of television texts with the expression of issues, debates, and moods operating in the society; to identify established traditions and practices; and to identify frames, perspectives, and positions operating in the social construction of meanings.
2. Dates and Barlow, *Split Image*; Schulman, "Laughing Across the Color Line."
3. Schulman, "Laughing Across the Color Line," 2.
4. Dates and Barlow, *Split Image*.
5. Schulman, "Laughing Across the Color Line," 5.
6. Schulman, "Laughing Across the Color Line," 4.
7. Schulman, "Laughing Across the Color Line," 5.
8. Harris, "Late Night's Real Problem."
9. Hall, *Representation*, 258.
10. Most one-hour-drama writing staffs gather in the same way, but there are exceptions. Because dramatic stories do not rely on the group humor dynamics prevalent in sitcoms, some one-hour dramas do not utilize the traditional writers'

room. Instead, they rely on one-on-one meetings between the writer who has an idea for an episode and the head writer/executive producer, who helps the writer shape the idea before assigning him/her the script to write.

11. During the 2008–2009 season, Mara Brock Akil, the creator and executive producer of *The Game*, a spin-off of the UPN/CW show *Girlfriends*, agreed to allow the author to observe the writers' room, with no rules, every day for two weeks. During this time, the author was allowed access to the entire writing staff, cast readings of new scripts, and production rehearsals on the stage. It is also worth noting that, as the photograph of the writers demonstrates, this writing staff was equally split between black and non-black writers. While this is common with black-themed shows, the dynamic is never repeated on mainstream shows, which tend to have one writer of color on a writing staff.

12. Kravets, "Court Rejects *Friends* Trash Talk Case."

13. Kravets, "Court Rejects *Friends* Trash Talk Case."

14. Kravets, "Court Rejects *Friends* Trash Talk Case."

15. Powdermaker, *Hollywood, the Dream Factory*.

16. Box Office Prophets, *Rush hour 2*.

17. Internet Movie Database. "All-Time USA Box Office."

18. Hilton and von Hippel, "Stereotypes," 283.

19. Hilton and von Hippel, "Stereotypes," 283.

20. Casey et al., *Television Studies*; Wilson et al., *Racism, Sexism, and the Media*.

21. Bowes, "Only When I Laugh"; King, *Film Comedy*.

22. King, *Film Comedy*, 129.

23. Denzin, *Reading Race*.

24. Malanowski, "Colorblind Buddies in Black and White."

25. Haggins, *Laughing Mad*; King, *Film Comedy*.

26. Bowes, "Only When I Laugh"; Hall, "The Whites of their Eyes."

27. Bogle, *Toms, Coons, Mulattoes, Mammies, and Bucks*; Hall, "The Whites of their Eyes"; King, *Film Comedy*; Means Coleman, *African American Viewers*; Omi, *In Living Color*; Wilson et al., *Racism, Sexism, and the Media*.

28. Omi, *In Living Color*; Hall, "The Whites of their Eyes."

29. Omi, *In Living Color*, 121.

30. Schulman, "Laughing Across the Color Barrier."

31. Schulman, "Laughing Across the Color Barrier," 6.

32. Bogle, *Toms, Coons, Mulattoes, Mammies, and Bucks*, 182.

33. King, *Film Comedy*.

34. Means Coleman, *African American Viewers*, 130.

35. Myers and Williamson, "Race Talk."

36. Essed, *Understanding Everyday Racism*; Myers and Williamson, "Race Talk"; Van Dijk, *Prejudice in Discourse*; Van Dijk, *Communicating Racism*.

37. Hall, "The Spectacle of the 'Other.'"

38. Schauer, *Profiles, Probabilities, and Stereotypes*.

39. Ogunnaike, "The Perks and Pitfalls," E1.

40. Omi, *In Living Color*.

41. Lo, "Double Negations," 474.

42. Teo, *Hong Kong Cinema*.

43. King, *Film Comedy*, 149.

44. Marchetti, *Ethnicity, The Cinema and Cultural Studies*, 279.

45. Jhally and Lewis, *Enlightened Racism*.

46. Fiske, *Television Culture*.

47. Dave, *Indian Accents*.

48. Sims, *"Master of None."*

49. Warner, *The Cultural Politics of Colorblind Casting*, 3.

50. Rogin, *Blackface, White Noise*, 58.

51. Beltrán and Fojas, *Mixed Race Hollywood*; Chito Childs, *Fade to Black and White*; Entman and Rojecki, *The Black Image in the White Mind*; Gray, *Watching Race*; Hall, *Representation*; Jhally and Lewis, *Enlightened Racism*; Vera and Gordon, *Screen Saviors*.

52. Omi and Winant, *Racial Formation in the United States*.

53. Gans, "Symbolic Ethnicity."

54. Takaki, *Strangers from a Different Shore*; Prashad, *The Karma of Brown Folk*; Wu, *Yellow*.

55. Takaki, *Strangers from a Different Shore*; Tuan, *Forever Foreigners*.

56. Maira, *Desis in the House*; Prashad, *The Karma of Brown Folk*; Purkayastha, *Negotiating Ethnicity*; Shankar, *Desi Land*.

57. Bagdikian, *The New Media Monopoly*; McChesney, *The Problem of the Media*.

58. Berg, *Latino Images in Film*, 42.

59. Gates, "Bringing the Black," 153.

60. Marx, "Industry Lore and Algorithmic Programming on Netflix"; Sienkiewicz, "Neighed to Order: The Case of *Bojack Horseman*."

Works Cited

Bagdikian, Ben. *The New Media Monopoly*. Boston: Beacon Press, 2004.

Beltrán, Mary, and Camilla Fojas. *Mixed Race Hollywood*. New York: New York University Press, 2008.

Berg, Charles R. *Latino Images in Film: Stereotypes, Subversion, and Resistance*. Austin: The University of Texas Press, 2002.

Bogle, Donald. *Toms, Coons, Mulattoes, Mammies, and Bucks: An Interpretive History of Blacks in American Films*. Bloomsbury Publishing, 2001.

Bowes, Mick. "Only When I Laugh." In *Understanding Television*, edited by Andrew Goodwin and Garry Whannel, 128–140. London: Routledge, 1990.

Box Office Prophets. *Rush hour 2*. One of Us Inc. Retrieved March 3, 2005. http://www.boxofficeprophets.com/tickermaster/listing.cfm?TMID=169:Rush_Hour_2.

Casey, Bernadette, Neil Casey, Ben Calvert, Liam French, and Justin Lewis. *Television Studies: The Key Concepts*. London: Routledge, 2002.

Chito Childs, Erica. *Fade to Black and White: Interracial Images in Popular Culture*. Lanham, MD: Rowman and Littlefield, 2009.

Dates, Jannette, and William Barlow. *Split Image: African Americans in the Mass Media*. Washington, DC: Howard University Press, 1990.

Dave, Shilpa. *Indian Accents: Brown Voice and Racial Performance in American Television and Film*. Champaign: University of Illinois Press, 2013.

Denzin, Norman K. *Reading Race: Hollywood And The Cinema Of Racial Violence*. London: Sage, 2002.

Entman, Robert M., and Andrew Rojecki. *The Black Image in the White Mind: Media and Race in America*. University of Chicago Press, 2000.

Essed, Philomena. *Understanding Everyday Racism: An Interdisciplinary Theory*. London: Sage, 1991.

Feagin, Joe R. *The White Racial Frame*. New York: Routledge, 2009.

Fiske, John. *Television Culture*. New York: Routledge, 1987.

Gates, Racquel. "Bringing the Black: Eddie Murphy and African American Humor on *Saturday Night Live*." In *Saturday Night Live and American TV*, edited by Ron Becker, Nick Marx, and Matt Sienkiewicz, 151–172. Bloomington: Indiana University Press, 2013.

Gans, Herbert. "Symbolic Ethnicity: The Future of Ethnic Groups and Cultures in America." *Ethnic and Racial Studies* 2, no. 1 (1979): 1–20.

Gray, Herman. *Watching Race: Television and the Struggle for Blackness*. Minneapolis: University of Minnesota Press, 2004.

Haggins, Bambi. "Laughing Mad: The Black Comedian's Place in American Comedy of the Post–Civil Rights Era." In *Hollywood Comedians: The Film Reader*, edited by Frank Krutnik, 171–186. London: Routledge, 1995.

Hall, Stuart. *Representation: Cultural Representations and Signifying Practices*. Thousand Oaks, CA: Sage, 1997.

———. "The Spectacle of the 'Other.'" In *Representation: Cultural Representations and Signifying Practices*, edited by Stuart Hall, 223–290. London: Sage, 1997.

———. "The Whites of their Eyes: Racist Ideologies and the Media." In *The Media Reader*, edited by Manuel Alvarado and John O. Thompson, 7–23. London: BFI, 1990.

Harris, Lynn. "Late Night's Real Problem." *Salon*, January 10, 2010. http://www.salon.com/mwt/feature/2010/01/10/women_writers_late_night/index.html.

Henderson, Felicia D. "The Culture Behind Closed Doors: Issues of Gender and Race in the Writers' Room." *Cinema Journal* 50 no.2 (2011): 145–152.

Hilton, James L., and William von Hippel. "Stereotypes" *Annual Review of Psychology* 47 (1996): 237–271.

Internet Movie Database. "All-Time USA Box Office." Amazon. Retrieved March 3, 2005. http://www.imdb.com/.

Jhally, Sut, and Justin Lewis. *Enlightened Racism: The Cosby Show, Audiences, and the Myth of the American Dream*. Oxford: Westview Press, 1992.

King, Geoff. *Film Comedy*. London: Wallflower Press, 1992.

Kravets, David. "Court Rejects *Friends* Trash Talk Case." *Associated Press*, April 20, 2006. http://www.breitbart.com/article.php?id=D8H3SVKoM&show_article=1 (accessed May 8, 2008).

Lo, Kwai-Cheung. "Double Negations: Hong Kong Cultural Identity in Hollywood's Transnational Representations." *Cultural Studies* 15 (2001): 464–485.

Maira, Sunaina. *Desis in the House: Indian American Youth Culture in New York City*. Philadelphia: Temple University Press, 2002.

Malanowski, Jamie. "Colorblind Buddies in Black and White." *New York Times*, November 10, 2002. http://www.nytimes.com/2002/11/10/movies/colorblind-buddies-in-black-and-white.html?mcubz=3.

Marchetti, Gina. "Ethnicity, the Cinema and Cultural Studies." In *Unspeakable Images: Ethnicity and the American Cinema*, edited by Lester D. Friedman, 277–307. Urbana: University of Illinois Press, 1991

Marx, Nick. "Industry Lore and Algorithmic Programming on Netflix." *Flow* 21, no.6 (2015). http://www.flowjournal.org/2015/04/industry-lore-and-algorithmic-programming-on-netflix/.

McChesney, Robert. *The Problem of the Media: US Communication Politics in the 21st Century*. New York: Monthly Review Press, 2004.

Means Coleman, Robin R. *African American Viewers and the Black Situation Comedy: Situating Racial Humor*. New York: Garland, 2000.

Myers, Kristen A., and Passion Williamson. "Race Talk: The Perpetuation of Racism through Private Discourse." *Race and Society* 4, no. 1 (2001): 3–26.

Ogunnaike, Lola. "The Perks and Pitfalls of a Ruthless-Killer Role." *New York Times*, October 13, 2003.

Omi, Michael. "In Living Color: Race and American Culture." In *Cultural Politics in Contemporary America*, edited by Ian Angus and Sut Jhally, 111–122. London: Routledge, 1989.

Omi, Michael, and Howard Winant. *Racial Formation in the United States: From the 1960s to the 1990s*. 2nd ed. New York: Routledge, 1994.

Prashad, Vijay. *The Karma of Brown Folk*. Minneapolis: University of Minnesota Press, 2000.

Powdermaker, Hortense. *Hollywood, the Dream Factory: An Anthropologist Looks at the Movie-Makers*. Boston: Little, Brown, 1950.

Purkayastha, Bandana. *Negotiating Ethnicity: Second-Generation South Asian Americans Traverse a Transnational World*. New Brunswick: Rutgers University Press, 2005.

Rogin, Michael. *Blackface, White Noise: Jewish Immigrants in the Hollywood Melting Pot*. Berkeley: University of California Press, 1996.

Shankar, Shalini. *Desi Land: Teen Culture, Class, and Success in Silicon Valley*. Durham, NC: Duke University Press, 2008.

Schauer, Frederick. *Profiles, Probabilities, and Stereotypes*. Cambridge: Belknap Press, 2003.

Schulman, Norma M. "Laughing Across the Color Line: *In Living Color*." *Journal of Popular Film and Television* 1 (Spring 1992): 2–8.

Sienkiewicz, Matt. "Neighed to Order: The Case of *Bojack Horseman*." *Flow* 21, no.6 (2015). http://www.flowjournal.org/2015/04/neighed-to-order/.

Sims, David. "*Master of None* Is Aziz Ansari's Best Work Yet." *The Atlantic*, November 5, 2015. http://www.theatlantic.com/entertainment/archive/2015/11/master-of-none-is-aziz-ansaris-best-work-yet/414439/.

Takaki, Ronald. *Strangers from a Different Shore: A History of Asian Americans*. Boston: Little, Brown, 1989.

Teo, Stephen. *Hong Kong Cinema: The Extra Dimension*. London: British Film Institute, 1997.

Tuan, Mia. *Forever Foreigners or Honorary Whites? The Asian Ethnic Experience Today*. New Brunswick: Rutgers University Press, 1999.

Van Dijk, Teun. *Prejudice in Discourse: An Analysis of Ethnic Prejudice in Cognition and Conversation*. Philadelphia: John Benjamins, 1984.

———. *Communicating Racism: Ethnic Prejudice in Thought and Talk*. London: Sage, 1987.

Vera, Hernán, and Andrew Gordon. *Screen Saviors: Hollywood Fictions of Whiteness*. Lanham, MD: Rowman and Littlefield, 2003.

Warner, Kristen J. *The Cultural Politics of Colorblind Casting*. New York: Routledge, 2015.

Wilson, Clint C., Felix Guitierrez, and Lena Chao. *Racism, Sexism, and the Media: The Rise of Class Communication in Multicultural America*. Thousand Oaks, CA: Sage, 2003.

Wu, Frank. *Yellow: Race in American beyond Black and White*. New York: Basic Books, 2002.

7.

Gender & Sexuality

INT. COURTHOUSE — DAY

A JURY of twelve sits around a table on a hot summer's day. Tension fills the room. The FOREMAN rises to speak.

FOREMAN

Ok, so it's got to be a 12–0 vote either way, that's the law. So, gentlemen, raise your hands, if you think that Amy Schumer is not hot enough to be on television.

The men begin to raise their hands. They eye each other with suspicion.

FOREMAN (cont'd)

One, two, three, four, five, six, seven, eight, nine, ten, eleven. That's eleven votes for Amy Schumer, not hot enough for television. Anybody voting the other way?

One man, JUROR 12, raises his hand reluctantly. JUROR 3 looks on in disbelief.

JUROR 3

Are you kidding me?

JUROR 12

I think she might be hot enough.

The remaining jurors explode in anger.

* * *

This sketch from *Inside Amy Schumer*, part of an episode-length parody of *Twelve Angry Men* in which "jurors" satirically debate the comedian's attractiveness versus her funniness, presents a simple, yet salient, critique of the comedy world's gender bias. "Hotness" is rarely, if ever, a criterion through which male comedians are deemed worthy of being on screen. If comedians from W. C. Fields to Woody Allen to Chris Farley are any evidence, there might actually be an inverse relationship between male comedians' looks and their funniness. Female comedians are not often afforded that option. They must first meet the media's already-distorted standards for beauty, the sketch suggests, before even getting a chance to have their funniness debated by a mostly male jury of their "peers." This dynamic is of crucial importance to the student or theorist of comedy, as it dispels the notion that success in the business of commercial humor is tied directly to pure comedic meritocracy. Power matters in the world of comedy, and power, in comedy as anywhere else in life, is deeply intertwined with gender norms and expectations.

The entirely male makeup of the jury in the sketch highlights this reality in a stark but very effective fashion. Men are much more often in positions of power in the entertainment, advertising, and criticism communities that decide which women will be on screen, the financial value of their programs, and the opinions viewers ascribe to them. Men often not only stack the metaphorical jury but also serve as judge and executioner, adjudicating the terms of comedy's gendered hierarchy and banishing those who defy it.

From the perspective of the more formalized comedy theories of this volume's first five chapters, it is easy to assume that all are welcome to joke equally, and the best jokers will rise to the top of the industry. But starting with the previous chapter on race and ethnicity, we suggested that one's identity position—and now here, specifically, one's sexuality and gender—creates powerful variations in how comedy is both performed and processed at the individual level. In other words, the same joke won't be funny to everyone equally. Therefore, the American entertainment industries must consciously decide who gets to make comedy and which audiences they will target. *Schumer* is calling out and mocking this process, asking its audience to consider, and laugh at, the existence of unjust double standards. *Schumer*'s critique is made all the more trenchant by its place on Comedy Central, a network that targets the heterosexual young male viewership long assumed to be the natural audience of comedic media.

Schumer is a paradigmatic example of what Kathleen Rowe Karlyn describes in the first essay of this chapter as the "unruly woman," a female comedian who transgresses both physical and verbal norms for female propriety. Rowe examines Miss Piggy, The Muppets character whose body defies conventional beauty standards and whose comedic persona fits uneasily alongside traditional notions of femininity. Unruly women like Miss Piggy, Roseanne Barr, Leslie Jones, and Schumer expose the often unseen gender bias of how we understand comedy and arm viewers with the critical tools for combatting that bias.

Linda Mizejewski updates Rowe Karlyn's concept in order to examine the industrial and cultural forces dictating that female comedians must either be pretty (utilizing their comedic talents in roles as the objects of romantic pursuit) or funny (lampooning traditional feminine beauty). In many ways, the *Schumer* sketch combats this binary directly, arguing that female comedians can be both. It suggests, too, that the pretty/funny dichotomy is an entirely false one that limits the broad range of female comedic personae normally made available to male comedians. Mizejewski further deconstructs "pretty/funny" by using queerness as an additional critical lens in a case study of comedian Ellen DeGeneres. DeGeneres's uniquely comedic physical presence, she suggests, provides a site for the complex and sometimes contradictory intersections of feminist and queer discourses to be seen and discussed by a multitude of audiences.

Finally, Alfred L. Martin, Jr. adds an industrial perspective to this intersectional approach to comedy in his study of the BET sitcom *Let's Stay Together*. Considering the interplay of race, gender, and sexuality, Martin argues that producers often assume that African American comedy audiences will balk at depictions of gay black men. Historically, he suggests, these characters were omitted entirely from the TV landscape. Today, they find themselves trapped in the "generic closet," as gay black men are relegated to limited storylines in the relatively safe space of the black sitcom. Although television has made progress in many areas of its representational politics, Martin shows that comedy writers, often pressured by risk-averse producers, tend to employ one-off jokes and throwaway storylines when depicting black gayness.

A: *The Unruly Woman,* Kathleen Rowe Karlyn[i]

The figure of the unruly woman contains much potential for feminist appropriation, for rethinking how women are constructed as gendered subjects in the language of spectacle and the visual. The parodic excesses of the unruly woman and the comedic conventions surrounding her provide a space to "act out" the "dilemmas of femininity," in Mary Russo's words, to make not only "fantastic" and "incredible" but also laughable those tropes of femininity valorized by melodrama.[1] Russo asks in what

i. From Kathleen Rowe Karlyn, *The Unruly Woman: Gender and the Genres of Laughter*, 11-12, 26-31. Copyright © 1995. Courtesy of the University of Texas Press. All rights reserved.

sense women can produce and make spectacles of themselves *for* themselves. The unruly woman points to new ways of thinking about visibility as power. Masquerade concerns itself not only with a woman's ability to look, after all, but also with her ability to affect the terms on which she is seen.

Such a sense of spectacle differs from the one that shaped early feminist film theory. Granting that visual pleasure and power are inextricably bound, this position would see that relation as more historically determined, its terms as more mutable. It would argue that visual power flows in multiple directions and that the position of spectacle isn't necessarily one of weakness. Because public power is predicated largely on visibility, men have long understood the need to secure their power not only by looking but by being seen, or rather, by fashioning—as subject, as author, as artist—a spectacle of themselves. How might women use spectacle to disrupt that power and lay claim to their own?

The connection between spectacle making and power was clear in Hellenic Greece, where men played out their existence in a public sphere sharply demarcated from the invisible private sphere, in which women and slaves tended to the body. It was understood in early Christian culture which worshipped God through "graven images" and spectacular cathedrals. In Renaissance England, Elizabeth I consciously manipulated her image to consolidate her power; and throughout the courts of Europe, the upper-class body was celebrated by adorning it with sumptuous clothing. Yet as capitalism tightened the structure of the patriarchal family, Protestantism and the Enlightenment fostered a turn from the pleasure of the image toward visual austerity and utilitarianism. The sartorial flamboyance men shared with women through the eighteenth century became increasingly restricted to women. Women retained their attachment to spectacle, but a spectacle exiled to the private sphere and severed from the exercise of official power. One could argue, following Michel Foucault, that as power has become more dispersed, the need to display it has diminished; however, in a postmodern culture of the image and the simulacra, power also lies in possession and control *of* the visible.

I want to suggest that women might begin to reweave the web of visual power that already binds them by taking the unruly woman as a model—woman as rule-breaker, joke-maker, and public, bodily spectacle. . . . In acts of spectatorial unruliness, I believe, we might examine models of *returning* the male gaze, exposing and making a spectacle of the gazer, claiming the pleasure and power of making spectacles of ourselves, and beginning to negate our own invisibility in the public sphere.

* * *

In a 1,000-piece jigsaw puzzle of Jim Henson's Muppets, Miss Piggy's face, coquettishly tilted to one side, beams out from a group of close to twenty of the puppets. She stands behind her beloved frog Kermit who, as hero of the Muppets, occupies front row center and whose sympathetic presence sets the tone of their adventures. Yet Miss Piggy rises a full head above him to the visual center of the puzzle. This dominance over the apparent leader of the Muppets is central to Miss Piggy's persona. It is also central to a larger tradition of female unruliness—that of the woman on top—which resonates in her image.

As a group, Henson's puppets encompass a range of human and animal characteristics. Some, such as the old men Statler and Waldorf, are clearly human. Others, such as Kermit the Frog, Miss Piggy, and, of course, Animal, are clearly animal. However, the distinction between animal and human blurs in a sea of fuzzy textures, bright fabrics, and similar voices (spoken primarily by a handful of men). In fact, it seems irrelevant in the whimsical vision of their creator, who endowed his creatures with qualities that are meant to be seen as, above all, human. While Kermit may muse on the difficulties of being a frog ("It's not easy being green," he sings, in one of the most lyrical ballads in the classic Muppet repertoire), the source of that pain is really not his frogginess but his humanness, his awareness of how a certain alienation is the price of being human. (If it's possible to miss this point when Kermit sings the song, it certainly isn't when Frank Sinatra does.) And while such sensitivity and pain might seem reminiscent of the romantic male hero, Kermit's masculinity—even in his courtship of Miss Piggy—is never the focus of our attention. His gender is as unobtrusive as his attire, which, except on rare occasions, consists only of a subdued green, jester-like collar.

Indeed, at first glance, the distinction between female and male appears to be as irrelevant among Henson's puppets as the one between animal and human. Except for the humanoids, who are marked as humans by their unambiguous gendering as male or female, the rest of the puppets, the animals, are "generic" humans—that is, male. There is one important exception, however: Miss Piggy. As her name indicates, two aspects are basic to her identity: she is a "Miss," both the most strongly gendered of the main Muppet characters and the only female among them; she is also "Piggy." It is no accident that the most obviously gendered Muppet is a female, that the female is an animal, and that the animal is a pig. Gender is Miss Piggy's raison d'être, and the issues of sexuality in the Muppet world condense most extravagantly around her porcine body.[2]

Like her name, Miss Piggy's persona and her humor arise from the tension between two precariously combined qualities: an outrageously excessive, simpering, preening femininity and a wicked right hook. Miss Piggy's femininity is evident in her awareness of her "to-be-looked-at-ness." With cleavage-baring costumes, wigs, jewelry, coy and flirtatious body language (leg-crossing, hair-flouncing), she cultivates an appearance designed to appeal to males. She also uses her voice to enhance her femininity by adopting a mannered, whispered French. She calls herself "moi."

The essence of conventional femininity is the pursuit of heterosexual love, and wherever Miss Piggy is, the story of her love affair with Kermit is not far behind. A sequence in *The Muppet Movie* (1979) depicting the origin of their romance parodies the conventions of romantic love, from love at first sight to storybook weddings. Love is one of the few areas where Hollywood allows women to take charge, and the Muppets are no exception: Miss Piggy initiates her affair with Kermit. On stage, after establishing herself as female spectacle par excellence by winning a hometown beauty contest, she deploys her gaze like one of her famed karate chops when she first lays eyes on Kermit. The camera zooms in on his face in a point-of-view shot, as romantic music swells. A reverse shot shows a bright flash issuing from her eye, emphasizing not only the "sparkle" of love but the fact that she is the one who first looked. What follows is a montage of clichéd courting scenes, from slow-motion romps in flowery meadows, to rowing by waterfalls, to a rendezvous on a foggy London street, to a wedding. The sequence closes with the couple framed in a heart-shaped iris like the one made famous by *I Love Lucy*, while Miss Piggy screeches the finale of the love song, "Never Before and Never Again." In *The Kermit and Piggy Story* (1985), mostly songs and production numbers from *The Muppet Show* compiled for home video release, she and Kermit continue to spoof romantic love. As in the screwball comedy film, their declarations of love take the form of verbal sparring and actual screaming. Even the film's B-movie title is mock-heroic, casting their story in the context of the great love affairs of history, and the myths and movies they have generated.

At the same time, however, Miss Piggy's apparent femininity is constantly undermined aurally and visually. Her voice, a tremulous falsetto, is provided by a man, Frank Oz. Even more strikingly, Miss Piggy physically dwarfs Kermit. She is enormous beside him, and her body is voluptuously physical. In the courting sequence of *The Muppet Movie*, for example, the two lovers run to each other across a meadow. Instead of meeting in an embrace, Miss Piggy plows into Kermit and continues to bulldoze him across the field. When they finally fall to the ground and disappear beneath the eye of the camera, she is on top. Fat jokes are sprinkled through *The Ker-*

mit and Piggy Story, and while Miss Piggy isn't exactly fat she is undeniably large, and she loves to eat. One scene in the film shows the two characters seated at a cozy, romantic dinner. On the table in front of Kermit is a modest salad. Miss Piggy has a huge platter of spaghetti and meatballs. The film repeatedly detours from the dinner to their memories then returns to the dinner. With each return, the mountain of spaghetti gets smaller and smaller until it disappears. The movie ends with Miss Piggy bolting from the table to get pizza and assigning the dish-washing to Kermit.

As Judith Williamson has argued, Miss Piggy's unabashed hedonism subverts the ideologies of both capitalism and patriarchy. In *Miss Piggy's Guide to Life*, a mock self-help and etiquette book, Miss Piggy borrows *Cosmopolitan* magazine's style of using imperatives and checklists ("do this, check that") to tell women how to improve themselves. On the surface, she seems to accept the norms of femininity. But when she tells women how they can "snack" their way to "slimness," she abandons *Cosmo*'s line on deferred gratification in favor of the pleasure principle, mocking the bourgeois Protestant ethic of work and investment that pervades women's magazines and that helps support the identity of self-sacrifice and masochism with femininity.[3]

Miss Piggy only barely conceals the power, coarseness, and aggressiveness of her physicality beneath a simpering and submissive mask of femininity, which she drops the moment her own interests are threatened. These interests are defined largely but not exclusively in terms of her love object, Kermit. When such threats occur, she responds verbally with one-line insults delivered in a clearly masculine voice. (She calls a chicken "Buzzard Beak" and a rival pig "Bacon Brain.") She also displays her well-known skills in the martial arts. In one episode in *The Kermit and Piggy Story*, she wears a black belt and violently demonstrates her skills on a hapless Kermit. More typically, it is his enemies or hers that she tosses around. In *The Muppet Movie* she bursts her own chains to rescue a bound Kermit and demolishes a crew of bad guys with a series of violent lunges, punches, leaps, and karate kicks. In *Miss Piggy's Guide to Life*, she uses a "quick movement" of her hand to knock to the floor a bookseller who tries to sell her a romance novel instead of her own book.[4] Miss Piggy will have nothing to do with melodrama. Yet, despite her disdain for such a feminine genre, she also appears generally content to operate within the confines of conventional heterosexuality. That is because for her, femininity is a masquerade, a costume like any other, which she can relish—or wallow in, if you will—but discard in an instant. Feminine passivity and weakness are artificial ploys, took to utilize toward her own ends.

More an image than a character fleshed out in narrative, Miss Piggy exists in a hazy realm, triggering multiple and contradictory responses. No one could deny that on one level she provides the occasion for laughter at women. Yet at the same time, she mobilizes laughter against the posturing and illusoriness of a femininity that encourages such silliness as diminutive names ("Piggy") and girlish ways for full-sized, fully grown women. It is this masquerade more than the feisty and funny "woman" who plays it that she renders ridiculous. In one study of children and television, girls said they liked Miss Piggy the best of the Muppets. It was her aggressiveness, not her femininity ("She crashes Kermit the Frog to pieces," one girl said), that seemed to appeal to them.[5]

The Muppets have had enormous popularity in our culture, their images widely circulated through television shows, movies, books, records, toys, games, clothing, and other products. Yet consider how Peter Jennings described three of the most popular of them when he eulogized Henson on the ABC Evening News after his death in 1990: Cookie Monster taught us that "monsters can be lovable"; Big Bird showed us "grace in awkwardness"; and Miss Piggy was "a study in self-centeredness." Miss Piggy is admittedly self-centered, but she is other things as well. Moreover, her self-love draws attention to the self-*denial* we expect to accompany all the other signs of femininity Miss Piggy exhibits so abundantly. Jennings's reading—misreading, really—overlooks the exuberance and humor in the Miss Piggy character, which was modeled on Mae West, another female female impersonator. It also shows how easily the feminine—even among puppets—is held to a different, and harsher, standard than is the masculine.

Historian Natalie Zemon Davis might explain this phenomenon by identifying Miss Piggy as an unruly woman, a topos (a "place" or stock rhetorical theme) of female outrageousness and transgression which often evokes such ambivalence—on the one hand, delight; on the other, unease, derision, or fear. Davis first identified this figure in "Women on Top," an essay in her book *Society and Culture in Early Modern France*. The topos of the unruly woman isn't limited to the historical period Davis examines, however, but reverberates whenever women disrupt the norms of femininity and the social hierarchy of male over female through excess and outrageousness. Davis does not provide an inventory of qualities associated with female unruliness but instead a wide-ranging collection of examples of "women on top" and a powerful theoretical framework for understanding them.[6] Still, from her examples and others, such as Miss Piggy, a cluster of qualities tends to emerge:

1. The unruly woman creates disorder by dominating, or trying to dominate, men. She is unable or unwilling to confine herself to her proper place.
2. Her body is excessive or fat, suggesting her unwillingness or inability to control her physical appetites.
3. Her speech is excessive, in quantity, content, or tone.
4. She makes jokes, or laughs herself.
5. She may be androgynous or hermaphroditic, drawing attention to the social construction of gender.
6. She may be old or a masculinized crone, for old women who refuse to become invisible in our culture are often considered grotesque.
7. Her behavior is associated with looseness and occasionally whorishness, but her sexuality is less narrowly and negatively defined than is that of the femme fatale. She may be pregnant.
8. She is associated with dirt, liminality (thresholds, borders, or margins), and taboo, rendering her above all a figure of ambivalence.

These are some of the tropes or signifiers of female unruliness. Ideology holds that the "well-adjusted" woman has what Hélène Cixous has described as "divine composure."[7] She is silent, static, invisible—"composed" and "divinely" apart from the hurly-burly of life, process, and social power. Such is not the case with the unruly woman. Through her body, her speech, and her laughter, especially in the public sphere, she creates a disruptive spectacle of herself. The tropes of unruliness are often coded with misogyny. However, they are also a source of potential power, especially when they are recoded or reframed to expose what that composure conceals. Ultimately, the unruly woman can be seen as prototype of woman as subject—transgressive above all when she lays claim to her own desire.

B: *Pretty/Funny*, Linda Mizejewski[ii]

The question is no longer whether to read [Ellen] DeGeneres as a lesbian but rather how to read this lesbian body: soft butch in her baggy trousers, groundbreaking gay role model, wholesome talk-show host, middle-age female superstar, spokesperson for CoverGirl cosmetics—that is, "pretty"—and for JCPenney, a trustworthy version of the average shopper. Some critics have argued that she is most legible as gay in her dancing, which has been interpreted as her queer signature, a repeated gesture of self-outing. Candace Moore persuasively links DeGeneres's dancing to the physical comedy on her sitcoms and her "discursive skirting" as evidence of how she performs her sexuality "as multiple self-outings."[8] The "dance with herself," Moore says, is "a daily declaration of queer identity."[9] After her 2008 wedding DeGeneres began more openly to dance around her sexual identity with jokes and allusions on her talk show and in other television venues as well. The references are indirect, relying on audience acknowledgment of what's unsaid. For example, in the episode when she hosts Mormon "sister-wives" from the reality show of the same title, DeGeneres describes in her monologue how the four women live together, sharing the household work as well as the husband. DeGeneres says she has several questions for the women, including "Why do you need a husband?"—playing on audience knowledge about DeGeneres without directly citing it. Along the same lines, in a talk-show skit in 2011 she Photoshops herself into a scene from the movie *The Fighter* (2010) so that she becomes the Mark Wahlberg character, who was supposed to yell at his brother Dicky. DeGeneres changes the dialogue, explaining, "I'm not saying 'Dicky, I want you.' It's not gonna happen."

This type of joking about sexual orientation derives from DeGeneres's comic style of digression, evasion, and equivocation. Describing her work as a judge on *American Idol*, Alessandra Stanley notes that DeGeneres "finds a way to remind audiences of her sexual status on almost every episode." Stanley cites a moment when DeGeneres teases a young male contestant about his good looks, telling him that "for most women, their hearts are going to start racing just looking at you, right, but then, for people like *me*. . . ." The audience began to laugh, but DeGeneres held the beat a moment longer before her punch line: blonds. Like her interpretive dance and her refusal to say she wants Dicky, the joke depends on what's not said, which Candace Moore would characterize as "discursive skirting."[10] It is also a joke that refers, directly and indirectly, back to Ellen's body, its sexuality, and its blondness. It is a reminder of her difference from the other, more traditionally feminine female bodies on *Idol* so that her punch line, "blonds," not only reverses expectations but makes an ironic contrast to what "blondness" as glamour usually means on television. And because white blondness is the iconic identity of the girl next door, the gag sums up the contradictory components of DeGeneres's celebrity.

These contradictions play out in a 2010 article by chick-lit novelist Jennifer Weiner. The article was the cover story for *Shape* magazine, and as *Shape*'s cover girl, DeGeneres was being held up as a healthy role model. Weiner's assignment was to fill in the details of that ideal. DeGeneres is an updated version of "Hollywood's girl next door," she writes, "blond-haired and blue-eyed . . . cute instead of sexy," even though she dresses in "a wardrobe of men's vests and ties that Doris Day would have immediately handed off to her brother."[11] The reference to Doris Day is telling, given that Day was unwittingly the beard for Rock Hudson, one of the most famous closeted gay men of the twentieth century. DeGeneres's stardom uncannily combines both poles of that iconic 1950s romantic couple: Day's identity as all-American girl, Hudson's yet undisclosed identity as gay. For Weiner, the latter is abject, the element that gets discounted in the all-American body being promoted by *Shape*. Weiner may also have forgotten or overlooked Doris Day's own status as a lesbian icon, further queering her appearances with Hudson. Thus in Weiner's list of the attributes that make DeGeneres likable and hip, the lesbian marriage is a footnote: "With a vegan diet, a dedication to yoga, a vocabulary salted with self-help buzzwords, and, lest we forget, a wife instead of a husband, Ellen embodies the modern version of everyone's neighbor and friend."[12] The vegan, yoga, self-help snapshot guarantees DeGeneres's credentials as white and upper class, making it easier for her to be, lest we forget, a lesbian in a marriage that a majority of California voters in 2008 regarded as illegal with the passing of Proposition 8 six months after DeGeneres's wedding. The political antipathy toward gay marriage appeared again in 2011 when several Republican candidates for the presidency apparently believed they would be more attractive to voters if they signed a pledge by the National Organization for Marriage vowing to push a federal constitutional amendment outlawing same-sex marriage. For the 2011 Iowa caucuses, a group named the Family Leader offered an even more stringent pledge it called the Marriage Vow and succeeded in having a few candidates sign.

Given these signals of continued homophobia and controversy about gay rights, the question remains what an article like Weiner's contributes to the construction of a post-gay DeGeneres persona, a return to the 2001 sitcom character who just happened to be gay in a world that did not need to acknowledge it. Academic discussions around DeGeneres's lesbian presence are often polarized around the question of whether she performs as homonormative, a lesbian presence careful not to disrupt conservative, heterosexist structures and thinking.[13] Her associations with American Express, CoverGirl cosmetics, and JCPenney seem to confirm the consumability of her gayness as "commodity lesbianism," a strategy that makes sexual diversity another consumerist choice or a colorful life-style option. However, my argument here is that DeGeneres maintains popular interest and succeeds as a comic by resisting those binary options of complicity/subversion and that she does so precisely by drawing attention to a body that as a comic body agile enough to bend the rules and open the boundaries is a comfortable presence, as seen at the 2001 Emmy awards broadcast.

In her influential 2001 essay on the relative consumability of certain lesbian images, Ann Ciasullo asserts that the butch creates an uneasiness that makes her less "consumable" for mainstream representation than a femme lesbian, who can be the object of multiple identifications and de-sires. The butch not only defies straight male desire but presents a threat that needs to be disavowed, for she has "the capacity to disrupt the notion that masculinity is an inherently male attribute."[14] Ciasullo emphasizes the supposed "ugliness" of the butch lesbian as an undesirable working-class stereotype. With her short hair and identification with the "tool-belt crowd . . . the butch's perceived unattractiveness renders her invisible in an image-based culture," Ciasullo writes.[15] Her primary argument is that the "lesbian chic" trend that emerged in the 1990s enabled only one kind of visibility, the consumer-friendly femme, and continued the ongoing invisibility of the butch in mainstream representations.

Ciasullo is one of several critics who claim that DeGeneres's popularity has been enabled by her ability to eschew working-class associations and take on the more attractive class and femme qualities of the consumable lesbian in popular culture. Looking at DeGeneres's famous *Time* maga-zine cover photo in which the comic wears a fashionable, low-cut, black shirt and subtle diamond on a necklace, Ciasullo argues that "*this* les-bian body—comfortable and comforting—doesn't look anything like the stereotypical lesbian body, the 'mannish,' makeup-less butch in boots and flannel so often associated with lesbianism. Here, Ellen is attractive (nice smile, light but appealing makeup), feminine (low-cut shirt—unusual for DeGeneres—and diamonds?), and inviting"—Ciasullo makes an impor-tant point about DeGeneres's attractiveness and its class and feminine markers in the cover photo.[16] But especially since DeGeneres's talk-show debut in 2003 she has often veered closer to the stereotypical lesbian body in her self-presentations, never unattractive but never far from a soft-butch identity. She is likely to show up without makeup or jewelry, wear-ing loose-fitting slacks and her signature sneakers, when she makes a guest appearance on *The David Letterman Show* (1980–) or *So You Think You Can*

Dance (2005–). She has maintained the image of a butch body that is comfortable and comforting but still decidedly lesbian, an affect that propels her mainstream popularity.

As popular as well as scholarly critics have noted, DeGeneres's whiteness, blondness, and associated signs of middle- to upper-class privilege are pivotal to the public comfort with her image. Bociurkiw argues that these factors were the very grounds of DeGeneres's public coming-out on television; in the season following her coming-out on the sitcom *Ellen*, the Ellen character's upward mobility was literalized in a subplot about buying her own home, so that "coming out and buying real estate were narratively presented as inextricable."[17] Bociurkiw emphasizes how DeGeneres relied on racial metaphors to talk about her sexuality during the months-long coming-out saga, comparing herself to Rosa Parks and using Oprah Winfrey on the coming-out episode to make the point about parallel oppressions.[18] More than a decade later, when it was clear that DeGeneres had become one of the most powerful women on television, *Esquire* writer A. J. Jacobs went back to the Rosa Parks comparison to note that the NAACP had been exceedingly cautious about who could be fronted as the icon for the seat-on-the-bus protest. A black teenager who was arrested for that very crime was considered too risky because she later became pregnant, and civil rights leaders "waited for Rosa Parks, the amiable middle-aged woman." Ellen DeGeneres is gay culture's Rosa Parks, Jacobs says, not so much for her bravery but for her safe fit with middle-class ideals.[19] Ironically, then, DeGeneres is most Rosa Parksish in being blond and white.

However, DeGeneres's popularity as a talk-show host may be better described in terms of audience comfort not with a butch lesbian but with a woman who is herself comfortable in her own body. It is true that her vegan diet since 2008 has slimmed DeGeneres down into magazine-model parameters and accentuated her cheekbones. But neither DeGeneres nor the show has fetishized or flaunted this development of a gradually healthier body, as opposed to the sensationalized weight fluctuations of Oprah Winfrey, who once wheeled onstage a wagon of fat to show how much weight she'd lost. Winfrey was frank in her discussions about her disappointments and anxieties regarding her weight, and given the health issues involved, this was a serious concern. But it was also a concern about appearance, as seen in Winfrey's use of tight jeans, for example, to emphasize her diet successes in the 1980s. My point here is that these anxieties about bodily appearance are simply not present on DeGeneres's talk show. One current of response to DeGeneres may indeed be the simplistic one that because she's butch, her appearance doesn't matter to her or anyone else. But because she engages the audience on many different levels, as a lesbian (which still matters deeply to many gay followers) and as a sweet-tempered host, a silly comic, a music fan, a feel-good entertainer, the effects of her bodily presence cannot be easily dismissed.

* * *

Rather than discussing DeGeneres's body as a code or sign of something else, I would like to conclude by considering what her body does and how it works in process among various social registers at the same time. Susan Bordo's concept of how bodies speak, how they make an impact that is visceral, emotional, affective, is particularly relevant to the female stand-up comic, who offers her body for scrutiny in a visual dynamic that is traditionally male. Certainly in a predominantly white culture, the raced bodies of comics such as Margaret Cho and Wanda Sykes have an immediate impact in their difference, but DeGeneres's body attests to the plurality of sexualities among women, a less culturally obvious difference than race. The difference is physical, thus the "unnatural" effect that occurs when she wears feminine clothes, and cultural, an embodiment of historical meanings of the butch lesbian. This is a body that provokes specific currents of desire and anxiety, an anxiety immediately dismissed by her self-deprecating comedy and her persona of niceness, that is, the willingness to accommodate and make others feel comfortable despite the explicit queerness of the persona. As a talk-show host and previously as a closeted and then open lesbian on her sitcoms, DeGeneres acts as a relay point for multiple, often contradictory social desires evoked by her meanings as clown, celebrity, outsider, butch, blond, CoverGirl model, and groom to a femme bride.

* * *

People buy tickets to see a particular comedian not simply because they desire to laugh; they desire something the comedians make them feel and respond to. Margaret Cho's fans clearly desire her moments of manifesto and defiance; Silverman's fans desire her edginess, her ability to transgress the boundaries of taste and decency. Tina Fey's female fans so strongly desired a smart, funny, feminist voice on television that some were furious that Fey isn't feminist enough in their eyes. Obviously, any pop culture success depends on the ability to fire up, create, and sustain desire.

* * *

[N]o matter how bourgeois and consumable some of her images may be, such as clowning with Justin Bieber on her talk show, it is impossible to unremember more transgressive images, such as posing with her bride on the cover of *People* magazine. One can think of DeGeneres's celebrity body as leaky, like that of Princess Diana's, far messier and less organized than a model of star elements that are negotiated or in tension. Leakiness is a function of the disruptiveness and disorder of comedy, its basic thrust of anti-authoritarianism, as ideal bodies.

* * *

The comic bodies of these performers likewise generate palpable energy and presence that defy categories and stereotypes and, by virtue of their mainstream stardom, likewise defy dismissal. Throughout this book I have emphasized the ways women comedians have challenged, satirized, and often savaged the pretty versus funny dynamic that has dominated traditional comedy. They have called out what is funny about prettiness and have colonized funny as a place where the stories are more interesting than the place where only pretty bodies have a story, the story of romantic comedy. The comic body—unpredictable, leaky—is particularly apt at keeping the meanings of prettiness up for grabs and not necessarily at the disposal of conventional stories, as seen in corporate CoverGirl model Ellen DeGeneres, who cannot stop being a queer icon. Comedy itself defies dismissal because of the bonding power of laughter, which in Deleuzian terms is a force, both physical and psychological, that can make things happen for better or for worse—the racist and homophobic comedy that shores up hatred but also the queer and feminist comedy that opens up the flow of the possible.

C: "Generic Closets: Sitcoms, Audiences, and Black Male Gayness," Alfred L. Martin, Jr.

The closet becomes an implicit TV form—a logic governing not only the ways in which gays and lesbians are represented but also the generation of narratives and positions on and for TV.
LYNNE JOYRICH[20]

The closet, whether in or out of it, refers to the notion of one's disclosure of one's (homo)sexual identity. To be "in the closet" means that a disclosure of one's homosexuality has not been made to family, friends, coworkers, and others. This interplay with the closet has historically played a central role in defining television's engagement with gayness. As Joyrich rightly suggests, the closet—and being in or out of it—provides a compelling comedic narrative device, particularly for the sitcom. However, Joyrich's understanding of the closet as a television motif is both temporally and racially specific. It assumes a gayness that is implicitly white and tied to the industrial norms of television's network era. Today, examining the closet through the lens of race reveals that white gayness and black gayness create distinct possibilities for stories and jokes, especially in the domestic sitcom.

This essay examines the predominantly white-cast sitcom *Sirens* (USA, 2014–2015) and the black-cast sitcom *Let's Stay Together* (BET, 2012–2015). I ask: why do predominantly white-cast sitcoms grant black gayness tenure within the ranks of their recurring cast whereas black-cast sitcoms do not? I focus on the ways the industrial discourses about genre and audience intersect with black gayness. In particular, I draw on interviews with black-cast sitcom writers who discuss how these industrial discourses construct black gayness differently in black-cast and largely white-cast sitcoms.

Television's first attempts to engage with gayness relied on the closet to provide the narrative thrust and comedic possibilities for white gay characters. In an early example, the 1972 *All in the Family* (CBS, 1972–1979) episode "Judging Books by Covers," Archie discovers that one of his friends is gay. The show plays this revelation for humor, as Archie's gay friend defies the semiotics of stereotypical gayness, while another straight character displays stereotypical flamboyance. The episode couples its coming-out of the closet story with the "liberal" idea that one should not judge others based on appearances. By *Soap*'s (ABC, 1977–1981) 1977 premiere, gayness had been integrated into the sitcom's construction of family. In five short years (and eight years after the Stonewall Riots, commonly understood as the beginning of the modern gay rights movement), gay characters had graduated from being interlopers simply there to provide the sitcom a trite, one-off lesson or joke. Instead, gay men (and at this point it was only men) had been welcomed into the domestic space. That is not to suggest that *Soap* was without its representational failures.[21] However, it is clear that by the 1980s white gay men were integrated into the televisual family fold.

Soap aired its final episode on April 21, 1981. Several weeks later, the Centers for Disease Control reported the first official, documented case of AIDS, then called Gay-Related Immune Deficiency, or GRID.[22] The overwhelming power of the AIDS discourse pushed the sitcom's gay storylines back into the closet until the 1990s. Although sitcoms including *The Golden Girls* (NBC, 1985–1992), *Mr. Belvedere* (ABC, 1985–1990), and *A Different World* (NBC, 1987–1993) would feature storylines seeking to educate their audiences about AIDS, those stories did not have gay characters of any race.

When gayness re-emerged from the sitcom's closet, it first did so with white gay characters in white-cast sitcoms, employing coming-out narratives to frame gayness jokingly in single episodic arcs. Domestic sitcoms including *The Golden Girls*, *Roseanne* (ABC, 1988–1997), and *Dear John* (NBC, 1988–1992) featured stories with guest-starring gay characters who came out, allowed the main cast of characters to demonstrate their liberalness, and then were discarded. By the mid-1990s the television industry had deemed white audiences, long assumed to be less homophobic than their black counterparts, to be ready for gay programming.

Black gay characters first emerged as recurring characters in the "gay 90s" on the workplace sitcoms *Cutters* (CBS, 1993) and *Spin City* (NBC, 1996–2002). *Cutters* concerned the merging of a white barbershop and a black beauty shop in Buffalo and featured the black gay character Troy King in the core cast. Later, in *Spin City*'s pilot episode, the New York City mayor's office hires as the director of minority affairs Carter Heywood, an out, proud, black gay activist.

Importantly, when black gayness emerged in a sustained fashion within the sitcom, it was within the multicultural-cast sitcom. Multicultural-cast sitcoms could include black gayness because their audiences were largely understood as belonging to the "slumpy" demographic—one defined by Ron Becker as being comprised of demographically desirable "socially liberal, urban-minded professionals."[23] Although Becker does not explicitly engage with questions of race, the slumpies that networks targeted with gay programming were imagined as white. Accordingly, the television industry portrayed gayness within a largely white, urban context that avoided the sitcom's traditional domestic setting to make way for the inclusion of a differently raced character. In other words, series regular black gay characters on sitcoms coincided with the television industry's pursuit of slumpies via the workplace sitcom. By the time *Sirens* hit the airwaves in 2014, a few black gay characters had starred in multicultural-cast (or otherwise white-cast) sitcoms including *How I Met Your Mother* (CBS, 2005–2014), *Don't Trust the B---- in Apartment 23* (ABC, 2012–2013), and *Brooklyn Nine-Nine* (FOX, 2013–). Accompanying the appearance of black gay men in white-cast sitcoms is a move away from the domesticom's focus on the nuclear family and socio-economically and racially homogenous groups.

However, BET's *Let's Stay Together* emerges from a somewhat differ-

ent tradition—the black-cast sitcom, a subgenre with its own unique relationship to the closet. The black-cast sitcom is rarely set in the workplace. Rather, the domestic sphere is the industrial setting of choice for
the genre. Since the "broken home" black-cast sitcoms of the late 1960s
and 1970s, which featured single parent–headed households such as *Julia*
(NBC, 1968–1971), *Sanford & Son* (1972–1977), *What's Happening!!* (ABC,
1976–1979), and *That's My Mama* (ABC, 1974–1975), the black family was
largely "rehabilitated" to mirror normative nuclear families with father,
mother, and well-behaved children. Certainly, successful black-cast sitcoms of 1970s series like *Good Times* (CBS, 1974–1979) and *The Jeffer-
sons* (CBS, 1975–1985) featured nuclear black families. However, the en
masse movement of black families into the nuclear model of the domesticom largely followed the success of the upper-middle-class comedy of
The Cosby Show (NBC, 1984–1992). Following in this tradition, today, the
black-cast domesticom implies a sense of normativity that always/already
excludes homosexuality. This family centricity excludes black gayness, in
part, due to industrial assumptions of black audiences as monolithic and
more anti-gay than their white counterparts.

I argue that this exclusion of gayness from the home works according
to what Timothy Havens calls "industry lore"—overarching (and often
unfounded) ideas among culture industry workers about what audiences
want, what they will accept on TV, and how those perceptions shape
industrial practices.[24] For these reasons, with respect to black gayness,
the black-cast sitcom remains trapped in what I call a "generic closet."
The generic closet refers to the ways the black-cast sitcom functions as an
industrial representation of an imagined, monolithic black audience, and,
as such, contains black gayness into specific coming-out episodes/story
arcs before discarding these characters for other "mainstream" stories.
From the first appearance of black gay men in black-cast sitcoms on the
1977 *Sanford Arms* (NBC, 1977) episode "Phil's Assertion School," to the
recent appearance on *Let's Stay Together* (BET, 2012–2015), such characters
have served one narrative purpose—to come-out within these black-cast
sitcom worlds and demonstrate the "liberal" leanings of the core cast of
characters. I now turn to *Sirens* to discuss the ways black gayness functions
in a multicultural-cast sitcom.

Sirens: Black Gayness in White Televisual Spaces

Sirens was a single-camera workplace comedy about a group of Chicago-
based emergency medical technicians. Although the show was positioned
as an ensemble comedy, the narrative most frequently centers on three

male EMTs: Michael Mosley's Johnny (who is white and the series' heterosexual axial character), Kevin Bigley's Brian (also white and straight), and Kevin Daniels's Hank, a black gay man—who, in a rarity for television, is coincidentally also played by a black gay man.

USA positioned this series as being for white audiences, despite the obvious fact that the program had a number of black viewers. Following trends within recent white/multicultural-cast television, *Sirens*' Hank announces his gayness early in the pilot episode in the series' opening scene.

> Johnny: You know who I've got a thing for? The new anchor on *Action News*.
> Hank: (Entering the set) Oh that little blonde girl. She's cute.
> Johnny: Yeah, you get the idea that she'd be nice behind the scenes. Like, the crew would love her. You know what I mean?
> Hank: You know who I've got a thing for? The new sports guy on WGN.
> Johnny: That guy? I don't think he's gay, dude.
> Hank: Oh . . . he's gay.
> Johnny: How do you know?
> Chief: He knows. He's the Dick Whisperer.
> Hank: Yes, I am. Besides, I slept with him last week.
> Johnny: Shut up!

This "coming-out" can barely be understood as a coming-out. It is not concerned with creating the narrative problem of the week. The other characters in the scene already have this information and display an attitude (or lack thereof) about Hank's gayness that positions it as inconsequential, thereby, instructing viewers to understand his gayness in a similar way. In other words, his gayness is not the butt of the joke. Hank mentions his gayness a second time in the pilot as he, Johnny, and new EMT member Brian are transporting a patient:

> Johnny: I don't think he [the new partner] looked like Denzel [Washington]. I think he looked like Dennis Rodman, maybe.
> Hank: That's because you're looking at him through angry ex-boyfriend cock goggles. Take it from me as your best friend who is looking at him through single, extremely horny gay goggles. He's hot. Denzel banging hot. [turns to Brian] I'm gay, by the way.

Because of the matter-of-factness with which Hank's gayness exists within *Sirens*, his black gayness in this otherwise white-cast sitcom world is understood as "a *subject*, certainly, but not a *topic* that is framed by coming-out stories."[25] Rather, *Sirens* designs Hank's gayness as a form of character development and as an opportunity to expand forms of comedic dialogue and narrative.

Because *Sirens* is ultimately unconcerned with making gayness an "issue," it plays instead with discourses of post-raciality and post-gayness. Post-raciality is the much-contested belief that, in a post-civil-rights-era America, "racism is no longer embedded in the US social structure and no longer serves as an obstacle to success. If racial inequality persists, then it is due to actions (or inactions) on the part of minority group members."[26] Similarly, post-gayness embraces the notion that "public discussion about one's sexuality is so common . . . that sexual orientation is akin to personal characteristics . . . being known as gay seems like no big whoop."[27] Under post-racial and post-gay logics, both race and gayness cease to have cultural specificity. Rather, those who are black just happen to be black while those who are gay just happen to be gay. There are no differences between the races, and the differences between someone who is gay and someone who is not is simply the gender of their romantic and sexual object of affection.

Hank embodies both of these "post" logics. Put another way, as a character on a white-cast sitcom, Hank is not a black gay character; he is a character happens to be black and gay. As with the opening scene from the *Sirens* pilot episode, the show constructs same-sex sex as simply a matter of fact. Concomitantly, *Sirens* positions Hank's blackness within post-racial discourses. While Hank's skin makes his blackness legible, it does not otherwise define him. *Sirens*, then, subscribes to an assimilationist discourse, which Herman Gray describes as televisual worlds constructed according to "the complete elimination or, at best, marginalization of social and cultural difference in the interest of shared and universal similarity."[28] In this way, Hank exists within two discourses: First, he is constructed within what Catherine Squires calls "race neutral characters."[29] These characters have no sense of attachment to a broader Black community. Furthermore, Hank's home life is rarely considered, something common in the construction of post-racial characters.[30]

While Hank's mother (played by Loretta Divine) appeared in a few episodes, *Sirens* gives no sense about where Hank lives or from what kind of community he *really* comes. Although many scenes were set in Johnny's apartment (including sexual liaisons with his girlfriend/fiancée), Hank's apartment is never shown. Hank is rarely involved in a relationship, sexual or otherwise, with another gay man. His romantic involvements tend to be presented in the past tense or as fleeting moments that do not fundamentally impact the series' narrative. Ultimately, *Sirens* scripts Hank in ways that lack cultural specificity, emphasizing the post-everything discourse of the contemporary moment. This effectively underscores that black gayness can exist within the fabric of the series, but the show does not confront white slumpy viewers with the specter of homosexuality/homosexual acts which would likely result in the series being understood as "too gay." Does this model hold true in black-cast sitcoms? In the next section, I explore the ways the black-cast sitcom *Let's Stay Together* deploys black gayness.

Black Gayness in Black Televisual Spaces

Let's Stay Together was a black-cast, multi-camera, proscenium-style sitcom that centered on two couples and the antics of their romantic and personal relationships. Unlike *Sirens*, which features a black gay character among its core cast, *Let's Stay Together* does not. However, the series features a six-episode arc across its second and third seasons with such a character. When Darkanian Le'Johnson (played by actor Tony Bravado) first appears in the series in the second-season episode "Leave Me Alone," as a womanizing NFL running back for the fictional Atlanta Stallions who has been wooing series costar Kita (played by Erica Hubbard). His first line of dialogue, shouted from across a crowded bar/restaurant is "Yo Kita! You ready to have my baby yet?" Sexual intercourse, sexual prowess, and procreation are, stereotypically, among the ways black men culturally signify their masculinity. For some gay men, particularly those who are not yet ready to disclose their homosexuality, a bravura demonstration of heterosexuality via sexual intercourse can provide a cover for one's true feelings. Darkanian's insistence on not necessarily *dating* Kita, but making a baby with her, suggests a desire not necessarily to have sex with her female body, but rather to make manifest the sexual encounter through procreation and thus silence any questions about his sexuality.

The second scene in which Darkanian appears is the episode's third act, again featuring a first line of dialogue that suggests he is most interested in procreation:

Darkanian: Kita! Or should I say future baby mama?
Kita: Do all your greetings involve impregnating me?

Even as Darkanian appears to have a laser-like focus on Kita, once she rebuffs his advances for the third time, he immediately turns his romantic

Let's Stay Together's **Darkanian** boasts of his (hetero)sexual prowess before later emerging from the televisual closet.

attention to Crystal (played by guest star Kyla Pratt). Crystal succumbs to his wooing and, when directed to do so, writes her phone number on his abdomen. The next episode in which Darkanian appears finds Crystal moving into one of Darkanian's extra condos in downtown Atlanta after being asked to move out of her cousin Kita's condo. On the first night Crystal lives in the condo, she and Darkanian share a quiet moment on the couch that Crystal wants to take further.

> Crystal: And now that we have our own place and we are all alone . . . [she begins to remove her shirt].
> Darkanian: Baby, baby, baby. Hold on. We don't need to do all that.
> Crystal: Well I don't know about you, but I have needs. So . . .
> Darkanian: Hold on now. Crystal Whitmore. I don't want to get into your panties. I want to get into your heart.
> Crystal: For real? Oh Darkanian, you're so romantic.
> Darkanian: Girl, you are tempting me. I better get home though. Good night.

This scene begins to lay the groundwork that something is not quite as it appears with Darkanian. On one hand, this scene suggests a move away from the "sex-crazed" Darkanian of the first few episodes. On the other hand, when taken together with the previous scenes and the ways he sexually approached Kita, the "romantic" Darkanian seems inconsistent. Given that Darkanian only wanted to impregnate Kita, his denying Crystal raises questions about his claim to stereotypical black masculinity, particularly because the other men in the series (either via innuendo or explicit representation) are having sex with their wives and girlfriends.

The Darkanian storyline re-emerges in the second season finale. Crystal discusses what makes her relationship with Darkanian so wonderful while lounging with friends in Darkanian's extra condo. She suggests, "In order to be in a great relationship, you have to be with the right guy. I mean, Darkanian and I are compatible. We respect each other. We have fun together. And we're completely honest with one another." Then the three women hear a noise as if someone is trying to enter the apartment. When the door opens she asks:

> Crystal: Um, sir. Where did you get that key?
> Greg: From Darkanian.
> Crystal: Oh, ok. I'm Crystal, Darkanian's girlfriend.
> Greg: Oh, so you're Crystal, I've heard so much about you. I'm Greg, Darkanian's boyfriend.
> Crystal: Say what now? [Fade to black.]

Unlike many other episodes of black-cast sitcoms, Darkanian's homosexuality is never explicitly made an issue for the cast. Nor is the realization of his homosexuality (or deviation from heterosexuality) punctuated by a canned audience reaction.[31] Rather, once Crystal and her friends verify that Greg is, in fact, Darkanian's boyfriend, the discussion re-centers on Crystal and Darkanian's relationship and its future because Darkanian and Greg both knew that Crystal's function was that of a "beard," a colloquial term that refers to a woman who is dating a gay man to help him conceal his sexuality. The episode quickly turns to the language of deceitfulness rooted in heterosexual relationships when Crystal suggests "Darkanian's been using me."

Although the show itself makes clear that homosexuality cannot exist in its long-term narrative, *Let's Stay Together* uses paratexts to mitigate this conservative televisual treatment of black male gayness. Lest there be any confusion about the way BET be perceived, the network uses its website as a site of paratextual discourse. BET creates paratexts designed to control the parameters within which a text can be interpreted. The network attempts to open a conversation about homosexuality in sports, suggesting that professional athletics is, in fact, a welcoming place for openly gay athletes. In April 2013, shortly after the season 3 premiere wherein Darkanian successfully convinces Crystal to continue to be his "beard," BET.com featured a slideshow of past and present NFL players who would support

Darkanian's fictional coming-out, based on their past as LGBT rights supporters. The slideshow begins with a letter from Crystal that reads:

> Dear Darkanian . . .
>   You may never read this, but given the complex nature of our relationship, I thought it would be in my interest to compile a list of football players (and ex-football players), who would support you if you came out no matter what team you play for (no pun intended).
>   Sincerely,
>   Crystal[32]

Televisually, homosexuality can only be "real" if one makes a public declaration. Otherwise, even as Darkanian has had a long-term relationship with Greg, it is shrouded in a cloak of alleged secrecy. Because of that need for a "loud and proud" public declaration, the fictional character Crystal takes to the "real" BET.com to show support while attempting to get Darkanian (and by extension, other men who have not publicly proclaimed their homosexuality) to come out.

On May 17, 2013, BET continued its paratextual support of black gay men publicly coming out with a two-part video featuring Wade Davis, a "former athlete and LGBT activist" who ultimately suggests that Darkanian's having a "beard" is wrong.[33] Davis indicates that Darkanian could forgo having a fake girlfriend, legitimating his prescription by providing details about the ways that he navigated closetedness while he played for various football teams. Ultimately then, as Jonathan Gray suggests, these paratexts are "controlled and produced by a text's authors or producers [which] allows them ample opportunity, using networks of intertextuality, to construct meanings for their texts outside of the texts themselves."[34] Despite the series suggesting in some ways that Darkanian's sexuality is his own and that he does not need to come out unless he is ready to do so, the series' paratexts suggest otherwise. Shortly after this coming-out, Darkanian disappears from the series' narrative landscape.

Conclusion

Unlike the contemporary white-cast sitcom, *Let's Stay Together*, like other black-cast sitcoms, follows a distinct three-step progression: detection, discovery, and discarding. The detection and discovery modes provide the narrative frameworks. But after that, black gayness advances into a third stage: discarding. In this stage, which can last several episodes, black gay characters are not imagined to exist outside of coming-out narratives. While this model has been adapted from white-cast sitcoms in their early engagement with respect to white gay characters, black-cast sitcoms have become industrially trapped in this model. Additionally, because the series do not sustain an engagement with black gay characters, they do not include much in the way of character development, and therefore, must use paratexts to try to amend some of the possible readings in which the script engages.

Although white and black gayness have been integrated into the white-cast/multicultural-cast sitcom, black gayness in black-cast sitcoms remains useful only within "coming-out." This is not necessarily because this "coming-out" model guarantees ratings success, but because black-cast sitcoms remain beholden to the illogics of culture industries. Long-time television writer and producer Ed. Weinberger suggests executives developing black-cast sitcoms have to expand the ways they think about black audiences. He says:

> Here's the problem: the only people right now doing black-cast TV shows are TVOne and BET. There are black executives running those networks. I don't think they have encouraged gay black characters because they are fearful of alienating their audience. I think they're afraid that there is still a prejudice. TVOne did two gay characters on *Love That Girl* (2010–2012), but they weren't black. They were Hispanic. They could be allowed to be as stereotypical without alienating the black audience. I have a feeling that, if they tried to make those characters black, they wouldn't have been able to get on the air.[35]

Weinberger suggests that black audiences are understood in monolithic ways that positions them (wholly) as holding anti-gay prejudices. Some writers understand what needs to happen to change this model, but they remain unable to effect that change. In an interview I conducted with long-time television writer Jackie McKinley, she suggested that writers "have to start developing shows for black gay characters outside of [coming-out]. The only way that could change is the character has to come back, that's the only way that it will change. So far it has been difficult. I think that's the challenge, getting that [black] gay character as a regular character."[36] McKinley has attempted to engineer this revolution in black-cast television by writing more recurring black gay characters into her scripts. But, aside from writers, there are still network executives who remain resistant to a recurring or regular black gay character within black-cast sitcoms. McKinley said, "I had a black gay character in a pilot that was a recurring character that's now not gay."[37] McKinley recalled how network executives changed the character's sexuality in her pilot episode. Because network executives did not want to explicitly deal with homosexuality on a black-cast situation comedy, her two options were to either change the character's sexuality or risk not having the pilot picked up. In this way, even as McKinley understands what must happen in order to shift the representational paradigm, industrial practices continue to create roadblocks to fuller representations of black gay characters within black-cast sitcoms.

Demetrius Bady, a black gay writer who has worked on *Moesha* and *Single Ladies*, concurred with McKinley's assertion:

> For black shows they couldn't imagine a situation in which a gay character could sustain a series like NBC's successful *Will & Grace*. It hasn't changed much since writing "Labels" for *Moesha*. I went to pitch over at BET. A gay person at the network told me that I should not write any gay characters. That's their directive because they think their audience would never accept a recurring gay character, which I just think is ludicrous.[38]

Here, Bady underscores the differences that emerge with respect to industrial understandings of audiences. It is not wholly about the exclusion of gayness from black-cast sitcoms (although Bady suggests that to be the case at BET at the time) but is more deeply rooted in an inability to imagine a world in which a black gay character could sustain a series. Beretta Smith-Shomade concedes, while homosexuality was becoming more visible on television broadly, "On BET, heterosexual black masculinity maintain[ed] a ratcheted up personification . . . [and] the notion and discussion of homosexuality garnered very little airtime on BET."[39] Showrunners and, in some cases, writers, cannot yet imagine stories about black gayness that are decentered from coming-out narratives.

The television industry has made no space for the imagining of a BLAMPY viewer—ones who are black, liberal, affluent, metropolitan professionals and who understand that gayness can be a part of the fabric of black television families. These black gay characters are imagined as temporary intruders designed to reify broad cultural understandings of blackness broadly and the black family unit specifically. And there is little expectation that the black-cast sitcom's model for engaging with black gayness will change anytime in the near future.

Notes

1. Russo, "Female Grotesques," 225.

2. Kinder, *Playing With Power*, 65.

3. Williamson, *Consuming Passions*, 55–61.

4. Beard and Henson, *Miss Piggy's Guide to Life*, xii.

5. Hodge and Tripp, *Children and Television*, 150–157.

6. That framework is based on the notion of sexual inversion, which I will discuss in more detail later in this chapter. I substitute *gender inversion* for *sexual inversion*, to avoid any ambiguity that might arise from the latter's associations with homosexuality in psychoanalytic discourse. While the list that follows is my own, it is largely indebted to Davis, as is this entire study. Like Mary Russo, her work has made immeasurable contributions to my own.

7. Cixous, "The Laugh of the Medusa," 246.

8. Moore, "Resisting, Reiterating, and Dancing Through," 20.

9. Moore, "Resisting, Reiterating, and Dancing Through," 23.

10. DeGeneres herself has identified the comedy of her persona as "skirting"—evading issues, glossing over the topic at hand, pointing to distractions to avoid a direct statement. In her book *My Point . . . and Do I have One*, she writes that someone asked why she always wears "pants and never skirts," and her reply is that "if they mean the *verb* skirt, well, they're dead wrong. I'm always skirting" (93). John Limon and Candace Moore have cited this pun as a rich entry into DeGeneres's comic style for very different reasons, and they both make elegant arguments about its significance. Limon pinpoints the joke as DeGeneres's constant evasion of the status of her body (116–117), while for Moore, skirting is the performance of queerness. Moore's focus is "the multiple queer appearances and disappearances of Ellen DeGeneres" on her sitcoms and her talk show (18). Moore argues that the verbal skirting, "distancing her comedy from the bodily, from her body and the material consequences of the world," ends up nevertheless "leaking other meanings." For Moore, this leakiness complements the physical displays that "convey and rely on utter embodiment" (30). In short, Moore comes down on the side of the body precisely because visibility, no matter how playful and ambiguous, is central to LGBTQ politics.

11. Weiner, "How I Stay Strong and Centered," 59.

12. Weiner, "How I Stay Strong and Centered," 59.

13. Lisa Duggan has introduced and defined the term "homonormative" as "a politics that does not contest dominant heteronormative assumptions and institutions but upholds and sustains them while promising the possibility of a demobilized gay constituency and a privatized, depoliticized gay culture anchored in domesticity and consumption" (50).

14. Ciasullo, "Making Her (In)Visible," 604.

15. Ciasullo, "Making Her (In)Visible," 602.

16. Ciasullo, "Making Her (In)Visible," 584.

17. Bociurkiw, "It's Not about the Sex," 179.

18. Bociurkiw, "It's Not about the Sex," 177–179.

19. Jacobs, "Ellen (The Knife) DeGeneres," 63.

20. Joyrich, "Epistemology of the Console," 27.

21. Streitmatter, *From "Perverts" to "Fab Five."*

22. Gross, *Up from Visibility*, 95.
23. Becker, *Gay TV and Straight America*, 81.
24. Havens, *Black Television Travels*, 5.
25. Walters, *All the Rage*, 105.
26. Doane, "Shades of Colorblindness," 15.
27. Healy, "How Celebrities Come Out Now."
28. Gray, *Watching Race*, 85.
29. Squires, *African Americans and the Media*, 219.
30. Beltrán, "Meaningful Diversity."
31. The series is shot without a live studio audience with laughter and other "re-actions" added in post-production.
32. "Football Players Who Would Support Darkanian Coming Out," BET .com, BET Interactive, April 2013, http://www.BET.com/.
33. "Let's Stay Together Exclusive," BET.com, BET Interactive, May 17, 2013, http://www.bet.com/video/letsstaytogether/season-3/exclusives/wade-davis-on -darkanian-pt-1.html.
34. Gray, *Watching with* The Simpsons, 37.
35. Ed. Weinberger (television writer and producer), tape recorded interview by author, February 23, 2013, Austin, TX.
36. Jackie McKinley (television writer), tape recorded interview by author, March 22, 2013, Austin, TX.
37. McKinley, author interview, March 22, 2013.
38. Demetrius Bady (television writer), tape recorded interview by author, February 27, 2013, Austin, TX.
39. Smith-Shomade, *Pimpin' Ain't Easy*, 169.

Works Cited

Becker, Ron. *Gay TV and Straight America*. New Brunswick, NJ: Rutgers University Press, 2006.
Beltrán, Mary. "Meaningful Diversity: Exploring Questions of Equitable Representation on Diverse Ensemble Cast Shows." *FlowTV* 12, no. 7. (August 27, 2010). http://flowtv.org/2010/08/meaningful-diversity/.
BET.com. "Football Players Who Would Support Darkanian Coming Out." BET Interactive. April 2013. http://www.bet.com/.
———. "Let's Stay Together Exclusive: Wade Davis on Darkanian, Pt. 1." BET Interactive. May 17, 2013. http://www.bet.com/video/letsstaytogether/season -3/exclusives/wade-davis-on-darkanian-pt-1.html.
Bociurkiw, Maryusa. "It's Not about the Sex: Racialization and Queerness in *Ellen* and *The Ellen DeGeneres Show*." *Canadian Women Studies* 24, no. 2/3 (2005): 176–181.
Bordo, Susan. *Twilight Zones: The hidden Life of Cultural Images from Plato to O. J.* Berkeley: University of California Press, 1997.
Ciasullo, Ann M. "Making Her (In)Visible: Cultural Representations of Lesbianism and the Lesbian Body in the 1990s." *Feminist Studies* 27, no.3 (2001): 577–608.
Cixous, Hélène. "The Laugh of the Medusa." Translated by Keith Cohen and

Paula Cohen. In *New French Feminisms*, edited by Elaine Marks and Isabella de Courtivon, 245–264. Brighton: Harvester, 1980.

Davis, Natalie Zemon. *Society and Culture in Early Modern France*. Stanford: Stanford University Press, 1975.

DeGeneres, Ellen. *My Point . . . and I Do Have One*. New York: Bantam, 1995.

Doane, Ashley. "Shades of Colorblindness: Rethinking Racial Ideology in the United States." In *The Colorblind Screen: Television in Post-Racial America*, edited by Sarah Nilsen and Sarah E. Turner, 15–38. New York: New York University Press, 2014.

Duggan, Lisa. *The Twilight of Equality?: Neoliberalism, Cultural Politics, and the Attack on Democracy*. Boston: Beacon, 2003.

Gray, Herman. *Watching Race: Television and the Struggle for Blackness*. Minneapolis: University of Minnesota Press, 2004.

Gray, Jonathan. *Watching with* The Simpsons*: Television, Parody, and Intertextuality*. New York: Routledge, 2006.

Gross, Larry. *Up from Visibility: Lesbians, Gay Men, and the Media in America*. New York: Columbia University Press, 2001.

Havens, Timothy. *Black Television Travels: African American Media around the Globe*. New York: New York University Press, 2013.

Healy, Patrick. "How Celebrities Come Out Now." *New York Times*, June 9, 2012. http://www.nytimes.com/2012/06/10/sunday-review/how-celebrities-come-out-now.html?pagewanted=all&_r=0.

Hodge, Robert, and David Tripp. *Children and Television: A Semiotic Approach*. Stanford University Press, 1986.

Jacobs, A. J. "Ellen (The Knife) DeGeneres: Soft Power Comes to American Idol." *Esquire*, February, 2010.

Joyrich, Lynne. "Epistemology of the Console." *Critical Inquiry* 27, no. 3 (2001): 439–467. http://www.jstor.org/stable/1344216.

Kinder, Marsha. *Playing With Power in Movies, Television, and Video Games: From Muppet Babies to Teenage Mutant Ninja Turtles*. Berkeley: University of California Press, 1991.

Limon, John. *Stand-Up Comedy in Theory, or, Abjection in America*. Durham, NC: Duke University Press, 1996.

Beard, Henry, and Henson Associates. *Miss Piggy's Guide to Life*. New York: Knopf, 1981.

Moore, Candace. "Resisting, Reiterating, and Dancing Through: The Swinging Closet Doors of Ellen DeGeneres's Televised Personalities." In *Televising Queer Women: A Reader*, edited by Rebecca Beirne, 17–31. New York: Palgrave Macmillan, 2008.

Russo, Mary. "Female Grotesques: Carnival and Theory." In *Feminist Studies, Critical Studies*, edited by Teresa de Lauretis, 213–229. Bloomington: University of Indiana Press, 1986.

Smith-Shomade, Beretta E., *Pimpin' Ain't Easy: Selling Black Entertainment Television*. New York: Routledge, 2007.

Squires, Catherine. *African Americans and the Media*. Malden: Polity Press, 2009

Streitmatter, Rodger. *From "Perverts" to "Fab Five": The Media's Changing Depiction of Gay Men and Lesbians*. New York: Routledge, 2009.

Walters, Suzanna Danuta. *All the Rage: The Story of Gay Visibility in America.* University of Chicago Press, 2001.

Weiner, Jennifer. "'How I Stay Strong and Centered': The Real Reason Ellen DeGeneres Looks So Amazing at Age 52." *Shape,* May 2010.

Williamson, Judith. *Consuming Passions: Dynamics of Popular Culture.* New York: Marion Boyars, 1986.

8.

Nation & Globalization

Introduction, Peter Kragh Jensen and Matt Sienkiewicz

CURB YOUR ENTHUSIASM, SEASON 3, EPISODE 6, "THE SPECIAL SECTION," DIRECTED BY BRYAN GORDON, STORY BY LARRY DAVID, FIRST AIRED OCTOBER 20, 2002, ON HBO.

In this improvised, mockumentary-style American sitcom, Larry discovers that his recently deceased mother will be moved into a particularly undesirable section of the local cemetery. Through bribery and deceit he works to move her remains into a more prestigious area with surprising and embarrassing results.

* * *

KLOVN, SEASON 1, EPISODE 10, "FARVEL IGEN MOR" ("GOODBYE AGAIN, MOM"), DIRECTED BY MIKKEL NØRGAARD, WRITTEN BY CASPER CHRISTENSEN, FIRST AIRED APRIL 11, 2005, ON TV 2 ZULU.

In this improvised, mockumentary-style Danish sitcom, Frank discovers that his recently deceased mother will be moved into a particularly undesirable section of the local cemetery. Through bribery and deceit he works to move her remains into a more prestigious area with surprising and embarrassing results.

* * *

Think of the longest, most satisfying laugh you've ever had. It's possible this took place at a stand-up show or in the midst of watching your favorite Adam Sandler film (you don't have great taste). But probably not. Far more likely, you were with your friends or family and something happened that, for that particular group of people at that particular moment, was utterly uproarious. You probably refer back to that situation from time to time when the same group gets together, enjoying aftershocks of laughter based on the original earthquake of hilarity you all experienced together. This, of course, is what is known as an "inside joke."

Comedy, as evidenced by the phenomenon of the inside joke, has a powerful capacity to create in-groups and out-groups. It ruthlessly sorts individuals by whether or not they have the requisite background experience to understand and enjoy that which is making everyone else laugh. This is particularly important at the level of the nation. Nations, regardless of how natural and eternal they may feel, are products of social convention and require constant upkeep. As the scholar Benedict Anderson notes, you are quite unlikely to have firsthand experience of every member of your national community. Thus, in order to feel really a part of something, conationals must imagine themselves as an "imagined community" of people who, while different in many ways, share a certain set of common ideas and experiences. Comedy, by creating a set of national "inside jokes," can play an important part in this process. A nation, at least in some small way, might be understood as a group of people who, for the most part, understand the humor of their country's top comedians. Accordingly, comedy theorists must address the fact that there are localized, national approaches to humor that encourage a sense of belonging for those on the inside and serve to alienate those on the outside.

And yet, comedy travels. Jerry Lewis, a peculiarly American comedian who reached his height in the 1960s, remains a popular figure in France. *The Hangover*, which would seem to be a very American film at first glance, made nearly as much at the international box office as it did at the domestic. And dare we tempt the easily distracted reader with the fact that right now, no matter what country you're in, there's a very good chance that *Friends* is being rerun on a local station? Certainly there are limits to comedy's ability to cross national borders. A YouTube video making fun of various regional American accents is not likely to become a worldwide hit. However, comedy flows globally, if generally only in one direction. American and British comedies have, for decades, succeeded in finding success in a variety of global markets, with relatively little material travelling the opposite vector. As important as comedy can be in the creation of national identity, some aspects of it are quite apparently able to achieve international, if not quite global, appreciation.

Klovn, a hit Danish sitcom from the early 2000s, is an excellent example of the tension that exists between the national and the global in the realm of comedy. As the episode descriptions above attest, the show draws amply from American media conventions, stealing its plotline and style more or less directly from the HBO series *Curb Your Enthusiasm*. In fact, *Klovn*'s dependence on *Curb* may even be seen as a straightforward case of "media imperialism," in which the US has infiltrated a smaller culture and reshaped its sense of humor in Uncle Sam's image and interest. The global popularity of the sitcom genre itself provides evidence of Anglo-American comedic dominance. From *I Love Lucy* to *The Big Bang Theory*, global audiences have often preferred US-based comedies to their own local productions.

Looking at the history of the sitcom in Denmark, globalization and Anglo-American influence are both readily apparent. For fifteen years following the introduction of the medium, little on Danish television could be described as comedy and certainly there was no programming featuring the consistent generic codes and conventions of the sitcom. This all changed in 1964, however, when DR, the Danish public broadcaster, imported *I Love Lucy* from America's CBS, relabeling it *Lucy Show*. The program was a success, not only proving that the sitcom could work in Denmark but also establishing American hegemony over the genre. As DR came to allow a greater proportion of international programming in the 1970s and '80s, Danes were introduced to shows like *Fawlty Towers*, *Cheers*, *The Cosby Show*, and *Roseanne*. When commercial television first came to Denmark at the end of the 1980s, the floodgates opened and less family-oriented fare like *The Simpsons* and *Seinfeld* also became available. During 1992, *The Cosby Show*, locally known as *Cosby & Co.*, garnered roughly one-fifth of the Danish television audience, proving that American comedy could draw large, sustained audiences throughout the country.

During the 1980s, DR did create a handful of local sitcoms, but they remained vastly overshadowed by their more famous American counterparts. In DR's own analysis, these local efforts failed in significant part due to an inability to merge local humor with the globalized sitcom format. It wasn't until 2001 that the concept of a successful Danish sitcom morphed from punchline to reality. In that year, Frank Hvam and Casper Christensen, who would later come to star in *Klovn*, created *Langt fra Las Vegas* (*Far away from Las Vegas*), an indigenous Danish program that leaned heavily on American and British genre conventions while nonetheless creating countless "inside jokes" that only a Danish audience could truly appreciate. Running for five seasons, the show brought an edginess to the sitcom that meshed perfectly with the sensibilities of young Danish viewers. *Langt fra Las Vegas* is significant both for breaking down the notion that Danes could not make locally popular sitcoms and for its special relationship to *Klovn*. *Klovn* is a highly improvised sitcom about Frank and Casper after finishing *Langt*. It is, thus, exactly analogous to *Curb Your Enthusiasm*, a highly improvised sitcom that details Larry David's life in the wake of having created *Seinfeld*.

The similarities between *Klovn* and *Curb* go beyond plot, character, and style. Most significantly for the comedy theorist, the shows share a sensibility. Actual punchlines are rare, and the laughs are mostly found in the social faux pas of the clueless main character and the painfully awkward situations he finds himself in. This often involves testing taboos and letting the profane put its grimy hands on the sacred. Both *Curb*'s "The Special Section" and *Klovn*'s "Farvel Igen Mor," engage with taboos of death and burial. In their respective episodes, Larry and Frank make enemies and awkward moments by bribing grave diggers and treating burial arrangements as crass business interactions. Not surprisingly, the comedians also proceed to have a lot of inappropriate fun with the severe taboo of disturbing the earthly remains of the deceased. These overlaps prove both that some comedy crosses cultures quite easily and that American culture plays an outsized role in the sorts of humor that traverse the globe.

Nonetheless, *Klovn* is a thoroughly Danish sitcom, far better enjoyed by viewers with a grasp of local language and culture. Peppered with references to Danish history and society, the program differs from *Curb* in key ways, lending credence to Henri Bergson's claim that "laughter is always the laughter of a group." Even when there is an apparent narrative likeness, the story is given a local spin, which becomes apparent when one digs deeper into the texts. In *Curb*, Larry's mother has violated Jewish dogma and is moved to a section for people who are sinners according to (the writers' misunderstanding of) Jewish tradition. In *Klovn*, Frank's mother has been moved due to cemetery renovation, and he tries to have the grave moved next to a beech tree, which is attractive solely for personal, sentimental reasons. *Klovn*'s gallows humor is devoid of any theological undertones, which is typical of a secularized Danish culture, in which organized religion is thought of as largely antiquated. Likewise, Frank manages to desecrate his mother's remains in a way that is culturally specific and in stark contrast to *Curb*. He (spoiler alert for those readers who just made a DVD purchase from Amazon.dk) brings his mother's urn to a "gentleman's lunch," a type of all-day drinking event that is common in Denmark but foreign to the American eye. The ham salad that he intended to bring somehow ends up in an urn of its own and is buried in his mother's newly secured grave plot. Suffice to say, gentlemen's lunches and ham salads do not appear in material written by David, a Jewish comedian from Brooklyn.

Klovn leans heavily on both *Curb* and a generic format that has been fine-tuned to attain global reach, but still it manages to connect with a Danish sense of belonging. This dynamic is echoed in the essays that comprise this final chapter of this book. The opening essay comes from Andy Medhurst's analysis of the British comedian Chubby Brown. Just as *Klovn* often pushes boundaries of taste as it portrays Danish culture, Brown's humor aggressively defines its audience as people who meet a certain, limited understanding of what it means to be British. Brown traffics in the uglier, more provincial side of comedic nationalism but, in doing so, displays the theoretical ways in which comedy can serve to solidify local identities.

In the essays that follow Medhurst's analysis, contemporary media scholars grapple with the globalizing side of comedy and the ways in which national and subnational sensibilities always seem to re-emerge. Inger-Lise Kalviknes Bore offers an empirical look at *The Office*, interviewing both British and Norwegian viewers of the original BBC version starring Ricky Gervais. Bore shows that both sets of viewers have a tendency to describe the show as idiosyncratically British, a fact belied by its wild success throughout the globe. She argues that nationalist understandings of humor are important tools by which viewers craft their local identities, even in cases when jokes are demonstrably successful across cultures. Along similar lines, Danish critics often celebrate *Klovn* as unique Danish comedy, ignoring that fact that the show has resonated with audiences throughout Scandinavia and was spun off into a film that did well on the American festival circuit. This speaks to the communal, nationalized nature of what we find funny.

Turning to India, Sangeet Kumar argues that a cultural export can only attain lasting success if it achieves a minimum of resonance at its site of importation. Looking at Indian political satire, he points to the local innovation necessary in cultural exchange. From this perspective *Klovn* can be understood not just as a result of media imperialism, but also as an example of the dynamic interplay between similarity and difference that is inherent in cultural globalization. Comedy, it seems, often works best when culturally transcendent concepts are customized for the sensibilities of specific local audiences.

Finally, the chapter returns to Britain, as Brett Mills offers an analysis of the humor found in the BBC television series and film *The Trip*. Much like *Klovn*'s attention to Copenhagen and *Curb*'s embrace of the physical space of Los Angeles, *The Trip* revels in the British countryside, using the road trip format as a means through which to map the comedic boundaries of British space and identity. In doing so, Mills notes, *The Trip* creates inside jokes for Britons while, at the same time, refereeing which people and places are central to British national identity.

A: *A National Joke*, Andy Medhurst[i]

When [comedian Roy "Chubby" Brown] turns his attention to topical events and the foibles of celebrities, he is merciless, and often finds ways of saying the otherwise unsayable through the licensed space his commitment to obscenity has afforded him. He returns more than once to the royal family, especially in the context of the death of Princess Diana. "If she'd have been a fat tart with boils nobody would have fucking sent one bastard flower," is one interesting thought he shares, before speculating on how her campaign against landmines increased the likelihood of unemployment for those who worked in factories that made artificial limbs. Elsewhere he notes that Elton John sang at Diana's funeral because "he's the only queen that gives a fuck." As these Diana jokes show, one of Brown's favorite tropes is the provocation of outrage. He and his audience are engaged in a game of dare—will he dare to say these outrageous things and will they dare to laugh at them? He rampages through taboo areas, unleashing jokes about pedophilia, making fun of disabilities, treating famines in Africa and earthquakes in India as source material for jibes. When even his audience finds the going hard, he rounds on them—"Just got out of church, have you?"—and after especially on-the-edge remarks he takes satisfaction in confirming his status as the man who will go further than any other—"Only me that can get away with that one." Very occasionally, he miscalculates and pays the price—performing in a town at the center of a much-publicized child abuse investigation, his opening line was "I'm surprised there are so many of you here, I thought you'd all be at home fucking the kids," and his reward was to be booed off stage.[1] His reputation, perceived attitudes and turbulent private life have led several local councils to propose banning him from appearing in venues that they administer.[2] Unsurprisingly, such incidents only add to his scandalous appeal in the eyes of his devotees. He is the censor-baiter, the scourge of municipally funded cultural policing, the speaker of the unspeakable. This relish for disrespecting boundaries is often seen at its fullest and richest

---

i. From Andy Medhurst, *A National Joke: Popular Comedy and English Cultural Identities* (London: Routledge, 2007), 189–191, 194–199. Copyright © 2007, reproduced by permission of Taylor & Francis Books UK.

in his parodic songs, which take a special delight in shredding decorum and undermining codes of taste, rewriting the lyrics of hitherto innocuous pop songs so they are rendered gapingly obscene through the introduction of excessive detail. Brown performs a kind of carnival surgery on these songs, for example turning a saccharine ballad like Ronan Keating's "When You Say Nothing At All" into a saga of farting, menstruation, and unusually messy oral sex, hauling into the public sphere the sounds, secretions and suctions conventionally hidden away beneath the surface pieties of romantic love. Romance is always a fake in Brown's gleefully corporeal world, a deception that must be erased to reveal the pulsations, juices, lusts, embarrassments and compromises that make up the actuality of sex.

In addition to casting himself as both the risk-taker and the taboo-breaker, Brown has an occasional habit of electing himself as a political spokesman. Politicians across the political spectrum are fair game, since it isn't any specific policies he wants to attack but the sheer fact that such people have power over the ordinary folk he sees as his peers. As with his jokes that make fun of teachers or social workers or the legal system, it is authority figures who are targets—those who control, those who clamp down, those who make decisions that compel the less powerful to comply. There are other moments, however, when he flexes rhetorical muscles against even less powerful groups than the white working-class English whose self-appointed jester figurehead he has become. Hence his overtly racist jokes, a handful of which can be found on most of his videos—in 2001's *Stocking Filler*, for example, he announces, "If there's any asylum seekers in [the audience], fuck off home"—and "home" here does not mean indoors but overseas. The cheer that greets this hue barely leaves the theater roof intact. Such a line is startling not so much for the viewpoint it expresses, a viewpoint entirely congruent with the outlook of Brown's core following, but for its abrupt directness, jettisoning any pretense of wordplay or comic invention in favor of the articulation of undisguised prejudice. In an earlier video the line "if there's any poofs in, fuck off" serves an identical purpose and garners an equally rapturous roar. Such lines are unusually explicit in the way they draw lines between those who belong and those who do not, the lines which are essential to any comic utterance or event, though they are rarely so nakedly revealed. It is moments like these which make it easy to label Brown a mouthpiece for bigotry, and it is undeniable that the jokes he makes about ethnic and sexual minorities only work for audiences who are unassailably convinced that whiteness and heterosexuality are higher in any conceivable social and cultural pecking order than non-whiteness and non-heterosexuality. Many reading these pages would doubtless proceed from that point to damn the man and all he stands for, banishing him to the lands of the ideologically irredeemable where, to invoke the names of two other English comedians often accused of ultra-conservative views, Jim Davidson is heir apparent to Bernard Manning's ageing monarch. Nonetheless, as this book has argued on every available occasion, the politics of comedy are rarely free of ambiguity, and this chapter will later argue that alongside such crowd-pleasingly reactionary lines there are other, deeper facets of what Brown says and means which deserve closer consideration and even respect.

* * *

A comedy of resistance

A recurring concern of this book is the relationship between comedy and belonging, a relationship that is intensely important when considering the comedy of Roy "Chubby" Brown. In an era characterized by the fragmentations of postmodernism and the disorientations of globalization, his comedy waves a battered, often shabby, but always defiant flag for wholeness and locality. His comedy offers its white working-class English audiences a welcome, a place of refuge, a sense of belonging, a space that is simultaneously warmly familiar to those whose faces fit and ferociously unforgiving to those who faces do not. To borrow a phrase from the social theorist Anthony Giddens, Brown is in the business of dispensing onto-logical security. There is, perhaps, something unavoidably absurd in using such a luridly highbrow term to explain the appeal of such a ruthlessly lowbrow comic, but this is yet one more way in which Brown crystallizes and focuses some of the key agendas of this book. Anyone who approaches popular comedy intent on academic analysis must encounter the risk of being told one is "reading too much into things," but it seems profoundly implausible to me that Brown should attain such heroic significance for his audience simply as a result of his technical skills in joke-telling, brilliant though these are. The intensity of his success in this precise period of English cultural history suggests that he is tapping into complex and troublesome issues of identity, belonging, location, community and home, and I want to explore how he does so over the next few pages.

[Earlier] I looked briefly at those debates over globalization and cosmopolitanism which contend that contemporary life, especially for those in affluent cultures, is defined by its rootlessness, its migratory drift, and its dissolution of established boundaries in favor of unfixed, mobile and hybrid identities. Economic and technological change have led, it is argued, to new forms of cultural self-understanding in which we are unable to rely on older versions of making sense of ourselves and our relationship to social life. In the appropriately unfettered words of Alberto Melucci:

> Individuals find themselves enmeshed in multiple bonds of belonging created by the proliferation of social positions, associative networks and reference groups. . . . We are migrant animals in the labyrinths of the world metropolises; in reality or in the imagination, we participate in an infinity of worlds. . . . The rhythm of change accelerates at an extraordinary pace. The multiplication of our social memberships, the constant surge of possibilities and messages floods the field of our experience. The traditional co-ordinates of personal identity (family, church, party, race, class) weaken. It becomes difficult to state with certainty who we are . . . we search for permanent anchors, and question our own life stories. Are we still who we were?[3]

Melucci is not expecting any other answer to that question but "no," but Brown's comedy is, in effect, a sustained and resounding shout of "yes." Such an answer may be a fiction—a harking back to a romanticized and selective version of the past, a denial of diversity in the present, and a refusal to embrace the changes offered by the future—but it remains a source of comfort to Brown's core audience, and collective comfort is the heart and soul of popular comedy. What the proponents of hybridity and fragmentation have often overlooked is that the opportunities such cultural shifts make possible are not equally open to all, or indeed beneficial to all, and it could be argued that one of the groupings least able to benefit from what Melucci calls the "surge of possibilities" is that segment of the white English working class whose identities were rooted in traditional heavy industries.[4] Years before he reinvented himself as Roy "Chubby" Brown, Royston Vasey, it should be remembered, was born in the steel industry fiefdom of Grangetown, the same Grangetown that the black writer Darcus Howe nominated in *White Tribe*, his astute Channel 4 series about changing ideas of Englishness, as emblematic of the declining, abandoned, stranded-by-change, hope-starved white English North. Michael Billig has written of how people excluded by postmodern and globalizing cultures, people for whom "there is no rapture in ambiguity," feel themselves to be "dispossessed and insecure," and that pair of adjectives seems very telling in this context.[5] Those who see Brown's comedy as nothing more than bigotry rendered comedic would be delighted to note that Billig's prime examples of where such feelings of dispossession and insecurity can lead are the figures of the "fascist thug and ethnic cleanser," but I would regard it as shockingly reductive to put Brown in such company.[6] He does indeed make racist jokes and ethnically prejudiced asides, and these are inexcusable. They are also, however, explainable, if the concept of ontological security is looked at more closely.

For Anthony Giddens, ontological security means "the confidence that most human beings have in the continuity and constancy of their self-identity and in the constancy of the surrounding social and material environments."[7] The key words here are continuity and constancy, since it is they which are most under threat from the dislocations and fragmentations of postmodern life. Giddens sees postmodern existence as characterized by a process of "disembedding," which he defines as "the 'lifting out' of social relations from local contexts of interaction and their restructuring across indefinite spans of time-space."[8] There could hardly be a more concise antithesis of what popular comedy strives to do, since popular comedy is a practice founded on embedding, on knowable locality, on the recognition of shared and familiar reference points. It is a discourse of demarcation, of drawing lines rather than erasing them, it operates according to an imperative of unification, of sealing its reciprocal participants (comedian and audience, joke-giver and joke-receivers) into tight networks of manageable parameters. Brown's comedy is exemplary in this respect, forever patrolling its same small patch, its closely meshed landscape of white, working-class, mostly Northern, wholly heterosexual, English life. Hence the constant mention in Browns routines of everyday occasions, familial rituals, marital conventionalities, shared cultural touchstones, routine consumption practices, familiar holiday resorts, long-established leisure activities, and unquestioned presumptions about sexual and ethnic norms. "Ontological security," Roger Silverstone once said, "is sustained through the familiar and the predictable . . . expressed and supported by a whole range of symbols and symbolic formations. The symbols of daily life . . . are our attempts, as social beings . . . to manage others, and to manage ourselves," and this is precisely what Brown's recurring iconography of everyday life—pie and chips and egg and chips, Blackpool and Asda, nagging wives and boozing husbands, smelly farts and bushy fannies, ridiculed queers and resented immigrants—sets out to achieve.[9]

Brown's comedy offers, in effect, a rallying point for resisting globalization. It is not a carefully thought-out political program (it would be gauche, at best, to expect such a thing from a stand-up comedian), but a gut reaction, a beer-gut reaction perhaps, against changes that are consigning whole ways of life to the scrapheaps of outmodedness and irrelevance. He encapsulates a sensibility that can also be seen in films like *The Full Monty* and *Brassed Off* which, although they employ a far less abrasive tone than Brown and are consequently far more exportable across both class and national borderlines, manifest a similar anger about the dismantling of working communities (Brown has explicitly incorporated the first of those films into his act, performing a typically grotesque parody of its celebrated striptease routine). For some cosmopolitan critics, that anger is misplaced, a soft-hearted amalgam of nostalgia and sentimentality; consider, as an example, Iain Chambers' insistence that the 1980s Miners' Strike, that pivotal battle between organized labor and the government of Margaret Thatcher, was "articulated around the closed prospects of a single-economy working 'community' and the guarded secrets of a skilled trade . . . out of step not only with the temporality of modern capital, but also with modern life."[10] Such a view, where entire working cultures are written off with clinical accountancy and the word community can only be used if it is incarcerated within quotation marks that mark it out as delusional, is the polar opposite of the sensibility given comedic shape by Brown. In his act, as in the two films cited above (and in other vital tragicomedies such as Mike Leigh's film *Meantime* and Debbie Horsfield's BBC TV series *Making Out*) the sacrificing of community in order to fall at the feet of rapturous fragmentation is not an option. Such comedies cannot hope to overturn those social and cultural changes, but they can at least register the emotional damage that they cause and they can become temporary shelters where those ripped apart by and reeling from that damage can gather. There are, no doubt, dangers here of sentimentalizing what Brown's success and sensibility represents, but it is highly debatable as to whether that is a greater folly than loftily regarding his audiences as so much human silt washed away by the Melucci's tidal surge of change or as stumbling dinosaurs doomed by their inability to read the runes of postmodernity as perceptively as Chambers. As with most important comedians, Brown is a contradictory and ambivalent figure. Some of his jokes undoubtedly hinge on intolerant attacks against minorities, yet the sensibility he personifies is itself rooted in the life experiences and structures of feeling of another stigmatized group, those white working-class English left behind by the turn towards hybridized, globalized culture.

This is a sticky paradox, and not resolvable through any kind of facile checklist of trying to work out who is more oppressed than whom. Ien Ang, in a thoughtful article on the complexities of identity in contemporary life, has noted how "struggles for or on behalf of identity tend to be conservative, even reactionary . . . aimed at restoring or conserving established orders of things and existing ways of life . . . keeping at bay the unsettling changes that a globalizing world brings about," and this description fits Brown's comedy very well, up to a point.[11] Brown's comedy, self-evidently, posits an established order of things in which it is axiomatic that whiteness equals Englishness, that foreigners are made for ridicule, that homosexuals are inferior and that feminism is an untenable nonsense—so far, so reactionary. But the established order that Brown's comedy yearns for is also an order where white working-class identities are valid and valuable, where "classlessness" is revealed as a pernicious lie, where defending embattled communities against unemployment and deskilling still matters, where men and women mock each other's weaknesses but find ways of accommodating them within a framework of unvarnished but mostly amiable disputatiousness, and where humor helps people to make the best of low-expectation lives. The defining difference between those two lists is the place of class. In terms of sexual and ethnic politics, the outlook of Brown's comedy is far from progressive (though I would nonetheless still argue that his marital sex jokes find humor in the see-saw power struggles of heterosexual everyday life rather than in unrelieved misogyny); yet when studied through a class lens the picture is very different. That particular lens, however, is rarely used in contemporary academic studies of culture and identity, where works centered on gender, sexuality and ethnicity are immensely more numerous than those which place class center stage. Yet to understand Brown, to understand English comedy, and to understand Englishnesses in general, class must always be a prominent framework of analysis.

In a Britain so recently captivated by Tony Blair's New Labour project, however, class is a guilty secret, and the white working-class audiences who cheer Brown's every utterance are a cultural embarrassment. To understand why, it's revealing to look at a dazzlingly prescient essay written in 1982 by the historian Raphael Samuel. At that cultural moment, the Labour Party was in crisis following the defection of several prominent self-proclaimed moderates who had resigned in order to form the Social Democratic Party. The SDP, buoyed along by favorable media coverage, was briefly seen as threatening to replace Labour as the main opposition party to Margaret Thatcher's Conservative government. The relevance of that essay to this chapter lies in Samuel's brilliant anatomizing of how the SDP's messianic faith in new technologies and new industries was intimately connected to its distaste for organized working-class politics (in the shape of the trade union movement) and indeed to working-class life more generally. In doing so, he prefigures many of Giddens' arguments about the disembedded culture of postmodern society, with its concomitant undermining of settled identity and ontological security. For the SDP, according to Samuel, traditional working-class lives, cultures and politics were "anachronistic . . . backward-looking . . . insular . . . suspicious of progress and change . . . Luddite in relation to new technologies," all of which made them "offensive" to the SDP's "vision of society as a frontier-less open space."[12] The end result of this, he argued, was that the SDP "do not want to represent or help the working class. . . . They want to abolish it. In their mind's eye, with a speculative gaze fixed on the microchip revolution, and the impact of 'sunrise' technologies, the day does not seem far distant when the country may be inhabited by people as radical and reasonable, as up-to-date and mobile, as themselves."[13] Some of the language here is dated, but the underlying point seems indisputable: established working-class cultures were the product of specific industrial and economic practices in the process of being undermined by new technological changes. For the SDP, entranced as they were by rhetoric of newness and mobility and open spaces, that situation made working-class people, as traditionally conceptualized, supremely surplus to requirements. (And, as Sharif Mowlabocus has pointed out to me, how much better it has proved for the profit margins of globalized capitalism to transfer work from the politicized and truculent British proletariat to the nonunionized sweatshops of the developing world, filled with a much more docile and exploitable workforce.) The people traditionally accustomed to laboring in Britain's heavy industries could, in this SDP vision, either reinvent themselves and join the new world (though by waving which particular magic wand was never made clear), or risk becoming a dead weight, stranded by change. This, it should be clear by now, is the same kind of argument fostered in more theoretical circles by writers like Melucci and Chambers, and more importantly it is precisely the mindset of Tony Blair's New Labour, which swallowed whole the SDP's fetish for change, its managerialist rationalism, its trusting romance with technology and its impatient dismay at those people who failed to go with (what were selectively perceived as) the flow of the times. Worse still, to any cultural Blairite, it is exactly those same recidivists who failed to scramble on to the bandwagon headed for new times who compound their crime by insisting on spending time with Roy "Chubby" Brown. He is an important figure precisely because his popularity is a flagrant testament to the persistence of class as a meaningful category, an indispensable tool which English people use in recognizing, understanding and placing themselves. As long as he continues to flourish, then the specificities of white, working-class, heterosexual, Northern Englishness—with all its warm humor and inspiring solidarity, all its insular suspiciousness and its embittered fear of difference, all the gruff discourteous banter of its sex wars, and all its other ambivalences and contradictions—will still have their comedic champion.

B: "Transnational TV Comedy Audiences," Inger-Lise Kalviknes Bore[ii]

The relationship between nationality and humor has been debated across academic disciplines such as psychology, social anthropology, sociology, communication, and literary studies. Within television studies, this issue has been approached primarily through research on comedic representations of nationality, while more recent work has also looked at transnational adaptations of sitcom formats.[14] However, considering the continuing international trade in TV comedy programs and formats, it is also important to examine how audiences engage with transnational TV comedy. What are the constraints associated with such consumption? How do audiences make sense of nationally specific content? And why do essentialist notions of a national "sense of humor" persist, despite the international success of shows such as *Friends* (NBC, 1994–2004), *Yo Soy Betty, la Fea* (RCN TV, 1999–2001), and *The Office* (BBC2, 2001–3)?

* * *

[T]his article examines how [focus] groups discussed the pleasures and constraints of watching translated TV comedy, considers how transnational viewers made sense of these specific texts, and analyzes how participants constructed the programs in relation to notions of nationality. [This excerpt] also reflects on how Norwegian viewers compared *The Office* to other British programs. My discussion identifies key constraints associated with translated comedy viewing but also demonstrates that both Norwegian and British participants had a tendency to stress their comprehension of the translated comedy I screened while underestimating the ability of transnational viewers to make sense of the case study text that they, as national viewers, considered "theirs." Drawing on theories

ii. From Inger-Lise Kalviknes Bore, "Transnational TV Comedy Audiences," *Television & New Media* 12, no. 4 (2011): 347–349, 351–352, 355–361. Copyright © 2011 by Inger-Lise Kalviknes Bore. Reprinted by permission of SAGE Publications Inc.

of the relationship among humor, comedy, and nationality, I suggest that the recurring emphasis on difference served to reinforce a nation-based sense of distinctiveness.

* * *

Subtitled Comedy and Transnational Audiences

The role of subtitles was discussed in all of my groups, and the topic was sometimes introduced by the moderator and sometimes by participants. Both Norway and Britain tend to subtitle rather than dub foreign-language programming for adults. Dubbing was referred to in some of my focus groups, but no participants suggested that they preferred this translation approach to subtitles. Instead, dubbing was frequently both criticized and ridiculed. As Koolstra, Peeters, and Spinhof argue, viewers are used to the method adopted in their country and usually believe that this approach is the best.[15] However, in some focus groups, subtitling was constructed as a constraint associated with transnational audience engagement, and I discuss how this might be linked to patterns in TV trade, the specificities of TV comedy genres, and audience practices.

As previously noted, the Norwegian participants were all used to watching subtitled English language television. Many suggested that they normally did not give much thought to this process, which can be related to Antonini's argument that the subtitler should aim for "readability" and "invisibility."[16] In contrast, most Anglophone territories have had little need to import foreign-language programming.[17] Thus, while two of my British participants mentioned watching subtitled Welsh language TV programs, most referred to experiences of watching translated cinema rather than television.

In Norwegian focus group discussions, subtitles were often seen to supplement the dialogue. This can be illustrated by the following exchange between fifty-nine-year-old Marit and twenty-seven-year-old Kristine (group 13):

Moderator: Um, what do you think of watching subtitled things?
Marit: I prefer it when they're subtitled, because I think there are a few of these expressions that I'm too old to have picked up on, a lot that maybe the young people know, so I think it's handy if the English ones are subtitled, because the point might be more of a contemporary phrase that I didn't learn in school in the olden days, so I think it's an advantage when they're subtitled.

Kristine: Or they talk a bit fast, or not very clearly, and punch lines in
    particular should often be a bit quick.
Marit: [interruption] Yes.
Kristine: I prefer it when Norwegian programs are subtitled.
Marit: [interruption] Yes, that's often the case.
Kristine: because I think it's hard to follow it with only the sound.

However, while many Norwegian participants saw the reading of subtitles
as a way to fill gaps in their understanding of the dialogue, some also said
that they followed the subtitles whether they needed to read them or not.
In group 14, for example, Rune complained that he did it automatically:

It annoys me, because I'll just sit there, reading them. Even though,
even though, even though I am totally fine watching it without the subtitles, and understand everything, as soon as the subtitles are on, I end up
having to read them, just to check that I've got everything.

Participants in this group also criticized flawed translations and mocked
examples including the translation of "make up sex" as "cosmetics sex"
(*sminke-sex*) in Norwegian subtitles. Such mistakes could be seen to create new sources of humorous incongruity.

* * *

"British Humor" and *The Office*

Participants in eleven of the thirteen British focus groups highlighted the
Britishness of *The Office*, focusing on its incompetent characters, its drab
office setting, and its subtle humor. When asked what they thought viewers in other countries would make of the program, some British participants questioned the extent to which transnational viewers would be able
to make sense of it. This is an example from group 9:

Sophie: I think it's quite British humor, that sort of deadpan.
Kirsty: [interruption] I don't think they'd get it. I don't know how it's
    gone down, but I don't think they get it.
Sophie: No. I don't think they would, I think we've got quite cynical
    humor. [laughs] Cynical, deadpan.
Kirsty: [interruption] Like *Cheers* and what's the other one? *Frasier.*
Sophie: [interruption] *Frasier.*
Kirsty: I don't find them as funny as British humor. I do love British

humor. That's what I missed when I lived in Italy. A lot. So it'd have to be like a very British take on it.

Despite such misgivings, the potential of *The Office* for successful transnational engagement is demonstrated by the reported export of this BBC production to seventy countries. A number of countries have also bought the format and made their own versions.[18] This undermines the national specificity of *The Office*. The recurring emphasis on cultural differences in talk about *The Office* may thus reflect participants' desire to reinforce nation-based identities and us–them distinctions.[19] In this sense, humor can contribute to the imagining of the nation-state as an "inherently limited" and bounded community.[20]

However, six British participants also constructed *The Office* as "universal" rather than nationally specific. This idea was also evident in the Norwegian groups, where eleven participants suggested that one or more of the characters in *The Office* reminded them of people they knew or argued that similar people could be found in different workplaces. Focusing on the character of Gareth Keenan (Mackenzie Crook), twenty-two-year-old sales representative Tor (group 20) suggested that Gareth's behavior reminded him of his own colleague, "who's got his name on *everything* he has in the office." This form of character recognition relied on Norwegian participants drawing on their own social experiences in their engagement with *The Office* and their talk demonstrate the potential for transnational viewers to make sense of this sitcom.

There were also a number of other aspects that Norwegian participants laughed at and brought up in the subsequent discussions. A recurring topic was a scene where Gareth discovers that Tim (Martin Freeman) has put his stapler in gelatin because Gareth had refused to lend it to him. This scene has much more obvious comic cues than many of the other scenes in *The Office*, involving a rather overt incongruity and a moment of comic surprise. This is an extract from the all-male group 14:

Stian: [interruption] Yes, that's what I was going to say. Jell-O [laughs] or whatever it's called.
Torjus: Jell-O.
Stian: Yes, that was a bit good. [laughs]
Moderator: What was funny about that?
[laughter]
Rune: Cruel humor, that's fascinating. When someone else is the butt, that works.
Kristoffer: It would have been a fun trick. Yes.

In the scene, Gareth is clearly upset about his stapler and about manager David Brent's (Ricky Gervais) decision to side with Tim and crack jokes, instead of reprimanding him. This appears to have been a source of comic pleasure for twenty-two-year-old Rune, who described the scene as "cruel humor." Similarly, other Norwegian participants also described their pleasure at moments where Tim "gets one over" on Gareth. This is an example from the mixed-sex group 16, where Elin is referring to a scene in which Tim is refusing to respond to Gareth with anything but insults:

Elin: [interruption] Everyone laughed when he said that, "cock, cock, cock," every time he got those points, *everybody* laughed, so that is actually. . . . [pause]
Karin: [interruption] And the stapler in the jelly and that stuff.

. . . However, eighteen Norwegian participants also maintained that there were aspects of *The Office* that were specific to Britain. For example, participants in three groups suggested that its representations of workplace hierarchies are located in British experiences, arguing that interaction between Norwegian colleagues tends to be more egalitarian.[21] This exchange is from group 16:

Olav: But England is very [pause] I see that those colleagues who come from England, who come to Norway and started working here, and there, there is [pause] in *The Office* there is very much a hierarchy. [pause] You don't really talk to your boss. Right? They kind of just [pause] and it is obvious, that when people challenge things like that, then people start to, like, that is humorous for them. But here in Norway, then whether you are a boss, or a worker, there is usually a [pause] dialogue across.
Moderator: Mmm.
Olav: And then, for us, that might not be as humorous as it is for them, perhaps, who see that he is a challenge to that whole system.

Constructing humor as a corrective, thirty-three-year-old engineer Olav argued that the satirical representation of Brent's managerial style may not be as recognizable for Norwegian viewers.[22] Thus, while Olav had been a regular *Office* viewer, he suggested his transnational engagement with the text was nevertheless constrained by national differences.

Across the Norwegian groups, sixteen participants constructed the humor in *The Office* as specifically British, and this argument was sometimes used to explain why participants did not enjoy *The Office*. In this context, focus group members were at times reluctant, or struggling, to specify what they perceived such differences to be. This extract is from the all-male group 23:

> Henning: [interruption] Maybe you have to be English to see the humor in that show, I don't know.
> Moderator: Because this show was a hit in Britain, so do you have any thoughts on why that might be?
> Henning: They're very weird aren't they. English people.
> Moderator: [Laughs]
> Per: It's a British show and um, but I can't really see anything that strong, that's to do with the cultures.
> Moderator: Mmm.
> Per: It's certainly possible that it is, but um [pause] not that I can think of now. [pause] There's also nothing language-wise but obviously um [pause] the British may have a slightly different type of humor.
> Henning: Yes, they're really dry.
> Arve: Yes, yes.

Henning's description of "English people" as "weird" maintained the boundaries of imagined Norwegian-ness and rejected the "other" as incomprehensible. Per also failed to identify any specific cultural differences that could impede engagement with *The Office*, instead suggesting that the problem may be national differences in humor types. This essentialist construction of humor conflicts with other parts of their discussion, as all of the participants in group 23 had previously named British comedy series that they did enjoy, including *Absolutely Fabulous* (BBC1, 1992–96) and *Fawlty Towers*. This contradiction may suggest that speculations about more general cultural differences between Norwegian and British humor could instead be linked to textual elements specific to *The Office*. I now examine this possibility in more detail.

Discussions in four Norwegian groups constructed *The Office* as different from other British sitcoms. In group 25 Kristian argued that, unlike many other British imports, *The Office* excludes Norwegian viewers with low levels of English literacy because the verbal humor is difficult to translate. In other groups, it was also described as more demanding or slower than many previous British comedy series. This is an extract from group 18:

> Hege: . . . But British TV has always had, like Mum and them, they always say that they prefer watching British series to American series,

because they think the American series, at least Mum thinks that they
get [pause] it gets a bit superficial and phony, and a bit like, right?
Linn: [interruption] Yes, my parents as well. *Heartbeat* they watch.
Hege: [interruption] Yes, *Heartbeat* and *Peak Practice* and series like that.
[laughs]
[laughter]
Hege: Because the British series, they are so real.
Linn: [interruption] [high-pitched voice] "It's such lovely scenery!"
Hege: Yes! That's what they say as well!
[laughter]
Hege: It is, kind of, so real, they are just like normal people, right, so that
is, but maybe *The Office* was a bit too different, because it isn't exactly
like *Peak Practice*. [laughs]
Linn: No, it isn't exactly great scenery and lovely people.
Hege: [Laughs]
Linn: I don't think my parents would have fallen head over heels for this
one.

Group 18 here suggested that, for their parents, the appeal of British fiction was linked to notions of verisimilitude as well as to sympathetic characters and attractive rural settings. Medhurst argues that "English popular
comedy in the twentieth century . . . is overwhelmingly urban."[23] However, two of the exceptions that he highlights, *The Darling Buds of May*
(ITV, 1991–93) and *To the Manor Born* (BBC1, 1979–81), have both been
shown on Norwegian television, and this could suggest that their "comic
wallow in retrospective rurality" may offer some Norwegian viewers a
pleasurable engagement with romanticized notions of rural Englishness.
In contrast, *The Office* provides very different representations of Englishness or Britishness. As Brabazon points out,

> *The Office*, by focusing on Slough, creates an alternative Britain for the
> United States, after the death of Diana, the birth of Austin Powers and
> the recycling of Jane Austen. It is not heritage television but set in a
> (post)industrial business park.[24]

Hege suggested that *The Office* is too "real" to appeal to Norwegian viewers of her parents' generation. The generic hybridity of *The Office* also
appeared to be a problem for several of my Norwegian participants, who
struggled to identify the comic intention of this program. This is an example from group 15:

Solveig: I don't think it had a proper story, really, it was just. . . .

Vilde: [interruption] No, there were kind of a few funny points, but far too much filler in between.

Solveig: Yes, there was.

Nora: It's very documentary [pause]. Like, very typical, it was kind of too much of a documentary, really, to be funny, sometimes.

The perception that *The Office* lacks jokes and comic situations may be partly related to the absence of a laugh track. Antonini notes that foreign-language comedy can be particularly perplexing if viewers fail to understand comic moments that are signaled by laugh tracks.[25] However, as Elise (group 19) jokingly suggested, a laugh track might have helped her "understand when it's funny."

Discussions problematizing the comic intention of *The Office* often focused on David Brent's insensitive behavior. While some Norwegian participants constructed this as a source of humor in the program, others argued that these scenes were often too uncomfortable to be amusing. This can be related to what Klages sees as a "typical response" to what she terms "sick" humor. It includes

a laugh-wince, which represents a moment of simultaneous resistance and reification. The resistance occurs in the laughter, with which one recognizes, and happily participates in, a violation of social taboos and standards of polite behaviour. The reification of these social standards occurs with the wince which immediately follows the laugh; the wince is an acknowledgement of the self-enforcement of the social taboo, when the laughter chides herself for laughing at something that, when you think about it, is really NOT FUNNY.[26]

While audience engagement with *The Office* may involve this simultaneous laugh—wince, it is also complicated by the idea of comic intent. Who do viewers feel that they are being invited to laugh at? The bully or the victim or both? Several participants expressed confusion and frustration with scenes showing Brent's abuse of managerial power, and Mills argues that this discomfort is because of the program's use of docusoap devices. The employees are clearly aware of being filmed by the documentary crew, and they frequently address the camera directly.[27] As Mills notes, this removes the comic distance that encourages audiences to laugh at characters rather than feeling sorry for them.

British and Norwegian viewers who were unfamiliar with *The Office* often expressed uncertainty about how they were meant to respond to uncomfortable moments in the text, while those Norwegian participants who had watched several episodes were more likely to argue that they enjoyed this tension. This might suggest that viewers can "learn" to engage with the comic intention in a way that makes *The Office* more enjoyable. This process was also suggested by twenty-three-year-old British participant Peter, who said, "When it first came out, I didn't like it, but it's grown on me, steadily. So, sometimes with comedy, you have to almost get used to it."

Through this analysis of participant talk about *The Office*, I have considered the ways in which British and Norwegian participants constructed the national specificity or "universality" of *The Office*. Providing examples from the Norwegian focus group discussions, I have demonstrated the potential for pleasurable transnational engagement with this sitcom, but also examples of comic failure. The analysis examined perceived constraints to such engagement and suggested that these may primarily be linked to the program's generic hybridity. Audiences unfamiliar with *The Office* often struggled to identify its comic intention and were unsure about what and whom they were meant to laugh at.

C: "Transgressing Boundaries as the Hybrid Global: Parody and Postcoloniality on Indian Television," Sangeet Kumar[iii]

This study investigates the case of political comedy, whose translation is tricky due to culturally coded category of humor. In India this translation is further complicated by a rich and ancient indigenous tradition of comedy and satire as a means of speaking truth to power. Its lineage can be traced to the ancient Indian theory of drama within which the tropes of *rasa* or moods includes the *hasya rasa* or the trope of comedy.[28] From its ancient origins to its ripening as a fully developed mode of political resistance during colonial rule, political satire has thrived in India prior to the airing of the two shows analyzed here.[29] The notable contribution of these shows is popularizing the genre on television while also adapting already successful formats to India. While the Western tradition of satire has been well documented by scholars, this article illustrates how the merger of these seemingly different strands of humor within the shows allows them to inhabit an interstitial space located between Western and Indian aesthetics of humor.[30]

An analysis of Indian political satire must also locate its emergence within ongoing changes in the country's political landscape. Despite being a multiparty democracy that theoretically allows for equal representation and accountability through a system of checks and balances, India has entered a phase of extreme disillusionment with its political institutions and their ability to represent and empower the weakest in society. Instances of egregious abuses of power by politicians for personal gain have galvanized civil society leaders to take to Gandhian forms of national protest, forcing the state to negotiate with them for stringent anti-corruption laws. If political satire is a particularly apt mode of resistance during periods of "social and political rupture" or those of "manufactured realities," then the current political impasse in India provides ample cause for its thriving.[31] It allows for a "momentary form of aggression" against institutions of power that otherwise remain largely unaccountable and unreachable for the common people.[32] This political impasse provides ammunition for programs of satire to tap into and build upon the disillusionment.

* * *

Situating the Hybrid Global in Indian Television

Inspired by successful formats abroad and launched within short periods of each other on competing networks, the two shows analyzed here are prime instances of political humor on Indian television today. *The Week That Wasn't* (launched in 2006 and henceforth referred to as *TWTW*) airs weekly on Sunday nights. Hosted by the comedian Cyrus Broacha, it is a mix of news parody and skits that poke fun at news events by caricaturing and impersonating characters in the news. The show airs for 30 minutes each Sunday night on the network CNN-IBN, a 24-hour news network produced in collaboration with CNN. *Gustakhi Maaf* ("Excuse the Transgression"; launched in 2003) is a satirical puppet show in Hindi that airs for four minutes twice a day and then is compiled together to create a half hour show called the *Best of Gustakhi Maaf* on Sundays. . . .

TWTW is loosely based on the format of the American news parody program *The Daily Show*, while *Gustakhi Maaf* is a copy of the successful French puppet show *Les Guignols de l'info* ("News Puppets") that has run for more than 25 years on French television. Similar to the styles of Jon Stewart on *The Daily Show* and Stephen Colbert on *The Colbert Report*, *TWTW* follows the format of humorous video montages of news footage, fake reporters pretending to do on-location reporting, and fake "experts" pontificating on news events of the day/week. Similar to Stewart's straight-faced interviews, the reporters and experts on *TWTW* too begin in all seriousness (after having their expert credentials declared by Cyrus) until he begins to feign surprise at the ridiculousness of their answers. The juxtaposition of a serious news format with inexplicable and perplexing behavior or answers is the key to laughter on the show.

Akin to Stewart's constant penchant for ridiculing his own show through self-deprecating humor, *TWTW* also regularly indulges in self-bashing aimed to point out that its creators do not take themselves too seriously. A particular case in point is its celebration of 200 episodes in October 2010. As a part of its celebration, the show conducted interviews with several celebrities as well as journalists from the IBN channel on which *TWTW* aired. Almost every interviewee either feigned ignorance about the show and its anchor or dismissed it while hurling expletives. In one particular scene, the network's top executives in an editorial meeting show complete ignorance about the program and its anchor Cyrus. In another, the chief film critic on IBN reviews *TWTW* and gives it a rating of 0 out of 5. In an expanding and fiercely competitive television landscape caught in a ratings war and featuring outlandish claims about the relative success of networks and shows, this self-deprecating attitude, even coming from a parody show, stands out as odd.[33]

As opposed to the unofficial and informal relationship between *TWTW* and the American *TDS*, *Gustakhi Maaf* is an officially sanctioned Indian version of the French *Les Guignols*. The launch of the Indian version was preceded by a training workshop in which technicians and producers from the French show visited Delhi for over a month and taught their Indian counterparts (including the current anchor of the show) the skills of creating and maintaining the puppets. The program began with a short four-minute clip each weekday, but due to its rising popularity the frequency was increased to twice a day and later to three times a day before settling on a regular schedule of telecasting twice a day (the second one repeats the first airing).

Les Guignols and *Gustakhi Maaf* have identical-looking puppets as the technique of gradually constructing and then maintaining the cast was transferred to the Indian staff during the workshop. It currently takes about 25 days for the staff at *Gustakhi Maaf* to build a puppet and add it to the show's repertoire. Given the time and labor involved, the process of adding a puppet to the show depends on following the public actions of politicians and celebrities to gauge their ability to stay continuously in the news.

An innovative way in which the team has added a uniquely Indian flavor to the show is by confronting the real life characters (mostly politicians) with their puppets or that of their rivals. These face-offs have been extremely popular since coaxing a celebrity or a politician into conversations with their puppets (who speak as their alter ego) invariably leads to hilarious situations. "In these situations we realized that politicians respond best when the puppets speak in the plural 'us' as though the person and the puppet were one and the same," explains Shukla (personal communication, September 4, 2011). Among the topics between puppet and politician are strategies for the future, "malicious" media allegations, and private conversations presented as though the real people are speaking to themselves. Not all politicians take this face-off sportingly and the team has also had rude encounters in the process. When confronted with her political rival's puppet at a political event, the politician Uma Bharati was visibly upset and refused to engage in any conversation. Later, however, when mollified she agreed to a long conversation with her puppet (but not with her rival's) (Shukla, personal communication, September 4, 2011). For the most part, publicity hungry politicians jump at these opportunities, especially during election time.

Besides these face-offs between puppets and real people, the show has also introduced a distinctly Indian ethos through the use of musical numbers from Hindi movies. The cultural dominance of the film industry in India ensures that popular songs from successful movies provide readily available metaphors for explaining political events that the show frequently deploys to amplify themes of love, betrayal, and loyalty to describe shifts in political coalitions and changes in personal fortunes in Indian politics. The writers on the show routinely write their own lyrics set to the tunes of popular numbers from movies.

As is evident, *Gustakhi Maaf*'s success must be attributed as much to its borrowed format as to the innovative ways in which it has managed to reflect uniquely Indian themes and motifs. These adaptations allow it to resonate with Indian audiences especially in the nonmetropolitan areas of the country. "News reporters from our network who travel to rural areas frequently narrate instances of immediate recognition when introducing themselves from the same channel that airs *Gustakhi Maaf*," explains Shukla (personal communication, July 8, 2011). The diverging ways in which both the comedy shows have Indianized themselves points to the unique case of the Indian audience as well as the fragmented Indian national identity itself. The historical processes instrumental in creating this fractured identity inform the analysis of the two shows.

* * *

The Language of Humor

Both shows play upon the linguistic and accent diversity within India to create humor. While *TWTW* uses the distinction between the Hindi and non-Hindi speaking populations, *Gustakhi Maaf* taps into the variations and dialects within Hindi itself. Given the rich multiplicity within the linguistic space in India, the issue of language creates ample opportunities for jokes aimed at politicians and celebrities. For *TWTW* the inability to speak English, or in the correct accent, is a frequently recurring cause for ridicule. A case in point is the show airing June 26, 2011, in which the Indian Finance Minister Pranab Mukherjee's accent is exaggerated to create comic effect. Even though the person ridiculed on the show is not the minister himself but his spokesperson, it is clear that the show makes the latter stand in for Mukherjee as the skit repeatedly exaggerates his accent and makes fun of his inability to speak grammatically correct English. Moreover the skit, which is based on allegations of Mukherjee's office being spied upon through a wiretap, ends when the spokesperson mentions that bugging his office was a useless exercise as no one could understand what he was saying anyways. The joke is clearly targeted at the finance minister's thick accent that is at odds with the polished Anglicized accent considered "proper" within the English-speaking world of *TWTW*.

Several of the shows jokes are language based relying on puns or phrases that require an advanced familiarity with the language. For instance, Cyrus recently (May 8, 2011) poked fun at a politician by saying that "he put his foot in his mouth" and adding, "and it fit perfectly well." In yet another instance he clarifies accusations against the Prime Minister by saying that instead of calling him a "lame duck," he was actually a "sitting duck." An earlier episode about the President's visit to China played on the phrase "bull in a China shop." Many of these linguistic wordplays also utilize a uniquely Indian way of speaking English that may be lost on speakers of English in other nations. In an interview celebrating 150 episodes of the show, Cyrus interviews Kunal Vijaykar, an actor on the show, who frequently uses words/phrases such as "motherswear," "one nut loose," and "get your kidney checked." Each of these phrases, even though spoken in English, are translations of common Hindi phrases that have been incorporated into the lexicon of Indian English and are far more likely to resonate with an Indian speaker of English than English speakers from other countries.

Similarly, the use of language on *Gustakhi Maaf* relies on regional variations in Hindi accents to create humorous situations. These depictions rely on stereotypical conceptions about regional accents and privilege a North Indian way of speaking Hindi over other region's accents. Distinctions from the norm are marked either by overtly Sanskritized "pure" Hindi that sounds comically highfalutin or by an Anglicized Hindi that is interspersed with English words. While the former is often used to mock a purist right-wing position, the latter is used to ridicule an elite incapable of speaking in Hindi without using English words. On the show, both religious gurus (e.g., well-known yoga guru Baba Ramdev speaking in accentuated Hindi) and English-speaking politicians (e.g., Rahul Gandhi using English words when speaking) are frequently the target. The attack on politicians unable to speak Hindi is a surreptitious condemnation of the elites in the English speaking India who either cannot speak Hindi or avoid speaking it in order to mark social distinction. It is a way to reassert the primacy of Hindi, the language of the program, within the political discourse of the country.

The complex politics of English in postcolonial India are not merely symbolic but also have material stakes as language and accent become means of upward social mobility.[34] While certain regions in India (specifically in Southern and North Eastern India) have welcomed the hegemony of English as a counter to the dominance of Hindi, regional parties in the North have opposed that imposition as they see English as a vehicle through which the English-educated elite perpetuate their rule. It is also a potent issue in the electoral politics of India with some regional parties frequently threatening legislation against the use of English and others seeking a more widespread role for it to counter the dominance of the North over Southern India. The different ways in which the two shows deploy linguistic difference in India to humorous effect allow us to interrogate the political stakes masked behind the comedic gesture. While English remains an aspirational language for all, there is a clear disdain against those who differentiate themselves on the basis of the supposed cultural capital the language and a certain accent gives them.

Looking Inside versus Looking Outside

Related to the issue of language is the emphasis each program places on foreign versus domestic stories. Aimed towards an English speaking urban audience, *TWTW* is focused on foreign stories and events far more than *Gustakhi Maaf*. Its jokes and skits ridicule foreign (usually Western) celebrities and politicians almost as often as they pick on Indian targets. This tendency to focus on Western stories shows the extent to which the show's targeted demographic already consumes and is familiar with non-Indian news and cultural events.

* * *

Commenting on another news report that noted that a certain section of the US population blamed the recent Japanese tsunami on retribution for their attack on Pearl Harbor, Cyrus claims, "but these are the same people who kept the show *Two and a Half Men* running for eight seasons!" The reference to the Charlie Sheen show is noteworthy because were it not for the recent scandal involving him, the show would be quite unknown in India. In a single joke he ties together several cultural and news events that are US-specific and hence foreign to Indians unless they regularly consumed American popular culture through media or travel. These jokes rely on an existing knowledge base about the United States, presumably created due to the global proliferation of US culture through Hollywood and globalized television that *TWTW* is both inspired by and a beneficiary of.

The desire created by this access is frequently tapped into by *TWTW* and in sharp contrast to *Gustakhi Maaf*, it is Hollywood and not India's own film industry that is the source for plotlines and themes to be parodied. An instance of this is a skit inspired by news that James Bond would be shooting his next film in India. In the skit, Bond (played by Cyrus) goes around discovering what the show would consider to be the most remarkable things about India seen from a Western perspective. To begin, Bond visits a high-society party where upper-class women are talking in whispers about the fact that they illegally employ underage maids for household work. Having made note of this common malpractice in India, Bond moves to a bar where he is informed that he can only be served drinks if he is over the age of 25 (referring to recent legislation in the province of Maharashtra where the city of Mumbai is located). Bond then moves to the popular Juhu beach in Mumbai expecting to meet women there but instead only comes across a few drunken men dancing to Bollywood songs.

This short skit is notable because it picks up on those aspects of Indian life that the makers of the show perceive would strike a Westerner as odd. The skit therefore refracts the Western gaze on Indian society. More importantly, the interstitial space that the show occupies allows it to reflect the gaze back onto the West as it simultaneously mocks both the oddities of India and the Western gaze that would find certain things to be odd.

As opposed to this, the Hindi show *Gustakhi Maaf* rarely uses or makes reference to events and celebrities from the West. In the rare case this occurs the reference is strictly in the realm of politics and rarely popular culture. The most frequent non-Indian context mentioned on the show is that of India's neighbor Pakistan, which given its rivalry with India in the realm of politics and cricket, continues to occupy a large share of the conversation in Indian media. The show regularly takes a dig at the country's internal instability and its close relationship with the US with frequent skits that show presidents of both countries meeting in private to plan their public strategy. The most recent of these skits occurred after the killing of Osama Bin Laden. The skit offers a prehistory of the killing as it shows former US President George Bush teaching the former Pakistani President Pervez Musharaf to feign public anger against the US presence in Pakistan in order to allay opposition against him. The skit then repeats the exact scenario with the current Prime Minister of Pakistan Yousuf Geelani first practicing in private with President Obama and then publicly getting an apology out of him after feigning displeasure. The message about the failure of the Pakistani state is clear and is part of efforts by the show to create Pakistan as India's inferior Other.

* * *

In exploring the distinct ways in which the two shows have Indianized themselves, . . . this article points to the innovativeness engendered within global cultural exchanges.[35] It responds to the invitation of scholars who see the global amalgamation of culture as a story of gain rather than one of loss. In so doing it takes seriously Pieterse's contention that the coming together of cultures in a syncretic mix, while frequently seen as erasing global difference, could also be seen as emphasizing similarities.[36] The latter perspective begins with the position that cultural texts must meet the threshold of a bare minimum resonance with audiences in order to be translatable to new locations. A text entirely at odds with the cultural sensibilities prevalent at its new site may arouse initial interest but will invariably meet opposition and face steep odds unless it allows space for local specificities to seep in. The category of humor is a helpful heuristic tool in this investigation as it allows for the interplay of sameness and difference to emerge quite clearly. Causes for laughter around the world are both common as well as culturally contingent and the two shows analyzed here show this duality at play.

They display humor strategies that could have worked in a different cultural setting as well as those that are specific to the cultural framework of India. The most prominent instances of the former, found already embedded in the borrowed formats for both shows are juxtaposing incongruities and mimicry. As *TWTW* relies on professional reporters and "experts" to do and say the incomprehensible and *Gustakhi Maaf* allows respectable public figures to be caricatured through puppets, they both rely on the juxtaposition of seemingly incompatible elements to create laughter. Moreover the puppets in *Gustakhi Maaf* as well as the characters on *TWTW* are also copies of an original that they mimic with a "critical ironical distance" thus subverting the original through parody.[37] The tropes of juxtaposition and mimicry commonly seen in Western aesthetics of comedy are also deeply embedded in the ancient Indian treatise on drama the Natyashastra and hence point to the commonalities within the category of humor.[38] Focusing on it affirms Pieterse's contention that cultural globalization hinges as much on similarities as it does on difference.[39] Exploring the two shows as a story of gain must emphasize how the genre of political comedy is enriched through its interaction with a new cultural site.

D: "Comedy and the Nation in *The Trip*," Brett Mills

The comedy series *The Trip* (BBC, 2010) features the writer-performers Rob Brydon and Steve Coogan travelling around the rural areas of northern England sampling restaurants as Coogan has been commissioned to write food reviews for a UK national newspaper. In the program, Brydon and Coogan play characters with the same names as themselves, and the series draws on their longstanding working relationship perhaps best exemplified in the film *A Cock and Bull Story* (Winterbottom, 2006). Furthermore, the restaurants the characters visit are ones that exist in the real world too—many of them extremely well-regarded on the UK culinary scene—and the program therefore places itself within a recognizable world that viewers can, if they wish, choose to enter outside of the program. While not a mockumentary, the program draws on ideas of comic realism by placing its characters in the real world, and as Coogan and Brydon play versions of themselves, the viewer is invited to ponder to what extent we are witnessing their "real" relationship.[40] While all cultural products can be examined in order to think about the nation that produced them, this attempt to place a comedy program within a recognizable, real-world UK renders it a ripe site for the examination of the comedic representation of, and relationships with, the nation.

Before discussing the specifics of the program, however, it is worth noting the broader relationships between a British sense of identity and humor. National identities are always "imagined communities" which require restating and reaffirming in order to justify their existence and to suggest that they are natural and inevitable.[41] This process is carried out via a range of techniques, such as the structuring of governments and tax systems, but is perhaps most evident in an everyday manner via ideas of culture. All nations have conceptions of their own particular inflections of culture and celebrate these in things like national galleries, anniversaries of the births or deaths of "great" artists, and statues of exemplars of cultural producers. National school curricula similarly inculcate learners into the specifics of the culture they are assumed to belong to. Such processes result in a sense of "belonging, [which is] a feeling of mostly illusory yet deeply sustaining togetherness."[42] Belonging is central to the idea of the nation because it is also a process which can exclude, as those unable to understand or emotionally respond to forms of culture deemed central to a particular nation can be argued to not "properly" belong to that community. It is in this way that immigrant cultures, for example, can be seen as problematic to dominant ideologies of the nation, and the failure for those new to a country to properly "get" the imagined community can be used to suggest that they don't properly "belong" and therefore should leave.

Comedy can be a particularly interesting site for the examination of these tensions as humor "is a prime testing ground for ideas about belonging and exclusion."[43] As humor commonly functions by inviting an audience to be amused by a comic butt, it can both include and exclude; the audience comes together to affirm its shared humor, while the butt is excluded as worthy of nothing but laughter. That comedy might function in a "disciplinary" manner to police behavior and render the outsider as laughable has long been one of the key criticisms of it, and a wide range of work on sexist and racist humor argues that comedy is a powerful tool for policing what enters the mainstream and what is perceived as "normal."[44]

Thinking about this in terms of television comedy is often difficult, because it can be unclear who is telling the joke and who the audience is. That is, in a sitcom the comedy may come from things characters do or say that they know are funny (in which case the teller is that character) or may instead come from the audience being invited to find laughable the actions of a character who does not know they are doing something humorous (in which case the teller is the program itself). Traditionally, the sitcom has attempted to reaffirm the collective nature of its consumption via the laugh track, whereby viewers get to hear others finding the comedy funny. This "electronic substitute for collective experience" insists the comic nature of particular moments is unarguable, and invites viewers to join in with the mass of others finding it funny.[45] In that sense, the laugh track functions as an indicator of the "imagined community," a textual component stating that "we" find this funny, and here's the aural evidence of this process taking place. Like many contemporary sitcoms, though, *The Trip* does not have a laugh track, and therefore cannot use this aural tactic to imply a unified response to its comedy. While the loss of the laugh track could be seen as evidence of a wider range of possible interpretations, I want to show here how the idea of the nation *The Trip* relies on remains secure, evident in its depiction of locations, the kinds of humor it employs, and its status as a comedy program made by the BBC.

This is because even though comedy is a useful topic for thinking about all national and cultural identities, its role in a British sense of identity is more prominent than for many other nations. As Andy Medhurst notes, "English comedy . . . contributes significantly to how English culture has imagined its Englishness."[46] Medhurst highlights the complexity in referring to this comic Englishness, partly because of the confusion between Britain and England, but also because regions within Britain can be seen to have particular comic inflections too. Citing a number of examples, Medhurst argues that the characteristics of English comedy are not coherent or cohesive, and therefore cannot be definitively defined. Their potency instead lies in the assumption that "it is impossible to conceive of them [British jokes] coming from anywhere else."[47] Whether certain kinds of jokes *do* exist in other countries is irrelevant; what matters for a British sense of comic identity is simply the assumption that that humor is unique and exclusive.

It is in these ways that a sense of identity, and a sense of comic nationhood, is "imagined." The suggestion that comedy is central to notions of British national identity is demonstrated by the fact that, since 2013, it has become part of the ways in which the British government assesses those new to the country. That is, immigrants wanting to apply for British citizenship have to pass a "Life in the United Kingdom" test, which aims to help those new to the country learn the "values and principles at the heart of being British."[48] Debates about what should be excluded and included in that test are highly political, but since 2013 what has been included has been "an exploration of Britons' unique sense of humor and satire."[49] Such statements make clear claims for the specificity of a national sense of humor, which is not only "unique" but also a key "principle" related to everyday interactions. Newspapers reporting on the inclusion of this material noted that no other country places comedy within their citizenship tests, and proudly proclaimed the self-evidently unique nature of British comedy.

In more practical terms, the ways in which these "imaginings" play themselves out can be seen in the workings of the institution that made and broadcast *The Trip*, the BBC. One of the oddities of television as a cultural form is that "for most of its history, in most places where it is available, television has been a national medium."[50] While all forms of culture are related to nation, the organization of television (and other forms of broadcasting, such as radio) has been much more strongly tied to the nation than is the case for things like literature, music, and film. The BBC is funded by a license fee, charged to households resident in the UK, placing the responsibility for funding television on the citizens of the nation. Comparable license fees for other countries work in the same way. The BBC also functions as public service broadcaster, whereby television is seen as a public, rather than commercial, good that can productively serve the nation. Because of this, the BBC is given purposes to fulfil, and these center on the ideas of the nation. The BBC's current remit requires it to "represent the UK, its nations, regions and communities" and "bring the UK to the world and the world to the UK."[51] While similar remits apply to pretty much all public service broadcasters, the BBC version of this is unlike some comparable institutions in that it repeatedly argues comedy is a genre through which these goals can be achieved. The BBC argues that "good comedy continues to resonate with audiences, particularly when it reflects the texture of British life."[52] That comedy can supposedly "reflect" the nation demonstrates the assumption that Britishness is something coherent and self-evident, which comedy merely draws on. However, such programming also helps restate and reinforce these national ideals, showing how "in so many little ways, the citizenry are daily reminded of their national place in a world of nations."[53]

In *The Trip* Brydon and Coogan function as citizens who remind themselves and their viewers of the ever-presence of nationhood. This is done not only through comedy but also via aesthetic choices. Key comic moments in *The Trip* center on Brydon and Coogan eating in the restaurants they are reviewing, doing impersonations of a wide range of actors, writers, and other celebrities. As performers, the two are highly skilled mimics, and the program's format allows them to display these skills, in a semi-improvisational style that enables them to riff off one another. In one sequence the two battle over who does the best Michael Caine impersonation, even going into the detail of how that actor's voice has changed over his career. The comedy of the sequence comes from the accuracy of their impersonations, but also the bickering they employ to critique one another's performance. In these sequences Brydon is usually the more affable and keen to please, while Coogan's character is more detached and cynical, commonly offering cutting demolitions of Brydon's impersonations and his enthusiasm. Much of the pleasure on offer here comes from the free interplay between the two performers, and the suggestion that, as viewers, we might be getting some insight into how the real Coogan and Brydon are when they are together, in a manner comparable to much work carried out by Brydon, where he often plays versions of himself.[54]

The actors Brydon and Coogan choose to impersonate are evidence of the normalization of certain ideas of nation in the program. As already noted, Michael Caine is a recurring figure, but others over whom the two battle include Sean Connery and James Mason. All of these are British. While the program does include impersonations of non-British actors (such as Arnold Schwarzenegger and Al Pacino), it is those from the UK that dominate. Caine, Connery, and Mason are, of course, internationally successful film performers, whose fame is not limited to the UK; their inclusion in the program is not one likely, then, to cause confusion for international audiences, least of all in the United States. But it is significant that each of them has been successful internationally via a performance of different kinds of Britishness, and are emblematic of a variety of ways that the UK is understood internationally. Michael Caine's performances in *The Italian Job* (Collinson, 1969) and *Get Carter* (Hodges, 1971) illustrate that he has appeared in films that have been read as "functioning as propaganda for British culture and industry" and as "expressly English."[55] Sean Connery's portrayal of James Bond embodies a version of Britishness which is perhaps one of the most famous in the world. And Paul Ward argues that, although James Mason had complex on- and off-screen relationships with his English identity, his "sense of rootedness in locality" repeatedly signaled his foreignness to American audiences.[56] For all three, their fame and success has been dependent upon selling a version of Britishness to the world which makes sense to international audiences. One of the key ways in which this takes place is via the voice.

It is the very distinctive voices of these actors which Brydon and Coogan emulate and mock in *The Trip*, working from the assumption that the audience knows who these people are and are aware of the films that are being cited. All of this may seem obvious; parodies and mockery always assume audience knowledge of the original. But this is evidence of the very ordinary, everyday way in which ideas of nation recur, and are drawn upon. In *The Trip* we have two British comedy actors demonstrating their comic skill in performing a range of iconic national voices, taken from actors who have represented different versions of British national identity to international audiences. That the program makes no attempt to explain who any of these people are shows how the specificity of Britishness on offer here is *assumed* to be intelligible and to make sense. It is precisely in the reiterations of these assumptions that the supposed normalness of national identity is restated. And in order for the comedy to make sense, audiences have to buy into this idea, whether this is a viewer from the UK seeing their own nation reflected back to themselves, or one from another country enjoying the presentation of a foreign national identity.

That said, tensions exist within this vision of Britain, as they do within all ideas of nation. And *The Trip* plays on those tensions sometimes for its humor. As noted above, the UK is a complex country made up of four discrete nations, whose union is a quirk of historical accident, politics, and invasion. These tensions ebb and flow, perhaps most evident in the Brexit debate and the 2014 Scottish referendum in which that country voted whether or not to leave the UK. While globally Englishness and Britishness are often conflated, they are instead very different entities, and the inclusion of Connery in the pantheon of targets for mockery in *The Trip* is significant because of his pronounced Scottishness, whereby he has routinely made pronouncements about the possibility of that country's independence. Furthermore, these national tensions exist for Coogan and Brydon, for while the former is English, the latter is Welsh, and jokes about these two nations recur across the series.

Indeed, Brydon has spent much of his career drawing on his Welsh identity not only for comic purposes but also in serious documentaries about nation, such as *Rob Brydon's Identity Crisis* (BBC4, 2008) in which he examined whether there was something specific about a Welsh comic identity. In comic terms, Wales commonly represents a cultural backwater, less sophisticated than urbanized, modern England; this is perhaps best exemplified in the comedy series *Gavin and Stacey* (BBC3/1, 2007–10), which centered on the romantic relationship between the eponymous characters, one of whom lived in Wales, while the other resided in England. In that series Brydon played a Welsh character repeatedly astonished by modern technology who marveled at the sophisticated ways of the English characters he met. Indeed, Brydon has spent much of his career playing wide-eyed naivety, and the success of this can be linked to his being Welsh and the ways in which Welshness is stereotyped in British comic culture.

Coogan, on the other hand, comes from Manchester, and exemplifies the sophisticated urbanite, coupled with the sense of "cool" that that city connotes. Their comic battles in *The Trip* therefore play on the English/ Welsh contiguity which both binds them together as British, but which also divides them into more specific national identities. This is evidence of how ideas of national identity can acknowledge the tensions that exist within them, while simultaneously rendering those tensions as not significant enough to seriously threaten the coherence of the nation. Here the differences between Brydon and Coogan sit alongside their similarities, the nation being a collective unit within which difference can persist. It is via such processes that national identities remain stable, accepting "the particular and the universal" that are assumed to underpin their naturalness.[57]

The content of the comedy in *The Trip* can therefore be seen to derive from ideas of the nation, and to contribute to the coherence of the nation. This program is particularly interesting in terms of nation, though, because of its visual engagement with ideas of location and geography. For much of its history, sitcom has been a studio-bound genre, which has meant that even though particular programs are nominally situated in real-life locations, they rarely offer up those spaces as part of the pleasure of the program. For example, while series such as *Friends* (NBC 1994– 2004) and *Seinfeld* (NBC 1989–1998) display iconic New York landmarks in some of their establishing shots, and draw on some comic mannerisms associated with New York urbanism, their location is not central to their comedy, nor for much of the time are those locations visually represented. The recurring locations in these series are indoors, and their being situated in a particular city is not vital to the comedy. Indeed, for sitcoms to be comprehensible to mass national and international audiences, it is essential that programs do not situate themselves too strongly in a location, or employ localized references which are likely to be unintelligible to wider audiences. A sense of place in much sitcom, then, is predicated more often on those internal spaces whose geographical specificity is limited, such as the coffee shop in *Friends* or Jerry's apartment in *Seinfeld*.

This is quite different in *The Trip*. As already noted, the program is located in real-world restaurants, placed diegetically in geographical locations congruent with those of the viewer. Indeed, while much sitcom has

Brydon and Coogan traverse the pastoral terrain of northern England, inviting viewers to take pleasure in *The Trip*'s comedic construction of British identity.

recurring sets, *The Trip* lacks these, with each episode about a different location, and much of the narrative often taken up with the characters travelling to that location. If there is a recurring set in the program, it is the car the two travel across the country in, with many scenes depicting them comically bantering as they drive. This setting functions in a manner similar to much sitcom, enabling the characters to engage in comic dialogue which is filmed in a shot-reverse-shot style evident in much comedy. But that setting, as a vehicle on the move, is also different to those recurring locations in other sitcoms, precisely because it symbolizes movement. It is also functional rather than domestic, when much sitcom instead uses spaces such as apartments and coffee shops as reassuring, familiar spaces in which domestic activities occur. Perhaps most importantly, all scenes in the car in *The Trip* show the countryside outside the window passing by, the sense of movement permanently evident. In that sense, the outside is always present in the program, and the program repeatedly encourages the viewer to take pleasure in the locations on offer. For a viewer unfamiliar with these landscapes their specificity is unmarked, and they instead function as a generalized, northern rural environment conforming to the ways in which the British countryside is "imagined." That they can be meaningful without being specific demonstrates the certainty of the imagining, inviting viewers—both British and international—to recognize their Britishness without the need for reference to the specificity of the locations.

This is evident in the number of very wide shots the program employs, with the characters, or their car, located in the distance, situated within the geography. Sitcom is traditionally shot in close-up, enabling humor to be derived not only from comic action but also from reaction shots. For comedy, space and location are pretty much irrelevant, for comic mileage is garnered through the activities of the performers. *The Trip* is shot quite differently. A recurring joke in the series is Coogan's inability to get a signal for his mobile phone due to the remote landscape they are in, and he is required to trudge to the tops of hills, holding his phone aloft, in search for a signal. In these shots Coogan is often a small figure in a very wide shot, and his powerlessness is comically emphasized by his lack of status in the frame. But these shots are also often very beautiful, depicting sunsets behind valley ridges, or the morning mist settling on lakes, while the dawn chorus stirs. That is, there is (non-comic) pleasure on offer here from the depiction of a particular kind of rural English landscape. Felix Thompson, in his analysis of the British factual series *Coast* (BBC2 2005–), shows how British national identity draws on ideas of particular kinds of geography, with television offering "visual pleasures of landscape," and a recurring suggestion of a "uniqueness of place."[58] While Coogan's inability to get a phone signal comically highlights the problems in the unique aspects of geography, the program repeatedly reasserts the specialness of the locations the characters visit, and offers these up for pleasure. So, as the characters journey across the Lake District so do we as viewers, with recurring depictions of a certain kind of rugged, rural English landscape rooting the series within a location emblematic of a certain kind of Englishness. It is unlikely that foreign viewers (and, for that matter, many British ones) would have in-depth knowledge of these locations, or have visited them themselves. However, this specificity does not matter; what is relevant here is how these locations connect to an idea of English landscape repeatedly presented across a range of media as being British, as shown in films such as *The Full Monty* (Cattaneo 1997) and television series like *Downton Abbey* (ITV 2010–). This is part of how Britishness is "imagined."

Of course, central to the process of imagining a nation is the need to exclude as well as include; there are things an imagined Britishness does *not* look like as much as there are things it does. As noted above, there are tensions in the coherence of a British identity because of the multiple nations which constitute it, and a wealth of media has attempted to embrace "cultural diversity" and therefore "constitute a powerful critique of traditional ideas of Britishness."[59] *The Trip*'s focus on rural vistas posits preindustrial landscapes as ones of peace and tranquility, and the depictions of the city—as seen in the first and last episode—situate these as isolating. The Britishness evident in *The Trip* is resolutely white, not only in terms of the characters depicted but also the historical places Brydon and Coogan visit (in particular, those associated with the Lake Poets) and the food which is eaten; there are, for example, no curries here. So while the comedy on the program draws on the tensions and complexities within contemporary middle-aged masculinity, it situates such contested selfhood within solid, recognizable national contexts that ignore the multiple ways "Britishness" might be conceived. Its focus on landscape and food means it "imagines" these as untroubled, uncontested categories, and therefore coherent contexts within which comic debates about masculinity can take place.

The Trip therefore repeatedly draws on ideas of the nation, both for its comic matter and for its visual aesthetic. It presents a version of Britishness which acknowledges the tensions within the nation, while rendering these unthreatening by making them comic. It places its protagonists in a recognizable landscape, offering up those locations for an additional pleasure. And it narratively presents travel across the countryside as a worthwhile and pleasurable pursuit, locating the specificity of the Lake District within a broader British context. Here, a sense of space and place naturalizes the nation; and via the comedy, it suggests the British sense of humor is similarly unique and natural too. In these ways, *The Trip* can be seen to be evidence of how "humour is an important means to negotiate identity and belonging."[60]

A significant footnote: in 2014 a sequel to *The Trip* was broadcast, called *The Trip to Italy*. In that series Brydon and Coogan travelled around Italy, once again reviewing restaurants, via a route that enables them to retrace the journeys taken by the Romantic poet Lord Byron in the nineteenth century. The kinds of jokes the program tells remain the same, even while the locations and geography are noticeably different. While this chapter does not explore this program, it is worth highlighting because it demonstrates the ways in which ideas of national identity are transportable. Indeed, as Brydon and Coogan haltingly interact with Italians in a manner congruent with stereotypes of the reserved, embarrassed British person, their national identities are thrown into even sharper relief. Their "belonging" to a natural and unarguable Britishness is all the more evident because they are in places where they resolutely do not belong.

Notes

1. Brown, *Common as Muck*, 332.
2. See Quade, "A Slap in the Face"; Brown, *Common as Muck*.
3. Melluci, "Identity and Difference," 61–62.
4. For a spirited and moving defense of white English working-class culture, albeit in a southern rather than a northern setting, see Collins, *The Likes of US*.
5. Billig, *Banal Nationalism*, 136.
6. Billig, *Banal Nationalism*, 136.
7. Giddens, *The Consequences of Modernity*, 92.
8. Giddens, *The Consequences of Modernity*, 21.
9. Silverstone, *Television and Everyday Life*, 19.
10. Chambers, "Narratives of Nationalism," 159.
11. Ang, "Identity Blues," 4.
12. Samuel, *Island Stories*, 265.
13. Samuel, *Island Stories*, 271.
14. Dobson, "Mister Sparkle Meets the *Yakuza*"; McCallum, "Cringe and Strut"; Sørenssen, "I Have a Plan!"; Beeden and Bruin, "*The Office*"; Griffin, "The Americanization of *The Office*."
15. Koolstra, Peeters, and Spinhof, "The Pros and Cons of Dubbing," 326.
16. Antonini, "The Perception of Subtitled Humor in Italy," 212.
17. Horan, "Quality US TV," 111.
18. BBC News, "*The Office* to be Remade in Russia."
19. Critchley, *On Humour*, 67–68.
20. Anderson, *Imagined Communities*, 6.
21. For a further discussion of the ideals of egalitarianism in Norway, see Gullestad, "Invisible Fences."
22. Paul, *Laughing Screaming*, 48.
23. Medhurst, *A National Joke*, 48–49.
24. Brabazon, "What Have You Ever Done on the Telly?," 104.
25. Antonini, "The Perception of Subtle Humor," 222.
26. Klages, "What to Do with Helen Keller Jokes," 17.
27. Mills, *Television Sitcom*, 64.
28. Arogyasami, "Shakespeare's Treatment of Comic Sentiment"; Schwartz, *Performing the Divine in India*; Vatsyayan, *Bharata*.
29. Freedman, *The Offensive Art*; Hasan, "Political Satire in Modern India."
30. Connery and Combe, *Theorizing Satire*; Hutcheon, *A Theory of Parody*.
31. Gray, Jones, and Thompson, "The State of Satire," 15.
32. Gray, Jones, and Thompson, "The State of Satire," 12.
33. Kohli-Khandekar, *The Indian Media Business*; Sanghvi, "News TV."
34. Sonntag, "The Changing Global-Local Linguistic Landscape."
35. Havens, "Globalization and the Generic Transformation."
36. Pieterse, "Globalization as Hybridization."
37. Hutcheon, *A Theory of Parody*.
38. Arogyasami, "Shakespeare's Treatment of Comic Sentiment."
39. Pieterse, "Globalization as Hybridization."
40. Hight, *Television Mockumentary*; Mills, *The Sitcom*, 128.

41. Anderson, *Imagined Communities*.
42. Medhurst, *A National Joke*, 35.
43. Medhurst, *A National Joke*, 39.
44. Billig, *Laughter and Ridicule*, 39.
45. Medhurst and Tuck, "The Gender Game," 45.
46. Medhurst, *A National Joke*, 1.
47. Medhurst, *A National Joke*, 54.
48. Booth, "Want to Become a British Citizen?"
49. Booth, "Want to Become a British Citizen?"
50. Turner, "Television and Nation," 54.
51. BBC, *Annual Report 2013/14*, 2.
52. BBC, *Annual Report 2011/12, Part 2*, 18.
53. Billig, *Banal Nationalism*, 8.
54. Mills, "Being Rob Brydon."
55. Foster, "Snobs, Yobs, and Italian Jobs," 1015; Fuller, "Brute Force," 35.
56. Ward, "Did You See James Mason," 418.
57. Perkins, "The Banality of Boundaries," 388.
58. Thompson, "*Coast* and *Spooks*," 431; Thompson, "*Coast* and *Spooks*," 432.
59. Higson, "The Instability of the National," 35.
60. Kessel, "Landscape of Humour," 3.

Works Cited

Anderson, Benedict. *Imagined Communities*. London: Verso, 1991.
Ang, Ien. "Identity Blues." In *Without Guarantees: In Honor of Stuart Hall*, edited by Lawrence Grossberg and Angela McRobbie, 1–13. London: Verso, 2000.
Antonini, Rachele. "The Perception of Subtitled humor in Italy." *Humor* 18, no. 2 (2005): 209–225.
Arogyasami, M. "Shakespeare's Treatment of Comic Sentiment (*Hasya Rasa*): An Indian Perspective." In *Acting Funny: Comic Theory and Practice in Shakespeare's Plays*, edited by Frances N. Teague, 153–163. Cranbury, NJ: Associated University Presses, 1994.
BBC. *BBC Annual Report 2011/12, Part 2: The BBC Executive's Review and Assessment*. London: BBC, 2012.
———. *BBC Annual Report 2013/14*. London: BBC, 2014.
BBC News. "*The Office* to be Remade in Russia," *BBC*, July 25, 2008. http://news.bbc.co.uk/go/pr/fr/-/1/hi/entertainment/7525248.stm.
Beeden, Alexandra, and Joost de Bruin. "*The Office*: Articulations of National Identity in Television Format Adaptation." *Television & New Media* 11 (2010): 3–19.
Billig, Michael. *Banal Nationalism*. London: Sage, 1995.
Billig, Michael. *Laughter and Ridicule: Towards a Social Critique of Laughter*, London: Sage, 2005.
Booth, Robert. "Want to Become a British Citizen? Better Swot up on *Monty Python*." *The Guardian*, January, 27, 2014. http://www.theguardian.com/uk/2013/jan/27/british-citizenship-test.

Brown, Roy "Chubby." *Common as Muck: My Autobiography*. London: Time Warner, 2006.

Brabazon, Tara. "'What Have You Ever Done on the Telly?' *The Office*, (Post) Reality Television and (Post) Work." *International Journal of Cultural Studies* 8, no. 1 (2005): 101–117.

Chambers, Iain. "Narratives of Nationalism: Being 'British.'" In *Space and Place: Theories of Identity and Location*, edited by Erica Carter and James Donald, 145–164. London: Lawrence and Wishart, 1993.

Collins, Michael. *The Likes of Us: A Biography of the White Working Class*. London: Granta, 2004.

Connery Brian A., and Kirk Combe. *Theorizing Satire: Essays in Literary Criticism*. New York: St. Martin's Press, 1995.

Critchley, Simon. *On Humour*. London: Routledge, 2002.

Dobson, Hugo. "Mister Sparkle Meets the *Yakuza*: Depictions of Japan in *The Simpsons*." *Journal of Popular Culture* 39, no. 1 (2006): 44–68.

Giddens, Anthony. *The Consequences of Modernity*. Cambridge: Polity, 1990.

Gray, Johnathan J., Jeffrey P. Jones, and Ethan Thompson. "The State of Satire: The Satire of State." In *Satire TV: Politics and Comedy in the Post-Network Era*, edited by Johnathan J. Gray, Jeffrey P. Jones, and Ethan Thompson, 3–36. New York: New York University Press, 2009.

Griffin, Jeffrey. "The Americanization of *The Office*: A Comparison of the Offbeat NBC Sitcom and its British Predecessor." *Journal of Popular Film and Television* 35, no. 4 (2008): 145–163.

Gullestad, Marianne. "Invisible Fences: Egalitarianism, Nationalism, and Racism." *Journal of the Royal Anthropological Institute* 8, no. 1 (2002): 45–63.

Freedman, Leonard. *The Offensive Art: Political Satire and Its Censorship around the World from Beerbohm to Borat*. Westport, CT: Praeger Publishers, 2009.

Foster, Kevin. "Snobs, Yobs, and Italian Jobs: European Union, British Identity, and the Crime Film." *Journal of Popular Culture* 44, no. 5 (2011): 1010–1026.

Fuller, Graham. "Brute Force." *Film Comment* 36, no. 5 (2000): 35–37.

Hasan, Mushirul. "Political Satire in Modern India." *The Hindu*, April 6, 2003. http://www.thehindu.com/thehindu/lr/2003/04/06/stories/2003040600010100.htm.

Havens, Timothy. "Globalization and the Generic Transformation in Telenovelas." In *Thinking Outside the Box: A Contemporary Television Genre Reader*, edited by Gary R. Edgerton and Brian Geoffrey Rose, 271–92. Lexington: The University Press of Kentucky, 2005.

Horan, Dermot. "Quality US TV: A Buyers Perspective." In *Quality TV: Contemporary American Television and Beyond*, edited by Janet McCabe and Kim Akass, 111–117. London: I. B. Tauris, 2007.

Hight, Craig. *Television Mockumentary: Reflexivity, Satire and a Call to Play*. Manchester University Press, 2010.

Higson, Andrew. "The Instability of the Nation." In *British Cinema, Past and Present*, edited by Justine Ashby and Andrew Higson, 35–47. London: Routledge, 2000.

Hutcheon, Linda. *A Theory of Parody: The Teachings of Twentieth-Century Art Forms*. New York: Methuen, 1985.

Kessel, Martina. "Landscapes of Humour: The History and Politics of the Comical in the Twentieth Century." In *The Politics of Humour: Laughter, Inclusion and Exclusion in the Twentieth Century*, edited by Martina Kessel and Patrick Merziger, 3–21. University of Toronto Press, 2012.

Kohli-Khandekar, Vanita. *The Indian Media Business (Vol.2)*. New Dehli: Sage Publications, 2006.

Koolstra, Cees M., Allerd L. Peeters, and Herman Spinhof. "The Pros and Cons of Dubbing and Subtitling." *European Journal of Communication* 17 (2002): 325–354.

Klages, Mary. "What to Do with Helen Keller Jokes: A Feminist Act." In *New Perspectives on Women and Comedy*, edited by Regina Barreca, 13–22. Philadelphia: Gordon and Breach, 1992.

McCallum, John. "Cringe and Strut: Comedy and National Identity in Post-War Australia. " In *Because I Tell a Joke or Two: Comedy, Politics, and Social Difference*, edited by Stephen Wagg, 202–220. London: Routledge, 1998.

Medhurst, Andy. *A National Joke: Popular Comedy and English Cultural Identities*. London: Routledge, 2007.

Medhurst, Andy, and Lucy Tuck. "The Gender Game." In *BFI Dossier 17: Television Sitcom*, edited by Jim Cook, 43–55. London: BFI, 1982.

Melluci, Alberto. "Identity and Difference in a Globalized World." In *Debating Cultural Hybridity: Multi-Cultural Identities and the Politics of Anti-Racism*, edited by Pnina Werbner and Tariq Modoods, 58–69. London: Zed, 1997.

Mills, Brett. *Television Sitcom*. London: BFI, 2005.

———. *The Sitcom*. Edinburgh University Press, 2009.

———. "Being Rob Brydon: Performing the Self in Comedy." *Celebrity Studies* 1, no. 2 (2010): 190–202.

Paul, William. *Laughing Screaming: Modern Hollywood Horror and Comedy*. New York: Columbia University Press, 1994.

Perkins, Chris. "The Banality of Boundaries: Performance of the Nation in a Japanese Television Comedy." *Television and New Media* 11, no. 5 (2010): 386–403.

Pieterse, Jan Nederveen. "Globalization as Hybridization." In *Media and Culture Studies: Keyworks*, edited by Meenakshi Gigi Durham and Douglas M. Kellner, 658–680. Malden: Blackwell, 1994.

Samuel, Raphael. *Island Stories: Unravelling Britain*. London: Verso, 1998.

Sanghvi, Vir. "News TV: Tripping on TRP." *Hindustan Times*, September 9, 2011. http://blogs. hindustantimes.com/medium-term/2011/09/09/news-tv-tripping -on-trp/.

Schwartz, Susan L. *Performing the Divine in India*. New York: New York University Press, 2004.

Silverstone, Roger. *Television and Everyday Life*. London: Routledge, 1994.

Sonntag, Selma K. "The Changing Global-Local Linguistic Landscape in India." In *English Language Education in South Asia*, 29–39. New Dehli: Cambridge University Press, 2009.

Sørenssen, Bjørn. "'I Have a Plan!' The Olsen Gang Captures Denmark and Norway: Negotiating the Popular Culture Gap." *Velvet Light Trap* 34 (1994): 71–83.

Thompson, Felix. "*Coast* and *Spooks*: On the Permeable National Boundaries of British Television." *Continuum: Journal of Media and Cultural Studies* 24, no. 3 (2010): 429–438.

Turner, Graeme. "Television and Nation: Does This Matter Any More?." In *Television Studies After TV: Understanding Television in the Post-Broadcast Era*, edited by Graeme Turner and Jinna Tay, 54–64. Abingdon: Routledge, 2009.

Quade, Anita. "A Slap in the Face." *Brighton and Hove Leader*, January 9, 1997.

Vatsyayan, Kapila. *Bharata: The Natyasastra*. New Delhi: Sahitya Akademi, 1996.

Ward, Paul. "Did You See James Mason in Town Today? A Case Study in Transatlantic and Local Identities in British Stardom." *Journal of Transatlantic Studies* 11, no. 4 (2013): 403–422.

Contributors

Mikhail Bakhtin was a Russian philosopher and literary critic. His many works on semiotics, aesthetics, and literary theory include *Rabelais and His World* (1965) and *The Dialogic Imagination* (1975).

Henri Bergson was a French philosopher. His works include *Time and Free Will* (1889) and *Matter and Memory* (1896).

Inger-Lise Kalviknes Bore is a senior lecturer in the Birmingham School of Media. She is author of *Screen Comedy and Online Audiences* (2017), and she has published work on comedy audiences, fandom, and climate change communication.

Ariel R. Chernin holds a PhD in communication from the University of Pennsylvania.

Donald Crafton is the Joseph and Elizabeth Robbie Professor of Film, Television, and Theatre at the University of Notre Dame. He is the author of *Shadow of a Mouse: Performance, Belief, and World-Making in Animation* (2013), which won the Award of Distinction in the Anne Friedberg Innovative Scholarship from the Society for Cinema and Media Studies.

Amber Day is an associate professor in the English and Cultural Studies Department at Bryant University. She is the author of *Satire and Dissent: Interventions in Contemporary Political Debate* (2011) and editor of *DIY Utopia: Cultural Imagination and the Remaking of the Possible* (2016). Her research focuses broadly on the intersections of popular culture and political speech, including ironic and satiric communication, political performance and activism, and public debate.

Umberto Eco was an Italian novelist, critic, and literary theorist. His many works include *The Name of the Rose* (1980), *Foucault's Pendulum* (1988), and *A Theory of Semiotics* (1976).

Evan Elkins is an assistant professor of media and visual culture in the Department of Communication Studies at Colorado State University, where he researches and teaches on various issues regarding media industries, digital culture, globalization, and transgressive comedy. His writing has appeared or is forthcoming in *Television and New Media*, *The Historical Journal of Film, Radio, and Television*, *The International Journal of Cultural Studies*, and several edited collections. He is currently working on a book about regional restrictions in digital entertainment platforms.

Paul Flaig is lecturer of film and visual culture at the University of Aberdeen, where he teaches and researches early and silent-era cinema, film comedy, Weimar cinema, animation, psychoanalysis, critical theory, Hollywood cinema abroad, feminist media theory, and theories of sovereignty.

Sigmund Freud was the founder of psychoanalysis. His many works include *The Interpretation of Dreams* (1899), *The Ego and the Id* (1923), and *Civilization and its Discontents* (1930).

Kathryn Fuller-Seeley teaches in the Radio-Television-Film Department at the University of Texas at Austin. Her research explores the cultural contexts surrounding media history and their audiences. Recent publications include *Jack Benny and the Golden Age of American Radio Comedy* (2017) and *One Thousand Nights at the Movies: An Illustrated History of Motion Pictures, 1895–1915* (2013).

Nadine G. Gabbadon holds a PhD in communication from the University of Pennsylvania. Her research and teaching interests include advertising, mass media industries, and the social and industrial construction of age.

Herman Gray is professor of sociology at the University of California, Santa Cruz, and has published widely in the areas of black cultural theory, politics, and media. He is the author of *Watching Race* (1995) and *Cultural Moves* (2005).

Felicia D. Henderson is an American television producer, screenwriter, and director who has worked on series such as *Family Matters*, *The Fresh Prince of Bel-Air*, *Moesha*, *Sister, Sister*, and *Everybody Hates Chris*. She holds a master of fine arts from UCLA's School of Theater, Film, and Television.

Bilal Hussain is a doctoral student in sociology at Loyola University Chicago. His research interests include race and ethnic relations along with the sociology of religion.

Linda Hutcheon is University Professor in the Department of English and of the Centre for Comparative Literature at the University of Toronto. Her works include *Irony's Edge* (1994), *A Theory of Parody* (1985), and *A Theory of Adaptation* (2006).

Peter Kragh Jensen is a PhD student in Screen Cultures at Northwestern University. His research focuses on contemporary political satire and digital culture.

Kathleen Rowe Karlyn is a professor in the Department of English at the University of Oregon, where she teaches and researches film studies and cultural studies, with an emphasis on film history, genre studies, and feminist theory.

Frank Krutnik is reader in film studies at the University of Sussex where he teaches and researches film history, US cinema and popular culture, film and television comedy, *film noir*, stardom, popular music, the Hollywood Left, radio broadcasting in the US (1930s–1960s), stardom, contemporary US television, and issues of cultural representation.

Sangeet Kumar is an assistant professor in the Department of Communication at Denison University. His publications include "A River by Any Other Name: Ganga/Ganges and the Postcolonial Politics of Knowledge on Wikipedia" in *Information, Communication & Society* (2017) and "Online Entertainment: YouTube Nation: Precarity and Agency in India's Online Video Scene" in the *International Journal of Communication* (2016).

Alfred L. Martin Jr. is an assistant professor in the Department of Communication Studies at the University of Iowa. Martin's research focuses on black media studies, queer media studies, production studies, reception theory, and television genre theory. He has published essays in *Feminist Media Studies, Popular Communication, Television and New Media, The Journal of Black Masculinity*, and *Spectator*.

Nick Marx is an assistant professor of media and visual culture in the Department of Communication Studies at Colorado State University. His research on film, television, and internet comedy has appeared in *Television and New Media, Communication and Critical/Cultural Studies*, and *The Velvet Light Trap*. He is coeditor (with Matt Sienkiewicz and Ron Becker) of Saturday Night Live *and American TV* (2013) and author of *Flexibly Funny: Sketch Comedy and American Television* (2019).

Andy Medhurst is senior lecturer in media, film, and cultural studies at the University of Sussex, where he teaches and researches British popular culture (both contemporary and historical), gender and sexuality, and the genre of comedy and constructions of Englishness.

Brett Mills is a senior lecturer in television studies at the University of East Anglia. He is the author of *Television Sitcom* (2005) and *The Sitcom* (2009), and coauthor of *Creativity in the British Television Comedy Industry* (2017). The latter drew on the three-year Arts and Humanities Research Council–funded "Make Me Laugh" project, which followed the working practices of UK television comedy writers, producers, and commissioners for over three years.

Linda Mizejewski is a professor in the Department of Women's, Gender, and Sexuality Studies at Ohio State University. Her books include *Ziegfeld Girl: Image and Icon in Culture and Cinema* (1999) and *Divine Decadence: Fascism, Female Spectacle, and the Makings of Sally Bowles* (1992).

Steve Neale is professor emeritus of film studies at the University of Exeter and academic director of the Bill Douglas Centre for the History of Cinema and Popular Culture.

Andrew J. Owens currently teaches in DePaul University's Department of Media and Cinema Studies. His work has been published in *Feminist*

Media Studies and *Television and New Media*. He is currently completing a book manuscript that traces the cultural and industrial history of queer occult film and television since the 1960s.

Jerry Palmer is an emeritus professor based in the Sir John Cass School Department of Art Media and Design at London Metropolitan University.

Ji Hoon Park teaches in the School of Media and Communication at Korea University.

Philip Scepanski is an assistant professor in the School of Communication and the Arts at Marist College where his research focuses on American television history, cultural theory, crisis and catastrophe, and comedy and humor. His current book project examines the ways that television comedy engages and manages collective American traumas from the assassination of John F. Kennedy to the present.

Matt Sienkiewicz is an associate professor of communication and international studies at Boston College. He is the author of *The Other Air Force* (2016) and coeditor (with Nick Marx) of Saturday Night Live *and American TV* (2013).

Bhoomi K. Thakore is assistant professor and chair of the Department of Sociology at Elmhurst College. Her research interests include race/ethnicity, media studies, South Asian Americans, and mentoring in higher education, and she has published extensively on these issues.

Ethan Thompson is an associate professor in the Department of Communication and Media at Texas A&M University–Corpus Christi. He is coeditor (with Jason Mittell) of *How to Watch Television* (2013) and (with Jonathan Gray and Jeffrey P. Jones) of *Satire TV: Politics and Comedy in the Post-Network Era* (2009) and author of *Parody and Taste in Postwar American Television Culture* (2013).

Index

Page numbers in italics refer to figures

36; social hierarchies, inequalities, mores and, 2–3, 18, 59. *See also* carnivalesque, the

Bakley, Bonnie Lee, 113, 114

Baldwin, Harry, 156

Ball, Lucille, 8, 147. See also *I Love Lucy* (1951–1957)

Barker, David, 148–149

Barlow, William, 174

baroque syllogism (*syllogismus in modo barocco*), 53

Barr, Roseanne, 209

Barrymore, Drew, 116

Bateman, Jason, 151

bathroom humor, 18–19. *See also* bodily humor

Baudrillard, Jean, 128

Baumgardner, Jody, 118

Baym, Geoffrey, 12, 121

BBC, 137, 138, 242, 248, 256, 257, 269, 270, 272, 275. *See also individual shows*

Becker, Ron, 224

Bee, Samantha, 12

Beloin, Ed, 163

Belushi, John, 19

benign violation theory, 62

Benny, Jack, 153–165; audiences and, 163, 165; Sadye Marks Benny (Mary Livingstone) and, 158–159, 161; *Canada Dry Program* and, 154–159; characters and, 153, 154, 157–160, 161–165; Chevrolet and, 159–160; comedy and, 163, 166n33; commercialism and, 155, 159–160, 163–164, 165; Harry Conn and, 154, 156–165, 166n33, 167n41; as "the Fall Guy," 161–165; gags and, 156; genres and, 136; humor and, 155, 159, 160, 161, 164; Jell-O and, 161, 162; jokes and, 154–155, 155–156, 161; masculinity and, 161; narrative and, 153, 157–158, 163; NBC (network) and, 154, 156, 159, 162; parodies and, 163; radio and, 153–154, 163–165; as showrunner, 160, 164; Sid Silvers and, 159; sitcoms and, 136, 153–154, 157,

163, 166n33; television and, 153, 163; vaudeville and, 154–155, 156, 161

Benny, Sadye Marks (Mary Livingstone), 158–159, 161

Berg, Charles Ramírez, 197

Bergson, Henri: absurdity and, 46; childhood games and, 49–51; clowns and, 48; comedy and, 3, 5, 49, 50; comedy mechanics and, 3–4; the comic and, 25, 49–51; *The Eric André Show* (2012–) and, 60, 66; "How Animals Eat Their Food" (YouTube video) and, 13; laughter and, 3–4, 46, 241; *Laughter: An Essay on the Meaning of the Comic*, 47–51; the mechanical and, 59, 68n11; slapstick comedies and, 46

Berlant, Lauren, 34, 42n3

Best of Gustakhi Maaf, 260. See also *Gustakhi Maaf* ("Excuse the Transgression") [2003–]

BET (channel), 210, 223, 224–225, 230–231, 233. *See also individual shows*

Bewitched (1964–1972), 137, 142–143

Bharati, Uma, 262

Bialik, Mayim, 89

Bieber, Justin, 221–222

Big Bang Theory, The (2007–), 73, 89–97, 154, 158, 197, 240

Bigley, Kevin, 225–226

Billing, Michael, 246–247

Bin Laden, Osama, 116, 266. *See also* 9/11

black audiences, 9, 66, 210, 225, 226, 232, 233

black male gayness, 222–233; African Americans and, 210; audiences and, 210, 228; BET and, 230–231; black sitcoms and, 225, 231–233; gender and, 210; *In Living Color* (1990–1994) and, 174; jokes and, 210, 223; race/sexuality and, 210; *Sirens* (2014–2105) and, 223, 224, 225–228; sitcoms and, 223, 224; "slumpy" demographic and, 224. See also *Let's Stay Together* (2012–2015)

wit and, 120. See also *Onion, The* (news satire)

Satire TV: Politics and Comedy in the Post-Network Era (Gray, Jones, Thompson), 12

Saturday Night Live. See *SNL* (1975–)

Saved by the Bell (1989-1992), 195

Scepanski, Philip, 19, 33-42

Schleifer, Ronald, 111

scholarship. *See* comedy scholarship

school shootings, 34, 36, 37

Schulman, Norma M., 174, 176, 177, 185

Schumer, Amy, 208-210

Sconce, Jeffrey, 63

Scotland, 272

Scott, Adam, 199

screwball wordplay, 88, 99n30

Scriptures, 31

Seinfeld (1989-1998), 11, 147, 240, 241, 273

Seinfeld, Jerry, 112

serials, 136-137, 144, 164

sex, 14. *See also* gender

Sex (Madonna), 110

sexism, 71-72, 123, 195, 268. *See also* misogyny

sexual comedy, 73, 179

sexual harassment, 181

sexuality, 208-233; *The Big Bang Theory* (2007–) and, 73, 90-95; blacks and, 228-230; Roy "Chubby" Brown and, 247, 249, 250-251; Ellen DeGeneres and, 216-222; Sigmund Freud and, 94; *Friends* (1994-2004) and, 181; Rudy Giuliani and, 114; identity and, 249; *In Living Color* (1990-1994) and, 174, 175, 177, 178-179; jokes and, 141-142; *Let's Stay Together* (2012-2015) and, 228-230, 231; masculinity and, 228; Miss Piggy (character) and, 212; *Pretty/Funny: Women Comedians and Body Politics* (Mizejewski), 216-222; psychoanalysis and, 94; racial stereotypes and, 228-230; *Sirens* (2014-2015) and, 227; sit-

coms and, 89; television and, 176; unruly women and, 216; writers' rooms and, 181-182. *See also* black male gayness; gender; homophobia; homosexuality; lesbianism; queerness

Shakespeare, William, 22

Shanghai Knights (Dobkin, 2003), 184, 187-188

Shanghai Noon (Dey, 2000), 187-188

Shape (magazine), 218

Sheen, Charlie, 265

Short Circuit (1988), 195

Shukla, Brij Bhushan, 262

Shutta, Ethel, 154, 155-156, 159

Sienkiewicz, Matt, 103-104, 111-119, 122, 128, 200

sight gags, 57, 68n7, 68n8. *See also* gags

signifier, the, 81-87, 114, 115

silent films, 8, 47, 55, 68n1. *See also* slapstick comedies; *individuals and individual films*

Silverman, Sarah, 221

Silvers, Sid, 159

Silverstone, Roger, 247

Simon, Paul, 115

Simpsons, The (1989–), 12, 40, 43n19, 154, 157, 163, 197, 200, 240

simulation/simulacrum, 128

Sinbad (performer), 64, 65

Single Ladies (2011–), 233

Sirens (2014-2015), 223, 224, 225-228

sitcoms, 136-143; AIDS and, 223-224; animation and, 153; audiences and, 136, 142, 144-145, 153, 240, 268-269; Jack Benny and, 136, 153-154, 157, 163, 166n33; black male gayness and, 223, 224; camera shots and, 275; characters and, 135, 136, 140-141; class and, 137-138; comedy and, 268-269; comedy codes and, 136; comedy scholarship and, 15; comedy verité and, 144, 146, 152-153; commercialism and, 155, 160; communalism and, 141-142; cultural change/identity and, 137-138, 141; *Curb Your Enthusiasm* (2000–)

Trahair, Lisa, 84
"Transgressing Boundaries as the
  Hybrid Global: Parody and Post-
  coloniality on Indian Television"
  (Kumar), 259–267
"Transnational TV Comedy Audiences" (Bore), 251–259. *See also*
  nations
Transparent (2014–), 9
trash talk, 181–182
Trip, The (BBC, 2010), 242–243,
  267–276
Trip to Italy, The (Winterbottom,
  2014), 276
Trip to the Moon, A (Méliès, 1902), 8
Tucker, Chris, 184, 186, 187–188, 190–
  193. See also *Rush Hour 2* (Ratner,
  2001)
TVOne (network), 232
TV 2 Zulu (Danish station), 238
22 Jump Street (Lord/Miller, 2014),
  134–135
Two and a Half Men (2003–2015), 265
2 Broke Girls (2011–2017), 57–58
two-reel comedies, 55, 56–57
two-world conditions, 20, 22, 32, 35

uni-culturalism, 182–183
United Kingdom, 267–268, 269–270,
  271, 272. *See also* BBC; British audiences; British comedy; British
  identity; *Office, The* (BBC) [2001–
  2003]; *Trip, The* (BBC, 2010)
*Unruly Woman: Gender and the Genres
  of Laughter, The* (Karlyn), 210–216
unruly women, 209, 210–216, 234n6
UPN (network), 179, 203n11
upside-down worlds, 26–27, 32. *See also*
  two-world conditions
Upworthy (online site), 123, 125, 127
USA Network, 223, 226

Vanity Fair (magazine), 110
Variety, 96
Vasey, Royston. *See* Brown, Roy
  "Chubby"
vaudeville, 8, 56, 60, 87, 99n30, 154–
  155, 156, 161

verbal skirting, 234n10
Vietnam War, 11, 37
Vijaykar, Kunal, 263
Vilanch, Bruce, 65
viral comedy videos, 10
Vogue (magazine), 110

Wagner, Richard, 108–109
Wahlberg, Mark, 217
Wales, 272–273
Walküre, Die ("Ride of the Valkyries")
  [Wagner], 108–109
Walth, Natasha, 118
Ward, Paul, 271
Wareheim, Eric, 63
warmedies, 140
Warner, Kristen, 195, 197
Warner Bros. Television, 181
Warren, Caleb, 62
*Watching Race: Television and the
  Struggle for Blackness* (Gray),
  173–179
Watergate scandal, 11
Wayans, Damon, 177, 178. See also *In
  Living Color* (1990–1994)
Wayans Bros., The (1995–1999), 186
"Wayne's World" (*SNL*), 112–113, 117
Week That Wasn't, The (*TWTW*)
  [2006–], 260–267
Weide, Robert, 147, 149
Weinberger, Ed., 140, 232
Weiner, Jennifer, 218
West, Mae, 110, 215
West, the, 14, 259–260, 265–267
What's Happening!! (1976–1979), 225
Wheen, Francis, 141
"When You Say Nothing At All" (bal-
  lad), 244
white American men, 13, 66, 67
whiteness, 194, 199, 200, 201, 218, 220,
  244, 249
whites: blackness and, 195–196;
  bodily appearance and, 221; Roy
  "Chubby" Brown and, 244, 245–
  251; homosexuality and, 223–224;
  In Living Color (1990–1994) and,
  175, 176, 177; *Key & Peele* (2012–
  2015) and, 170–172; *Lethal Weapon*

(Donner, 1987) and, 185; *Master of None* (2015–) and, 201, 202; *Parks & Recreation* (2009–2014) and, 199; racial hierarchies/stereotypes/racism and, 185–194, 196; *Rush Hour 2* (Ratner, 2001) and, 184, 187–194; *Sirens* (2014–2015) and, 225–227, 228; *The Trip* (BBC, 2010) and, 276
White Tribe (television series), 246
Will & Grace (1998–2006), 233
Williamson, Judith, 214
Wilson, Don, 160, 161
Winfrey, Oprah, 175, 176, 220
Winokur, Mark, 98n28
Winston, Brian, 150
wit, 25, 32, 76, 78, 120, 124
Wit and its relation to the Unconscious (Freud), 74–75

Witherspoon, Reese, 115–116
"Women on Top" (Davis), 215
Wood, Natalie, 65
working class. *See* class
workplace sitcoms, 154, 163, 165, 224, 225. *See also individual shows*
world literature, 22, 24. *See also* literature
writers' rooms, 179–183, 202n10, 203n11. *See also individual writers*
Wunderblock (mystic writing pad), 86

Yahoo, 160
Yo Soy Betty, la Fea (1999–2001), 251
YouTube, 9, 10, 239. *See also individual shows*

Žižek, Slavoj, 84, 86
Zupančič, Alenka, 80–81, 98n15, 98n23

CPSIA information can be obtained
at www.ICGtesting.com
Printed in the USA
LVHW050922220322
714020LV00003B/20

9 781477 316009